Dividing the Isthmus

Dividing the Isthmus

Central American Transnational Histories,
Literatures, and Cultures

BY ANA PATRICIA RODRÍGUEZ

University of Texas Press ◆ *Austin*

Copyright © 2009 by the University of Texas Press
All rights reserved
Printed in the United States of America
First edition, 2009

Requests for permission to reproduce material from this work should be sent to:
Permissions
University of Texas Press
P.O. Box 7819
Austin, TX 78713-7819
www.utexas.edu/utpress/about/bpermission.html

⊗ The paper used in this book meets the minimum requirements of
ANSI/NISO Z39.48-1992 (R1997) (Permanence of Paper).

Library of Congress Cataloging-in-Publication Data

Rodríguez, Ana Patricia, 1963–
  Dividing the Isthmus : Central American transnational histories, literatures,
and cultures / by Ana Patricia Rodríguez. — 1st ed.
      p.   cm.
  Includes bibliographical references and index.
  ISBN 978-0-292-71909-5 (cloth : alk. paper)
    1. Central America—History.   2. Central America—Civilization.   3. Central
American literature—20th century—History and criticism.   I. Title.
  F1436.R68   2009
  972.805—dc22
                                                              2008042296

*Con todo mi corazón dedico este libro a mi querido papi, Mario
Rodríguez Duarte, a mis hermanas, Claudia, Nancy y Cynthia
Rodríguez, a mi cuñado, Sean Hayes, y a mi sobrino, Cassius Benicio
Rodríguez-Hayes*

With all my heart, I dedicate this book to my father, Mario
Rodríguez Duarte, to my sisters, Claudia, Nancy, and Cynthia
Rodríguez, to my brother-in-law, Sean Hayes, and to my nephew,
Cassius Benicio Rodríguez-Hayes

Contents

Acknowledgments

The writing of this book has been an exciting voyage of discovery, taking me to literary and real spaces that I never would have known had I not been granted the opportunity to do graduate work at the University of California, Santa Cruz (UCSC). On that beautiful campus atop a mountain facing the Pacific Ocean, I encountered many people who encouraged my study of Central American histories, literatures, and cultures and often stood back and allowed me to travel alone that rocky discursive terrain. Although pursuing Central American Studies in the United States can be a lonely endeavor, it is always a labor of dedication for those of us who pursue it. For me, it has always also been a labor of love, love for an imaginary homeland that I left much too young (at the age of five) but one that I return to with abandon in my reading of Central American literature. The fruit of that labor is this book, for which I am indebted to the many wonderful people who have guided me on the path to that land between seas and continents.

Over the decade that I spent researching and writing this book, many people guided and enlightened me with their intelligence, advice, and foresight. Among them at UCSC, my first mentor, adviser, and reason for going to Santa Cruz, Roberto Crespi, introduced me to revolutionary literature, *indigenista* novels, and Latin American *testimonio*. In 1992, when he passed away, I was fortunate to fall into the intellectual care of Norma Klahn, who taught me to leave no book unread and no border uncrossed in Latin American and Latina/o Cultural Studies. She paved the way for my explorations in Central American transnational and transisthmian thinking. This book has her name written all over it, as it does the name of Lourdes Martínez-Echazábal, who always challenged my thinking in positive ways.

Everything that I learned early in my studies about Chicana/o and Latina/o literature I owe to José D. Saldívar, who shared with me the excitement of initial readings in the "Latina/o literary boom" in several independent studies. My debt to Susan Gillman is great for she refocused my vision toward Inter-American Studies in the various courses in which I was her teaching assistant and student. At UCSC, I had the good fortune to learn from critical scholars of popular culture, gender/queer studies, and meta-historiography: Carla Freccero, Earl Jackson Jr., and Hayden White. They have influenced my thinking in more ways than they will ever know. In language teaching pedagogies, I can only thank M. Victoria González-Pagani, who took me under her wing and single-handedly taught me how to teach the Spanish language. Her lessons have served me well.

For financial support to conduct research in graduate school for a dissertation on Central American and U.S. Central American literature, I am grateful to the UCSC Department of Literature for several dissertation fellowships and to the Chicano/Latino Research Center for Research Mini-Grants that allowed me to travel as a graduate student to Costa Rica, where this book was really born under the midwifery of mentors associated with the Universidad de Costa Rica at San José. In spring 2001, I was awarded a Smithsonian Institution Postdoctoral Fellowship through the Latino Studies Fellowship Program to develop a project titled "Transnational Deportee Cultures." At the Smithsonian Institution, I would like acknowledge the mentoring of Olivia Cadaval, Magdalena Mieri, Marvette Pérez, and Cynthia Villarutia. That year, I also received a Grant-in-Aid from the Recovering the U.S. Hispanic Literary Heritage Program at the University of Houston, Texas, to conduct transnational research on the writer Máximo Soto Hall, which allowed me to travel to Buenos Aires and spend time in the archives of the venerable hemispheric newspaper, *La Prensa*. The National Endowment for the Humanities and Community College Humanities Association (NEH/CCHA) granted me a fellowship to participate in the Summer Institute, "The Maya World: Cultural Continuities and Change in Guatemala, Chiapas and Yucatán," from June 23 to August 3, 2002. George Scheper, Laraine Fletcher, and David A. Berry produced an excellent program, where many ideas for classes and articles began to germinate, including chapter 4 of this book. At the University of Maryland, a Graduate Research Board fellowship in summer 1999 began what would be the long process of rewriting this book. Ultimately, each award has allowed me the opportunity to develop and write new chapters.

I would like to express my deepest gratitude to my colleagues in the

Department of Spanish and Portuguese at the University of Maryland (UM), College Park, where I arrived as a newly minted Ph.D., found a warm home on the East Coast, and continue to grow with the support of Jorge Aguilar-Mora, Tony Barilla, Carmen Benito-Vessels, Laura Demaría, Regina Igel, Manel Lacorte, Roberta Lavine, José María Naharro-Calderón, José Emilio Pacheco, Juan Carlos Quintero-Herencia, Mehl Penrose, Karen Remson, Ivette Rodríguez-Santana, Graciela Palau de Nemes (Professor Emerita), and Hernán Sánchez de Pinillos (a.k.a. the Tangerine Man). In particular, I would like to thank Saúl Sosnowski (then chair of the department), associate provost for International Affairs of the Office of International Programs, who hired me, and the rest has been history. From the first day, Sandra Cypess has mentored and opened her heart to me. I have enjoyed every minute of our ongoing in-person and online conversations about literature, learning, and life. If it were not for Regina Harrison, I would not be at UM, and I thank her for her brilliance and professionalism. Finally, in my department, I would like to thank Eyda Merediz, who has been a friend and colleague since we arrived at UM as a team.

In the School of Languages, Literatures, and Cultures (SLLC), I extend my gratitude to Mike Long, Pierre Verdaguer, and Lauretta Clough for their support and to the wonderful staff who have made my life a little easier in ways only they know how to do. They include Peilei Chow, Mike Fekula, Laura Glockner, Phoenix Liu, Ida Seibert, and Mildred P. Yen. A special thank you goes to Peter Beicken, Joseph Brami, David Branner, Caroline Eades, Giuseppe Falvo, Inas Hassan, Ahmad Karimi-Hakkak, Jianmei Liu, Cynthia Martin, Michele Mason, Rosemarie Oster, Elizabeth Papazian, Robert Ramsey, Mel Scullen, Gabriele Strauch, Lindsay Yotsukura, and untold others whose kind words I have appreciated in and about Jiménez. Janel Brennan-Tillmann and John Grimm have saved me electronically more than once, especially in organizing materials for this book and other projects.

My appreciation also goes to colleagues with whom I have had the pleasure of interacting in various capacities throughout my years at UM, among them, Cordell Black, Robert Waters, Gloria Bouis, Christine Clark, Bonnie Dill Thornton, Judith Freidenberg, William Hanna, Robb Hernandez, Victoria María MacDonald, Martin Johnson, Edna Mora Szymanski, Claire Moses, Randy Ontiveros, Angel D. Nieves, Phyllis Peres, Ruth Zambrana, and the librarians at McKeldin, especially Patricia Herron. I would like to pay special homage to folks who have touched my life beyond the workplace, including Mark Brimhall-Vargas, Sandra Jiménez, David Jones, Mónica Mora Herrera, Hugo E.

Nájera, and Irene Zoppi. I am honored to have called Carolina Rojas-Bahr my *hermana*, friend, and partner-in-projects, until her untimely passing on June 20, 2007. I learned from her true commitment to students, service, and community-based scholarship.

Many undergraduate and graduate students at UM have enriched my work with their trials and tribulations. I would like to acknowledge the following undergraduate students, among many others: Evelyn Aguilar, Ashley Bennett, Sandra Buitrago, Arquimen Chicas-Navarro, Lino Contreras, Colleen Esper, Matthew Goldmark, Arelis Hernández, Edvin Hernández, Leslie Hernández, Patricia Graf, Cristina Lee, Irene Liu, Joshua Lieberman, Evelyn López, Raúl Marín, Vilma Nájera, Krystle W. Norman, Gisela Paredes, Corina Rivera, Manuel Ruiz, Julie Sarmiento, Leimer Tejeda, and Katie Tracey. I have had the pleasure of working with former and present graduate students in the Department of Spanish and Portuguese and the College of Education, among them, Leonel Alvarado, Patty Alvarez, Jason Bartles, Agnieszka Bolikowska, Marja Booker, Loredana Di Stravolo, Jennifer Dix, Bianca Laureano, Silvia Mejía, Elaine Miller, Hugo E. Nájera, and Nilda Villalta. An Unknown Student Tribute goes out to all my students whom I do not identify here. I would like to recognize, however, Ronald Luna, whom I met as an undergraduate student in my classes at UM and from whose doctoral research in geography I have learned a great deal about Central American demographics in the greater Washington, D.C., metropolitan area.

Along the way, I have had the good fortune to meet and work with a host of scholars in Central American Studies. My scholarship began in classes with Carlos Cordova—my first mentor in Central American history and heritage during the two years I was an undergraduate student at San Francisco State University. My life has not been the same since I took two extension classes on Central American literature and culture with the Salvadoran writer Manlio Argueta in the late 1980s. Another mentor, Arturo Arias, graciously and generously served as a reader of my dissertation on Central American and U.S. Central American literature, from which this book originated. I would also like to recognize colleagues, far and wide, in Central American immigration and cultural studies who continue to inspire and inform my work, among them, Ramón Luis Acevedo, Douglas Carranza, Norma Chinchilla Stolz, Susanne Jonas, Ellen Moodie, David Pedersen, Manuel Orozco, Horacio Roque Ramírez, Rhina Toruño-Haensly, and Marc Zimmerman.

Through the years, I have enjoyed the support of a group of inspiring women scholars in Central American transnational immigration and cultural studies. In summer 1999, Sarah Mahler invited me to participate in "Central America 2020," a seminar on immigration in San Salvador. In fall 2002, Susan Coutin, Esther Hernández, and I crossed the San Diego–Tijuana border to interview migrants and deportees, and we continue to talk about that and other border-crossing interview projects. Cecilia Menjívar has been a friend and role model, trailblazing in her publications on gender and immigration and offering me sound advice and good cheer along the way. Beatriz Cortez not only brought me to speak at California State University, Northridge, the home of the first Central American Studies Program in the United States, but also gave me the key to her house in Antigua, Guatemala, from which we traveled to the center of the world, Lago Atitlán. My knowledge of Central American and U.S. Central American literature has been enriched by conversations with Linda J. Craft and Astvaldur Astvaldsson, as well as with Maya Chinchilla, Gustavo Guerra Vasquez, and Yajaira M. Padilla, my former students at UCSC, where as a graduate student I taught the first class on Central American literature in 1997. They have gone on to do great things with Central American (spoken) words.

This book is a transnational endeavor that has drawn from my intersections with many scholars, researchers, and writers in the north and the south. I wish to recognize the influence of many people whom I can only list here for lack of space: Soledad Bianchi, Rosa Campos-Brito, Christopher Conway, Cary Cordova, KarenMary Dávalos, Gwen Kirkpatrick, Francisco Lomelí, Muriel Hasbun, William Nichols, Suzanne Oboler, Ricardo Ortiz, Alicia Partnoy, Yansi Pérez, Mary Louise Pratt, Ileana Rodríguez, David Román, Kirsten Silva Gruesz, and Uriel Quesada. In Costa Rica, I thank Ligia Bolaños Varela, Elba Espinoza Retana, Martha and Eugenia Gómez, Emilia Macal, María Pérez Yglesias, Dennis Quiros, the late Álvaro Soto Quesada, and other people at the Universidad de Costa Rica, San José, where I studied Central American literature in 1993–1995. In El Salvador, I thank Katharine Andrade-Eekhoff, Ricardo Roque Baldovinos, Carlos Dinarte, Carlos Martínez Lara, Miguel Huezo Mixco, Consuelo Roque (R. Cruz), and the personnel at the Museo de la Imagen y la Palabra, Universidad de El Salvador, and Universidad de Centroamérica José Simeón Cañas. Also, I cannot forget the artists and writers who have given me of their talents and time for interviews: Manlio Argueta, Quique Avilés, Mario Bencastro, Maya Chinchilla, Maya Cu, Martivón Galindo, Lilo González, Otoniel Guevara, Claudia Hernández, Leticia Hernández-Linares, William

Huezo Soriano, Daniel Joya, JC Mendizabal, Karla "Karlísima" Rodas, Ric Salinas and Herbert Siguenza of Culture Clash, Héctor Tobar, and Marcos McPeek Villatoro.

This book would not have materialized without more than a little help from a group of special people, whom I could always count on for friendship, support, and a shoulder to cry on at various points in my life. Michelle Habell-Pallán, Maylei Blackwell, Deb Vargas, Luz Calvo, Catriona Rueda Esquibel, and Victoria Bañales have been a source of uplift since our years in graduate school. Marge Lasky, Otieno Kisiara, and Ronald Webb became lasting friends after our NEH/CCHA research trip to the Maya world. Sergio de la Mora has given me enduring *confianza*, encouragement, and inspiration through the ups and downs of academic life. Through thick and thin, too, Barbara Ige has been a pillar of strength and ethical teaching. Christopher A. Shinn has always been an important presence in my life, enlightening me with his intelligence, integrity, sincerity, and unwavering affection. Angelo J. Gómez and Marina Riquelme have been my family in Washington, D.C., giving me shelter, food, and laughter when I most needed them. My former office mate in the Department of Spanish and Portuguese, Virginia M. Bouvier taught me fortitude in the face of adversity at the university; the luncheon divas, Evelyn Canabal-Torres and Teresa Cabal-Krastel, have shown me that there is life after UM, and Carmen Román has reminded me to breathe and live amidst the work. Millie Lanauze, my first housemate in graduate housing at UCSC, has been a steadfast friend from Santa Cruz to Washington, D.C., proving that there must be some truth to the theory of synchronicity.

Words fail me when it comes to expressing my undying gratitude to my family, who have loved me, respected me, and supported my work even at a distance. With great sacrifice, my father and mother made the decision to emigrate from El Salvador to the United States to give my sister Claudia and me the opportunities they never had. By the goodness of God, my father has been with me in heart and soul every day of my life, and my mother, I believe, has been with me in spirit. I honor them with images of Central America in this book. My sisters, Claudia and Nancy, have given me the greatest gift—immeasurable love—when I could not write another word or spend another sleepless night at the computer. My sister Cynthia, too, has given me love and insight into her world. My brother-in-law, Sean Hayes, has shown me how to rise above conditions that would seem to be beyond us, and the light of my life, my nephew, Cassius Benicio Rodríguez-Hayes, gives me hope that the future will be lighter and brighter than the present. I also honor my late cousin Mayte Ramírez Wembes, who never failed to remind me that I should never forget "mis raíces" and that one day I must return to my family and my City by the Bay, San Francisco. I am working toward that return. Last but not least, I wish to thank my extended family in the United States, Australia, and Central America, especially *mi tia* Chabelita Pantoja de Carranza, *mi prima* Silvia Ramírez de Lemus *y mi hermano* Mauricio Rodríguez *y su familia* who remain in El Salvador. We are a transnational family divided only by the miles.

All the people named here have shaped me as a person and scholar and have contributed to the writing of *Dividing the Isthmus*, but some individuals have read it from cover to cover at various stages. I am most grateful to Christopher A. Shinn for reading and editing the manuscript in its first incarnation as my doctoral dissertation. Otieno Kisiara and Virginia M. Bouvier read and commented on early drafts of the book manuscript, and the anonymous readers for the University of Texas Press made recommendations that could only improve my work. Finally, I am indebted to the editorial staff at the University of Texas Press for their diligence, professionalism, and critical eye. Theresa May has been the most patient of editors, allowing me more than ample time to bring the book to a close and offering expert editing advice and kind e-mail messages. Allison Faust, Megan Giller, Leslie Tingle, and other editorial personnel shepherded the book at different stages. I have taken their suggestions and incorporated them into the book to the best of my ability. The responsibility for any and all errors is mine.

Early versions of chapters 4, 6, and 7 were published previously in different forms and are republished herein with permission. Chapter 6 was originally published as "'Departamento 15': Cultural Narratives of Salvadoran Transnational Migration," *Latino Studies* 3.1 (April 2005): 19–41. Chapter 7 was published as "Wasted Opportunities: Conflictive Peacetime Narratives of Central America," in *The Globalization of U.S.– Latin American Relations: Democracy, Intervention, and Human Rights*, edited by Virginia M. Bouvier (Westport, CT: Praeger, 2002), 227–247. A part of chapter 4 appears in "The Evidence of *Testimonio*: The *Return of the Maya*," *Community College Humanities Review* 24 (Fall 2003): 67–80. An early incarnation of the epilogue appeared as "'Sueños de un collejero': The University, the *casa*, and the Streets of Salvadoran Transmigrant Communities in the Longley Park Area," *Journal of Latino–Latin American Studies* 2.2 (Winter 2006): 48–61.

In closing, I would like to echo the words of a shaman who on a sunny day on a mountain outside of Chichicastenango allowed me to see that, indeed, I have been blessed with good guides. They have taken and will continue to take me where I need to be. With this book, I honor that shaman's vision, as well as all those who have had faith in me. *Muchísimas gracias por todo.*

Dividing the Isthmus

Central American Transisthmian Histories, Literatures, and Cultures

This is the coast of Darien. And here the Spanish adventurer Balboa, in 1513, was told by the chief of the Indian fishermen about another sea beyond the mountains, and [he] put his men ashore and marched across to find the Pacific Ocean—and started a passionate dream, the dream of cutting a canal to join the seas, which was only fulfilled four hundred and one years later. The coast that one sees today is exactly the same as it was when he saw it: it is only one's knowledge that is different.
—DAVID HOWARTH, *The Golden Isthmus*

Columbus did not discover Central America and its history does not begin with him. In fact, the relevance and importance of the history of aboriginal Central America does not depend on Spain or any other nation. It is the history of highly creative and successful autonomous peoples, and, as such, it deserves its own place, alongside the histories of the most important civilizations of the world.[1]
—ROBERT M. CARMACK, Introduction to *Historia General de Centroamérica*, vol. 1

In my classes on Central American literatures, cultures, and histories, I often begin by giving students cutout pieces representing Central American countries and asking them to (re)construct mappings of the geographic isthmus. Often Belize and Panama fall off the map, Guatemala topples over a ragged strip of land, El Salvador acquires an Atlantic coast, Honduras borders Mexico, Nicaragua becomes an undistinguishable green expanse, and Costa Rica does not quite fit in with the others. More often than not, Central America as a whole lies suspended somewhere between amorphous masses on the north and south and the east and west. As if it were an island, Central America appears without physical, geographic, and historical ties to the rest of the western hemisphere and the world. On reading these student maps, I have pondered why, for many people, Central America figures as an unknown, nebulous zone.

In this book I explore the ever-shifting literary, cultural, and histori-cal configurations of the Central American isthmus as an in-between discursive space linking regions, peoples, cultures, and material goods. I offer the trope of the *transisthmus*—an imaginary yet material space— as a spatial periodizing term and as a "cultural provision" for reading Central American literatures and cultures outside of categories that up to now have elided larger regional complexities.[2] I read a range of texts that bring to the fore the connections among material, cultural, and lit-erary productions in the region and across nations and the overarching economic conditions that make them possible throughout the isthmus at specific historical moments. I purposefully divide, organize, and assem-ble Central American texts into cultural, temporal spaces linked by so-cial and economic flows that transcend geopolitical borders. Rather than read Central American literatures as discrete national units, I attempt to read selected texts across national divides, drawing connections be-tween them while producing other transisthmian and transnational cul-tural and literary spaces. In a sense, I follow Fredric Jameson's "cultural logic" as a way to link cultural and symbolic texts with their sites of material production. Accordingly, Central American transisthmian cul-tural and literary production, as I understand it here, emerges from the linkages of material and symbolic capital situated in specific geographic, historic, and discursive locations. Because the material and economic basis and imaginary terrain of the isthmus is ever shifting, like the fault lines that run along the region's tectonic plates, the discursive isth-mus fully lends itself to constructions of social imaginaries of Central America. The project of this book is thus to reconfigure the imaginary transisthmus through readings of texts produced in economic, political, and symbolic relationship to the physical geographic location of Central America.[3]

To this end, I seek to provide spatial-cultural readings of Central America as a region shaped by and responding to wider global forces with locally inflected and entwined narratives. These narratives speak to the imaginary construction of Central America as an isthmian whole and Central American countries, cultures, and literatures in synecdochal relationship to one another and to the isthmus. I argue that Central American narratives transect and transcend national political boundaries and traverse the entire region, destabilizing not only insular and isolationist notions of national literatures but also integrative and holistic readings of the Central American region and its cultures and peoples. I examine Central American literary and cultural productions as linked practices emerging from overarching conditions, yet speaking from and to specific local contexts. Indeed, Sergio Ramírez, in his essay "Seis falsos golpes contra la literatura centroamericana" (Six False Blows against Central American Literature) (1985, 117–128), reminds us that Central American cultures and literatures are produced in particular locations and under special circumstances, for which perhaps hegemonic critical categories may be inappropriate, inadequate, and insufficient. He suggests that local referents (signifying realities, not *one* reality) and social, historical contexts hold important social functions in Central American narrative, although this may not be the case for literature produced in other postlocal sites. Despite globalizing trends in the region, Central American texts also follow local imperatives and injunctions and benefit from locally produced strategies of analysis. It is fair, then, to acknowledge the claim made by Central Americanist scholars that specific Central American contexts continue to be of significant consideration in the analysis of Central American histories, cultures, and literatures (Ramírez 1985, 1995; Beverley and Zimmerman 1990; Torres-Rivas 2006). The challenge here is to read Central American texts in relation to globalizing tendencies and local specificities.

In *Taking Their Word* (2007), Arturo Arias analyzes Central American literature as "'narrative textuality,' an approach that encompasses all genres (the novel, short story, *testimonio*, essay, and even some variants of epic poetry such as Ernesto Cardenal's *El estrecho dudoso* [The doubtful strait]" (xiv). He encourages us to read Central America through "the varied textual discursive production of the region, the tapestry of languages, characters, conflicts, and cultural locations of Central America" (xiv). From Arias's discussion of Central American literary and cultural production, I take to heart and task in *Dividing the Isthmus* the suggestion to "pay closer attention to Central American words themselves, mostly written, but some spoken and then transcribed by others," and to engage Central American narrative textuality as a meta-reflexive "symbolic comprehension of itself" (xv). As (self-)defining representations, Central American texts are not solely interpretive ends in and to themselves (though they can be in some forms of literary criticism) but may more critically serve as tools for "understanding cultural and cross-cultural practices" (xi) and for defining and assuming ideological and subjective positions in world orders, hegemonic and otherwise, as Arias recognizes in his work. In this age of the devaluation of literature and the humanities, critically reading Central American texts in various forms as signs of local realities and global tendencies remains a vital endeavor. As Arias puts it so well, Central America and its narratives can be read as an "invisible hinge between North and South" (2007, xvi) and as an intersection of bodies of knowledge, which I examine further here.

Dividing the Isthmus thus seeks to (re)assemble Central American narratives into transisthmian bodies of knowledge, connecting texts across nations of the region. It, moreover, analyzes the production of *transnational* literatures in different periods of Central American history. But, as cultural and literary genealogists would remind us, a term such as "transnational" cannot be used loosely and indiscriminately; thus, in this project, I use it situationally to describe Central American texts produced in ever-shifting historical trans/national configurations. Simply put, *Dividing the Isthmus* is about reading Central American narratives across national boundaries and about producing transnational, or rather transisthmian, "narrative textualities." Each chapter reads an assemblage of Central American texts produced across Central American countries and against insular national traditions. The reading of foundational literature, social realist novels, crisis testimonials, diasporic narratives, and other texts written under globalizing forces will show the possibilities and limits of reading Central American literatures, cultures, and histories in transisthmian and transnational fashion.

The (Re)Signifying Isthmus of Central America

The geophysical and geographic isthmus of Central America lies between the landmasses of North and South America and the Atlantic and Pacific Oceans. It extends across seven countries: Guatemala, Belize, El Salvador, Honduras, Nicaragua, Costa Rica, and Panama. A relatively recent land formation, Central America acquired its present-day isthmian configuration about three million to four million years ago.[4] Before that time, what are now the Americas North and South were separated by approximately 1,900 miles of water. An archipelago of volcanic islands consolidated into a narrow terrestrial strip, forming a land bridge between North and South America and a partition between the waters later named the Pacific and Atlantic Oceans. Central America is the only region in the world whose geophysical landmass is both intercontinental and interoceanic. It serves as a hemispheric land corridor and as a pathway between waters. Its narrowest lowland routes are located at Tehuantepec (southern Mexico), the waterways of the San Juan River and Lake Nicaragua, and the present-day canal in Panama. As a terrestrial bridge, the isthmus serves as a platform for the dispersion of plants and animals, the migration of peoples, the diffusion of cultures, and the movement of global economic capital. It is a site of unparalleled but quickly deteriorating biological and cultural diversity as manifested in its varied land formations, climate, vegetation, animal life, peoples, and cultures. The region is characterized by tropical climate, transitional flora and fauna of North and South America, long volcanic chains with extending seismic fault lines, mountain ranges that run from north to south, dividing Central America into east and west, and lowlands on both the Pacific and Caribbean coasts, where in some places precipitation is bountiful almost year-round. Successively, the most important agricultural and industrial products of global export economies— among them, cacao, indigo, coffee, rubber, timber, bananas, sugarcane, and cotton—have been cultivated in the isthmus. In the twenty-first century, Central America exports its greatest commodity—its people as labor migrants.

For thousands of years, the Maya people have believed the northern isthmus to be the *axis mundi*, from which all life is generated and connected to the upper- and underworlds.[5] Sixteenth-century Spanish conquistadors were convinced that a waterway leading to the East Indies was located somewhere in the isthmus. For seventeenth- and eighteenth-century European profit seekers, the isthmus, especially at the key ports of Portobello and Nombre de Dios (now Panama), represented boundless treasure-hunting opportunities. In his epic poem, *El estrecho dudoso* (1966), the Nicaraguan poet Ernesto Cardenal retraced the Spanish conquistadors' elusive search for the doubtful strait long after Vasco Nuñez de Balboa had reached *la mar del sur* (the southern sea), the Pacific Ocean, by land in 1513. Cardenal's exhaustive use of *exteriorista*, or concrete, images of land, rain, mud, swamp, and other natural boundaries in *El estrecho dudoso* serves to represent the isthmus as an inhospitable land to be conquered and transformed by (neo)colonial powers. As David Howarth suggests in the epigraph that opens this introduction, the isthmus, or rather the neocolonial idea of the isthmus, so relentlessly represented in Cardenal's narrative poem has been used historically to authorize successive imperial and imperialist claims to the region and its wealth.[6] Although the conquistadors did not find the elusive strait cutting through the isthmus, in their wake they left a trail of (dis)illusions that have drawn many fortune seekers to Central America throughout the centuries. Recognizing the material and signifying power of the isthmus, nineteenth-century Latin American nation builders further envisioned Central America as the crossroads of the Americas, where the capital of the western hemisphere might one day be based. In "The Jamaica Letter" (1815), Simón Bolívar writes:

> The States of the Isthmus from Panama to Guatemala will perhaps form a confederation. This magnificent location between the two great oceans could in time become the emporium of the world. Its canals will shorten the distances throughout the world, strengthen commercial ties with Europe, America, and Asia, and bring that happy region tribute from the four quarters of the globe. Perhaps someday the capital of the world may be located there, just as Constantine claimed Byzantium was the capital of the ancient world. (Quoted in Leiken and Rubin 1987, 62)

Bolívar's vision of the isthmus as the "emporium of the world" and Francisco Morazán's subsequent proposal for a united transisthmian federation would prove as elusive and illusory as the long-standing struggle for autonomy, development, and progress in the region. Possessing "great strategic and commercial importance" and "a favorable situation for a city,"[7] the isthmus has been recast in the global imaginary as a land route, water canal, duty-free zone, strategic military portal, and, more recently, a series of interconnected roadways producing an extended network of dry canals.

Since the mid-nineteenth century, the imperial forces of Great Britain, the United States, and other world powers have repeatedly besieged the region, each competing relentlessly for concession rights to territory, resources, and capital. In 1850, the Clayton-Bulwer Treaty granted dual custodianship over canal rights in Nicaragua to the United States and Great Britain, ensuring that "neither the one or the other will ever obtain or maintain for itself any exclusive control over the said ship-canal."[8] The long-sought interoceanic canal, of course, would be completed by the United States in Panama in 1914, after the U.S. government orchestrated Panama's secession and independence from Colombia in 1903 (McCullough 1977; LaFeber 1989). Carolyn Hall dully asserts that for foreign powers, "la principal significación de América

Central ha sido su posición interoceánica [the main significance of Central America lies in its interoceanic position]" (1985, 9). First, Spanish conquistadors and merchants transported riches from South America, especially gold from Peru, by land and sea through Panama to the Spanish metropolis. Then Great Britain and the United States competed for control over Panama and Nicaragua, each at different moments representing the two most viable sites for the construction of a canal. After the completion of the canal through Panama, the United States would come to control the ten-mile-wide and fifty-mile-long (553-square-mile) Canal Zone until December 31, 1999, as decreed by the Panama Canal Treaties, signed by General Omar Torrijos (1929–1981) and President Jimmy Carter in 1977. The biggest cut through Central America at the Canal Zone came thus to epitomize U.S. economic, military, and political intervention in Central America, which continues well into the present. Indeed, while revolutionary and popular movements might have attempted to set other courses for the region in the 1970s and 1980s, Central America at the foot of the twenty-first century is central to the expansion, consolidation, and implementation of the Free Trade Area of the Americas (FTAA).[9]

The Isthmus as Nature and/or Culture

Perhaps because of its long history of crossings, interventions, and mediations, Central America remains anchored to its isthmian geographic, historical, and cultural location, but this is not to say that geography or even history has predetermined Central America's socioeconomic, political, and cultural conditions.[10] As Gabriela Nouzeilles makes clear in *La naturaleza en disputa* (2002), there is little that is "natural" about physical configurations of nature, for nature is always perceived, conceptualized, and constructed ideologically, historically, linguistically, and culturally. Furthermore, as a field of intellectual inquiry into geophysical natural formations, geography has epistemologically shaped thinking about the world and produced various notions of space, place, and location. The idea of nature at any one time is filtered through systems of thought, culture, language, and rhetorical figures that serve as interpretive lenses through which to see the material "natural" world. Concepts and representations of nature, as in all things deemed natural, are subject to interpretive shifts and variations (16–17). As such, the significations of the Central American isthmus have varied across time. While the

Maya people may well perceive the isthmus as an organic cosmic center awaiting cataclysmic change on December 21, 2012, capitalist free trade agents contemporaneously conceive the isthmus as a material site of factories, products, patents, migrants, and high-speed rail/road transportation systems otherwise known as "dry canals" ensuring the movement of high-value commodities in the present global market economy (Warpehoski n.d., 34–35). Nouzeilles's claim that representation gives shape to "empirical reality" (15) holds true for the isthmus and its people.

Along these lines, in *Transatlantic Topographies* (2004), Ileana Rodríguez examines the conceptualization of physical space in the Americas, more specifically, the "representations of American space" informing colonial and postcolonial projects (xi–xix). Among other things, she draws attention to "space and the representation of space as it mutates from landscape into sugar fields, milpas into haciendas, forests into plantations, rivers and lakes into transoceanic canals" (xiv). In a key chapter titled "Banana Republics: Nineteenth-Century Geographers and Naturalists," Rodríguez discusses the early corroboration of the burgeoning fields of geography, archaeology, and ethnology and U.S. commercial expansion in the isthmus (131–162), concentrated in the construction of the interoceanic and transisthmic railroads and canals. For agents of these projects, "Central America is first represented as a metonymy, enjoining space and time contained in the proposition of trans-isthmic routes" (137). Synecdochally, the isthmus as a whole and the countries located in it would be measured according to their use value as ocean and land-crossing instruments for the United States and other world powers. The shorter the crossing span and time, the greater value the particular country or region would have for the United States. Hence the United States historically has exercised great control and power over Nicaragua and Panama (the shortest land and water routes throughout the isthmus), as well as other countries that more recently have provided the U.S. and the global economy with copious quantities of agricultural, industrial, and material resources such as bananas, coffee, and migrants. At the beginning of the twenty-first century, El Salvador, which possesses one of the largest underemployed populations concentrated in one of the smallest countries in the western hemisphere, has become a main exporter of migrant labor to the United States, providing inroads for the expansion of U.S. markets in the global economy. Against this historical context, Rodríguez judiciously claims that, for the United States, "Central America is just a geographical medium" (138) to be appropriated, divided, and exploited by those with the knowledge, technology, capital, and power to do so.

Following the work of Rodríguez and other scholars, my intention in *Dividing the Isthmus* is not to naturalize the relationship of Central American societies to their physical geographic location, or to essentialize geographic, spatial, and materialist readings of Central American cultures. Rather, I ponder Central America's geographic location and locution as an isthmus, giving rise to spatial-cultural metaphors, synecdochal discourses, and entwined narratives transcending national imaginaries. The conceptualizations of the isthmus that I describe in this introduction are but a few examples that cast the isthmus as a cultural space bound by real and imagined tensions, conflicts, and contradictions.[11] As a cultural space-in-between continents, oceans, and geopolitical spheres, Central America has been imagined by world powers and those serving them as a transitional region to be conquered, civilized, cultivated, charted, mapped, modernized, and pacified (Dunkerley 1988, 1994; Benz 1997; I. Rodríguez 2004) and open to continual exploitation and expropriation of its natural resources, territories, and peoples. Alternate Central American imaginary configurations and transisthmian discursive assemblages, however, are made possible when reading texts and discourses across borders, regions, nations, languages, traditions, and genres, as this book seeks to show.

The Isthmus as Discursive Space-in-Between

Dividing the Isthmus examines cultural and literary assemblages that may allow us to look beyond the forces that have kept Central American histories, cultures, and literatures compartmentalized, isolated, and divided. In the introduction to *The Location of Culture* (1994), Homi K. Bhabha argues that it is in the interstitial, the liminal in-between, or, as posited here, the "transisthmian" space, that postcolonial or neocolonial cultures and literatures speak to, back, and against the unifying narratives of imperialism, neocolonialism, and globalization. Furthermore, it is in these contact zones, or spaces of cultural encounter, that "peoples geographically and historically separated come into contact with one each other and establish ongoing relations" (Pratt 1992, 7). While Mary Louise Pratt speaks about the (neo)colonial encounters between colonizers and colonized, the cultural and literary contact zones of Central America may be read as spaces of internal division, as well as crossings and exchanges between Central American cultures and societies. From these spaces of intersection of diverse Central American traditions, cultures, and peoples, as Silviano Santiago suggests in *The Space In-Between*

(2001), Central Americans produce texts that respond to, dialogue with, speak to, and write against narratives imposed on the region (31). The isthmus, to use Santiago's words, "is the space in which, although the signifier may remain the same, the signified disseminates another inverted meaning" (35) and generates liminal discourses. The isthmus, thus, concomitantly represents a cultural space of divisions and intersections, as I argue in this book.

It is important here to acknowledge the groundbreaking work of Edelberto Torres-Rivas (1980, 2006), Sergio Ramírez (1982, 1985, 1995), Héctor Pérez-Brignoli (1989), Arturo Arias (1998a, 1998b, 2007), Ralph Lee Woodward Jr. (1999), and other Central Americanists who have studied the region's history, culture, and literature as intersecting local, regional, and international productions. In *La piel de Centroamérica* (The Skin of Central America) (2006), Torres-Rivas recognizes that projects covering the region as a whole and as discrete units may be potentially superficially synthetic (15) but nonetheless useful for examining general tendencies converging across Central American countries. Thus he uses the metaphor of the epidermis to describe tenuous forces such as modernization on national and regional terms (16–18). For Torres-Rivas, it is important to examine what he identifies as "la piel centroamericana" (16) as an interpretive membrane or filter by which to understand historical developments in the region. Similarly, Pérez-Brignoli, in *A Brief History of Central America*, uses the paradigm of the puzzle to piece together Central American national histories into a regional historiography, covering the pre-Columbian period through the revolutionary apex of the 1980s. Woodward, in *Central America: A Nation Divided*, also engages in a comparative, regional, and transisthmian historiographic project. In the words of Woodward, such a project seeks "to provide representative examples of general trends rather than a comprehensive chronicle, while also explaining the major political, social, and economic events of the region's history" (1999, ix–x). One of the first scholars to theorize Central American comparative cultural studies, Ramírez further examines the intersections of Central American histories, cultures, and literatures in *Antología del cuento centroamericano, Balcanes y volcanes y otros ensayos y trabajos*, and *Hatful of Tigers*. According to Ramírez, Central American literary texts, like the "particular conducts" of Central American nations and peoples, not only acquire specificity but also represent "general conditions" that connect them in significant ways (1985, 14). Reading Central American literatures comparatively to reveal shared Central American traditions, Ramírez suggests that cultural texts such as short stories, music, and folk art could be read to analyze regional sociohistorical conditions, issues, and problematics. Following the work of these critics of Central American Studies and others, I explore ways of reading Central American literary and cultural production in transcultural, transnational, and transisthmian ways.

Furthermore, Magda Zavala and Seidy Araya, in *La historiografía literaria en América Central (1957–1987)* (1995), along with other contemporary scholars of Central American cultural and literary studies (Bolaños Varela 1988; Cortez 2000; Barbas-Rhoden 2003; Mackenbach 2004; Ortiz Wallner 2005; Leyva 2005), recognize the need to examine Central American literatures and cultures comparatively and inter- and transregionally, a project that Rafael Cuevas Molina engages critically in his *Traspatio florecido* (1993) and *Identidad y cultura en Centroamérica* (2006). Based on critical cognitive remappings of Central America, Zavala and Araya propose a regional analytic grounded on "la idea de Centroamérica, entendida como zona cultural o patria grande de los siete países del istmo [the idea of Central America, understood as a cultural zone, or supra-nation of the seven isthmian countries]" (1995, 21).

Although Zavala and Araya's idea of a Central American cultural zone would seem to allude to the nineteenth-century ideal of a federated Central American isthmian imaginary, they argue instead for the study of cultural intersections across nations, produced especially under the strain of globalizing and homogenizing epistemological projects. *Dividing the Isthmus* responds to Zavala and Araya's call for a transisthmian cultural criticism that enables critics to reconfigure texts and locations into new synecdochal groupings as representative of larger cultural dynamics extending across the isthmus. A regional, comparative transisthmian approach to Central American literatures and cultures can only offer new provocative ways of reading Central American texts in specific and transhistorical locations, in relation to regional, hemispheric, and global contexts, and in intertextual relation to one another. More than ever at the beginning of the twenty-first century, transisthmian critical practices are needed to respond to hegemonic (i.e., developmentalist and economist) regional cultural agendas sweeping through the isthmus. *Dividing the Isthmus* links cultural productions across Central America and offers critical readings of a broad range of isthmian cultural and literary productions.

Methodologically, I draw from an investigative process that I identify as fiction-finding, as opposed to the fact-finding missions that in Central America often turn out to be equally fictive. In my fiction-finding fieldwork, I have conducted interdisciplinary and intersectional research drawing from literary studies, cultural studies, feminist/gender studies, critical race theory, trauma studies, transnational migration studies, popular culture, ethnography, geography, history, politics, economics, and Latin American and U.S. Latina/o Studies, to name only a few disciplinary fields that inform my critical practice. I have conducted research in national archives, university libraries, public libraries, and private holdings and engaged colleagues and subjects through in-person and electronic discussions, papers commented on and exchanged at conferences, personal communications, interviews, oral histories, and field visits across the isthmus and beyond. I draw from a spectrum of Central American and Central Americanist scholarship that is gaining critical attention in the United States.

I read the isthmus as central to the discourses of the Americas from the end of the nineteenth century through the beginning of the twenty-first century. This book covers a little over one hundred years, 1899–2007, of modern cultural and literary production and modern empire building in Central America. In my analysis of the Central American context, 1899 and 2007 represent key years in the history of Central America, as well as periodizing concepts in Central American literary and cultural production. In 1899, the ubiquitous United Fruit Company (UFCO) was officially incorporated in Boston, Massachusetts, not only branding an era of economic, diplomatic, and economic interventions in the region but also marking the inception of the struggle for economic, political, and cultural autonomy in Central America, as (re)presented in Máximo Soto Hall's novel, aptly titled *El problema*, published in 1899, which I analyze in chapter 1. The epilogue reads a series of Central American texts produced through the year 2007, when the Costa Rican government ratified the Dominican Republic–Central America Free Trade Agreement, despite wide opposition by the citizenry of Costa Rica. (On May 28, 2004, leaders of El Salvador, Guatemala, Honduras, and Nicaragua met with President George W. Bush to sign the Central American Free Trade Agreement without the presence of Costa Rica. In January 2004, the Dominican Republic entered into the Free Trade Agreement. Subsequently, on July 28, 2005, the U.S. House of Representatives ratified DR-CAFTA by a narrow midnight vote of 217 to 215, and Bush signed the agreement into law [P.L. 109–053] on August 2, 2005. By the end of 2006, DR-CAFTA had been approved in the Dominican Republic and the Central American countries, with the exception of Costa Rica, which finally entered the agreement on October 7,

2007.) The years 1899 and 2007, thus, mark over one hundred years of continued (U.S.) foreign intervention and local resistance to empire building in the isthmus. With the United States as its neighbor, Central America has responded to foreign interventions and homegrown inequities, injustices, and impunities in creative and critical ways, which this book explores in specific chapters organized chronologically, thematically, and spatially as transisthmian configurations.

In his acceptance speech on receiving the Nobel Prize in literature, "The Solitude of Latin America" (1982), Gabriel García Márquez described "the outsized reality" of Latin America given U.S. hegemony in the Americas and paid homage to Central America, which has been subject to multiple U.S. interventions throughout the years.[12] He spoke of countless massacres, genocides, dictatorships, and seemingly larger-than-life events and figures, often interpreted by "patterns not our very own" and deemed magical, exotic, and *supra-real*. These extreme realities in Central America, according to García Márquez, include the actions of "General Maximiliano Hernández Martínez, the theosophical despot of El Salvador who had thirty thousand peasants slaughtered in a savage massacre," and the "diabolic dictator [Efraín Ríos Montt?] who [in 1982 was] carrying out, in God's name, the first Latin American ethnocide of our time" (García Márquez 1982). In the 1980s Central Americans lived through a period of destructive civil wars in the isthmus; in the twenty-first century they face even greater levels of violence as the region plunges into greater poverty, scarcity, and migrancy. All this can be read as part of the "outsized realities" of Central America and as what the historian Eric Hobsbawm has called "the age of extremes" (1994). *Dividing the Isthmus* draws attention to the more than one hundred years of "outsized realities" and extreme (hi)stories of Central America as represented in selected works by Central American writers and artists. This book is thus an exercise in (re)reading Central American texts in and against extreme realities and grand narratives.

Rewriting the Isthmus: The Next Chapters

Each chapter of *Dividing the Isthmus* focuses on the grand narratives of (anti)imperialism, revolution, subalterity, globalization, and transnational migration, as well as other discursive, historical, and material configurations of the region. In Central America, the neocolonial capitalist production of cacao, coffee, indigo, bananas, canals, waste, and excess migrant labor has shaped the production of what I identify here as a transisthmian cultural and literary production.

Geoculturally, *Dividing the Isthmus* examines texts produced in Costa Rica, El Salvador, Guatemala, Honduras, Nicaragua, and Panama and their extraterritorial, transnational extensions in the United States. I do not examine Honduran Belizean cultural production at great length, although I can only hope that my work incites scholars to write about Belizean and other Central American cultures and literatures. I do not use one interpretive lens, critical framework, or theoretical language but draw from various critical interpretive lenses, or *membranes*, as Torres-Rivas would have it, to produce a bricolage of interdisciplinary materials and provisional readings of the transisthmus, always subject to reelaboration, reinterpretation, and interrogation. Each chapter may be read as a discursive "splice," or intersectional study, of the isthmus, generically, historically, and otherwise analyzing texts from one or more Central American countries. The material and cultural production of cacao, indigo, coffee, bananas, canals, waste, and "disposable workers" (Harvey 2005, 169–170) central to each chapter serves as the "glue" holding the transisthmian bricolage together. In my analysis of Central America, these material and symbolic products are key to the discussion of the relationship of culture and nature and are deployed as cultural metaphors giving interpretive coherency to Central American conditions of cultural production. The nation- and empire-building narratives, social protest novels, *testimonios*, diasporic and immigrant stories, and other narrative textualities discussed in *Dividing the Isthmus* are cultural responses to local historical and material conditions, as well as global, "general trends" in Central America, as Sergio Ramírez and others have suggested.

Chapter 1 begins with a study of nation- and empire-building novels written in Central America at the turn of the twentieth century. Costa Rica is of particular interest here since, in 1830, it was one of the first countries in the isthmus to produce coffee for export and has since served as the model of a now highly contested exceptional Central American nation. In Costa Rica and elsewhere in the coffee-producing regions of the isthmus, the golden grain came to symbolize the positivist aspirations of Central American nations seeking modernization, industrialization, and progress. On the grounds of coffee, the oligarchy and intellectual elite class sought to fashion Costa Rica into an exemplary "coffee republic" to be replicated across the isthmus. In various period pieces, transisthmian writers such as the Nicaraguan Ruben Darío, the

Guatemalan Máximo Soto Hall, the Cuban José Martí, and the Costa Rican Carlos Gagini examined the predicament of Costa Rica and Central America in the modern era and on the eve of its imaginary annexation to the United States. The Central American caficulture intelligentsia would respond with a contradictory blend of anti-imperialist, nation-building novels, true to modern aspirations, patriotic ideals, and liberal economic agendas at the beginning of the twentieth century.

Chapter 2 revisits a corpus of social realist texts associated with the production of bananas and the construction of the Panama Canal, most of which were published between 1930 and 1960. During this thirty-year period, foreign powers, national oligarchies, and military forces forged alliances with multinational corporations across the isthmus. Produced by some of the most outspoken, progressive, and militant writers of Central America, the social protest literature challenged not only the corporate order but also national rule and foreign economic intervention in the isthmus. In their writings, the Panamanian Joaquín Beleño, the Costa Rican Carmen Lyra, the Guatemalan Miguel Ángel Asturias, and the Honduran Ramón Amaya Amador scrutinized the impact of U.S. intervention on local populations, as well as the realignment of race, class, and gender relations in the isthmus. No stone was left unturned or unthrown by writers of this genre that up to now has not been examined as a significant unifying discursive force across the isthmus.

Chapter 3 provides a case study in the wide production of testimonial narrative transecting the Central American isthmus during the civil war period and thereafter. Specifically, this chapter examines the significance of testimonial literature in El Salvador within the larger production of narratives of decolonization, resistance, and revolution in Central America in the 1970s, 1980s, and 1990s. Rather than elaborate a comparative study of different testimonial texts produced in various sites in Central America, this chapter focuses on the production of testimonial narrative in one site of convergence—El Salvador—where I argue the Foucaldian will to give testimony and to retell history informed various narrative practices, including the production of *testimonios* per se, testimonial novels, life and oral narratives, television and radio programming, graffiti, academic writing, school projects, and even university theses. In El Salvador, *testimonio* became a life practice that could not be silenced or obscured. Produced locally across Central America in the 1980s and 1990s, *testimonio* thus may be read as a veritable transisthmian narrative textuality, as Arturo Arias proposes (2007), with local inflections such as those manifested in Manlio Argueta's works.

Through an in-depth reading of Argueta's novel *Cuzcatlán donde bate la mar del sur* (1987) and Roque Dalton's heteroglossic historiography titled *El Salvador (Monografía)* (1979), this chapter examines the deep structures of testimonial narrative and the grand narrative of (neo)colonialism in Central America as codified by the sign of indigo (*añil*) in these texts. This chapter willfully reads testimonial literature as a transisthmian cultural phenomenon coming into scrutiny as a consequence of the so-called Rigoberta Menchú controversy. It examines the transformation of testimonial narrative into a historiographic record of neocolonialism in the isthmus, hence its enduring vitality and significance.

The remaining chapters and epilogue of the book examine Central American cultural production and practices as they expand and extend beyond the geophysical isthmus, all the while relocating, transforming, and negotiating new contradictions and realities in other sites. Chapter 4 revisits the effects of posttrauma and war in the diasporic novels *Return of the Maya* by the Maya Q'anjob'al writer Gaspar Pedro González and *The Tattooed Soldier* by the U.S. Guatemalan writer Héctor Tobar. Published originally in 1998, these novels may be read as literary companions to the Truth Commission's Report, *Guatemala, Never Again! REHMI (Recovery of Historical Memory Project in The Official Report of Human Rights Office, Archdiocese of Guatemala)* (1999), whose Spanish version was also published in 1998. The REHMI compiles data on human rights violations committed during the Guatemalan Civil War (1954–1996) and documents survivor *testimonios* gathered after the signing of the Peace Accords in Guatemala. In this chapter, fiction and fact become indistinguishable in the telling of the larger (his)story of violence, trauma, and diaspora in and outside of the isthmus. The migrant, or disposable worker (Harvey 2005), figures in both novels as the sign of the inhumane treatment of Central Americans in the late twentieth century.

Chapter 5 examines a corpus of transnational solidarity literature produced by Central American refugees, Latinas/os, and others in the United States at the end of the twentieth century. It focuses on texts written by U.S. Latina/o writers, including Ana Castillo (*Sapogonia*, 1990), Alejandro Murguía (*Southern Front*, 1990), Demetria Martínez (*Mother Tongue*, 1994), and Maya Chinchilla ("Solidarity Baby," 2007). Fleeing the civil wars in the isthmus and seeking refuge in the United States in the 1980s, Central Americans joined an increasing critical mass of Latinas/os, who were also transformed by the presence of Central Americans. In these Latino contact zones, solidarity networks, sanctuary sites, political activism, and the immigrant rights movement were reignited, benefiting not only Central American asylum seekers but also the U.S. Latina/o population as a whole who connected with the plight of the isthmus. Aligning with the struggles of Central Americans during the 1980s, a score of authors began to produce a Latina/o transnational literature mobilized against the wars and interventions in Central America.

Chapter 6 focuses on the transnational migration of Salvadorans and their production of cultural and literary space in Washington, D.C., a major destination for a growing number of Salvadoran immigrants. The Salvadoran media have identified Salvadorans residing outside of the isthmus as "Departamento 15." This chapter traces Central American migratory experiences after the 1990s and explores the cultural production of District of Columbia "wachintonians" Quique Avilés, Mario Bencastro, Lilo González, Karla Rodas, and others. In their work, the transisthmian divide takes yet a new turn as Central American communities occupy other spatial and cultural locations beyond Central America. The Salvadoran nation occupies not only San Salvador but also, among other sites, San José, Nuevo Laredo, Sydney, Los Angeles, and Washington, D.C. From these translocal sites, Salvadorans like other Central American diasporic subjects, produce transisthmian narratives.

Chapter 7 returns to a dystopic Central America still recuperating from past and future wars. The sign of waste (garbage), a constant in this reconstruction literature, represents the consumptive and tropicalized state of Central America within the neoliberal order. Through interlinked readings of Carmen Naranjo's story "And We Sold the Rain" (1989), Fernando Contreras Castro's *Única mirando al mar* (1994), Manlio Argueta's *Milagro de la Paz* (1994), and Gioconda Belli's *Waslala: Memorial del futuro* (1996), this chapter grapples with the devastating imaginary state of postwar Central America.

If literature can be said to incubate the political unconscious of a society and its greatest anxieties, as some critics have argued, then the texts examined in the epilogue represent a Central America grappling with its own tenuous future as the FTAA and the DR-CAFTA reconfigure yet again the isthmus according to intervening interests. In her groundbreaking work, Beatriz Cortez (2000) has identified these texts as narratives of disenchantment and discontent, for what else is left to take from Central America but the fighting spirit of its people. We can only hope that Central America will weather this latest intervention, as it has weathered previous ones. In these latest texts published across the isthmus, however, injury, dispossession, homelessness, hunger, suicide, homicide, and crime prevail. The living carnage and the undifferentiated multitude of Central America lay exposed, for example, in Werner Mackenbach's edited volume *Cicatrices* (Scars) (2004), Daniel Joya's *Sueños de un callejero* (2003), Sergio Muñoz Chacon's *Urbanos* (2003) and *Los Dorados* (2000), Claudia Hernández's *Mediodía de frontera* (2002), Waldina Mejía Medina's *La Tía Sofi y los otros cuentos* (2002), Rocío Tábora's *Guardarropa* (2001), and Franz Galich's *Managua Salsa City (¡Devórame otra vez!)* (2001), among other texts. I read these texts as red flags for Central America(ns), signaling the escalation of global violence, the uncurbed expansion of free markets, the careening race or push of local populations to the very depths of the global economy.

To understand (and challenge) the troubled narrative of Central America unraveling before our very eyes, I have written *Dividing the Isthmus*, for I wish finally to read beyond the endings that would ultimately seek to erase, silence, destroy, and scatter to the winds the narratives, cultures, and peoples of Central America. I believe that it is never too late to reconfigure and reimagine the isthmus along other coordinates and story lines; therein lies the power of the latest disenchanted narrative textuality of Central America, where imaginary characters live out the extreme realities that García Márquez sought to elucidate. Perhaps we can learn from these prescient Central American narratives and reinvent the isthmus for present and future generations. The devolving course of Central America's future history, as Gioconda Belli forewarns in *Waslala*, can be reversed and redirected, if and when we read the past judiciously, critically, and creatively to produce alternate, viable narrative scripts premised on literary drafts of the isthmus. In the chapters that follow, I retrace the history of Central America by examining its narrative life. As such, readers can begin at the beginning or at the end. For in the end all chapters lead to the same place, the reconfiguration, reelaboration, and reinterpretation of Central American histories, cultures, and literatures. It is my hope, as the author of this book, that we may gain greater understanding and respect for Central America by reading its signs and (his)stories in local, regional, and transisthmian configurations.

CHAPTER 1

Costa Rican Grounds and the Founding of the Coffee Republics

W hen the National Theater first opened its doors in San José in 1897, Costa Rica was beginning an era of progress, modernization, and urbanization. The inauguration of the theater, with its neoclassical architecture and imported Italian artwork (Ferrero 2004, 146), marked over two decades of the fortification of the national economy and the consolidation of the nation's cultural identity. According to the Costa Rican literary critic Álvaro Quesada Soto, the theater was viewed by many as a "réplica en miniatura de una ópera europea [miniature replica of a European opera house]" (1998, 31), representing not only the romantic ideals but also the positivist, modernizing agenda of the coffee oligarchy and its extended network known as the *caficultura* (caficulture).[1] A cornerstone of nation building in Costa Rica, the theater remains a symbol of the cosmopolitan aspirations of an oligarchic class for whom the theater was built (1998, 31) and its self-styled intelligentsia called El Olimpo (the Olympus) (Quesada Soto 1988, 1995, 1998; Rojas and Ovares 1995).[2]

Affiliated with the *caficultura* through family ties, education, profession, and economic, political, and cultural networks, the Olimpo wrote for an exclusive public, as literacy at the turn of the century was limited to the educated, wealthy class. It is estimated that in 1892 close to 69 percent of the population in Costa Rica was nonliterate (Segura Montero 1995, 12n4; Fumero 2002), compared to as high as 80 to 90 percent in the rest of Central America (Taracena Arriola 1993, 170; Fumero 2002). At best, in the 1860s 30 percent of the Costa Rican population was literate, while a far smaller percentage had access to print material (Vega Jiménez 1992, 117; Molina Jiménez 1995, 65).[3] Privileged by socioeconomic class and racial and gender status, a powerful "población maculina alfabeta" (male literate population) (Taracena Arriola 1993, 170) with "universal suffrage" ruled over the majority of people in Central America. According to Arturo Taracena Arriola, this ruling elite, comprising at most 10 to 20 percent of the population (1993, 170), determined how states would be run and how nations would be defined. That group in Costa Rica was El Olimpo—the male privileged class associated with the coffee-producing oligarchy.

From the start, the literate and literary culture of the ruling *caficultura* played a significant role in producing the founding cultural narratives of Costa Rica, as they would across Central America. Intellectuals, writers, and politicians associated with El Olimpo assumed the task of molding national identity through the development of political, economic, and cultural policies. Writers such as the Costa Rican national Carlos Gagini (1865–1925) and the Guatemalan émigré Máximo Soto Hall (1871–1944) expressed the caficulture's economic, political, and social values, as well as its cultural anxieties at the turn of the century. In their works, Soto Hall and Gagini represented the tensions of a brokered Central American cultural intelligentsia that sought economic, political, and cultural leverage on the eve of the construction of the Panama Canal. In his arguably anti-imperialist, futuristic novel titled *El problema* (The Problem) (1899), Soto Hall identified the subjection of the Central American national oligarchies and bourgeois classes to the United States as an ideological problem and social pathology that would continue to plague Central America well into the future. In a similar vein, Gagini, in *El árbol enfermo* (The Sick Tree) (1928), and José Martí, in his literary sketches of Costa Rica written during his short travels through the country, examined the crisis of a nation struggling to define itself as modern and cosmopolitan while staying true to its provincial traditions and ideals.[4]

The Making of a Nation in the Tropics

On the cusp of the twentieth century, Costa Rica would thus emerge as a modern Central American nation, with a tropical difference. Concentrated in the Central Valley—the coffee-producing region of the country—the Costa Rican intelligentsia consciously cultivated the image of Costa Rica as an exceptional nation (Molina Jiménez and Palmer 1992; Ovares et al. 1993; Ovares 1994; Molina Jiménez 1995) and laid the foundations of its national mythology as an arcadian coffee republic (Quesada Soto 1998, 35). According to Flora Ovares:

Esta visión del pasado, forjada sobre los mitos del paraíso y la edad de oro, se vinculan abiertamente con la imaginación del país como arcadia. Se construye un mundo rural, sujeto a una temporalidad cíclica, cuyos héroes son aquellos de la literatura de costumbres, vinculados por lazos de armonía social y familiar. La descripción idealizada del espacio acude al tópico del país vergel y el mundo diminuto, rural e idílico se cierra en sí mismo. (1994, 44)
[This vision of the past, forged over the myth of paradise and the Golden Age, is associated directly with the imaginary of the country as arcadia. This literature constructs a rural world, subject to cyclic time, whose heroes are those of local color, bound by the ties of social and familial harmony. The idealized description of space resorts to the topic of the bountiful country, and the small, rural and idyllic world closes in upon itself.]

The construction of an ideal pastoral Costa Rica required the production of heroes, monuments, institutions, and traditions, as well as an array of theater pieces, magazines, periodicals, newspapers, literary texts, and artwork forging a singular national history, mythology, and culture (Quesada Soto 1998, 32).

The Olympian image of Costa Rica as an arcadian nation or an idyllic coffee republic is nowhere more visible than in J. A. Villa's painting *Alegoría* (Allegory) (1897), which was commissioned for the inauguration of the National Theater. The painting, which still overlooks the foyer of the theater and whose image was once imprinted on national currency, provides a sweeping view of Costa Rican society at the end of the nineteenth century. The country's rich vegetation, complex topography, mixed economies, and diverse people are represented in a visual *cuadro de costumbre* (local color sketch). As its title suggests, the painting allegorizes the Costa Rican nation, drawing from stock figures associated with the highland Central Valley and lowland Atlantic Coast. Scanning from right to left, the scene moves from the coffee-producing region of the Central Valley toward ships adorned with Costa Rican flags on the Atlantic seaboard, ready to transport Costa Rican goods to world markets. The painting comes alive with white, robust, red-white-and-blue-clad female coffee bean pickers, mulatto stevedores carrying oversized banana stems, and dockworkers hauling coffee sacks labeled "Café de Costa Rica" onto the waiting steamships. On the docks, merchants, landowners, and spectators oversee the bustle of moving cargo and the industrial landscape of coffee trees, banana stems, and ships. Center stage, a single conspicuous electric light post rises out of the crowd as if heralding the arrival of modern technologies in the country.

In this foundational moment, Costa Rica was imagined as a prosperous modern republic tied to a diversified agrarian export economy powered by the labor of content campesinos and industrial workers. All of Costa Rica—urban and rural, agricultural and industrial, rich and poor, male and female, black and white—was represented in this *costumbrista* picture. This national portrait of the republic, part coffee and part banana, belongs to the mythology of the quintessential and exceptional Costa Rica, whose internal contradictions were melded into a colorful folkloric sketch. According to Ramírez, what was wrong with this picture of national harmony and bountiful prosperity was precisely the brand of "inoffensive folklore" cultivated by "the rich and powerful [who] are not prepared to see the world change" (1995, 62). In Ramírez's estimation, the literary aesthetic of *costumbrismo*, or local color, naturalized the power of the caficulture while romanticizing the material exploitation of coffee production.

Writing National Literatures in the Coffee Republic

Coffee beans—"the quintessential export crop"—and coffee production arrived in the Americas from Yemen, Java, and Africa in the seventeenth century (Topik 1998). Coffee quickly became a staple crop throughout the Caribbean islands and the tropical mainland and was widely produced in Central America and Brazil and other parts of South America by the mid-1800s (Jiménez 1995; Roseberry, Gudmundson, and Kutschbach 1995; Topik 1998, 37–41). An industrial "second conquest" of the region was aggressively pursued by profit-seeking foreign entrepreneurs and local oligarchies and governments desirous of modernizing their countries as quickly as possible (Topik and Wells 1998, 1). Many historians agree that the introduction of the coffee export economy in Central America is probably one of the most significant events in the region's history. Roseberry, Gudmundson, and Kutschbach claim that "the nineteenth century (that is, roughly, from 1830 to 1930) was *the* coffee century in Latin America" (1995, 3; original emphasis). Coffee provided the capital for Central America to produce crops for export, to build an internal market for global imports, and, as demand would have it, to initiate modernizing projects. These modernizing projects entailed the construction of roads, railroads, communications systems, shipping inlets, and transport routes; the import of migrant labor in some areas and the exploitation of local workers in others; and the investment of international capital.

By the 1870s, coffee production permeated the economies of the entire Central American region, with the exception of Honduras. Topik states that coffee became "one of today's leading internationally traded commodities, [and] it is likely the most valuable agricultural export in history" (Topik and Wells 1998, 37). A highly valued commodity in the world market from the start, the *grano de oro* was, in Topik's words, a "contradictory and controversial crop," the source of wealth for some and the burden of labor for others:

> Of all tropical export commodities, coffee is the most often credited with fostering a strong national bourgeoisie, industrialization, and a strong state. Yet coffee is also blamed for glaring inequalities, harsh labor conditions, the subjugation of local interests to those of foreigners, the creation of monocultural dependent economy, and the despoiling of indigenous people. (Topik and Wells 1998, 40)

While the coffee producing, exporting, and processing classes enjoyed a "foundation of wealth" (Paige 1997, 14; see also Stone 1990),[5] indigenous communities, especially in northern Central America, lost communal landholdings to coffee production and were subject to coercive labor codes associated with the Liberal Reforms of the 1870s. Designed to meet the modernizing agendas of each country, these reforms generally privatized lands and secured labor for coffee production. Northern Central America proved an ideal site for coffee production for it had the "required rich land, ample rain, and poor workers" (Topik and Wells 1995, 38) who could be forced to work under the systems of *colonato* and *mandamiento*. Vagrancy laws in Guatemala and El Salvador forced laborers to work annually on large *fincas* (farms) for at least 100 to 150 days, while *colonato* forced peasants to work on coffee *fincas* in exchange for housing or land use, *mandamiento* authorized forced recruitment, and *habilitación* substituted labor for loan payments (Peréz Brignoli 1989, 87; Samper 1993, 56–58, 86–88; Lovell 2000b, 392–444). From the start, the caficulture managed the new coffee economy and promulgated liberal reforms that made possible extreme means of labor extraction that linked Central America to larger global economic forces.

In *Balcanes y volcanes*, Ramírez situates the production of modern national literatures in Central America in the so-called golden age of coffee:

> Las primeras manifestaciones de un arte literario de importancia, se producen en Centroamérica en la época de oro del café, porque durante la colonia y los primeros decenios independientes del siglo XIX, sólo hubo casos aislados de creadores literarios, varios de ellos notables principalmente en Guatemala. (Ramírez 1985, 45)
> [The first manifestations of an important literary art were produced in Central America during the golden age of coffee, because during the colonial period and the first decades of Independence in the nineteenth century, there were only isolated cases of literary producers, many of them from Guatemala.]

The caficulture made possible the production of *costumbrista* literature and also literary texts associated with the latest modernist trends. At this juncture, Central American literature emerged as modern literature (Ramírez 1985, 45), splintering into literary nationalisms, national literatures, and literatures in the service of national politics (Franco 1994; Sommer 1991; Ramos 1989).[6]

Indeed, Central American nation-building literature was actively engaged in the articulation of political discourse and the formulation of cultural politics and practices. As Julio Ramos explains for other national literatures of Latin America, for the *caficulturas*, "las letras eran la política [literature was politics]" (Ramos 1989). The production of national literatures in Central America was tied to the emergence of an elite reading (ruling) class that possessed the means to produce and consume culture. At the same time modern print technologies and industries introduced by the *caficultura* served to naturalize a highly exploitative agrarian export economy and the authority of the ruling elite (Molina Jiménez 1992, 142). It is no coincidence, then, that the first printing press was introduced to Costa Rica in 1830, about the same time that coffee was initially produced for export, thus making possible the dissemination of print material and images of the nation. The elaboration of new reading subjects and new print media such as newspapers, periodicals, cultural supplements, and the *folletín*, or serialized novel, point to the "civilizing" effect of caficultures in Central America. In Costa Rica, as in other Central American countries, the product was a national literature tied to a dictating elite, whose tastes in literature were both conservative and innovative and increasingly informed by its exposure to Europe and the United States at the turn of the century (Vega Jiménez 1992, 109–135).[7]

At the beginning of the twentieth century, Costa Rican and Central American literature not only represented the tastes of the elite but also comprised an uneven blend of heterogeneous forms, some "inherited from the past" (Brushwood 1975, 4) and others just brewing on the horizon of modernity. Critics have pointed out that on the cusp of the nineteenth and twentieth centuries almost all major Latin American discursive tendencies and literary genres converged simultaneously in Central America, including those associated with *costumbrismo*, romanticism, naturalism, realism, and *modernismo*. Romantic historical novels, local color sketches, modernist writing, and anti-imperialist novels, to name only a few examples, circulated in Central America at the same time. In *Historia crítica de la novela guatemalteca* (Critical History of the Guatemalan Novel) (1985), Seymour Menton takes stock of the profusion of literary currents in Central America:

> En los últimos años del siglo XIX, ocurre en Hispanoamérica el espectáculo de una combinación de muchas tendencias novelescas fuera de orden cronológico. (1985, 84)
> [In the last years of the nineteenth century, a spectacular combination of many novelesque tendencies out of chronological order appear in Latin America.]

Ramón Luis Acevedo reads this confluence of cultural tendencies as a timely intersection of residual and emergent forms (1982, 65). The material and cultural conditions of Central America at the turn of the twentieth century were such that cultural flows intersected and interacted in the isthmus, giving way to *modernismo* while also reinforcing *costumbrismo*.

José Martí on the Modern Predicaments of Costa Rica

While visiting Costa Rica in 1893 and 1894 to meet with Cuban exiles, Olympian intellectuals, and supporters of the Cuban revolution-

ary cause (Oliva Medina 1995), José Martí had the opportunity to observe the complexities of modern Costa Rican culture. In his two brief
sketches, "El domingo en San José" (Sunday in San José) and "La parranda" (The Celebration) published in local newspapers, Martí depicted a Costa Rica striving to be modern and urban while preserving
its rural traditions. In "El domingo en San José," the streets of the small
capital come alive at daybreak. Before Martí's hotel window parades the
whole spectrum of Costa Rican society: silk-dressed madams, elegantly
frocked gentlemen, and cotton-clothed *mozos* (young male workers)
wearing colorful waistbands, flanked by black-shawled women, barefoot
"peons," and Indian women and their children. The red, white, and blue
of the Costa Rican flag waves over Martí's *tableaux vivant* (Oliva Medina
1995, 40–41). Likewise, in "La parranda," Martí depicts a countryside
fiesta, overflowing with colorfully dressed revelers, marimba and violin
music, *chicha* and *guaro* liquors, and homemade viands: "gallinas asadas,
pescado frito, frijoles y tortas, y el rompope de huevo y maíz, grato y
espeso [roasted chicken, fried fish, bean tortes, and egg and corn punch,
delicious and thick]" (Oliva Medina 1995, 41–42). In his descriptions of
traditional Costa Rican courting dances—the Torito cortés, the Boti-
juela, the Chiricano, and the Cajeta de leche—Martí reflects the image
of a bucolic modern nation, bringing together people from all walks of
life and nurturing the seeds of a democratic Costa Rican nation. Martí's
ideals of "nuestra Costa Rica" would influence writers such as Soto Hall
and Gagini, as well as successive generations of progressive writers such
as Carmen Lyra and Joaquín García Monge—founder of the Costa Rican journal *Repertorio americano*, which posthumously published many
of Martí's essays for Central American readers.

Martí's presence in Central America and his influence on Central
American writers cannot be underestimated. In particular, Martí's critique of the *criollo exótico* (exotic creole) (Martí 1987, 261–272) resonated
with the Europeanized sons of the Central American caficulture and
the members of the Costa Rican Olimpo.[8] Tellingly, the protagonists
of novels such as Soto Hall's *El problema* and Gagini's *El árbol enfermo*
are young male *criollos* who, having been educated in Europe, return
to Costa Rica on the eve of their country's subjugation to the United
States. Embodiments of a romantic sentimental European education,
the exotic creoles of Costa Rican Olympian literature represent a class
that itself has become alienated and has compromised its ideals of national sovereignty and cultural autonomy. Like Martí's *criollo exótico*, the
Olimpo creoles seem to lack the creativity, originality, and reflexivity to

construct fully democratizing social programs for Costa Rica, outside of those imported from Europe and the United States. Although Martí's influence in Costa Rica was far-reaching, the Olimpo would shun his meta-critique of the *criollo exótico*'s privileged status, instead opting to reify their exceptionality as a national signifier. Indeed, according to Martí:

> El genio hubiera estado en hermanar, con la caridad del corazón y con el atrevimiento de los fundadores, la vincha y la toga; en desestancar al indio; en ir haciendo lado al negro suficiente; en ajustar la libertad al cuerpo de los que se alzaron y vencieron por ella. (1987, 268)
> [It would have been the mark of genius to couple the headband and the professor's gown with the founding father's generosity and courage, to rescue the Indian, to make a place for the competent Negro, to fit liberty to the body of those who rebelled and conquered for it.] (Schnookal and Muñiz 1999, 117)

But in Costa Rica, as in most of Central America, the caficulture intelligentsia relegated its indigenous, black, and migrant populations to the jungle hinterlands, mountainous highlands, and Atlantic coastlands. In this drama, the *criollos exóticos* opened their countries to the international economy, collaborated with foreign agents (although many denied it), and enjoyed the privileged status made possible by the production of coffee and other export goods. In the novels of the Olimpo, the sins of Costa Rican exotic creole sons and fathers would be displaced and projected onto the protagonists of U.S. imperialism. By positioning themselves as victims of intervening forces, particularly those of the United States, members of the caficulture, through texts produced by its intelligentsia, virtually erased their corroboration and participation in imperialism in the isthmus.

As depicted in Villa's 1897 "Alegoría," the arcadian image of Costa Rica represented a singular criollo worldview in a romantic, local color sketch that excluded images of labor migration and exploitation, racial segregation and marginalization, and subjugation of all nonwhite and nonmale people. In effect, the caficulture rejected Martí's vision of an inclusive, egalitarian nation and his proposal for intellectual and cultural decolonization, although it celebrated his humanist ideals. Further, El Olimpo and the intelligentsia of other Central American nations notably became apologists for exploitative socioeconomic structures in the region. At the turn of the century, the cultural predicament of Central

America was the result of the collaboration of the *criollos exóticos* with imperialist market forces. The project of caficulture agents during the early nation-building period in Central America was to formulate, as Carlos Alonso identifies for Latin American nations in general, "a partial vision of cultural essence that willfully isolates certain elements . . . and advances them as representative of the totality of cultural experience" (1990, 3). By default, such representations could only privilege certain images of Central America, primarily those that could be assimilated and marketed to a modern world economy. Forging a good image of the nation through *costumbrista* signs was crucial to the Olympian nation builders.

In *100 años de literatura costarricense* (1995), the Costa Rican literary critics Margarita Rojas and Flora Ovares recognize the mercantilism upholding the autochthonous arcadian image of Costa Rica in the writings of El Olimpo:

> Una de las principales motivaciones de los escritores nacionalistas se encontrababa fuera del país: era el lector extranjero, pensando en el cual se escribieron muchas de las obras más típicamente pintorescas. Gagini (un autor del Olimpo) decía, por ejemplo, que los escritores costarricenses tenían que escribir sobre "los mil sujetos nacionales que pudieran dar motivo a otras obras literarias interesantísimas y llenas de novedad para los extranjeros." (34)
> [One of the main motivations of national writers was found outside of the country: it was the foreign reader for whom most typical picturesque texts were written. Gagini (a writer of the Olimpo) suggested, for example, that Costa Rican authors should write about "the thousands of national subjects that could generate interesting literary texts full of novelty for foreigners."]

Rojas and Ovares explain that the material interests of the caficulture prompted the production of an idealized *costumbrista* image of Costa Rica (see also Palmer 1992, 173). At the height of the Liberal Reforms and modernization projects, the leaders of Costa Rica sought to attract foreign investment to the country by granting concessions over territory, opening new markets for coffee and bananas, and promoting international diplomatic and economic ties, especially with the United States and Great Britain. The Olympian political leaders and cultural intelligentsia engaged also in the production of a marketable image of the nation. As Rojas and Ovares state:

Así, la imagen pictórica y literaria de lo costarricense en que se funda la identidad nacional, aparece motivada, en parte, por la existencia de un consumidor no nacional. Se escribía sobre Costa Rica pensando en el lector norteamericano o europeo. Por esto se explica la inclusión de un "glosario" de costarriqueñismos o tiquismos empleados en obras como "La propia" de Magón con su respectiva "traducción" al castellano "correcto." (1995, 34).

[As such, the picturesque and literary image of Costa Ricanness, upon which national identity was founded, is motivated, in part, by the existence of a non-national consumer. Costa Rica was written about with North American and European readers in mind. That is why a glossary of Costa Rican colloquialisms, or *tiquismos*, with their respective translations into correct Spanish, is included in texts such as "La Propia" by Magón.]

The marketing of Costa Rica relied on selling an idyllic rural image that came to naturalize the exceptionalism of Costa Rica. The ideologies of exceptionalism, expansionism, and interventionism, as I argue below, are closely tied to nation-building projects in Central America, especially Costa Rica. This concern for producing an exceptional image of Costa Rica would explain why, in 1894, a debate ensued over the best mode of representation. The debate, known as *La polémica* (the Polemic) occupied many writers of El Olimpo and filled the pages of Costa Rica's major newspapers (Segura Montero 1995).[9]

The Sick Tree and Its Redemption:
Carlos Gagini Writes a Drama for the Nation

In his novel, *El árbol enfermo* (1918/1989), translated into English under the title *Redemptions* (1985),[10] Carlos Gagini engages in the project of writing national literature in Costa Rica. He opts to use local color and colloquial language to represent the historical drama of the Costa Rican nation as it struggles to define itself against (neo)colonial forces. In the novel, multiple subplots ensue as the old and new creole guard represented respectively by don Rafael Montalvo and Fernando Rodríguez confront the U.S. banker and entrepreneur Mr. Ward, who, on arriving in Costa Rica, not only relentlessly pursues business deals but also seduces Margarita, don Rafael's daughter and rich coffee heiress. The resolution of the novel hinges on the questions, How will Margarita (Costa

Rica) be saved (redeemed) after she has betrayed her father and nation and given herself to the U.S. imperialist? How will her Costa Rican suitor and protector Fernando Rodríguez save her? What will happen to Costa Rica? The narrative crisis represents Costa Rica at the divide of subjugation and sovereignty, the cultural locus where it must forge a new identity and image. To move forward, the novel seems to suggest, Costa Rica must cast its fate with the United States and sever its ties to its colonial Hispanic heritage, as personified by the family patriarch, don Rafael Montalvo, whose house, lineage, and family are eclipsed by Mr. Ward. Don Rafael, a member of the ruling coffee oligarchy, owns property in the fertile coffee-producing Central Valley and in the city of San José; his holdings consist of coffee plantations, dairy farms, and cattle grazing lands. As foreign capital infiltrates Costa Rica, economic and political insecurity unsettles the nation, driving some of the novel's characters to question the traditional values and lifestyle of don Rafael's arcadian society.

> [Don Rafael] incarnated those splendid virtues of old Costa Rican gentlemen: little educated, yet wise and prudent; religious without being a fanatic; generous without being lavish; honest in every respect, un-compromising with laziness, lies, vices, dishonesty; faithful to his word; punctual in fulfilling his promises; a patriot without making a show of it; gallant without bragging; courteous but not obsequious; and respect-ful without fawning. (Gagini 1985, 30)

In sum, don Rafael embodies the values of common sense, Catholic faith, and male honor associated with his Spanish colonial heritage. An avid reader of Miguel de Cervantes's *El Quijote*, don Rafael personifies the quixotic ideal of the old Spanish nobleman on the verge of his de-mise in a modernizing world. His literary tastes represent the Olympian intelligentsia's conservative literary and cultural agenda for the con-struction of national identity: "He had no affection for the modern po-ets, whose verses he characterized as ridiculous, artificial, and immoral" (Gagini 1985, 30). Don Rafael's arcadian vision is shattered, however, with the arrival of new forces in the region, which are personified by Thomas Ward.

Costa Rica's dilemma is further complicated when Mr. Ward, after impregnating Margarita, abandons her and returns to the United States. In the fallout, don Rafael Montalvo dies, crushed by an ailing fig tree on his property; Margarita loses her child; and Fernando Rodríguez is exiled to Spain for plotting to topple the *comprador* government, which had invited Mr. Ward to Costa Rica. In the central metaphor of the sick tree of the Spanish title, the novel suggests that Costa Rica, too, is ill and fragile at its core, for it lacks the self-determination, historical character, and national fortitude necessary to overcome the forces of imperialism. In an inverse manner, José Martí's invocation of green metaphors in his essay "Nuestra América" seems to resonate throughout Gagini's novel, especially Martí's line, "Let the world be grafted onto our republics, but the trunk must be our own" (quoted in Schnookal and Muñiz 1999, 114). In Gagini's novel, the trunk of the tree in the center of don Rafael's property has been attacked by parasites and eventually topples because it has no solid roots. Like the sick tree and the impregnated Margarita, Costa Rica, too, has been infiltrated by outside forces and may not be salvageable. It is up to the sons of the nation to save Costa Rica, the novel seems to say. Through Ward, the United States grafts itself onto the land, politics, economy, and culture of Costa Rica, eating away at its core until the whole country seems to cede to U.S. domination. Martí's unheeded warning becomes a self-fulfilled prophecy in the novel, as Mr. Ward appears to win over Costa Rica. But the novel does not end with Ward taking possession of Costa Rica. Instead, the young oligarchic hero Rodríguez returns to Costa Rica, "redeems" Margarita by marrying her, and assumes responsibility for rehabilitating the nation. With Rodríguez's return, the novel suggests, the fate of Costa Rica on the eve of its takeover by the United States can be changed, or at least delayed.

In *El árbol enfermo*, Fernando Rodríguez returns to Costa Rica and its political, economic, and cultural predicament. As a member of the caficulture elite in a changing economy, Rodríguez seeks modernization, prosperity, and technological advancement for his nation and his socioeconomic class. If he is to save himself from imperialist takeover or neocolonial subjection, Rodríguez has little choice but to "redeem" Margarita, who serves as the sign of the nation throughout the novel. Indeed, by the end of the novel, the Costa Rica nation (vis-à-vis Margarita) has been rehabilitated by its patriot creoles, who, while "redeeming" Costa Rica from the imperialists, also exploit her for profit-yielding foreign investments and the production of agrarian export crops for the world market. Indeed, the coffee, banana, sugar, cacao, grain, and cattle industries have been historically exploited in Costa Rica (Meléndez 1981, 128–129). For both imperialists and the national caficulture in *El árbol enfermo*, Costa Rica represented a redeemable and exploitable source of wealth, providing not only optimum conditions for coffee production in Central America but also a compliant labor force and an elite class eager to exploit internal and external market forces. With Gagini's novel, the myth of Costa Rican exceptionalism would be canonized in the *costumbrista* literature of the period and the modernist literary aesthetic would meet a mixed reception (Barrantes de Bermejo 1997, 28).[11] In their respective works, Gagini and Soto Hall constructed narrative platforms to stage political and cultural debates and produced hybrid texts representing the ambivalent discursivity and modernity of Costa Rica at the beginning of the twentieth century. Indeed, as Rojas and Ovares point out, the project of writing literature in Costa Rica was part of larger ideological and discursive struggles:

> La polémica sobre el nacionalismo en la literatura fue mucho más que una simple discusión periodística, una divergencia entre los escritores jóvenes de entonces o la oposición entre los nacionalistas y los "europeizados." (1995, 34)
> [The debate on literary nationalism was much more than just a journalistic discussion, a disagreement between young writers at that time, or a confrontation between nationalists and Europeanists.]

The Problem of Writing National Literatures in a Transisthmian Context

Seemingly siding with Gagini, Máximo Soto Hall, who lived in Costa Rica at the turn of the twentieth century, participated in *La polémica* of 1894. Costa Rican literary critics identify Soto Hall as a member of Costa Rica's Olimpo, although he is Guatemalan by birth. Like José Martí, Rubén Darío, and other modernist writers, Soto Hall lived, traveled, and wrote throughout Latin America, Europe, and the United States. His older brother, Marco Aurelio Soto Martínez (1846–1908), was president of Honduras from 1876 to 1883, and Soto Hall, at various times, held international diplomatic posts for Guatemala and other Latin American countries. Early in Soto Hall's life, the dictator Manuel Estrada Cabrera (1857–1924), who ruled Guatemala from 1898 to 1920, befriended him. Estrada Cabreras's governance has been called the "twenty-two-year reign of terror" and "the longest uninterrupted rule in Central American history" (Kit 1996, 2:519–520). Under the auspices of Estrada Cabrera, Soto Hall traveled on diplomatic assignments to Costa Rica, El Salvador, Honduras, Panama, South America, Europe, and the United States. The author of an eclectic range of texts that include *El problema* (Costa Rica, 1899), *Un vistazo sobre Costa Rica en el siglo XIX* (Costa Rica, 1901), *La sombra de la Casa Blanca* (Buenos Aires, 1927), *Nicaragua y el imperialismo norteamericano* (Buenos Aires, 1928), and *Pedro de San José Bethencourt* (Guatemala, 1949), Soto Hall also edited his own newspaper and worked for various publications and newspapers throughout Latin America.[12] Toward the end of his life, he founded the Pan American Library and Archives in Buenos Aires, an extensive collection of materials on the Americas, for Argentina's foremost newspaper, *La Prensa* (Beteta 1949, 13–86). In the countries that he visited and that he resided in, Soto Hall participated in local intellectual circles, engaging a wide range of local and hemispheric topics, foremost among them Central American sovereignty and the autonomy of national cultures, issues that would remain significant throughout his career.

Soto Hall made his debut on the Costa Rican literary scene with his novel *El problema*. His work, however, has been largely ignored by Latin American literary criticism. Menton, among the few critics who comments on Soto Hall's novel, claims that "a Máximo Soto Hall le toca la distincción de haber escrito la primera novela anti-imperialista [Máximo Soto Hall holds the distinction of having written the first anti-imperialist novel]" (1985, 130). Ramón Acevedo claims that, as such, it serves as the "punto de partida de toda una producción novelística centroamericana que culmina en nuestros días con la triología bananera de Asturias [point of departure for a production of Central American novels that culminate, in our days, with the banana trilogy of Miguel Ángel Asturias]" (1982, 75). *El problema* occupies a significant place not only in Costa Rican literary history but also in Central American literature for it initiates a genre that engages hemispheric and transisthmian issues. Set in 1928 (almost thirty years in the future), the novel is considered one of the first Central American futuristic, science fiction novels, modeled on the work of Jules Verne (Durán Luzio 1985, 122). It foretells the completion of the transisthmian canal at the San Juan River border between Costa Rica and Nicaragua and describes Central America on the eve of its annexation to the United States (Durán Luzio 1985, 121–127).[13]

The title of the novel refers to the predicament of protecting national sovereignty in Central America at the beginning of the twentieth century. Struggling with the question of national identity and the problem of U.S. imperialism, Soto Hall's novel alludes to issues of Costa Rican literary canon formation, as well as the contradictions of Central American nation-building projects. According to Rojas and Ovares, in *El problema* Soto Hall tested Gagini's thesis "que se podía hacer literatura sobre asuntos locales sin utilizar el habla regional [that one could write literature about local subjects without using regional language]" (1995, 33). Instead, the novel uses a standard form of Spanish, although it mixes aesthetic codes associated with both *costumbrismo* and *modernismo*. The novel takes place in a country with allusions to Costa Rica after the completion of the transisthmian canal. It represents an oligarchic family caught up in a significant moment in national history and produces what John S. Brushwood calls a "picture of salon society" (1981, 14), or, in this case, a picture of Costa Rican *finca* society. Writers associated with the Olimpo represented rural oligarchic and urban bourgeois families as part of the larger folkloric tradition of Costa Rica.[14] *El problema* portrays the Costa Rican nation by focusing exclusively on its local gentry rather than also representing peasants or using colloquial language (*costarriqueñismos*) as signs of national autochthony. In *El problema*, the oligarchy is portrayed as the local color of Central America.

The novel is not about just one problem but many, among them, U.S. imperialism in Central America, the collaboration of creole elites with foreign intervention, and the project of defining national identity in Costa Rican literature. It is also about the problem of unrequited love as experienced by another young *criollo* educated in France and returning to Costa Rica after a twenty-five-year absence. In this national (anti-) imperialist romance, a young doctor, Julio Escalante, falls in love with his half-U.S., half–Costa Rican cousin Emma, who, in turn, loves and marries the U.S. industrialist Mr. Crissey. At the end of the novel, unable to bear the loss of his love and his nation to the imperialist, Julio commits suicide by charging his horse into a moving train carrying the newlyweds. With the death of Julio, the last of the Olympian sons of the coffee republic, the text suggests, the Costa Rican ruling class cannot protect the nation (and Central America) from the United States. Julio tellingly commits suicide on the day that he loses Emma and that Central America as a whole is to be annexed to the United States. With its dismal prognosis of the isthmus's future, the novel's anti-imperialist stance seems to warn of an imminent Central American defeat, if the course of history is not altered. Indeed, by 1855, the filibusterer William Walker had invaded Nicaragua and written about his invasion (Walker 1860/1985).[15] In response to repeated economic, military, and territorial aggression by the United States at the turn of the nineteenth century, Martí ("Nuestra América," 1891), José Enrique Rodó (*Ariel,* 1900), Darío ("A Roosevelt," 1904), Soto Hall, and others contested U.S. imperialism in Central America through their writings. Soto Hall's *El problema* not only alludes to the impact of the U.S. defeat of Spain in 1898 in the isthmus but also describes Central America under the threat of U.S. military intervention. Within a decade of the novel's publication, Panama would become a virtual protectorate of the United States (1903), the Roosevelt Corollary would authorize U.S. interventions in Central America (1904), and the United States would repeatedly invade the isthmus, especially Nicaragua, culminating in Augusto C. Sandino's last stand in 1927.

The first paragraph of the novel provides a point of entry into the plot of the novel, as well as the intersection of geopolitical discourses embedded in the text. After a twenty-five-year absence, Julio Escalante returns to a greatly transformed homeland: the canal has been built, English has become the national language, migrant laborers have been imported en masse from the United States, and the landscape of the region has been irreversibly altered and modernized. Prefacing Julio's grand entrance to the isthmus, the opening paragraph describes Julio's first impressions from the ship as it sails down "las dormidas aguas del Canal [the dormant waters of the canal]":

> A uno y otro margen, reflejando sus fachadas sobre la turbia linfa, quintas circundadas por altas verjas de hierro donde culebreaban, llovidas de flores, las tupidas madreselvas, dejando apenas ver, entre su verde tamiz, el blanco manchón de las escaleras de mármol que se iban estrechando al subir como una ola espumante; oficinas con sus amplias ventanas y sus piezas inundadas de luz; fábricas severas, claustrales, cortando el espacio con sus chimeneas altas, erguidas, que lanzaban constantemente sobre el diáfano azul del cielo bocanadas de humo negro y pesado. Era toda una gran ciudad, alargada, extendida en las riberas de aquel río hecho a medias entre Dios y los hombres; una Venecia moderna, con una sola calle anchísima, limitada por dos grandes océanos. (Soto Hall 1899, 55)
> [On the shores, the villas reflected their facades on the turbid waters, hiding behind high iron fences entwined with thick green honeysuckle vines and flowers that barely gave way to white marble stairs rising like foaming waves; offices with ample windows and rooms inundated with light; severely cloistered factories, slicing space with their tall, stiff chimneys that constantly hurled black smoke into the transparent blue

sky. It was a grand city, stretching alongside the levee of the river, which rose between God and man. It was a modern Venice, with one wide street dividing the oceans.]

The layered imagery of this paragraph suggests that Julio's vision is filtered through the lens of *modernismo*. The reference to the color *azul* (blue) in the middle of the paragraph, embedded in layers of metaphors, transports the reader to a highly aestheticized world that characterizes *modernista* literature. Following the lead of the Nicaraguan-born poet Rubén Darío, whose book *Azul* (1888) marked the debut of Spanish *modernismo*, *modernista* poets used chromatism (colors as signs) and other Parnassian and symbolist literary strategies to invent artful worlds and words. For the *modernistas*, blue was the color of creative possibility and the aesthetic veneer with which they transformed a neocolonialized and feudal Latin America into a modern cosmopolitan space.

In Soto Hall's hybrid *modernista* and *costumbrista* sketch, the young creole Escalante returns to a newly transformed and modernized Central America. On his arrival, he sees the canal awash in blue waters, representing not only a mechanical feat but also an aesthetic object. Etched into the tropical landscape, the canal is lined with factories, offices, stairways, mansions, and fences—utilitarian architectures and structures signifying development, progress, capital, and private property. Nature has absorbed the new installations, enveloping them with flowers, plants, and trees and neutralizing the rigid, noxious effects of the machine in the tropics. In this symbolic scene, the flora, the water, and the landscape soften the harsh reflections of the buildings, the smoke of the factories, and the impact of concrete against soil, water, and air. True to *modernista* fashion, the city of New Charleston at the mouth of the canal is transformed into a modern Venice, the floating city of Europe in Central America, as Darío and other *modernistas* envisioned the tropics. In subsequent references, New Charleston is called the linear city, the city-station, and a great city ("la ciudad lineal," "la ciudad-estación," and "una gran ciudad"). Indeed, New Charleston represents the city at the great divide, where nature and technology, the rural and the urban, and the modern and the traditional are melded. The canal city represents the modernization of Central America and the reconfiguration of the *costumbrista* nation into an entity divested of staple motifs and folkloric images and linked to new signs of development and progress as demonstrated by the construction of the canal built "entre Dios y los hombres," in the divide between nature and technology. Through the image of the naturalized canal, *El problema* suggests that imperialism will be grafted permanently onto the Central American landscape. Just like the flora and fauna of Central America have blended with the mechanical structures in the canal zone, Julio Escalante's family has facilitated the entry of U.S. imperialism into the region.

Between Coffee and Chocolate: Neocolonial Ambivalence

Although the production of coffee is not made explicit in *El problema* and the Escalante family wealth is linked to cacao production, by the end of the novel coffee and chocolate blend into one sign: neocolonial expropriation of capital. Teodoro Escalante, the anti-imperialist patriarch, has built a chocolate factory utilizing the latest machinery and a labor force imported directly from the United States. Teodoro takes great pride in the fact that the factory runs like clockwork because of the efficiency of his American foreman and technology. In the entire factory, there is only one laborer who is Costa Rican, and, on one fateful day, the chocolate factory comes to a fatal standstill due to his error. In a telling outburst of rage, Teodoro says:

> ¡Quién otro podía ser! ¡Claro! El del país. Que gente. Por eso no hemos podido hacer nunca nada. Somos una raza inferior, muy inferior. Mal hago en tratar de mantener esa gente en mi fábrica. (124)
> [Who else could it be! Of course! The one from this country. What people. That is why we have never been able to do anything. We are an inferior race, very inferior. I do wrong trying to keep those people in my factory.]

The novel's verbal irony and Teodoro's dialogic slips reveal the ambivalent position of the Costa Rican elite: on the one hand, ardent nationalists; on the other, U.S. economic partners and allies.

Throughout the novel, Costa Rican characters refer to the inferiority of the "Latino" race, their sickness in body, and their weakness in spirit, in contrast to the American race, which is full of youth, energy, strength, and will, capable of transforming the isthmus into "prodigious" and productive factories, mills, canals, and agricultural crops (Soto Hall 1899, 56). We are not just inferior, says Teodoro, but *very* inferior to the Americans, and the fault is not ours—the ruling class—but of *those* people, the Costa Rican and Central American folks, who fail to work efficiently, effectively, and seamlessly. To this end, the Olympian national imaginary makes invisible the popular discontent, except for the rare appearance of a laborer or two and the novel's sporadic explosions set off by members of European socialist, anarchist, and ultraist movements. Soto Hall, in the first part of *El problema*, alludes to a growing anarchist labor movement setting off bombs in churches and public places in France, where Julio has lived for twenty-five years. Julio explains to Margarita (his fiancée) that those bombs have a material cause—the poverty, hunger, unemployment, and homelessness of the masses with which he and those of his socioeconomic class have very little contact in France or Costa Rica (89–94). Julio says, "Nosotros los que tenemos todo, no sabemos ni pensamos en los que no tienen nada [Those of us who have everything do not know nor think about those who have nothing]" (92). Just shy of pronouncing a quasi-socialist idealism, Julio speaks not from conviction but rather in contradiction to the conservative position of his future father-in-law (95), who offers a Darwinist solution to the rise of social popular movements—the annihilation of the weak and the poor (94).[16] Repeatedly throughout the novel, Julio Escalante recognizes his race, his people, his nation, and himself as weak, impotent, inferior, and feminized,[17] and he offers no alternative to the Darwinist solutions proposed by U.S. imperialist and Central American liberal ideologues.

As the United States absorbs his family, his country, and the rest of Central America, Julio Escalante's personal response is one of self-victimization and self-annihilation—a complete relinquishment of accountability for his own (in)action and that of his socioeconomic class. Indeed, his father, Teodoro, is proud of his ability to use American technology, ingenuity, energy, manpower, and values while declaring himself opposed to U.S imperialism. He states, "Hago tragar mejor a estos sajones, lo que produce un latino, un verdadero latino incorrumpible [I make these Anglo-Saxons swallow what is produced by a Latino, a true incorruptible Latino]" (71). But the fact of the matter is that Teodoro has facilitated U.S. economic intervention in the isthmus, to the extent that the five Central American countries are to be annexed to the United States by the end of the novel. Although Costa Rican sovereignty could have been protected, Teodoro, his brother, Tomás, his son, Julio, and the other Costa Rican *criollos* hand Costa Rican over to U.S. industrialists, represented in the novel by the railroad robber baron Mr. Chrissey. Reflecting on his compromised position, Julio acknowledges that while Tomás and his children have all worked overtly for the U.S. annexation of Central America and Teodoro has relinquished his chocolate factory to U.S. control, he himself, in absentia, has contributed to the crisis in Central America. Identifying himself as a stranger in his own country (a *criollo exótico*), Julio declares himself incapable of addressing or changing its course toward U.S. annexation (115). What does Julio's inaction signify? How does it fulfill U.S. manifest destiny and Costa Rican exceptionality? How does Soto Hall's novel foreclose on the possibility of Costa Rican sovereignty in the face of U.S. imperialism in Central America? The answers to these questions may lie in Soto Hall's own intellectual and political biography.

In "La polémica de *El Problema* (1899) de Máximo Soto Hall" (2001), Iván Molina Jiménez discusses Soto Hall's early ties to the Guatemalan dictator Manuel Estrada Cabrera, which for Molina Jiménez cast doubt on whether *El problema* was originally written as an anti-imperialist novel or if it has been reinterpreted as such by its revisionist critics much later (see also Quesada Soto 1998). Molina Jiménez notes that the novel was recuperated in 1984 (and republished for the first time in Costa Rica in 1992), at the height of U.S. intervention in Central America. In this context, the novel was read and resignified anachronistically as anti-imperialist by critics such as Seymour Menton, Ramón Luis Acevedo, Juan Durán Luzio, and Álvaro Quesada Soto. Based on archival research on Soto Hall's political, economic, and intellectual affiliations, as well as an analysis of the reception of the novel when it was first published (Molina Jiménez and Ríos Quesada 2002; Ríos Quesada 2002), Molina Jiménez concludes that *El problema* cannot be read simply as an anti-imperialist novel. Rather it must be read in the context of the life and work of Soto Hall, whose family had ties to the political hegemony of Guatemala and Honduras and to U.S. mining capital in Honduras. During his lifetime, Soto Hall seemed to work under official patronage—the Estrada Cabrera regime in Guatemala, the Olimpo in Costa Rica, and, later, the Pan American diplomatic corps in Washington, D.C., as well as the conservative press in Buenos Aires. As a firm collaborator and "organic intellectual" of the Estrada Cabrera dictatorship, Soto Hall wrote speeches and school texts (including a biography of Estrada Cabrera for children), served as diplomat, edited publications, and promoted the governance of Estrada Cabrera (Molina Jiménez 2001, 158). Molina Jiménez believes that in the 1920s Soto Hall attempted to reinvent himself as an anti-imperialist writer, producing *La sombra de la Casa Blanca* (1927) and *Nicaragua y el imperialism norteamericano* (1928) (161–162). *El problema*, produced at the same time as his collaboration with Estrada Cabrera, was not written with an explicit anti-imperialist intent. Hence, Molina Jiménez argues, in Costa Rica Soto Hall quickly aligned himself with the Olimpo group, capitalizing on his contacts and becoming a successful émigré writer in San José. He gained, however, the distrust of writers affiliated with the cultural hegemony of the Olimpo, including Gagini, who considered Soto Hall his personal and professional nemesis (166–168).

Although Molina Jiménez seems to find it incongruent that *El problema* was written as an anti-imperialist novel, Soto Hall, critically articulates in his diverse writings the ambivalence of a class brokered to imperial(ist) forces at the beginning of the twentieth century. Like Teodoro Escalante, who repeatedly declares himself a fervent anti-imperialist, Soto Hall toyed with the idea of anti-imperialism, all the while benefiting from his work in diplomacy for various Latin American countries. As a "collaborator" of dictators and cultural elites, an internationalist writer, and a man with family ties to the United States, Soto Hall, like Teodoro and his brother, Tomás, was an insider to the workings of power. In *El problema*, Soto Hall was able to articulate an *apology* for his own personal collaboration with U.S. imperialism and Latin American dictatorships, as well as for the Olimpo with whom he shared ideological affinities. We are reminded of the position taken by Julio Escalante, who voices the compromised status of Soto Hall's own class and the caficulture of Costa Rica: "la anexión le importaba muy poco, habíala aceptado hacía largo tiempo y, quién sabe, quizá la acogía con entusiamo, con placer [he didn't care about the annexation, for he had accepted it long ago, and who knows maybe he waited for it with enthusiasm and pleasure]" (Soto Hall 1899, 169). And yet, at the end of the novel, Julio commits suicide beneath the wheels of an oncoming train built with U.S. capital. Was he an anti-imperialist or a pro-imperialist?

I would like to suggest here that Soto Hall's novel at its best articulates a compromised discourse on imperialism in Central America, from the side of those nationalist intellectual elites who collaborated with it. To my mind, Soto Hall's novel, then, does not rightly express an anglophilia, as Molina Jiménez claims, or an anglophobia, as Soto Quesada et al. claim; rather it articulates something in between—a neocolonial ambivalence attracted yet repelled by the presence of the United States in the isthmus. On making his first appearance in Soto Hall's novel, we are told, the imperialist Mr. Chrissey, "atraía" (attracted), not because of his (small) size, but because of his resolution, confidence, and business talk (143). Even Julio, observing his cousin Emma's attraction to

Chrissey, does not see that he, too, is drawn to Chrissey (143). Beholden to U.S. imperialism, Julio and the Costa Ricans of Soto Hall's novel cannot extricate themselves from the *problem* of imperialism in the region. They are subject not only to U.S. capital and power but also to a "fixed" symbolic order wherein they are tropicalized as inferior, weak, and feminized types, as manifested in the Social Darwinist discourse of the novel.

Indeed, Bhabha reminds us that colonial discourse "construe[s] the colonized as a population of degenerate types on the basis of racial origin, in order to justify conquest and to establish systems of administration and instruction" and in order to construct for colonial powers "a unified racial, geographical, political and cultural zone of the world" (1994, 70, 71). The discourses of U.S imperialism construe the isthmus as a degenerate tropical zone of sick, weak, and impotent national characters much like those seen in Soto Hall's *El problema* and Gagini's *El árbol enfermo*. Attracted and repelled by their tropicalized image under U.S. imperialism, the (male) nationals of the ruling class both reject and accept their image as subjects of imperialism. Julio recognizes himself as "un ser híbrido, cosmopolita, llenó de un falso patriotismo, que no era en el fondo una necia preocupación [a hybrid, a cosmopolitan, filled with false patriotism that was nothing but a nagging preoccupation]" (1899, 155). Julio, as Bhabha would have it, embodies the imperialized subject's neocolonial phobia and anxiety, his overt patriotism a fetish of national identity now defaced by U.S. imperialism in the region. As Uncle Tomás (Tom?) explains to Julio, national subjects in the shadow of U.S. hegemony are but poor copies or copies of copies because they absorb all external influences without having had a strong foundation to affirm their national sovereignty and subjectivity (1899, 110–111). Soto Hall's novel rejects the possibility of subversive neocolonial mimicry (Bhabha 1994, 85–101, 102–122), as Julio's suicide represents the ceding of Central America to U.S. control.

Both Soto Hall's *El problema* and Gagini's *El árbol enfermo* thus reveal how the leaders of the coffee republic facilitated U.S. presence in the region and benefited immensely from their collaboration. Members of the ruling class and its intelligentsia in the novels strategically identify themselves as victims of U.S. imperialism while deferring political responsibility and accountability on the imperialists. In absolving themselves of accountability, they adopt an imperialist (*costumbrista*) nostalgia that produces idyllic, exceptional images of the nation—forever traditional, rural, local, and, by virtue of their nationalist and patriotic char-

acter, resistant to foreign influences. A case in point is the position of
the Costa Rican family patriarch, Teodoro Escalante, whose ubiquitous
anti-imperialist ventriloquism only serves to magnify his privileged status as he enjoys the profits from his chocolate factory, the comforts of
his country manor, and his family connections to U.S. industrialists.
The respective sons of the newly imperialized nation in *El problema* and
El árbol enfermo, Julio Escalante and Fernando Rodríguez, return from
Europe to a homeland that has changed owners, yet still offers them
bittersweet repose in the comfortable family estate. In the novels, there
is no mention of crass matters like money and the exploitative modes
of its production. There is little mention of coffee and other mono-
agricultural products, which support Costa Rican and Central American nations and societies at the turn of the century. The political and
economic base of these novels is relegated to a political unconscious displaced across ambiguous and ambivalent signs. This is why Soto Hall
uses the sugar factor of *costumbrismo* to transform the industrial product
of coffee into the aesthetically and metaphorically ambivalent grain of
cacao, which as Sophie D. Coe and Michael D. Coe, in *The True History
of Chocolate* (2003), remind us is one of the truly autochthonous agricultural products of Central America.

The Escalante family's wealth comes from their brand of "Saint
Carlos Chocolate, the best in the world" (Soto Hall 1899, 60; note the
logo in English in the Spanish original and the interpolated linguistic
code-switching in the product name). They are in the business of cultivating, processing, and selling one of Central America's most prized
agricultural products. Cacao of the Americas has always figured as an
important object of ritual, erotica, consumption, and commodification.
Since pre-Columbian times, cacao, "the food of the gods," has been a
product of high value in Mesoamerica, cultivated by the Olmecs, Mayas,
Aztecs, and others for sacred ritual purposes and as monetary currency
(Coe 2000, 193; Coe and Coe 2003). Early production of cacao by European colonialists brought to the Americas slavery, empire, and technology that changed not only the chemical properties of cacao but also
the indigenous social relations attributed to it. As Coe and Coe explain,
cacao was "creolized" and hybridized by colonialists in the Americas,
who produced chocolate for the world market and for Europeans who
considered it medicinal, aphrodisiac, aristocratic, elite, and cultured.
Throughout Iberian America and Europe, cacao of the Americas would
be associated with Spain, Catholicism, and Hispanic traditions, for it
was the Spaniards who first introduced cacao to Europe and maintained

a monopoly over its production and export almost until the twentieth century. Coffee, on the other hand, would be associated with its mystical Eastern origins, philosophy, political economy, and revolutionary thought, (chemically) brewed in the coffeehouses of England and elsewhere (Coe and Coe 2003). Produced first for mass consumption, coffee was the industrial golden grain of the Americas, while chocolate was its more romantic companion.

Indeed, before the appearance of coffee in the Americas, chocolate set the scene for empire building and for the production and exchange of neocolonial commodity goods such as indigo, cotton, coffee, and sugar. In Soto Hall's novel, cacao embodies (in a nutshell) an archaeology of imperial(ist) relations in Central America, successively replicated in the production of coffee, indigo, canals, and migrant labors, as examined later in this book. In an apologetic discursive move accomplished through the use of the aesthetics of *costumbrismo*, Soto Hall's *El problema* transforms coffee production into the more benign, sweetened image of chocolate made in the family factory under the benevolent guidance of the Escalante patriarch. In resignifying coffee as chocolate, Soto Hall mystifies the exploitative modes of production of coffee on which the caficulture and national culture of *El problema* are based in Central America. While Roland Barthes, in *Mythologies* (1975), might have analyzed the naturalization of bourgeois cultures of consumption, Soto Hall's novel mythologizes, or "sugar coats," the socioeconomic and political apparatus controlled by the local coffee-producing elites of Costa Rica. In its conclusion, the novel thus seems to suggest that the Costa Rican intelligentsia sweetened, packaged, and marketed their national territory, culture, and people so well that the U.S. imperialists came back for more and took the entire isthmus as well—but not without fierce resistance, as we shall see in the following chapters.

CHAPTER 2

Nations Divided: U.S. Intervention, Banana Enclaves, and the Panama Canal

B etween 1930 and the 1960s a corpus of political literature representing and contesting the production of bananas gained wide currency across Central America. The transisthmian literature associated with banana production included Joaquín Beleño's *Flor de banana* (Banana Flower) (1962), Miguel Ángel Asturias's trilogy *Viento fuerte* (Strong Wind) (1950), *El papa verde* (The Green Pope) (1954), and *Los ojos de los enterrados* (Eyes of the Interred) (1960), Ramón Amaya Amador's *Prisión verde* (Green Prison) (1950), Joaquín Gutiérrez's *Puerto Limón* (Port Limón) (1950), Carlos Luis Falla's *Mamita Yunai* (United [States] Mother) (1941), and Carmen Lyra's "Bananos y hombres" (Bananas and Men) (1931).[1] These texts formed the basis of an enclave literature that linked dispersed geographic sites and struggles across the isthmus. At times identified as political novels, thesis novels (*romans à thèse*), social(ist) realist novels, proletarian novels, and company novels,[2] banana social protest literature generally articulated the internationalist agendas of Marxist-based popular social movements, as well as the discourses of local organic intellectuals schooled in the everyday hard labor and hard times of U.S. imperialism in the region. Although these texts document the experiences of marginal subjects in Central America in an age of foreign economic, military, and cultural intervention, most literary critics tend to dismiss them for their obvious ideological content and apparent lack of aesthetic merit. In this chapter, I revisit the genre of social realist literature in the historical context of banana production and the construction of the Panama Canal and reread the genre as it speaks to twenty-first-century concerns regarding empire building in the isthmus.

In *Authoritarian Fictions* (1983), Susan Rubin Suleiman defines the *roman à thèse* as "a novel written in the realistic mode (that is, based on an aesthetic of verisimilitude and representation), which signals itself to the reader as primarily didactic in intent, seeking to demonstrate the validity of a political, philosophical, or religious doctrine" (7). Attempting to represent in "realistic mode" life in the banana enclaves and to denounce the exploitation of laborers by international capital, the literary texts that critique banana production, like the *roman à thèse*, are didactic in nature and practice. They formulate an idea or thesis through the repetition of multiple levels of narrative (plot, characters, context, and intertextual references) and discourse (the order and systematization of narration) "in an insistent, consistent, and unambiguous manner" (10). According to Suleiman, the *roman à thèse* and by extension the social realist texts associated with banana production are rhetorically constructed to communicate their singular message and " 'correct' interpretation" (10). Hence, whether communicating conservative or radical ideas, according to Suleiman, these texts are "authoritarian" in that they leave very little room for discrepant interpretations: the reader is absorbed or repelled by the absolutist narrative but cannot remain neutral. For that reason, as Suleiman explains, these texts are deemed "too close to propaganda to be artistically valid" (3) and are often rejected as a literary genre by many readers and critics. Combining vanguard and sometimes radical ideas with local color, idioms, histories, and struggles, the banana thesis novels and short stories of Central America assault readers' attention with an anti-imperialist, anticapitalist message challenging inter/national power regimes in their immediate moment and context.

In Suleiman's words, the more tied these texts are to "specific historical circumstances" and a particular message, the more "perishable" (147) and dated they may become, as may be the case for the Central American banana social protest literature examined here. In fact, Suleiman argues that "written in and for a specific historical and social circumstance, the *roman à thèse* is not easily exported. And even in its native land, it becomes 'ancient history' as soon as the circumstance that founded it no longer holds" (147). Site-specific, historically situated, and referent-bound, the banana political and social protest narratives of Central America seem thus neither to withstand the test of time and ideological shifts of the isthmus nor to travel well to other sites of reception. With the waning of the cold war and Marxist-based resistance movements, these texts are now rarely read, but in their moment of production they were political manifestos of the revolution to come. Modern readers often relegate these political novels to the realm of "simplistic" literature, leaving them for the most part unexamined. I argue here, however, that there is more to banana social protest novels and that they should be critically reread. Indeed, Suleiman insists that "it is the very simplicity—or, to put it in more brutal terms, the simplistic character—of its rhetoric that makes the *roman à thèse* theoretically interesting" (73). Banana social protest literature has much to tell us about the relationship between form, content, context, and structures of power in the Central American isthmus. In defense of this type of novel, Suleiman assures readers:

> Certain literary and cultural traditions, as well as certain periods,
> are more apt to encourage the development of the *roman à thèse* than
> others. . . . [T]he *roman à thèse* flourishes in national contexts, and
> at historical moments, that produce sharp social and ideological
> conflicts—in other words, in a climate of crisis; furthermore, the genre
> is more likely to exist in a cultural tradition that fosters the involvement
> of writers in social and intellectual debates or problems. (1983, 16–17)

The copious production of transisthmian social protest novels during a relatively short span of time speaks volumes about the imperialist conditions of possibility that gave rise to them and the critical counterdiscourses that were available to Central American writers at the time. Many writers, including the Guatemalan Nobel Prize–winner Miguel Ángel Asturias, the Panamanian Joaquín Beleño, the Honduran Ramón Amaya Amador, and the Costa Ricans Carlos Luis Fallas, Joaquín Gutiérrez, and Carmen Lyra, took turns writing political literature in an effort to document the corporatization of human life and the regimentation of local cultures by foreign capital in the banana enclaves. They challenged the collaborations forged between internal and foreign powers, the concessions forced on sovereign states, and the abuse and exploitation of local populations. Moreover, through their writing they sought to advance a revolutionary agenda in Central America. We are reminded, thus, of the ending of Asturias's novel, *El Señor Presidente* (1946), when a student dissident newly released from prison returns to his house, located on a dead-end street. A survivor of the dictator's repression, the student in Asturias's experimental novel prefigures organized revolutionary action in Central America. The revolution, however, is more explicitly represented in Asturias's banana social realist thesis novels than in the magical realism of *El Señor Presidente*.

In its survey of the social protest literature associated with the production of bananas and the Panama Canal and the conditions that foreground this literature, this chapter explores the discursive and ideological battles waged against U.S. imperialism in the work of Carmen Lyra (e.g., "Bananas and Men" [1931]) and in *Flor de banana* by Joaquín Beleño. Lyra's literary sketch about life on the United Fruit Company banana plantations, published in 1931, is the first in a series of social protest texts that fell into decline after the publication of Beleño's *Flor de banana*.[3] These two texts mark the era of the banana republics, as Central American countries came to be known in the mid-twentieth century.[4] In a little over thirty years, military rule, massive repression, and popular uprisings would spread across Central America, resulting in the massacre of thirty thousand peasants in El Salvador in 1932, the U.S.-supported overthrow of President Jacobo Arbenz in Guatemala in 1954, the repression of student activists protesting U.S. presence in Panama in the 1950s, and the rise of leftist social movements throughout the isthmus in the 1960s. Although the revolution would not enter an armed struggle phase until the 1970s and 1980s, in the first half of the century a vanguard of organic intellectuals and writers such as Lyra and Beleño waged discursive war against power regimes in the isthmus. They challenged master narratives of progress, modernization, and the transnationalization of capital in Central America, and they constructed an alternate imaginary of social protest from within the banana enclaves—the underbelly of U.S. imperialism in Central America.

Dividing the Isthmus: The Business of Bananas

Of all the countries in Central America, Costa Rica served as the initial testing ground for U.S. imperialism and banana production on a massive scale. In 1890, Henry Meiggs and his nephews Henry Meiggs Keith and Minor Cooper Keith completed a railroad line linking the coffee-producing Central Valley of Costa Rica to the Atlantic port of Limón (Dosal 1993, 55–74; Murillo Chaverri 1995, 39–41). From this enterprise emerged one of the oldest, largest, and strongest corporate empires of all time—the United Fruit Company and its subsidiaries.[5] In 1871, the Costa Rican government granted the Keith family land concessions that amounted at that time to almost one-eighth of Costa Rica's territory.

The Keith brothers, in turn, began to build a railroad that not only started a corporate empire but also initially brought an imported labor force of Italian, Chinese, and Jamaican workers to Costa Rica and later to other parts of Central America. The introduction of modern transportation systems, corporate agricultural production, international investment, and a diversified labor force on a massive scale would change the social, economic, and political order of Central America. In 1878, seeking the means to finance his railroad project, Minor Keith began to produce bananas for export.[6] Through various land concessions granted by the Costa Rican government, Keith quickly amassed large holdings on the Atlantic coastal lands and opened the first large-scale banana plantations in Costa Rica.[7] According to Woodward (1999), by 1885, Keith was exporting over half a million bunches of bananas per year through the Tropical Trading and Transport Company (TTTC). By 1913 the company exported annually more than eleven million bunches under the auspices of the newly incorporated United Fruit Company (UFCO), a consolidation of the TTTC and the Boston Fruit Company (Kepner and Soothill 1935, 34; Woodward 1999, 178). For a short time, until the UFCO "extended its operations into the other Central American countries and soon dominated the isthmian banana industry" (Woodward 1999, 178), Costa Rica would be the main producer of bananas.

Like the corporate octopus, as it came to be known (Langley and Schoonover 1995, 170), the UFCO oversaw the International Railways of Central America (IRCA) with transcontinental railroad lines running through Guatemala, Honduras, Nicaragua, Panama, and El Salvador. It also ran the "The Great White Fleet" and its transatlantic line, "The Grey Fleet," which transported goods between Central America, Europe, and the United States until World War II (Woodward 1999, 179), when the fleets were folded into the war effort. Further, the UFCO owned commercial establishments, controlled banking systems, managed ports, and oversaw virtually all aspects of life on company-run lands. The UFCO (later known as United Brands and Chiquita Brands) and its competitors, such as the Honduras-based Vacarro Brothers (which consolidated as the Standard Fruit and Steamship Company in 1899) and the Cuyamel Fruit Company (1911), formed corporate entities that grafted themselves onto the economic, political and social landscape of the isthmus.[8] Writing in 1935, at the height of the UFCO's monopoly in the Central American Basin, Charles David Kepner and Jay Henry Soothill recognized that the modern production of bananas for commercial purposes is more than a simple agricultural operation. It is an industry whose mammoth undertakings require modern machines of many kinds and whose ramifications dominate many phases of the economic, political and social life of the Caribbean region. (27)

Through the implantation of the UFCO in the banana-producing regions, Central America would be tied to Boston and New Orleans, the industrial capitals of the U.S. banana industry, and the isthmus would be divided into Pacific and Atlantic socioeconomic regions, as well as enclaves possessing their own political, economic, social, racial, and gendered order (Putnam 2002).

Inaugurating a new era in foreign economic intervention and corporate occupation in the Central American and Caribbean Basin, the U.S. and its companies assumed custody of the production of bananas and established economic and political hegemony in the region. The United States quickly replaced Great Britain as the imperialist power in the isthmus. British presence in the Atlantic region of Central America dated back to the establishment of pirate and buccaneer camps, balsa wood plantations, and military outposts in British Honduras (Belize), the Honduran Bay Islands, and the Nicaraguan Mosquito Coast. The presence of British colonialism, the English language, and Protestant religions paved the way for U.S. imperialism. But it was banana production that served as the springboard for the ascendancy of the United States as a new hemispheric empire. In the 1890s, when the U.S. continental frontier was officially declared closed, the United States turned to Central America and the Caribbean for "an American frontier in reserve" (Pike 1992, 20). Fredrick B. Pike notes that "Americans turned instinctively to the Latin countries to their south as the repositories of wilderness necessary to prolong exceptionalism" (1992, 19). From the nineteenth century onward, the imperialist designs of the United States were played out in Central America through waves of military, economic, and political interventions and occupations. In 1855 William Walker invaded Nicaragua not merely because local political factions had invited him to do so but because he saw "Nicaragua as an extension of the less and less boundless West, an extension that promised rewards of mythic as well as economic dimensions" (19). Similarly, Minor Keith, the railroad entrepreneur and original "green pope" of banana production, as represented in Asturias's trilogy, saw Costa Rica and Central America as a region of untapped and unclaimed wealth, as would a series of entrepreneurs, traffickers, and diplomats succeeding him (Langley and Schoonover 1995). For them, Central America "mattered because it held an abundance of virgin land and untapped resources, as well as a plenitude of people . . . [who] could be disciplined into a subservient labor force" (Pike 1992, 43).

By the early 1900s, the United States had solidified its hegemony in the Caribbean and Central American Basin, defeating Spain and taking Puerto Rico as its territory while granting Cuba partial independence. The 1904 Roosevelt Corollary to the 1823 Monroe Doctrine granted the United States the right to intervene in Central America, rationalizing that given its instability and disorder, the region would "require intervention by some civilized nation" (quoted in Benz 1997, 61). That civilization was the United States. By authorizing U.S. military action in the resolution of internal conflicts in Central America, the Roosevelt Corollary ensured U.S. hegemony in the region and cast the isthmus under the might of the North. With the completion of the Panama Canal in 1914 and the enforcement of U.S. rule in the Canal Zone,[9] Panama was transformed into a virtual U.S. protectorate and the entire isthmus into a geopolitical hotspot.[10] Between 1900 and 1930, Big Stick and Dollar Diplomacies shaped U.S.–Central American relations, bringing with them military intervention, debt control, and "diplomatic pressure" to virtually every country of the isthmus but especially to Nicaragua, Honduras, and Guatemala, where U.S. economic investments were especially large (Woodward 1999, 177–202). Central America became an imperialized site where U.S. diplomacy could override and oversee local interests and peoples and where domestic ruling elites, national military forces, and U.S. business partners aided and abetted one another. Indeed, the traditional oligarchic class, new industrial sectors, and foreign investors in Central America found their greatest supporters in military dictators such as Guatemala's Manuel Estrada Cabrera and Jorge Úbico, El Salvador's Maximiliano Hernández Martínez, Honduras's Tiburcio Carías Andino, and Nicaragua's Somoza clan. As Peter J. Dosal claims in *Doing Business with the Dictators* (1993), it was almost always "good for business to collaborate with dictators" in Central America (12).

By the early twentieth century, the isthmus had been greatly reshaped by negotiations with and concessions to U.S. foreign economic interests. The governments of Costa Rica, Honduras, and Guatemala granted concessions with certain "advantages, assurances, and/or rights" to investors in the region. Although not all these concessions were equitable or in the common interest (Wilson 1947, 250), they served the immediate goal of securing capital and promoting the banana industry in Central America. Overseeing all aspects of banana production and operating railroads and steamship fleets, shipping docks, local public utilities, and commissaries, the UFCO grew to become "one of the world's oldest and most powerful United States–based transnational corporations" (Bourgois 1989, 3). In its most extreme form, the UFCO came to represent the United States, for as Kepner and Soothill explain, "the United is 'a State within a State.' It was more than that: It was an empire spreading across numerous American states and controlling many phases of inter-American relations" (1935, 255). Charles Morrow Wilson, in *Empire in Green and Gold* (1947), further affirms that the United Fruit Company became "virtually or practically synonymous with the United States of America" (255). Against the power of this corporate giant, or "Mamita Yunai," as Carlos Fallas titles his classic anti-imperialist novel, Central American banana social protest literature railed against the corporate monopoly of the UFCO and the regimentation of labor and life under corporate rule.

Transisthmian Banana Social Realist Literature: Carmen Lyra's "Bananas and Men"

As banana production expanded in the isthmus, social protest literature began to challenge foreign economic intervention and labor exploitation and to document the rise of vanguard social movements in the banana-producing regions. Almost template in form, Marxist-based, anti-U.S. imperialism banana social protest literature composed what Suleiman has called an "authoritarian fiction" grounded on the "insistent" repetition of a specific message and set of discursive elements. In her analysis of the internal workings of the thesis novel genre, Suleiman argues that the high frequency of structural "redundancies" ensures the communication of the ideological message and the "correct reading" intended by their authors. In a chapter titled "Redundancy and the 'Readable' Text," she identifies and classifies in precise detail numerous redundancies in the thesis novel that she claims can serve as "generic indicators" of a particular set of signifieds (1983, 159–170). Read as a "positive term," redundancy in linguistics, communications, computer science, and genetics, for example, ensures that a message (or trait or feature) is manifested. Suleiman concludes that through the use of multiple layers of narrative and discursive redundancies, "any text that aims at optimum communication or at a maximal reduction of ambiguity will tend to be heavily redundant, thus eliminating the interference of 'noise'" (154), or detractions from the message.

In her analysis of pre–World War II French thesis novels, Suleiman highlights the narrative duplication of events or sequence of events occurring to one or more like characters; the appearance of a character or characters who fulfill the same functions and/or have the "same qualities"; and the accumulation of interpretive comments made by the narrator or characters, who control the reading of the text (1983, 159–170). These redundancies in characters, plot elements, descriptions, and discourses in the *roman à thèse*, Suleiman tells us, are precisely what get the point or critique across to readers. The specific redundancies and repetitions in characters, narrative plot elements, descriptions, dialogues, monologues, information, intertexts, references, allusions, and less obvious structures of the narration in the banana thesis literature that I analyze here, following Suleiman, are not arbitrary but rather give this literature its shape and meaning. In combination, these features maximize the communicative effect of banana social realist literature, whose agenda is to denounce a certain mode of exploitative capitalist production and to offer a solution, often in the form of labor organizing and unionizing and general labor strikes. Inscribed in individual texts and the genre as a whole, these "redundancies" and repetitions can be seen as significant patterns. Indeed, intent on critiquing the exploitative human factor of banana production, convincing readers of this "reality," and moving readers to anti-imperialist and anticapitalist positions, banana social protest literature may present scenes, characters, and contexts that verge on propagandistic cliché.

As if the message of these novels were not didactic and transparent enough, they also employ other repetitive tactics such as "narrator's interventions, direct or indirect, with regard to the story" (Suleiman 1983, 158). Time and time again, narrators or authors intervene in the narrative and interject their pronouncements. In "Bananas and Men," for example, Lyra repeatedly comments on the situations faced by her characters on plantations owned by the United Fruit Company, thinly disguised in the narrative as the "United Banana Company." In mini-prologues to the literary sketches that comprise the text, Lyra calls attention to the importance of bananas over "men," hence the title of the text (Horan 2000, 48).[11] In addition, in other prologues, she states, "In the banana plantations more deference goes to a banana plant than to a laborer (50), and "In the banana zones a bunch of bananas is more valuable than a man" (58). Lyra also comments on the problems faced by the plantation laborers, such as the use of alcohol to drown illness and numb existential pain: "They carry bootleg rum and they drink. The campaign against alcohol is senseless in those places" (51). The narrator of the sketches describes the banana plantation as a vortex in which the laborers are "swallowed up"—"amid the banana trees" (50) and "amid the pitiless damp of the banana trees" (51)—and "dragged" like drift-wood and "deposited" on the banana plantation (48, 59). In like fashion, other banana social realist novels capitalize on the redundancy factor by repeating depictions of problems and abuses, as well as incorporating meta-commentaries by authors and narrators. In this manner, banana social realist novels are overloaded with redundant details and narrator interventions that at times make for tedious reading.

Indeed, one could almost create one master banana thesis novel based on the redundant features of Beleño's *Flor de banana*, Amaya Amador's *Prisión verde*, Asturias's *Viento fuerte*, *El papa verde*, and *Los ojos de los enterrados*, Falla's *Mamita Yunai*, and Lyra's "Bananos y hombres." These narratives focus exclusively on the banana enclave, its characters, plots, and issues, although allowing for local variations. More often than not, the narrative is told from the perspective of a laborer employed by a banana company or a labor organizer who instigates employees to take action against the company. The antagonists are almost always the fruit company and its top-layer administration, namely, U.S.-based execu-tives and local representatives of the company, both nationals and for-eigners. Nationality, race, class, gender, language, and migrant status anchor characters to the social hierarchy of the banana enclave, with U.S. Americans in the top tier, followed by inter/national middlemen, and a racially diverse workforce.

The product of different labor migrations, the banana enclaves ag-gregate without differentiation a transnational labor force of Caribbean, Southeast Asian, Chinese, and any number of Nicaraguan, Honduran, Salvadoran, or Central American transplants forced to cross each oth-er's borders in search of work on the banana plantations. Amaya Ama-dor's *Prisión verde*, set in Honduras, describes the diversity of the banana camps:

Blancos, indios, mestizos, negros y hasta algunos amarillos; salitreros del Golfo de Fonseca, tabaqueros de Copán, chalanes de los llanos de Olancho, morenos y zambos de Colón y la Mosquitia, isleños de Guanaja o de Roatán; de todos rumbos del país y no pocos también de

los demás paíes de Centro América y Belice y de más allá. . . . Todos,
arrastrados por el torbellino de la desocupación endémica y la descrimi-
nación social y política; hombres y mujeres que van vendiendo por un
par de monedas la energía de sus cuerpos y de sus vidas, en una constante lucha sin cuartel para obtener el pan negro y duro de cada día,
bajo el signo verde y oro del banano. (Amaya Amador 1950, 46–47)
[Whites, indians, mestizos, blacks and even some yellows; salt people
from the Gulf of Fonseca, tobacco workers from Copán, chalanes from
the valleys of Olancho, browns and zambos from Colón and Mosquitia,
islanders from Guanaja and Roatán; from all corners of the country and
not a few from the rest of Central America, Belize, and further out. . . .
All, dragged by the vortex of endemic unemployment and social and
political discrimination; men and women who sell the energy of their
lives and bodies for a few coins to the endless struggle to obtain the
black and hard bread of everyday, under the sign of the green gold of
the banana.]

In *Mamita Yunai*, Fallas also writes of the "huesos de nicas. Huesos de
ticos. Huesos de negros. ¡Huesos de hermanos! [Bones of Nicaraguans,
Costa Ricans, Blacks. Bones of brothers!]" deposited in the banana labor
camps (1941, 156). Meanwhile, in "Bananas and Men," Lyra notes how
women and children are dragged "toward these parts, just like the river's
current drags those sticks that one sees floating past" to the plantation
(Horan 2000, 48–50). Although women and children often recede into
the background of banana social protest literature, Lyra brings them
out of anonymity, emphasizing that the violence of banana production
is gendered and sexual. In satirical fashion, Lyra imagines the life of Estefanía, a woman drifting from "plantation to plantation, one guy today,
another tomorrow," while suffering at the hands of "the manager, who
kicked her, her daughter, and his dog" (48–50).

Banana social protest literature concerns itself with the extreme
exploitation of laborers on the banana plantation. Male workers are
whipped, injured, and maimed; women are exchanged, raped, and pros-
tituted; and children are abused and subjected to privations and diseases.
All are subject to inhumane living and working conditions, lacking access to proper nutrition, health care, and hygiene. In the labor camps,
laborer uprisings are common, as local movement leaders begin to organize workers. Asturias, in the final pages of *Los ojos de los enterrados*,
alludes to the political awakening of the banana plantation laborers as
they prepare for "la huelga general" (the general strike). In an apoca-

lyptic ending, Asturias announces that the strikers will not only bring down the banana company and the dictatorship but also bring justice to those who work and die in the service of the banana industrial complex (1960, 492). In the last lines of the novel, Asturias calls out the names of the banana men and women on hand to make the revolution:

> Tabío San, Malena Tabay, Cayetano Duendo, Popoluca . . . los capitanes, los ceniceros, los maestros, los estudiantes, los tipógrafos, Judasita, los comerciantes, los peones, los artesanos, don Nepo Rojas, los Gambusos, los Samueles, Juambo el Sambito, sus padres . . . unos vivos, otros muertos, otros ausentes, ya estaban cantando . . . (Asturias 1960, 492)
>
> [. . . the captains, the ashers, the teachers, the students, the typographers, Judasita, the merchants, the laborers, the artisans, don Nepo Rojas, the Gambusos, the Samueles, Juambo the Sambito, his parents . . . some living, others dead, others missing, all were singing . . .]

In juxtaposition to the popular heroes of the banana plantations, U.S. "gringo" characters in banana social realist literature are represented as villainous corporate heads, enclave foremen, plantation expatriates, and unscrupulous adventurers. They go by the names Mister Maker in Gutiérrez's *Puerto Limón;* Geo Maker Thompson, alias "the green pope," in Asturia's trilogy; Mr. Still and Mr. Foxter in Amaya Amador's *Prisión Verde;* Mr. Clinton and his assistant, Bertolazzi, in Falla's *Mamita Yunai;* and Mr. Sweetums and Dolly Darling in Lyra's "Bananas and Men." Highly satirical, these names, like the "gringo" appellation by which U.S. Americans are known in Central America and elsewhere, ridicule the overblown, hyperbolic presence of the United States in the isthmus. While readers may be familiar with U.S. stereotypes of Latin America—the banana republics—Central American writers invert neo-colonialist stereotypes to produce caricatures of "Americans" in the tropics and to challenge the social order of the plantation corporate system. Mr. Geo Maker Thompson oversees his banana empire from atop one of the tallest buildings in Chicago, far from the plantation site; while Mr. Still and Mr. Foxter cunningly steal the lands of poor Hondurans. Mr. Sweetums, the manager of the Fruit Company in "Bananas and Men," showers his American mistress, Dolly Darling, with gifts purchased on the backs of Costa Ricans. Moreover, the United Fruit Company comes to be known as "Mamita Yunai," the mother of all imperialist organizations in Central America, de facto representing the

United States in Central America. The omniscient narrator of *Prisión Verde* challenges the imperialist view of Central Americans as backward people, who need "whites" to civilize, or rather exploit, them: "estos eran pueblos atrasados y que necesitaban de los blancos para civilizarse por medio de la explotación del dólar [these backward people needed whites to civilize them through their own economic exploitation]" (Amaya Amador 1996, 121).

In a form of neoimperialist mimicry, these texts turn "gringo" figures into burlesque stereotypes of power, all shallow, sordid, violent, and inhumane. In their stead, the texts edify Central American common folks and plantation workers: Estefanía, Malena, Anastasia, Juan, José, Pedro, Silvano, Ignacio, Sandino, and Zapata. The names of the laborers, of course, are not gratuitous but rather serve as signs of future proletarian revolutions. Animated by their own ideological content, social protest texts build up to at least one big strike or labor uprising to which company personnel react with unyielding violence. Foreshadowing future revolutions, the texts close with a utopian vision of popular mobilization, the rise of organized labor unions, the socioeconomic transformation of the mono-agricultural economy, and the expulsion of U.S. imperialism from the region. Through the repetitive use of character (stereo)types, social satire, and political commentary, banana social protest texts make clear that Central Americans must form a united revolutionary front against "el corazón del monstruo verde [the heart of the green monster]" (Fallas 1941, 130).

From the Belly of the Green Monster:
Carmen Lyra's Silhouettes and "Bananas and Men"

During her lifetime, Carmen Lyra was recognized as a writer, editor, educator, anarchist leader, Communist Party member, and vanguard social movements leader in Costa Rica.[12] Born María Isabel Carvajal (1888–1949), Lyra was given her pen name (based on a bus route in Santiago de Chile) by her friend, mentor, and fellow writer, Joaquín García Monge. Her literary works include *En una silla de ruedas* (In a Wheelchair) (1918), *Fantasias de Juan Silvestre* (Fantasies of Juan Silvestre) (1918), *Cuentos de mi tía Panchita* (Tales of My Aunt Panchita) (1920), "Cuentos del Barrio Cothnejo-Fishy" (1923) ("The Cothnejo-Fishy District," 2000), "Siluetas de la Maternal" (1929) ("Silhouettes from the Maternal School," 2000), "Bananos y hombres" (1931) ("Bananas and Men," 2000),

"El grano de oro y el peón" (1933) ("Golden Bean: The Coffee Bean and the Laborer," 2000), and numerous articles and essays published in journals and newspapers that she and others edited. She was one of the first graduates (1901–1903) of the prestigious Colegio de Señoritas normal school. As such, she was a member of "a corps of modern [female] teachers imbued with a civilizing mission, a feminist identity, and a democratic ethic" (Palmer and Rojas Chaves 1998, 47). According to the historians Steven Palmer and Gladys Rojas Chaves, newly certified teachers who had been trained at the Colegio de Señoritas radically transformed the public education system in Costa Rica. Lyra would go on to subvert the patriarchal social order and conservative intellectual and political hegemony of her country.

In 1920 Lyra received a scholarship to study pedagogy in Europe, and on her return to Costa Rica, she was appointed professor of children's literature and pedagogy at the normal school (teacher's college) in San José. A dedicated and innovative educator in the public school system, in 1925, she and Luisa González and Margarita Castro Rawson founded the Montessori kindergarten system in Costa Rica and opened the first Montessori Escuela Maternal (kindergarten) in the nation. Iván Molina Jiménez explains that although Lyra rejected the feminist and suffrage movements, she mentored generations of young educators such as Luisa González, Corina Rodríguez, Adela Ferreto, and Emilia Prieto at the Escuela Maternal. Lyra trained her teachers in a self-styled pedagogy of liberation and social justice that focused on the human and civic rights of women and children (Horan 2000; Molina Jiménez 2002).

In *A ras del suelo* (At the Ground Level) (1989), Luisa González Gutiérrez describes the Escuela Maternal as a haven for poor children in San José where they were taught the "habits of hygiene, discipline, study and work" and where their artistic sensibilities were fostered, using modern scientific methods (1989, 123). According to González, Lyra imported a pedagogical system and transformed it to meet the material needs of her students (124–125). In her "Silhouettes from the Maternal School" (1929), Lyra acknowledged the limitations of the pedagogical theories that she learned in Europe as she and her teachers at the Maternal School dealt with the material realities of her students (Horan 2000, 43–46). In one literary sketch, she ponders:

How could God ever help these single women catch up, nearly all of them mothers with four or five little children to feed, pay for housing and dress? And all this by washing and ironing, as the women them-

selves put it, since almost all of them are washerwomen, and the ones
who aren't work as servants. (Horan 2000, 44)

Throughout her life, Lyra remained an engaged educator and writer,
seeking to tell the nation about the life conditions of the poor and teaching the urban and rural poor to transform society.

In her introduction to *The Subversive Voice of Carmen Lyra* (2000),
Elizabeth Rosa Horan calls Lyra a "sexual outlaw" because, as an ille-
gitimate daughter, an unmarried woman, and an unconventional female
public figure, she transgressed social prohibitions to become a leading
political activist. From 1930 to 1949, Lyra worked arduously as a social reformer, labor movement leader, director of the adult "open university," and editor of the Communist newspaper *Trabajo*. After openly
declaring her membership in the Communist Party in 1931, she became
one of its principal leaders, until she was forced into exile by the leaders
of the "1948 Revolution" of Costa Rica. Horan describes Lyra as "the
intellectual leader of Costa Rica's Communist Party . . . [who] terrified
Costa Rica's U.S.-backed junta in 1948" (2000, 1). Iván Molina Jiménez also notes the threat she seemed to pose to the U.S. government.
Indeed, a U.S. intelligence report in 1933 claimed, "Esta mujer será un
factor a ser tomado en cuenta en el futuro en cualquier radical movimiento en Costa Rica [This woman will be a significant factor in the
radical movements of Costa Rica in the future]" (Molina Jiménez 2002).
Despite Lyra's increasing popularity in Costa Rica after her death, repeated efforts to publish her collected works were rejected by the Costa
Rican establishment. Molina Jiménez (2002) attributes the excision of
Lyra from the public record to the post-1948 censure of Communism
in Costa Rica. Instead, Lyra is best remembered as a well-loved school-
teacher and writer of *Los cuentos de mi Tía Panchita*, which compiles the
folktales of Tío Conejo (Uncle Rabbit) and Tío Coyote (Uncle Coyote).
Like the Chilean Gabriela Mistral and other Latin American women
educators (Miller 1991, 35, 45–55), Lyra worked for educational reform
and progressive social movements, lending her support to Augusto
César Sandino in Nicaragua and other revolutionaries.

In the realm of literature, Lyra satirized the elite classes at the "very
top of the zoological ladder" (Horan 2000, 25) and denounced the
condition of the exploited and marginalized, in both urban and rural
areas of Costa Rica. She revamped the popular form of the *cuadro de
costumbre*, which she borrowed from the Costa Rican writer Manual
González Zeledón ("Magón") (1864–1936),[13] and transformed the form
into critical commentary on the plight of the urban and rural poor in

Costa Rica. In his introduction to *Antología del cuento centroamericano* (Anthology of the Central American Story) (1982), Sergio Ramírez describes "Bananas and Men" as "una de las primeras imágenes de la descarnada situación de los peones en las compañías bananeras [one of the first representations of the inhumane situation faced by workers on the banana plantations]" (1982, 23). Rather than attribute the condition of Central American workers to nature, fate, or God's will, Lyra links the exploitation of "man" to material conditions (Rojas and Ovares 1995, 77–82). In "Bananas and Men," she examines the condition of exploited migrant laborers, abandoned women, and abused children in the Atlantic banana enclaves of Costa Rica. Based on her personal observations of the Atlantic region, she deconstructs the romantic image of the coffee republic and denounces the rise of the banana republic, revealing the exploitation, degradation, and suffering on the Costa Rican banana plantations.

Not properly a *roman à thèse* or a collection of short stories, "Bananas and Men" is composed of literary sketches, vignettes, or what Lyra herself calls "silhouettes." In his introduction to *Relatos escogidos* (Selected Stories) (1977), Alfonso Chase describes Lyra's silhouettes as a highly original literary form:

> [Estos son] esbozos de narraciones en donde se plantea los problemas sociales de manera esquemática, [que] le sirve para construir narraciones posteriores, en donde esboza la vida, problemas intimos y externos de personajes apenas delineados. (25)
> [They are narrative sketches that delineate social problems in a schematic way and that allow her to construct later narratives about the lives, intimate and exterior problems of subjects rarely represented.]

Sparse and precise, Lyra's silhouettes bring into high relief the contours of social issues or problems while meticulously outlining the parts (of the problem) in relation to the larger social picture. Like cutout silhouettes, Lyra's silhouettes draw from personal observation and focus on human forms and impressions. Focus and detail are not lost in Lyra's silhouettes, which generally provide keen insight into the psyche and character of Costa Rican society. One of the few scholars to theorize on Lyra's literary silhouettes, Chase explains that in her invented form, Lyra

> mezcla sus opiniones—observaciones personales—con las palabras de sus personajes, tratando de establecer un contraste entre sus opiniones

conscientes, y el habla ingenua de sus biografiados, en donde se trasluce una cierta inconsciencia de lo terrible de la situaciones. (25)
[mixes her opinions—personal observations—with the words of her characters, trying to establish a contrast between her conscious opinions and the genuine discourse of her biographical subjects, from whom emanate a certain unconsciousness of the horror of the situations.]

Chase underscores Lyra's skill in representing Costa Ricans from all walks of life and making a political analysis based on her scientific observation of people and issues.

In "Silhouettes of the Maternal School," "The Cothnejo-Fishy District," and "Bananas and Men," Lyra engages in what she calls her "entomologist labor," whereby she explores social problems and outlines solutions. Lyra explains:

Like the entomologist armed with lenses, tweezers, tubes of cyanide and plaster or alcohol, etc., who goes out to hunt insects and to observe them, so we go to the Cothnejo-Fishy District to examine the form and manners of the distinguished people of an aristocratic center located in Costa Rica, a tiny country in Central America with a half million inhabitants. And we'll examine without passion, just as the entomologist would examine termites, flies, backbiting scorpions, butterflies, wasps, ants, cockroaches, spiders, etc., despite the blue blood that they think runs through their veins and the importance that money can give them. (Horan 2000, 25)

In her observations of the Cothnejo-Fishy District, Lyra dissects the most intimate secrets of the elite families of San José and pokes fun at their foibles and idiosyncrasies. Through her satire, Lyra takes apart the abject and corrupt social hierarchy of Costa Rica. The neighbors of Cothnejo-Fishy are members of the coffee elite class, the rising entrepreneurial sector, local politicians, and foreign diplomats who are plagued with bad manners, violence, and syphilis passed down from generation to generation. In one prescient scene, for example, an heir of the Cothnejo-Fishy District is shown to carry a strain of

syphilis still evident in the great-grandchildren of Lucho and Cristinita, manifest in the eyes that were like fountains of pus, in deafness, in foul-smelling noses, cleft palates and harelips, rickets, obesity, outsized limbs, sick hearts, still births, and all those monstrosities, madness, and deformations that chill the mind, meditating on them. (Horan 2000, 30)

Lyra focuses on a stratum of society whose privilege is gained by corruption, labor exploitation, "starvation wages" (34), and general disregard for "tragedies and dramas that occur a few steps away from them" (32). As the narrator explains, the founder of the neighborhood had become wealthy as "he squeezed and mistreated his fellow man" (24). Others in the district "achieved great honors in the fields of legalized robbery and exploitations," including smuggling, money laundering, and unscrupulous coffee speculation and business transactions (26–27).

Immersed in early-twentieth-century discourses of eugenics, pedagogy, dialectical materialism, and historical determinism, Lyra believed in the power and possibilities of social reform. Chase claims that in the banana silhouettes, Lyra perfected her technique by distilling her narration to the bare essence of "el problema humano"—the human problem of exploitation on the banana plantation (25). Upon being sent by the Communist Party in 1931 to investigate the conditions of the laborers of the United Fruit Company on the Atlantic side of Costa Rica, Lyra produced a series of bare silhouettes combining satire, "gritty realism," social criticism, and her entomological analytic skills (Horan 2000, 15–16). In these she examined the plight of women, children, and men reduced to their basic material energy, that is, purely exploitable labor and bodies.

In "Bananas and Men," Lyra describes her trip by train to the Atlantic region of Costa Rica, where for miles she sees only water and sky, green vegetation, and white sandy beach, until in the sand she encounters "the crude wooden cross, once painted black, now all but faded away" (Horan 2000, 48). Identifying as a traveler in this region, or more precisely, as the "entomologist" turned ethnographer, she sketches images of the plant life, people, and problems of this land. As eyewitness to life on the banana plantation, she produces five brief silhouettes that comprise "Bananas and Men": I. Estefanía; II. Christmas Eve; III. Children; IV. Upriver; V. The Laborer Who Seemed a Saint (Horan 2000, 47–61). In each silhouette, the narrator produces a still life of marginal figures on the banana plantation. In contrast to her silhouettes of the Maternal School and the Cothnejo-Fishy District, wherein Lyra writes in the first person, expressing familiarity with the urban contours of San José, in these sketches her "first person all but disappears" (Horan 2000, 16), and she writes with critical distance. However, there are a few instances in "Bananas and Men" in which Lyra uses her "I" point of view, as when she writes about Estefanía. The narrator meta-reflexively signals her narratological and subjective position in relation to Estefanía by using cues such as "I think," "I knew," and "I saw." These are the only instances in which Lyra uses the personal pronoun in the five sketches, thus drawing attention to her outsider status on the banana plantation and her subjective interpretation of life under extreme labor conditions.

In the first paragraph of the silhouette, the narrator encounters Estefanía only as a fading name on the "blackish cross anchored in the sand, the arms stretched out facing the vast blue," which the sea has dragged to the beach (48). On that cross is written the name "Estefanía R," "the surname" almost "completely illegible" (48). The narrator speculates on the identity of the woman—"maybe Rojas, maybe Ramírez, or Ramos." Because Estefanía is already dead at the beginning of the narrative, the narrator can only imagine her surname, genealogy, patrimony, and history. It is in this narrative gap and space of resignification that the narrator makes personal conjectures as to the identity of the banana plantation woman. In the absence of Estefanía's person, the narrator proceeds to invent her life story from the stories she knows of other women who have traveled from the plantations to seek medical care in San José and others whom she knows by hearsay. In reading Estefanía's name as an "empty sign" scratched on a fading black cross, Lyra comments on the absence of women's histories and stories in the anti-imperialist, social realist narrative. The narrator asks, "What of the woman who bore this name? What would she have been like? . . . How did she come to the banana plantations in the flatlands of the Atlantic Coast, between the Reventazón and Parismina River?" (48). Here Lyra alludes to the effaced stories of banana plantation women in Central American historiography; she can only fill in that gap, by sketching or outlining a silhouette of Estefanía, drawing from the life stories of other women and her own secondhand reconstruction of women's testimonies. It is telling, then, that the narrative begins and ends with "Estefanía R . . . "

Indeed, Estefanía might have been like any of the "row of women's outlines" seen on any banana plantation:

> pallid figures, wilted, darkened by the sun, fevers, and man's sensuality, amoral and innocent, like animals. One stands out in the sorrowful frieze: would she be called Estefanía? The name's been erased from memory. The face, a dark triangle amid the confusion of dark hair; teeth and sclera very white; feet bare, strong, and twining; very long arms. (48)

Having established Estefanía as any woman on the banana plantation, Lyra proceeds to fill in her silhouette and to tell the composite story of the plantation woman, who left Santa Cruz, Guanacaste, the folkloric heartland of Costa Rica, in search of work. She drifted to the Atlantic after having a child out of wedlock, leaving the child "at the first propitious house" and "roaming" with men and another child in tow (48). The narrator tells us, "Life deposited her, child and all, on a banana plantation along the Atlantic. And so she continued from plantation to plantation, one guy today, another tomorrow" (48). Continuing with her version of Estefanía's story, the narrator recounts the rapes, the abuses, the diseases, and the continued drifting of Estefanía and her daughter, who clings to her "like a mushroom to a broken branch" (49). On one return trip from the hospital in San José, where Estefanía is treated for malaria or an advanced case of tuberculosis, mother and daughter seem to be "coming to the end of the line" (50), as the text's verbal irony foreshadows. As they sit in the mule car used to transport bananas, the image is complete: mother, daughter, sacks, boxes, and bananas are rendered indistinguishable, recalling the title of the silhouettes, "Bananas and Men." Mother and daughter return to the banana plantation, only to be "swallowed up again amid the banana trees." The reader gets a last(ing) glimpse of Estefanía, her daughter, and the cemetery from which the cross with Estefanía's name might have drifted. The silhouette ends with the repetition of the name "Estefanía R . . . ," now filled in with the narrator's added epitaph: "One of so many women who have passed through the banana plantations" (50).

In "Estefanía" and the other silhouettes in "Bananas and [Wo]men" series, Lyra sketches an image of banana plantation life and fills in the blanks of Costa Rican and Central American popular history from the green belly of U.S. imperialism. Estefanía metamorphoses as an embodiment of women on the plantations, the "row of women's outlines," whose stories can only be approximated or sketched in the absence of their voices. Represented as outlines, figures, and body parts, "Estefanía R . . . " reembodies the broken and alienated lives of the women on the banana plantation, who have been raped, infected with diseases, and forced to migrate for their survival. Lyra's sketches thus represent the state of abjection produced in subjects forced to labor on the banana plantation. By the end, all that is left of Estefanía is the "cross," signifying the suffering and injustice that plantation women bear on the banana plantations.

In the second silhouette, "Christmas Eve," Lyra uses the motif of the holiday to satirize the plantation bosses, who are grotesquely caricatured by name. The reader is introduced to Mr. Sweetums, the United

Banana Company assistant manager; his vaudevillian mistress, Dolly
Darling; and their friends, the toilet paper heiress, Polly Flapper, and
the front-page headliner, Conny Fletcher. With his fruit company earnings, Mr. Sweetums showers Dolly with gifts, treating her to a Rolls
Royce, a Tiffany's diamond choker, and a fox-skin coat with no less than
thirty-two tails for Christmas (54). The redundancy of details drives
home the point that Americans squander the wealth they have made on
the backs of poor Central American workers on the banana plantations.
In New York and far removed from the malaria-ridden swamp of Estefanía's banana plantation, "they spent a delicious Christmas Eve . . .
[drinking] exquisite cocktails . . . [and listening] to 'Glory to God on high
and peace on earth to men of good will'" (55). In the meantime, back in
"the Zone," a high-ranking Costa Rican company official receives "the
order to reject the fruit," while his family "also celebrate their Christmas
Eve . . . in their comfortable houses with graceful wreaths of mistle-
toe . . . and little Christmas trees with many lights and fantastic glass
fruit" (53). At the house of an elected official "engaged in pushing
through contracts just as the United Banana Company wants them," another Costa Rican middleman has used bribe money to buy gifts for his
children and wife (54). Juxtaposed to these scenes of celebration and excess is the flooded labor camp on the same plantation, where the laborers suffer from pulmonary hemorrhage, malaria, and alcoholism. There,
the laborers work late on Christmas Eve, although no one will be paid
because company headquarters in New York has already rejected the
surplus of bananas. The narrator comments on the fruit's rejection:

> It didn't have the requisite grade. Of course it was the right grade, but
> there was a surplus of fruit on the market in the United States. The
> order came from above: reject the fruit. A Yankeefied Costa Rican, one
> of those who believe that speaking English is a great thing, received said
> order and fell all over himself to pass it along. . . . The cutters will lose
> all their work . . . Christmas Eve! (52–53)

The narrator closes the dismal scene at the labor camp with a biting
ironic understatement: "Everybody is drunk there, even the women and
the children" (53).

In the third sketch, "Children," the narrator describes the plantation
children, each in his or her turn being claimed by the abject conditions
on the plantation. Reflections of physical deterioration and material pri-
vation, the children are consumed by illness, alcohol, and starvation.

The repetition of the color green—in the vegetation, in the banana, in the water, in the malaria, and on the bodies of the laborers and their children—brands everything and everyone belonging to the United Banana Company. As the text explains, "The children are greenish, very brown, their bellies stuffed with worms, amoebas, ankilostomas, and God knows how many monsters. They don't shout or jump; they move slowly, and when they smile some anemic gums can be seen, which gives a painful depth to this smile" (55). The plantation children are juxtaposed to magazine advertisements and pedagogical materials produced by the UFCO, showing "smiling, healthy children" in the tropics waiting to be served bananas. Lyra quotes ironically from one U.S. ad: " 'For growing children bananas and milk are a nourishing luncheon' " (58). And she cites a medical source on the benefits of the fruit: "When a person eats a banana, the body takes in countless calories and vitamins" (57). As Suleiman explains, Lyra's repeated references and citations of banana advertisements, medical reports, pedagogical materials, and popular journalism highlight the UFCO's use of propaganda to market bananas as the "World's Perfect Food" (Jenkins 2000, 98). Lyra, fully aware of the market value of this promotional material, uses "Bananas and Men" to represent the abjection of banana production in Central America and to critique the U.S. public's consumption of bananas vis-à-vis the exploitation of "pallid" and "greenish" children, "swollen with anemia, prematurely aged" (56). Lest the reader miss her critique of banana production and consumption, Lyra nonchalantly explains at the end of the "Children" sketch:

> On the other hand, in the United States, where almost everyone is practical minded and on that account knows to take honest advantage of what has cost sweat and fatigue for everyone else, they eat all the bananas that the United Fruit Company offers them. (Horan 2000, 57)

The reader is thus reminded through the redundant and repetitive nature of Lyra's sketches that U.S. consumers of bananas are complicit in the exploitation and abuse of banana workers in Central America and that their consumption of the green gold is an eschatological and cannibalistic act.

Finally, in the last two silhouettes, "Upriver" and "The Laborer Who Seemed a Saint," the narrator alludes to a nascent American ecotourism industry tied to banana production. Tourists exploring the tropical rainforest of Tortuguero travel aboard the same decrepit banana boats that transport laborers from one plantation to another, sick workers and their families en route to the charity hospital in San José, and a fresh crop of migrant laborers to the banana enclave. It is not until the final sketch, "The Laborer Who Seemed a Saint," that the reader gets a glimpse of a future revolution, represented by Ignacio Parrales, who, like Estefanía, comes from Guanacaste. After arriving on the banana plantation, Parrales works in different capacities on the banana line, helping laborers to make traps for catching animals to augment their meager diets, teaching children how to read and write, and becoming a storyteller, healer, and leader of sorts (Horan 2000, 60). In the last sketch, however, he travels back to San José under armed guard after having killed a corrupt police agent who extorted money from laborers on payday (61). A revolutionary of sorts during the years of Augusto César Sandino's revolution in the Segovias of Nicaragua and Farabundo Martí's insurrection in El Salvador, Parrales embodies the larger revolution taking shape across the Central American isthmus. The sketch foretells of revolution and social change to come to the banana zone.

In "Bananas and Men," Lyra thus explores the transformative space of the banana enclaves, exposing the material conditions of labor exploitation, migrancy, disease, hunger, malnutrition, alcoholism, sexual violence, prostitution, and lack of alternatives, among other things. She constructs prototypical marginal subjects, who begin to articulate a collective denunciation and call to action (Rojas and Ovares 1995, 78). In the context of banana production, people are valued in proportion to their labor and productivity. In an effort to critique the extreme forms of human exploitation in the banana zone, Lyra seeks to bring Estefanía and others out of the shadow of anonymity and to recover their life stories from the larger narrative of U.S. banana production and imperialism in Central America.

The Banana-Canal Industrial Military Complex in Panama

Banana production, as we have seen, spread from Costa Rican enclaves to other regions in Central America, quickly becoming one of the principal agrarian exports of the isthmus. Once solidly (im)planted in Costa Rica, Honduras, and Guatemala—the original "banana republics"—the economic model of the banana enclave was exported to other Central and Latin American countries such as Ecuador and Panama, where literary production, too, responded with its local brand of social protest literature. In Panama, Joaquín Beleño (1922–1988), the son of Antillean workers on the Panama Canal and a leftist writer, intellectual, and activist, produced the final brand of banana social realist novels in Central America. In these, he not only contested the expansion of banana enclaves across the isthmus and the construction of the U.S.-controlled canal in Panama, but, more important, challenged the imperialist, racist apparatus operating in the country and turning it into a self-styled "Yankee colony" (Szok 2002, 151).

As a young man, Beleño worked in the Canal Zone. He later used his experiences in his journalistic and literary writing, particularly his novels focusing on the representation of West Indian, Panamanian, and ethnically diverse Central American migrant laborers in Panama. His social realist novel *Flor de banana* documents the expansion of banana production in the province of Chiriquí and the rise of organized labor among the exploited workers there. In addition to *Flor de banana*, Beleño produced a series of Canal Zone novels linking banana production to the construction of the canal, as laborers first recruited for canal labor turned to the banana enclaves for work. Beleño's Canal Zone trilogy begins with *Luna verde* (Green Moon) (1951). This novel represents the canal as one immense labor camp bringing together men from different nations to maintain and manage the canal. It focuses on the incessant hardships faced by canal workers in their daily struggle to survive in the diseased swamps and under the watchful eyes and wrathful hands of U.S. overseers. Beleño writes, "Allí el gringo no es hombre; es el amo, la bestia que marca sus pezuñas en los esclavos latinos o jamaicanos [There the gringo is not a man; he is the master, the beast that leaves his hoof prints on the Latino and Jamaican slaves]" (1951, 42). *Gamboa Road Gang* (1960) takes readers into the Canal Zone prison-plantation complex run by U.S. military personnel and used to extract extreme forms of labor from Panamanian and migrant laborers from Central America and elsewhere. The last novel in the trilogy, *Curundú* (1963), narrates the story of a young Panamanian man coming of age, as he is subjected to U.S.-style Jim Crow laws, otherwise known as "Gold and Silver Roll" in Panama.

To manage national and imported laborers from the Black Caribbean, the U.S. enforced Gold and Silver Roll in Panama, the system by which U.S. white laborers in the Canal Zone were paid in gold (dollars) and nonwhite laborers (Panamanian nationals included) were paid in silver (local) currency (LaFeber 1989). The institution of Gold and Silver Roll in the Canal Zone intensified racial stratification in the country as

public spaces were segregated and U.S. whites assumed superior positions over nonwhites, including Panamanian nationals. Michael L. Conniff, in *Black Labor on a White Canal* (1985), explains:

> Zone life was regimented and segregated. Virtually all facilities existed
> in duplicate, one set for gold (or white employees), another for silver.
> Americans did not admit that they practiced Jim Crow segregation
> because it was not permitted under the U.S. Constitution. Rather, they
> used the Gold-Silver system to disguise it. For their part, silver workers
> had difficulty fighting segregation because they were not citizens. (5)

Panamanian citizens were subject to U.S. racial laws in their own nation.
In *Luna verde*, the main character, Ramón de Roquebert, tells of receiving his work papers after undergoing an exhaustive medical examination
clearing him of tuberculosis, malaria, syphilis, and other diseases. Once
cleared and having declared his "unconditional fidelity" to the United
States, Roquebert was authorized to lift rocks, carry cement bags, and
break concrete and brush in the Canal Zone. His new ID card identified
him as laborer number 48,976, color *brown*, and nationality *Pana*. The
text juxtaposes his newly imposed "silver" status to his vital statistics,
as he knows them: white, straight blond hair, five feet nine inches tall,
eighteen years of age, Catholic, French descent, rural origins, and recent graduate with a Bachelor of Arts in literature seeking a job in car-
pentry. Attempting to correct his public "identity," Roquebert turns to
a black worker, who confirms Roquebert's greatest (internalized) racial
fear: "Los gringos te han convertido en brown. . . . Nunca serás Gold
Roll, aunque tengas todo lo que tienen los gringos [The gringos have
converted you into brown. . . . You will never be Gold Roll, even though
you have everything the gringos have]" (Beleño 1951, 28–29).

Beleño's Canal Zone trilogy and his banana thesis novel, *Flor de banana*, are all bildungsromans—stories of young men of color (Panamanian and other) coming of age with limited prospects due to their nationality, race, class, genealogy, and silver status in the U.S.-Panamanian
social hierarchy. All turn to the Canal Zone for work and to gain some
kind of understanding of their place in the world. In the Canal Zone,
they encounter a series of people, events, and trials ("adventures" in the
bildungsroman) that change them for the worse and induct them into
an official system of labor exploitation. Through the characters' experiences as laborers on the canal, readers are exposed not only to labor conditions under U.S. canal personnel but also to the racist banana-canal

industrial military complex, where all nonwhite laborers are subjected to the violent lessons of predatory capitalism at its most personal levels. In *Luna verde*, Ramón de Roquebert leaves his home in Río Hato in the Panamanian interior to work on the canal as an overseer, a job that causes his moral degeneration until he joins the labor movement. Only through his own conscience-raising does he recognize his alienated status in the Canal Zone and experience a political awakening of sorts. In *Gamboa Road Gang (Los forzados de Gamboa)*, Ata, the racially mixed Chombo son of an Antillean woman and a white man, is condemned to fifty years in the Gamboa prison for allegedly raping a white woman. Finally, in *Curundú*, the adolescent student Rubén Galván dreams of working in the restricted Curundú U.S. military base in Panama City. Once there, he goes through a series of degradations that break his fragile sense of Panamanian identity. Read as a whole, Beleño's canal novels are not just about young Panamanian men making their way in the world but rather the construction of national identity under the strain of U.S. neocolonialism and imperialism.

As Suleiman would have it, Beleño's novels can be read as bildungsroman, a principal form of the *roman à thèse*. According to Suleiman, what makes a bildungsroman an effective *roman à thèse* is the personal narrative of experience, learning, awakening, and possible transformation, features that one immediately identifies in Beleño's Canal Zone trilogy and *Flor de banana*. Suleiman's definition of the bildungsroman/*roman à thèse* can easily apply to Beleño's novels:

> It is the story itself, the lived *experience* (or transformation) of a subject over time. Here is where we encounter the structure of apprenticeship, which is a structure on the level of the story: the fictive subject who "lives" the story has his counterpart in the real subject who *reads*. The persuasive effect of a story of apprenticeship "with a thesis" results from the virtual identification of the reader with the protagonist. (1983, 73; emphasis in original)

Intended for national and international readers (his works have been translated into English, French, Chinese, and Russian), Beleño's novels articulate an anticolonial and anti-imperialist critique of Panama's so-called tutelage to the United States in the twentieth century, vis-à-vis the tutelage of his novels' young protagonists in the Canal Zone. As Ramón de Roquebert of *Luna verde* puts it, for the young subjugated Panamanians, the Canal Zone is "¡Tierra de odio, de blanco y negro, de

insulto y grajo! [Land of hate, of black and white, of insult and fraud!]"
(Beleño 1951, 28). As we might expect, Beleño's novels take readers into
the policed Canal Zone, the segregated Silver and Gold Roll public
spaces, the labor camps, the prisons, and the strips of land on both sides
of the canal waterway from Panama City on the Pacific and Colón on
the Atlantic that literally have divided the nation.

Going through a series of trials, which would amount to Suleiman's
redundancies in the *roman à thèse*, the protagonists of Beleño's novels
personify "one of the means by which the reader is led to a 'correct'
understanding, both of the story and of what it is designed to demonstrate" (Suleiman 1983, 79). It becomes clear to the reader that the problem in Panama is not its diverse racial inter/national population but
rather the social and racial hierarchy imposed by the United States and
its internalization and appropriation by the privileged ("rabi blanco";
white *criollo*?) establishment of Panama. Indeed, in an analysis of a canonical Panamanian novel, Peter Szok (2002) notes that the official literary canon of Panama is invested in promoting a Hispanic (whitened)
and sometimes Indo-mestizo national image, excluding black, Chinese,
Southeast Asian, and racially mixed populations. West Indians and migrant peoples associated with labor in the Canal Zone have been virtually made "invisible within foundational fiction" (160). In the 1930s
and 1940s, Caribbean blacks experienced great repression, and, in 1941,
the Panamanian government attempted to "strip West Indians of their
citizenship" (160). Emerging from this context of internalized national
racism supported by domestic policies in Panama, Beleño's novels representing the banana-canal racist apparatus take on new meaning, for
they are one of the few discursive spaces representing the diversity, exclusion, and marginalization of large numbers of Panamanian people of
color. Moreover, it can be said that Beleño's social realist novels come
close to articulating an antiracist and decolonizing critique in Panama,
a topic to which I return at the end of this chapter.

In *El tema del canal en la novelística panameña* (The Canal Theme in
the Panamanian Novel) (1975), the Panamanian literary critic Mélida
Ruth Sepúlveda notes that in his novels Beleño not only critiques U.S.
intervention and occupation of the Canal Zone but also expresses the
collective indignation, anger, and hurt pride of the Panamanian people (31). Along with others who write in this distinctly Panamanian literary genre, Beleño engages in the production of a "canal literature"
that addresses issues of national sovereignty, foreign occupation, and
racial identity. In her monograph, Sepúlveda analyzes a literary corpus

of social protest and political novels that challenge the presence of the United States and the canal. She insists that "la naturaleza 'transitista' de Panama queda marcada en sus primeros ensayos, es constante en su haber poético y en la evolución de su narrativa [the condition of transit in Panama is reflected in the first essays of the country, and is constant in poetic writing and the evolution of narrative]" (1975, 5). She identifies a number of literary texts that have represented Panama as a transit site and as the host country for the canal. This literature includes serial novels, romantic novels, thesis novels, and naturalist/social realist novels along the lines of Beleño's trilogy (7–30). This literature also includes a more recent production of literature by women and diasporic writers dealing with gender, race, and class in the canal regime of power.[14] The production of these texts suggests that a significant corpus of nonfoundational literary texts has opposed the omnipresence of the Canal Zone, supported the construction of a hybrid multiracial national imaginary, and interrogated official (inter)national imaginaries in Panama (7–30).

Sepúlveda further claims that the theme of the canal in Panamanian literature reflects the national problem ("la problemática nacional") of which Beleño is most explicitly critical (16–17). Of particular interest to Beleño is bringing to public discourse the condition of the "Chombos"—the mixed-race West Indian population in Panama that has been highly discriminated against in the U.S.-run Canal Zone and in Panama. Chombos are descendants of the Anglophone Afro-Caribbean laborers brought from Jamaica, Barbados, Santa Lucia, and other islands to build and maintain the canal.[15] Sepúlveda identifies Chombos as English-speaking, Protestant, Caribbean-origin persons of color and as the most marginalized racial subjects in Panama. As such, they are the subjects of much literature that deals with race in the country (Sepúlveda 1975, 41). Historically, Panamanian literature has made Chombos the collective scapegoat and metaphor of the "race" problem in the country under U.S. occupation, blaming them for intervention and neocolonialism, as well as racism. More critical of the condition of Panama, Beleño questions internal and external socioeconomic and political structures through his representation of the Afro-Caribbean characters that populate his novels. As Sepúlveda puts it:

La obra de Beleño puede catalogarse como una sorda y apasionada protesta contra una sociedad corrumpida por la ambición del dinero, una discriminación racial sistematizada y un régimen colonialista enclavado en el corazón mismo de la República de Panama. (51)

[Beleños's works can be cataloged as a muted and passionate protest against a society corrupted by ambition for money, systematic racial discrimination, and a colonial regime enclaved in the heart of the Republic of Panama.]

Beleño's texts are not only critical of U.S. occupation. They also highlight Panamanian complicity with the United States and the internalization of racist power structures.

Beleño's *Flor de banana*

In *Flor de banana*—his only novel to deal exclusively with banana production—Beleño is no less critical than Carmen Lyra of the impact of banana enclaves in the isthmus. His focus, however, is Panama, as the intertwined banana-canal complex grievously and perhaps irreversibly divides the nation. Another bildungsroman that deals with the question of Panamanian racial identity, *Flor de banana* takes up the story of Ramíro Vagones in a coming-of-age narrative that follows the main character in his furtive search for personal and national identity. Vagones is the son of an indigenous mother, who gives birth to him and abandons him in a freight car used to carry bananas to Puerto Armuelles. His name—Vagones (in Spanish, the word for railroad car or caboose)—links him to a mode of production that will control his personal development, although he attempts to redirect the course of his life. Throughout the novel, he tries to leave the banana plantation on which he was raised, but it calls him back repeatedly until he takes up the cause of the revolution.

After being abandoned by his biological family, Vagones is found by a plantation boss and taken to live in the home of the Walker family. They raise him as their "boy" and "foundling" but not as their "son." In the tradition of the bildungsroman, this tropical coming-of-age story of a "recogido" (foundling) follows Vagones's search for family, genealogy, and personal identity and fortune as he crosses various socioeconomic boundaries. He moves from the caboose, where he was left by his indigenous family, to the Anglo Walker family estate, and then back to the impoverished hut of his natural family, only to return to but be rejected by the Walkers. The movements back and forth convey the sense of instability, groundlessness, and nationlessness of this son of Panama. As in the Canal Zone novels, all roads in *Flor de banana* seem to lead

Vagones to Panama City, the center of economic production and the Canal outlet to the Pacific. There, he is a student for a brief time, until the Walker family disowns him and stops paying his monthly room and board. Once again homeless, Vagones starts his real trials and education. He learns about life on the streets when he becomes one of the *lumpen* living under the floor of the exclusive Club Union, to which only wealthy Panamanians and American Canal Zone personnel gain entry. Living literally underneath the Club Union floor gives Vagones the critical perspective, "from below," to channel his life into action—the message of many socialist realist novels, as Suleiman has suggested in her analysis of pre–World War II bildungsromans. In the streets of Panama, Vagones learns about the extreme poverty that pushes people to organize revolutions. Vagones returns to the plantation with his newly found consciousness, where, following the meta-narrative of social protest novels already described, he transforms himself into a labor organizer. His return to the Walker plantation fulfills not only the return-home imperative of the bildungsroman but also the plot requirement of banana social realist literature to stage a strike.

Vagones's coming-of-age narrative is first and foremost a narrative of coming to political consciousness and action in "la lucha sindical de los hombres de Chiriquí en la región bananera [the labor struggle of the men of the banana region of Chiriquí]" (Beleño 1962, 5). Through the personal story of Vagones, the novel describes the coming of banana production to the Chiriquí province, after the great world depression of 1929, an event of irreversible consequences for the region. Panama's traditional agricultural economies and their ways of life were traded, or conceded, to banana production by national leaders in Panama City. The novel explains:

> Los finqueros, decepcionados y en la ruina, abandonaban todas sus tierras y bajaban a las costas calientes para emplearse con la compañía frutera que arrendaba tierra y prestaba semillas de tallo para producir el oro verde. (13) [The dejected and financially ruined ranchers abandoned their lands and came to the steamy coasts to seek work with the fruit company that rented land and gave them banana stalks to produce the green gold.]

In the banana zone, amid a diverse population of indigenous, Afro-Caribbean, Nicaraguan, Salvadoran, Chinese, and Panamanian workers, Vagones finds his purpose in life, as he takes up the larger cause

against the fruit company and calls workers to the "sindicato de tra-
bajadores del banano" (banana workers' union) (170). The novel thus
comes full circle: it ends with Vagones's strike on the Walker plantation,
which then moves to Panama City to be taken up by students and urban
workers. Beleño's novel suggests that although the strike is inconclusive,
there is the possibility of social change in Panama, as prescribed by the
genre itself and as a prefiguration of the anti-U.S. student and proletarian strikes in Panama in the 1950s and 1960s. With *Flor de banana*,
Beleño completes his cycle of social realist novels about canal construction and banana production, perhaps pushing social realist literature to
other forms of revolutionary literature. While social realist literature
represented the harsh conditions of life on banana plantations and the
canal, this literature, with its tired and repetitive ideological message,
reached a literary and revolutionary impasse and had to make way for
other discursive modes of resistance.

Like other texts of its kind, Beleño's *Flor de banana* reached the limits
of a genre that had become saturated by its own message in an era that
began questioning the notion of "absolute truths" and absolutist ideologies or master narratives—the very reasons for being of the *roman
à thèse*. How, then, might we reread the *roman à thèse* of race in Central
America today? *Flor de banana* ends not just with the impending labor
strike but also with a prohibited romance. The main character of *Flor de
banana*, the indigenous Ramíro Vagones, like the Chombo Ata in *Gamboa Road Gang*, has desired a white woman. Estefanía, in Carmen Lyra's
"Bananas and Men," has slept with a series of men: black, Chinese, and
Central American. If we were to analyze the other novels of banana production identified in this chapter, we would see, too, that the novels address issues of race, sexuality, violence, and miscegenation. These novels
thus offer the opportunity to examine multiracial Central America outside of official national discourses declaring Central America Hispanic
and/or Indo-mestizo. The story of racial mixing, miscegenation, and
racism in Central America begins to surface in this brand of literature,
now rarely read but in which readers may catch glimpses of the Central
American Black Atlantic (Gilroy 1993).[16]

The transisthmian region of Panama northward through the Atlantic coasts of Costa Rica, Nicaragua, Honduras, Guatemala, and Belize is
part of the plantation economies and neocolonial cultures of the Black
Atlantic. Paul Gilroy and other critics inside and outside of Central
America, however, largely overlook Black Central America.[17] The cultural mythology of the region would have us believe in a Mesoamerican

mestizo (Indo-Hispanic) fusion (represented even in *Flor de banana* by the mestizo protagonist, Ramiro Vagones). The multiracial diversity of the isthmus is elided by the preeminent dividing of Central America into configurations of West/Pacific (Indo-Hispanic, mestizo) and East/Atlantic (Anglo and Indo-African) regions. Produced at a self-reflexive discursive moment in the twentieth century, Central American social protest literature (reinterpreted now as an interstitial literature of racial, gender, and sexual differences) can be read beyond an "authoritarian fiction" with a singular message. As dialogical literature, banana social protest literature speaks to and about untold issues, among them, race, class, gender, sexuality, miscegenation, migrancy, and imperialism. Instead of being obsolete, banana social realist literature pushes the discursive limits of its time, challenging the narrative of imperialism and producing other spaces of signification against global forces. In Lyra's "Bananas and Men" and Beleño's *Flor de banana*, the economy of bananas gives shape to a referential mode of representation and prompts the production of narratives that challenge the national mythologies of the banana republic.

CHAPTER 3

The Power of Indigo: *Testimonio,* Historiography, and Revolution in Cuzcatlán

With my reality, I have won the right to express it and share it
[Yo, con mi realidad. He ganado el derecho a expresarla y compartirla].
—MANLIO ARGUETA, *Cuzcatlán donde bate la mar del sur*

In the 1970s and 1980s, armed conflict swept through most of Central America, hitting Nicaragua, Guatemala, and El Salvador especially hard. Costa Rica, Honduras, Panama, and Belize did not escape the violence but served, at various times, as refugee camps, relocation centers, and military bases for the countries at war. More the rule than the exception in the isthmus, El Salvador in the 1980s was the scene of a twelve-year civil war that claimed over eighty thousand lives and displaced nearly 20 percent of its population (Lungo Uclés 1990, 97–98). Relative numbers of fatalities and displacements were also recorded in Nicaragua and Guatemala in the 1970s and 1980s. Despite great losses, Central Americans witnessed, documented, and resisted extreme forms of institutional violence. Under the sign of revolution, a testimonial narrative textuality emerged across most of the isthmus.

Testimonial literature crossed discursive genres, spanning personal and collective narratives representing social realities in the conflict zones. Pathbreaking Central American testimonial texts included works by Claribel Alegría, Manlio Argueta, Gioconda Belli, Omar Cabezas, Ernesto Cardenal, Roque Dalton, Nidia Díaz, Ana Guadalupe Martínez, Margaret Randall, and Daisy Zamora.[1] But it was Rigoberta Menchú's *Me llamo Rigoberta Menchú y así me nació la conciencia* (1983; *I Rigoberta Menchú: An Indian Woman in Guatemala,* 1984) that made the biggest impact on readers around the world and took the hardest hit when the testimonial boom came under scrutiny at the turn of the millennium (Arias 2001, 2007). This chapter explores the transformation of Central American testimonial narrative into historiography through a rereading of various testimonial texts, but most important Manlio Argueta's novel *Cuzcatlán donde bate la mar del sur* (Cuzcatlán Where the Southern Sea Beats) (1987) and Roque Dalton's *El Salvador (Monografía)* (1979).[2] It examines the deep structures of testimonial narrative against the grand narrative of (neo)colonialism in Central America as codified by the sign of indigo in Argueta's and Dalton's texts. More generally, this chapter revisits the transisthmian phenomenon of testimonial literature that came under scrutiny as a consequence of the so-called Rigoberta Menchú controversy and examines the transformation of testimonial narrative into a historiographic record of neocolonialism in the isthmus.

For the Testimonial Record

During the armed conflicts of the 1980s, Salvadorans found multiple spaces from which to protest, denounce, and attest to—albeit in clandestine ways—the repression they suffered. Within the growing culture of war, the streets of San Salvador at times teemed with demonstrators carrying signs, photographs, and other forms of visual resistance.[3] Political graffiti appeared overnight in San Salvador. Radio Venceremos reached listeners with news broadcasts coming directly from the war zones of Chalatenango and Morazán provinces.[4] Numerous *testimonios* were published inside and outside of the country, often as part of an extensive solidarity support network, which included artists, students, laborers, church activists, and solidarity workers. Under the imprint "Testigos de la historia" (Witnesses of History), the Universidad Centroamericana José Simeón Cañas (UCA) Press published various *testimonios*. These included Ana Guadalupe Rodríguez's *Las cárceles clandestinas de El Salvador* (The Clandestine Prisons of El Salvador) (1978); Francisco Metzi's *Por los caminos de Chalatenango* (Along the Roads of Chalatenango) (1988); and José Ignacio López Vigil's *Las mil y una historias de Radio Venceremos* (The Thousand and One Stories of Radio Venceremos) (1992). Volumes in the series *La iglesia en América Latina* (The Church in Latin America) included an anthology of slain Archbishop Oscar Romero's homilies, *La voz de los sin voz* (The Voice of Those Who Are Voiceless) (1980), edited by Jon Sobrino and Ignacio Martín-Baró, whose stories, in turn, are told in Salvador Carranza's *Mártires de la* UCA (Martyrs of the UCA) (1990). Other *testimonios* are María López Vigil's *Don Lito de El Salvador* (Don Lito in El Salvador) (1987a) and *Muerte y vida en Morazán* (Death and Life in Morazán) (1987b); and Charles Clements's *Guazapa: Testimonio de guerra de un médico norteamericano* (Guazapa: War Testimony of a North American Doctor) (1984). The UCA's Colección Premio Nacional UCA Editores and other literary imprints published works by Manlio Argueta, Roque Dalton, David Escobar Galindo, Claribel Alegría, Claudia Lars, Jacinta Escudos, and others. The UCA also published philosophical, sociological, psychological, pedagogical, historical, and political monographs on El Salvador at war, including works by the Jesuits Segundo Montes, Ignacio Ellacuría, and Martín Baró, all of whom were assassinated by the Salvadoran military on the campus of the UCA on November 16, 1989.

This massive site-specific production of testimonial narrative in El Salvador might be read as a collective heteroglossic response to official discourses of repression (Bakhtin 1981). Mikhail Bakhtin explains that in response to power certain speech acts proliferate, making possible denunciation and protest. According to him, "Alongside the centripetal forces, the centrifugal forces of language carry their uninterrupted work; alongside verbal-ideological centralization and unification, the uninterrupted processes of decentralization and disunification go forward" (1981, 270–271). In El Salvador, discourses deployed by the state and its institutions to control, silence, and repress the general population generated a counterdiscourse. Under normative and repressive conditions such as those experienced in El Salvador in the 1980s, the production of diverse responses was to be expected. In "A Dialogue on Power," Gilles Deleuze and Michel Foucault assert that since power engenders its own discursive resistances in clandestine (secret) spaces, it is from those discursive spaces that "the people involved could speak at last practically on their own" (1994, 11). Testimonial discourse in El Salvador, as in the rest of Central America, served thus as the channel through which people could speak out against institutional power.

The specific historical circumstances of the 1970s and 1980s in El Salvador prompted the production of dialogical, delinquent, and testimonial responses and opened wide discursive rifts, or discursive divides, wherein subversive discourses and subjectivities could be produced and disseminated. This volatile period served as ground zero for the elaboration of particular oppositional discourses and delinquent subjectivities. Salvadoran state propaganda and rhetoric identified all unauthorized discourses, dissenting opinions, and expressions of opposition as "insurgent" and "subversive" and classified as "guerrillas" and "terrorists" all those suspected of opposition. Leftist guerrillas, sympathizers, urban and rural workers, indigenous people, intellectuals, scholars, writers, student organizers, church activists, solidarity workers, families of the disappeared, innocent bystanders, refugees, exiles, and migrants—regardless of age, gender, class, and education level—all became suspect and delinquent subjects and targets of state repression during the war.

In the 1980s, the heightened production, reception, and dissemination of testimonial narratives challenged the propagandistic rhetoric of the government and opened spaces for the articulation of alternate subjects, identities, and histories. The poet Roque Dalton (1935–1975) recuperated the popular history of the Gran Matanza (Great Massacre) of 1932, when he documented the life of the labor organizer Miguel Mármol (Dalton 1982, 1987).[5] Manlio Argueta wrote about the role of peasants (men, women, and children) in the civil war, and Nidia Díaz, Claribel Alegría, and Ana Guadalupe Martínez, and others focused on the struggles of women in El Salvador. These testimonial texts challenged the official historical record and articulated oppositional discourses that emerged in the 1980s. Paraphrasing Foucault, it could be said that during this period there was an institutional incitement for other subjects to speak and to lay claim to their own histories and experiences, thus activating voices that had been long excluded from the historical record of El Salvador (Foucault 1987, 25–26). The decade of the 1980s, hence, was not a silent or lost decade for El Salvador. On the contrary, it was one of the most discursively productive periods in Salvadoran history. During this time, many used testimonial discourse to speak strategically and critically about power, although often under the threat of punishment and the cloak of secrecy. At this discursive juncture, subjects that had been formerly shut out of official history surfaced in a textual matrix that included Dalton's historiographic poetic works and Argueta's historica-testimonial novels.

From *Testimonio* to Historiography

In his most well known novels, *El valle de las hamacas* (Valley of the Hammocks) (1970), *Caperucita en la zona roja* (Caperucita in the Red Zone) (1977), *Un día en la vida* (A Day in the Life) (1980), *Cuzcatlán donde bate la mar del sur* (1987), and *Milagro de la paz* (Miracle of Peace) (1994), Manlio Argueta has elaborated an unofficial, testimonial history of El Salvador. Read as a corpus, the novels chronicle the history of El Salvador, from pre-Columbian times to the postwar period in the 1990s, as experienced by marginalized sectors of Salvadoran society. Until the decades of civil war, these subjects generally remained unaccounted for in Salvadoran literature and historiography. In *El valle de las hamacas* and *Caperucita en la zona roja*, Argueta narrates the rise of student militancy in the 1960s and 1970s, constantly referring back to crucial moments in the colonial history of the country. In *Un día en la vida*, *Cuzcatlán*, and *Milagro de la paz*, he represents the armed struggle and the political awakening of urban and rural groups, especially women who progressively become the protagonists of his narratives. Casting peasants, laborers, students, and militants, men and women, in title roles, Argueta produces unofficial historiographic narratives, or histories from below, wherein other subject producers of Salvadoran history take center stage.[6] In addition to reorienting the focus of Salvadoran historical and testimonial literature, Argueta's novels draw from alternate sources and archives, including oral testimonials of peasant men and women and interviews with revolutionaries. With regard to the writing of his novel *Un día en la vida* (1980), Argueta admits to having used newspaper reports on the Salvadoran crisis as well as personal interviews with Salvadorans who were adversely affected (Flores Zúñiga 1980). In an interview, Argueta explains, "Yo intercalo en el trabajo literario cosas ya elaboradas por la realidad [In my literary work I integrate things already elaborated in reality]" (Z. Martínez 1985, 47). Episodes in *Un día en la vida*, as in *Cuzcatlán* and *Milagro de la paz*, emerge from such *pieces* of Salvadoran popular lore, interviews with peasants, and Argueta's own childhood memories, especially in relation to the women in his family,[7] giving him insight into the lives of peasant women in particular. His narratives construct female figures whose daily experiences, quotidian language, and historical memories are legitimized.

Although women in El Salvador have played significant sociopolitical, historical, and economic roles, they have rarely been represented in print media—newspapers, history books, and canonical literature—as subject-producers of knowledge and agents of national history. In one rare text that speaks about women's history in El Salvador, Francesca Gargallo (1987) describes how market women, in 1921, protested living conditions under the successive oligarchic regimes (1913–1927) by taking over a police station. The following year, over six thousand women marched in the streets of San Salvador to show support for the presidential candidate, Miguel Tomás Molina, and they defended themselves when the army fired on them. Furthermore, many women participated in the 1932 uprising led by Farabundo Martí, and after the

Gran Matanza women continued the struggle to depose the dictator Maximiliano Hernández Martínez. During successive dictatorships and periods of repression in the country, countless unnamed women were captured, tortured, and disappeared, while others went about their lives, some becoming labor migrants and others filling the ranks of oppositional movements (Gargallo 1987). During the armed conflict, testimonial literature drew critical attention to women's historic roles,[8] although the history of women's participation in the war was to be subsumed by larger revolutionary narratives, as Ileana Rodríguez explains in *Women, Guerrillas and Love* (1996).[9] In this context, testimonial literature fills a significant void in Salvadoran women's historiography, presenting them as heads of households, guerrilla fighters, and labor migrants (A. Martínez 1979; Alegría 1983; Díaz 1990; Golden 1991; Centro de Estudios de la Mujer "Norma Virginia Guirola de Herrera" 1992).

Many of Argueta's novels published during and after the 1980s represent female peasants, workers, and militants breaking with Salvadoran tradition and adopting new forms of revolutionary femininity. The novels trace the construction of Salvadoran women in specific historical contexts, relations of power, and economic transformations that affect all strata of society but specifically the rural class embedded in a history of oppression. The term *peasant* itself is the product of the deterritorialization, proletarization, racialization, and marginalization of a large segment of the Salvadoran population. Indeed, Carlos R. Cabarrús, in "El Salvador: De movimiento campesino a revolución popular" (El Salvador: From Peasant Movement to Popular Revolution) asserts that "la revolución ha nacido del movimiento campesino [the revolution was born in peasant movements]," because it is out of peasants' discontent over land tenure, labor exploitation, and political repression that their resistance gained force (1985, 349). The peasants, workers, and, more concretely, the peasant and working women of Argueta's novels thus embody a history of neocolonialism, from the conquest to the peonage of more recent years. Argueta's decolonizing testimonial novels privilege the histories of those who struggle for survival along class, race, and gender lines.

The Poetic Militancy of Manlio Argueta

An active participant in revolutionary struggle, Manlio Argueta was a part of the the university literary circle of 1956, a cohort of students at the National University of El Salvador, who, according to the writer,

engaged in "poetic militancy." One of the principal objectives of the
university literary circle was to " 'exigir del escritor una actitud mili-
tante frente al problema político' [demand that a writer take a militant
position against the political problem]" (Redacción 1981, 11). The group
included the writers Matilde Elena López, Otto René Castillo, Roberto
Armijo, Roberto Cea, Tirso Canales, Alfonso Quijada Urías, Manlio
Argueta, and Roque Dalton, all of whom wrote poetry, *testimonios*, novels, and other kinds of texts focusing on the Salvadoran war effort. Most
of these writers participated in the formative stages of the revolutionary
movement in El Salvador, and some, like Roque Dalton, died within the
movement. From the beginning, these writers produced militant art, or,
as they put it, "arte puesto al servicio de la patria y en algunos casos,
puesto al servicio de la lucha revolucionaria [art put at the service of
the nation and, in some cases, put at the service of the revolutionary
struggle]" (Review of *Poesía de El Salvador* 1983, 11). Along with his con-
temporaries, Argueta tried to "llevar a la luz pública la discusión de la
situación social en El Salvador [make public the discussion of the social
situation in El Salvador]" (Blanco 1983, 11)—a project in which he continues to engage in his most recent work.

Translated into English, Dutch, Russian, Italian, German, Portuguese, Danish, Finnish, Swedish, Norwegian, Bulgarian, and Persian
(Hernández 1995, 400–403), Argueta's novels were disseminated widely
during the Salvadoran armed conflict and today are known worldwide
for their testimonial power, literary value, and political significance.
Within postwar El Salvador, Argueta's work has been virtually canonized. Even during the civil war, his writings circulated widely, although
they were considered subversive material. University students, guerrilla militants, dissidents, professionals, and perhaps even government
officials read his books, while outside of the country his novels served
to inform readers of the struggle in El Salvador and to elicit solidarity with the revolutionary cause. Along with Dalton, Alegría, Ernesto
Cardenal, and Sergio Ramírez, Argueta figures among the most recognized and respected Central American writers. His novels have received
national and international awards: *El valle de las hamacas*, the Premio
Centroamericano de Novela csuca, 1969; *Caperucita en la zona roja*, the
Premio de Casa de las Americas, 1977; and *Un día en la vida*, the Premio
Nacional de Novela uca Editores, 1980. In 2005, Argueta was awarded
the Guggenheim Prize to complete a novel on the Salvadoran diaspora.
A number of undergraduate and graduate theses have been written in
Salvadoran and foreign universities on Argueta's works. In an interview,
Argueta explained that his fiction "ha roto barreras de tipo cultural, lo

cual demuestra que posee un alto nivel de comunicación [has broken cultural barriers, which demonstrates its high communicative value]" (Blanco 1983, 11). Perhaps more than any other Salvadoran writer, Argueta has worked to inform the world about El Salvador's civil war and postwar crisis. In the 1980s, Argueta and Claribel Alegría were recognized as unofficial "cultural ambassadors" of the Central American revolutions ("War and the Writer in El Salvador" 1992, 3–5).

Barbara Harlow identifies Argueta's novels as resistance literature (1987). According to Harlow, *Un día en la vida* exemplifies a type of analytic and historical literature that emerged with national liberation, decolonization, and sociopolitical movements in Africa, Asia, Latin America, and the Caribbean toward the end of the twentieth century. In its multiple forms, resistance literature is manifested in exclusively local, historical, and political texts, which challenge canonical literary norms, hegemonic discursive forms, and power structures of a political and cultural regime. Harlow suggests that resistance texts incorporate elements of fiction and nonfiction reportage and develop "narrative analysis" of the political, economic, and cultural circumstances of a sociopolitical context. According to Harlow, resistance novels such as those produced by Argueta offer political analysis, historical interpretation, and symbolic resolution of the social crisis of El Salvador. Further, the literary critic Ramón Luis Acevedo states that Salvadoran novels such as those produced by Argueta in the 1980s focused on recurring themes in the history of El Salvador such as the exploitation of peasants within the *latifundista* system, the enforcement of dictatorial rule through military violence, the rise of popular insurrection, and foreign intervention in the country (Acevedo 1982, 1–7). Argueta's novels assume the critical "communicative" and denunciative role of journalism and the "investigative" function of social analysis when communication media and investigation (research) had all but been silenced in El Salvador. As narrative analyses of the Salvadoran civil war, Argueta's novels thus defied, denounced, and subverted Salvadoran hegemonic history, literary traditions, and dominant narratives while opening a space of representation for marginalized characters, issues, and (his)stories (Harlow 1987, 78–79).

Against Neocolonial Historiography: Argueta's *Cuzcatlán* and Dalton's *El Salvador* (*Monografía*)

Situated strategically against the panorama of Salvadoran history, Argueta's novel *Cuzcatlán donde bate la mar del sur* offers a narrative analysis of the neocolonial forces leading up to the civil war in the 1980s. The testimonial novel challenges the official record, representing peasants, laborers, men, women, and children as commentators on their history of exploitation, which is directly linked to the agroindustrial export economy initiated in Central America with the production of indigo. Indigo was the first major export crop and industrial product of Central America. Because El Salvador possessed fertile volcanic lowlands and a large indigenous population that could be used as a labor force, the region became the stronghold of indigo production during Spanish colonial rule. Subsequently, indigo production gave way to the production of coffee, sugar, cotton, and other agrarian and industrial products in the nineteenth and twentieth centuries (Browning 1982, 128–129). Between 1783 and 1792, however, El Salvador exported over eight million pounds of dried blue dye to Spain, reinforcing El Salvador's almost absolute economic dependency on indigo production (Browning 1982, 127; Contreras Sánchez 1996, 41–53). With the production of indigo, the landowning class grew increasingly reliant on a coercive labor system, which made possible the massive exploitation of indigenous and mestizo people. The production of indigo and the social-economic stratification it engendered across northern Central America would leave their mark to this day.

In his novel *Cuzcatlán donde bate la mar del sur*, Argueta presents indigo (and later coffee) production as the source of exploitation that prefigured the struggle for justice in El Salvador in the late twentieth century. His novel not only documents a history of labor exploitation and colonization encoded in the sign of indigo but also represents the rise of a revolutionary consciousness in the peasant class in El Salvador. As suggested by Harlow and Acevedo, Argueta's analytic novels require an informed historical reception as well as a politically receptive if not engaged readership. The ideal readers of Argueta's novels must read beyond the literary text and situate the novels within the geopolitical history of empire building in El Salvador, Central America, and the Americas, and they must be ready to navigate the mined discursive spaces of Salvadoran literature. Often heavy-handed in ideological and historical content, *Cuzcatlán* has been denounced by some critics as being provocatively polemic and classified by others as overtly political. In an early review, the U.S. literary critic Alfred MacAdam, for example, lauded the lyricism of popular speech re-created in the novel but condemned the novel's political revolutionary agenda for detracting from its artistic merit texts. According to MacAdam, "We sympathize with . . .

Argueta's peasants and . . . side with them against their oppressors, but we do not respond to the text as a work of art" (1987, 48). This chapter responds to such a reading of Argueta's texts by suggesting, with Harlow (1987) and Ramírez (1985), that testimonial nonfiction and fiction must be read with an informed perspective on location-specific issues, history, politics, and culture and a conscientious suspension of privileged First World sensibilities and tastes. *Cuzcatlán donde bate la mar del sur* is indeed a work of art, one that exemplifies the discursive strategies put to task and use by Central American writers to respond creatively to their historical, political, and economic predicaments. Indeed, the protagonist, Lucía, who by name and action plays the role of seer in Argueta's *Cuzcatlán*, declares in the name of Salvadorans, "Yo, con mi realidad. He ganado el derecho a expresarla y compartirla [With my reality, I have won the right to express it and share it]" (211). *Cuzcatlán* documents precisely that history in the name of countless Salvadorans denied a space and voice in official Salvadoran historiography.

A preliminary reading of the title reveals the complex forces at work throughout the novel, which represents a long history of Amerindian and European contacts and collisions. "Cuzcatlán" refers to the pre-Columbian name of the territory that in neocolonial times is known as El Salvador. In Nahuatl, Cuzcatlán signifies the land of jewels and precious things, or as Argueta repeats throughout the novel, "la tierra azul donde el venado cruza [the blue land where the deer cross]" (Argueta 1987, 37). On their arrival in 1524, the conquistadors led by Pedro de Alvarado christened the region, "El Salvador," land of the savior, imprinting on the region not only a name but also colonizing religious, linguistic, social, economic, and political codes. The second part of the title, *Where the Southern Sea Beats*, refers to the geophysical and political location of Cuzcatlán, bordering the Pacific Ocean, as Vasco Núñez de Balboa discovered in his early explorations of the isthmus in 1513. In 1522, Andrés Niño was the first Spaniard to set eyes on Cuzcatlán from his ship, which sailed into what is now known as the Gulf of Fonseca on the southeastern coast of El Salvador. Pedro de Alvarado, sent by Hernán Cortés to explore and claim lands in the region, arrived in Cuzcatlán in 1524, just as Pedro de Arias (Pedrarias), Cristóbal de Olid, Francisco de las Casas, Gil González Dávila, and other conquistadors from Veragua (Panama) were moving up the region (Dalton 1979, 26).[10]

In *El Salvador (Monografía)* (1979), Roque Dalton cites extensively from the letters of Pedro de Alvarado and Bartolomé de Las Casas's *Brevísima relación de la destrucción de las Indias* (1542) in order to produce

a metacritical, double-voiced, and parodic counternarrative of the conquest of Cuzcatlán. In particular, Dalton quotes repeatedly from Alvarado's second "Carta de relación," which describes the conqueror's first
violent contact with the warrior people of Cuzcatlán. Alvarado states
that in Cuzcatlán he saw "gente guerrera . . . con sus plumajes y sus divi-
sas y con sus armas defensivas, en la mitad de un llano, frente a la mar del
Sur, donde me estaban esperando [warrior people . . . with their feathers
and their coats and with their defense weapons, in the middle of a plain,
facing the South Sea, where they waited for me]" (Dalton 1979, 26).
This encounter is told differently in the *Brevísima relación de la destrucción de las Indias*, wherein Las Casas underscores Alvarado's description
of the resistant forces of Cuzcatlán and describes Alvarado as one of
the cruelest conquistadors who after attacking the Maya in Guatemala
descended with equal force upon Cuzcatlán (Las Casas 1989). Despite
being initially welcomed, Alvarado and his men violently subjugated the
Cuzcatlecos, killing their leaders and warriors, putting survivors into
large parcels of land known as *encomiendas*, taking possession of communal lands, transporting people as slaves to distant lands, and working
others to death (Las Casas 1989, 116–120). By referencing and citing
from Las Casas's and Alvarado's respective texts, Dalton not only shows
two sides of the same story, that of the conquerors and that of the vanquished, but he also brings to the textual surface the impossibility of
narrating the "whole" story of conquest. Alvarado's letters are as partial
and unreliable as Las Casas's *Brevísima relación*, for what is missing in
each case is the voice of the Cuzcatlecos, themselves denied a place in
neocolonial historiography, although Las Casas and other early ethnol-
ogists sought to gather "native" information for their natural and other
histories. Although Dalton seems to privilege Bartolomé de Las Casas's
prototestimonial narrative of resistance in his own revisionist history of
El Salvador, he also draws attention to the need to rewrite the history of
El Salvador using multiple sources, including the voices of Salvadorans
in the contemporary revolutionary moment and the Cuzcatlecos who
resisted the first Spanish conquistadors. Only through a multilayered,
palimpsest, and heteroglossic history can narratives be exposed, decon-
structed, contested, and reconfigured.

Dalton's monograph thus makes evident that the struggle for social
justice is also one that is waged over control of the historical record.
That Alvarado's letters are cited as primary and official historiography
gives proof of the power of the victors' voice over the vanquished. In the
neocolonial history that is recognized as "official" history, Alvarado's
forces of fewer than three hundred Spaniards defeated more than six

thousand indigenous allied forces. According to Alvarado's account, the conquering troops defeated the Cuzcatlecos by imposing their unmatched strength, ingenuity, and technology. Armed with heavy cotton armor and cumbersome lances (Dalton 1979, 29), the Cuzcatleco warriors could not resist the guns and horse power of the Spaniards, and the warriors of Cuzcatlán literally fell to their deaths under the power of the conquering force. Alvarado entered town after town, demanding obedience and tribute from the peoples of the isthmus. Dalton's citing of copious details of battles and defeats from Alvarado's letters recalls Las Casas's hyperbolic rendition of the conquest in *Brevísima relación*. Like Las Casas's use of abundant allusions to Alvarado and other conquerors' acts against indigenous peoples, Dalton's use of hyperbolic discourse serves to parody Alvarado's second letter and to deconstruct the master narrative of conquest, which not only describes how the Cuzcatlecos were subjugated but also how they resisted and fought back. In between the lines of Alvarado's accounts of battles, one can read how the people of Cuzcatlán armed themselves with their three-inch cotton armors and pointed lances, blocked roads, gave bronze as faux tribute, hid in the mountains for safety, and caused grave injury to Alvarado himself, who was crippled in battle.

Argueta begins *Cuzcatlán* with two epigraphs, one taken from an interview with a Farabundo Martí Liberation Front (FMLN) commander and the other from Alvarado's second letter to Cortés, in which he describes his first encounter with the armed people of Cuzcatlán. The use of an epigraph from Alvarado's text, like Dalton's double-voiced parody of the same letter, challenges the narrative of conquest with the image of indigenous and mestizo resistance. Argueta links the first revolts against European conquest and colonialism in Cuzcatlán with the resistance movements against U.S. imperialism in the 1980s, thus producing a genealogy of foreign intervention and local resistance in the isthmus. Chronologically, *Cuzcatlán* covers over five hundred years of neocolonial history in Central America. The novel thus may be read not just as a historical allegory of the colonization of El Salvador, but of the isthmus as a whole, for each of the Central American countries has been repeatedly conquered and colonized by foreign powers. This is the common history of the transisthmus.

Familiar/Familial History in Cuzcatlán

In *Cuzcatlán donde bate la mar del sur*, Argueta examines the greater narrative of neocolonialism, decolonization, and revolutionary struggle in El Salvador through the lives of the extended Martínez family, the novel's protagonists. Since they can remember, the Martínez family has been tied to the production of indigo in El Salvador. In the novel, indigo signifies historically rooted systems of exploitation and domination of the Salvadoran people, who have worked in *encomiendas* and haciendas until recent times. The novel is set in 1981 as Lucía Martínez, a former factory worker, union organizer, and now militant in the revolutionary movement, rides in a microbus headed for a clandestine meeting. Six chapters focus on Lucía's interlinked ruminations on the bus, wherein she recalls a series of episodes from her childhood: her life in the city, elopement, factory employment, and political awakening as a labor leader; her pain at losing her *compañero* in the war; and finally, her militancy in the leftist guerrilla movement as Ticha—her "nom de guerre"—in honor of her grandmother. The other nine chapters of the novel narrate the story of Lucía's extended family, going back to her great-great-grandfather Macario, her great-grandparents Emiliano and Catalina, her grandparents Ticha and Eusebio, and her parents, Jacinto and Juana, and sister, Antonia. In these chapters, we also learn about Lucía's estranged uncle, Pedro Martínez, who plays a crucial role in the novel. Through family history, flashbacks, and memories, the novel highlights key events in the recent history of El Salvador, recalling the Massacre of 1932, the era of dictatorships, and the rise of the revolutionary movements in the 1970s and 1980s. Through indirect discourse, textual allusions, epigraphs, and other peritextual strategies, the novel provides a narrative overview of the long history of conquest, neocolonialism, and imperialism in Central America, all symbolically bound by the motif of indigo.

For centuries, then, the Martínez family and their ancestors have worked in the production of indigo as pressers, fermenters, carriers, and *zacateros* (weed cutters). Some family members have died from exposure to the highly toxic fumes of indigo; others carry the mental and physical scars of their exploitation in the indigo mills. The omniscient narrator in the novel explains, "The product was known to be lethal at the turn of the century, but it could not be vanquished, particularly in the northern zones of Cuzcatlán. It was gasping its last breath" (Argueta 1987, 83). The indigo saga of the Martínez family begins with Macario, the great-great-grandfather, who was indentured to work in the indigo mills, and it ends in the 1980s with Lucía, who, though never having worked in the mills herself, carries the burden of that history. Pedro, the great-grandson of Macario and the uncle whom Lucía has never met, is the last of the Martínezes to have worked in the mills and the first to be conscripted into the Salvadoran army. He is also the first Martínez to turn against and kill his own people.

The Symbolic Economy of Indigo in *Cuzcatlán*

In its telling of the story of the Martínez family, *Cuzcatlán* offers a popular version of the history of the Salvadoran people, long marginalized and divided by larger economic and political forces. The main characters are all subjected to the power of indigo production in Central America, which dates to the seventeenth century and even before that to pre-Columbian uses of the blue dye. The Guatemalan historian Julio Pinto Soria points out that in Spanish colonial times, "el dominio del capital comercial no afectaba solamente la economía añilera de El Salvador, sino casi toda la actividad de la colonia [the domination of commercial capital affected not only the indigo economy of El Salvador but also almost every colonial activity]" (Pinto Soria 1993, 76). Not only did the colonial economy grow during the height of indigo production in Central America in the seventeenth and eighteenth centuries, but with the marketing of indigo in Europe, Central America entered the modern capitalist world system. During the colonial period, textile production and commerce (much of it centered in Great Britain) demanded dye, especially the "xiquilite" of Central America. In *El añil centroamericano* (Central American Indigo) (1981), María Eugenia Rojas Rodríguez and Flor de María Herrera Alfaro explain:

> El Salvador, por su parte, vino a contribuir de manera activa en el proceso de industrialización y consolidación del capitalismo en Europa, dado que la importancia de la industria textil fue clave en el desarrollo del capitalismo. La exportación del añil y su utilización como colorante en la industria textil indudablemente favoreció el desarrollo de la industrialización en Europa y en consecuencia del sistema capitalista. (1981, 48)
> [El Salvador, in its own right, came to contribute actively to the industrialization and consolidation of capitalism in Europe, given that the importance of the textile industry was key in the development of capitalism. The exportation of indigo and its use as a dye in the textile industry undoubtedly favored the development of industrialization in Europe and consequently the capitalist system.]

With the production of indigo, the hacienda system took hold in El Salvador, displacing small and communal landowners and making a native workforce available for exploitation. El Salvador's landed oligarchy would provide the raw materials and workers for the local indigo "latifundio" supporting the industrialization and textile market in Europe (Palma Murga 1993, 222–223).

The manufacture of indigo is particularly linked to El Salvador's Spanish colonial and early *criollo* period. In pre-Columbian times, the Pipil indigenous people cultivated "xiquilite" (the original name for the plant used to produce the blue dye) as textile coloring and as a "beauty enhancer," for ceremonial and medicinal purposes (Rojas Rodríguez and Herrera Alfaro 1981, 2). By 1575, when the region had been subjugated by colonial rule under the hegemony of the Captaincy General of Guatemala, the manufacture of indigo was extended throughout the Pacific northern zone of the isthmus, and indigo became the region's principal export product to Europe (Rubio Sánchez 1976, 20). In 1625, indigo was the main source of income for the colonial government and the local planters (Rubio Sánchez 1976, 42), whose economic interests were mostly concentrated in the territory known today as El Salvador.[11] In El Salvador, the hacienda system became the "fundamental nucleus" of indigo production, inaugurating the pattern of "economic dependence" and producing an "indigo elite" that accumulated capital and power harnessed on the "exploitation of indigenous labor" (Rojas Rodríguez and Herrera Alfaro, 1981, 1–2).

Argueta's text fills a void in the (post)colonial historiography of El Salvador and the isthmus by representing the other side of this "indigo boom,"[12] casting the Martínez family as the captive labor force of indigo production. The novel tells the story of the deadly conditions of indigo labor (Argueta 1987, 30). In *Cuzcatlán*, national, regional, and family history are shown to be part of the larger narrative of neocolonialism in Central America. To tell their (hi)story, the Martínez family will have to put it in the context of indigo production in Cuzcatlán. In constructing this subaltern history, the novel gives an account of the processes of decolonization, struggles of resistance, and histories-from-below, which together decenter the positivist master narratives of progress, development, and capitalist expansion associated with indigo production in the region.

The process of proletarization in El Salvador resulted in the violent persecution of indigenous peoples, the alteration of traditional social practices, the abolishment of the *pueblos de indios* (native settlements), the appropriation of land by the colonial administration and the ruling

elite, and the forced migrancy of workers (Palma Murga 1993, 223; Guevara 1975, 776). Landless mestizo peasants worked as migrant braceros
(776) or *poquiteros* (sharecroppers) on small land parcels (Pérez Brignoli
1989, 55), producing xiquilite, along with subsistence products—maize,
rice, beans, and pumpkins, among other crops (Guevara 1975, 780). In
regard to the Salvadoran racial "demographic phenomenon," Concepción Clará de Guevara explains:

> Por un lado, la introducción de esclavos negros, que al mezclarse con la
> población indígena produjo cierto tipo de mestizo moreno más ca-
> racterístico del departamento de San Miguel y otras poblaciones del ori-
> ente de la república. Por otro lado, el advenimiento de familias blancas
> de extracción peon, [estaban] destinadas a localizarse especialmente en
> la región del Norte del país o sea la más despoblada, donde se ubica ac-
> tualmente el departamento de Chalatenango. Respecto a los últimos se
> dice que en 1791, el Barón de Carardalet, gobernador general del Reino
> de Guatemala, envió un buen contingente de personas blancas a dicha
> región. (Guevara 1975, 775)
> [On the one hand, the introduction of black slaves, once mixed with the
> indigenous population, produced a type of dark mestizo more repre-
> sentative of those people found in the department of San Miguel and
> other eastern regions of the republic. On the other hand, white peas-
> ant families (from Europe) were destined to live in the least populated
> northern part of the country where the department of Chalatenango is
> located today. Regarding the former, it is said that in 1791 the Baron of
> Carardalet, governor of the Reino de Guatemala, sent a large number of
> white persons to that region.]

While the present-day departments of Chalatenango and Cabañas in
northern El Salvador are located in colonial indigo manufacturing regions (Guevara 1975, 773; Rojas Rodríguez and Herrera Alfaro 1981,
141), the town of Apastepeque began as a *pueblo de indios* (Rubio Sánchez
1976, 44). During the height of indigo production in Central America
(1760–1790) (Pérez Brignoli 1989, 55), Apastepeque was the seat of the
Feria de los Añiles (Rojas Rodríguez and Herrera Alfaro 1981, 98). At
this annual convention, *criollo* indigo growers, administrators, pickers,
producers, merchants, lenders, and others involved in the industry met
to set prices, to determine quality standards and export quotas, and to
negotiate with colonial authorities of the Diputación de Comercio, the
cabildos of San Salvador, San Miguel, and San Vicente, and to bring disputes before the Juez de Disputa (Court of Disputes) (Rojas Rodríguez

and Herrera Alfaro 1981, 96–99). According to Rojas Rodríguez y Herrera Alfaro, Apastepeque played a significant role in indigo commerce between 1758 and 1810. In the 1980s, this region formed part of the war zone in El Salvador.

It is not a coincidence, then, that *Cuzcatlán* is set in the region around the Apastepeque lagoon or that many of the characters have family ties to Chalatenango, both historic zones of indigo exploitation and scenes of the civil war in El Salvador. After leaving Chalatenango to escape indigo intoxication, Eusebio (one of the main characters in the novel) explains, "Toda mi niñez trabajé en obrajes, hasta que fui viendo que me iba a morir de hambre con los salarios raquíticos o que me iba a morir de los pulmones, como ha muerto casi toda mi familia [All of my childhood I worked in the labor until I began to see that I would die of hunger with the meager salaries, or that I would die of lung (disease) as has most of my family]" (Argueta 1987, 32). Eusebio arrives in Apastepeque, where he marries Ticha and has children and lives with his father-in-law, Emiliano, who gives testimony to the adverse effects of the agrarian export economy in El Salvador. On giving birth to Ticha, Emiliano's wife, Catalina died, "víctima del añil. Muerta por falta de aire. Tras el parto. Sus pulmones no soportaron el esfuerzo; minados por la emanaciones del añil [victim of indigo. Dead due to lack of air. After giving birth. Her lungs did not withstand her efforts; her lungs were mined by indigo fumes]" (37). Through Emiliano and others, the text denounces the unyielding use of Salvadoran peasants in the production of indigo while recounting the story of countless unknown peasants who suffered the exploitation of an agricultural export economy.

Although *Cuzcatlán* might be read as the tragic story of a Salvadoran peasant family, it attests to the peasants' collective will to live, to survive, and to resist—three distinct strategies of resistance that shape the larger process of decolonization in El Salvador and that the novel traces through its characters. Since his youth, the great-great-grandfather Macario has made grinding stones in order to supplement the family's income and to preserve the family's legacy of subsistence. Through his work, he keeps alive the ancient tradition of making stone tools to grind corn. The great-grandfather Emiliano works in the indigo mill, along with his wife, who dies from prolonged exposure to toxins from the blue dye. It falls on Emiliano to decide whether the family will continue to work in the service of indigo or work for themselves on their small plot of land. Displaced by the hacienda system, Eusebio has worked in the production of indigo, cotton, and coffee, yet he cannot provide for his family and finally succumbs to an indigo-related illness. The last of the indigo workers, Pedro, is conscripted into the army and forced to take up arms against his own people. As the novel puts it, Pedro breaks the "fuerza moral" (moral force) of the family when the family learns that he is the soldier responsible for causing the death of several of its members (260). Alienated from his land, family, community, and history, Pedro brings law, death, and destruction to Apastepeque.

Throughout the novel, the female members of the family (Catalina, Ticha, Juana, and Lucía) ensure that the family survives, despite its suffering and poverty (12). Lucía, the youngest daughter who works for the underground revolutionary movement, becomes the final reference point of the family, as she retells its history from a Marxian standpoint. The text seems to suggest that with Lucía the history of exploitation of the Martínez family, or the extended national family, reaches a breaking point. Lucía's revolutionary ideas and militancy embody new subaltern agencies in El Salvador, for it is Lucía who takes up the revolution in defense of her family and Salvadoran peasants. With Lucía as the central character who overturns the colonized history of the Salvadoran family, *Cuzcatlán* translates the "sabiduria popular" (popular wisdom) of her ancestors into armed insurrection (23).

In its presentation of a materialist history that extends from the Spanish conquest and colonial period to the civil war of the 1980s, *Cuzcatlán* seems to imply that the current moment of war marks the last cycle in the transformation of the country. The Marxist-Leninist Revolution is upon Cuzcatlán, referring not only to the imaginary location of the novel but also to an El Salvador free of neocolonialism, domination, and exploitation and restored to a more equitable pre- and postcapitalist state. Naming its ideological location "Cuzcatlán" (the land before colonialism and the land recuperated after the last stages of capitalism), the text represents the contemporary moment of war in El Salvador and seeks narrative resolution in the dissolution of exploitative economic systems and the social transformation of its characters, predominantly Salvadoran peasants, laborers, students, soldiers, guerrillas, men, women, and children, all of whom play significant roles in the revolution.

The Language of Decolonization in *Cuzcatlán*

In *Cuzcatlán*, Argueta constructs a collective biography ("biografía colectiva"), or rather a testimonial narrative of the Salvadoran nation (Redacción 1981, 11). According to Argueta, it is through this collective biography that the resilient and resistant voices of peasants transmit their history, their protest, and their hope for a just society.[13] Emerging from the conflictive social dynamic and history described in this chapter, Argueta's work translates oppression as experienced by Salvadoran peasants into popular symbols and idioms, that is, into the testimonial vernacular language of the novel (Flores Macal 1980, 4). The novel's characters are shown to speak about, ponder, and analyze their experience of exploitation from their own social locations. The interviews conducted with Salvadoran people and their *testimonios* are the source of Argueta's information. According to Argueta, these slices of life are "cosas ya elaboradas por la realidad [things already elaborated in reality]" (Z. Martínez 1985, 47). They are the verbal archives, bits of life, pieces of personal stories, and everyday expressions that Argueta assembles into his testimonial novels. By drawing from the experiential record, alternate historiographic sources, and histories-from-below (Sharpe 1992), Argueta's testimonial *Cuzcatlán* articulates and legitimizes the historical (d)enunciation and agency denied to the Salvadoran popular class by the state and its institutions. In its totality, *Cuzcatlán* represents Salvadoran peasants as historical, economic, political, social, and cultural agents and as "subject-producers of history" (de Certeau, 1989).

The character of Emiliano, the shamanlike father and guardian of people's history, is the voice of popular wisdom as he proclaims:

> "Los hijos son como los palos de frutas, hay que sembrarlos sin preguntarse cuándo se llenarán de frutales, porque si te lo preguntás decidís no sembrarlo, te desanimás al ver la semillita y que está lejano el día que esa semillita se levanta en un palo frondoso. Y sin embargo, uno siembra la semilla y cuando menos acuerda ya está recogiendo las huacaladas de frutas." Así pensaba Emiliano en aquellos tiempos, para darse esperanzas e inventarse sueños. (Argueta 1987, 46)
> ["Children are like the fruit trees that must be planted without asking when they will give fruit, because if you ask you'll decide not to plant them. You will be discouraged when you see the little seed so far away from becoming a tree in bloom. Nonetheless, you plant the seed and before you know it, you are picking up bowls filled with fruit." That is how Emiliano thought in those times to give himself hope and to invent dreams.]

Through the voice of Emiliano, the novel re-creates a peasant vernacular and structure of thought and feeling from the subjective location of

the Martínez family. In the lore of the novel, children are metamor-
phosed into the "palos" (trees) and "semillas" (seeds), or "cornucopias
of fruits"—the vegetal life that promises to (re)generate material and
social well-being for the peasant family and community at large. For the
peasants of the novel, having children signifies the possibility of reap-
ing "huacaladas" (helpings) of benefits for the survival of the family.
The hope of enduring the harsh peasant life and continuing the family
depends on the procreation of children. When Catalina dies, Emiliano
explains his hope and perseverance as forms of survival: "Si no fuéra-
mos fuertes como el palo o como las piedras, moriríamos después de
las primeras tareas en la hacienda [If we were not as strong as the sticks
and stones, we would have died shortly after the first tasks in the planta-
tion]" (1987, 30). Immediately following Emiliano's statement, the indirect discourse of the novel echoes his philosophy of life: "Moriría la
raza. Las condiciones de trabajo eran las condiciones de la muerte [The
race would die. Work conditions are the conditions of death]" (30). In
acknowledging his own right to live, Emiliano performs a silent protest against the economic system and the oppressive forces of the army,
church, and state, which seek to extinguish the "sueños de los pobres"
(dreams of the poor) (127).

In a defiant act of discursive power, Emiliano speaks in the Salvadoran vernacular and draws strength from an organic wisdom embedded in traditional cultural beliefs and practices. Guided by "sabiduría
popular" (popular knowledge), Emiliano and the peasants of *Cuzcatlán*
are carriers of local wisdom, or what Williams (1977) calls "structures of
feeling," that allow them to comprehend their experiences from other
epistemologies. Emiliano and his family give testimony to almost five
hundred years of exploitation. As presented in the novel, Emiliano and
the peasants of Cuzcatlán possess an intimate knowledge of and a special relationship to indigo production. They are critical interpreters of
the sign of indigo (the materialization of their oppression), which per-
meates the novel as a whole like the symbolic membrane to which the
historian Edelberto Torres-Rivas alludes in *La piel de Centroamérica*. For
the peasants of *Cuzcatlán*, indigo comes to signify the demise of ancient
traditions, the imposition of *encomiendas* and successive forms of coerced
labor, the loss of sovereignty and autonomy, the enforcement of repressive control mechanisms, and, finally, the resistance of the people.

In the novel, indigo doubly signifies a presence and an absence. It
is present as the industrial product that emits the blue dye that gives
color to European textiles; it is absent in that the color blue is virtually

extracted from Cuzcatlán and banned for use by the Cuzcatlecos. The peasants of Cuzcatlán thus lose to the world market the sensorial and aesthetic experience of the color blue in their land. Even their clothes lose the symbolic value color as they are forced to wear bleached white cotton garments, which come to be associated with Salvadoran peasants in folkloric representations. At one point in the novel, Emiliano reflects on the meaning of indigo for the peasants:

> Por un lado, el procesamiento de la tinta ocasionaba intoxicación lenta; por otro, ¡la concentración y monopolio del producto les vedaba el acceso a los colorantes para sus telas que antes habían sido de vivos colores! Ahora los trajes eran blancos. El añil se iba para otros mundos. Además habían perdido la tierra. El obraje les daba para sobrevivir, les procuraba el jornal diario; pero el obraje era inclemente y los barcos voraces para llenar sus bodegas. Cientos de niños tenían que trabajar apisonando las piletas, sumergiendo la hierba al nivel necesario para que despidiera la tinta de calidad. Los propietarios de la tierra no perdonaban la niñez ni la sensibilidad para obtener la mano de obra necesaria y satisfacer las necesidades de exportación. Por eso sus camisas, sus pantalones y fustanes y blusas y refajos eran blancos, de manta blanca. La tinta había dejado de pertenecer a los naturales. La tierra también. (Argueta 1987, 37)
>
> [On the one hand, the processing of the dye caused slow intoxication; on the other hand, the concentration and monopoly of the product prevented them access to the coloring for their cloth that had been so colorful before! Now their clothing was white. The indigo went to other worlds. They had also lost the land. Indigo labor gave them the means to survive, it paid their daily wage, but the labor was harsh and the boats voraciously filled their storage spaces. Thousand of children had to work stomping the indigo in the pools, submerged in the herb up to the level necessary to extract the quality dye. The landowners did not excuse age or health in order to obtain the labor necessary to satisfy export requirements. That is why their (peasants') shirts, pants, slips, blouses, and skirts are white, of white cloth. The dye had stopped belonging to the people of this land, as had the land.]

In Emiliano's rumination, indigo represents the absence of everything that the color blue might have signified in *Cuzcatlán*, namely, tradition, freedom, autonomy, and beauty. The removal of "blue" from the isthmus might be read as the erasure of pre-Columbian structures of being, wherein blue-green is often associated with the central, life-giving cardinal point of Mesoamerican (Maya) cosmology, which connects the human world with spiritual realms, deities, ancestors, heritage, nature, and life forces. All these cultural elements were forced to retreat with the arrival of the Europeans and as the Cuzcatlecos were severed from their former signification systems. Dislodged from its pre-Columbian signification system, indigo was reinvested with meanings associated with colonization, forced labor, and suffering. The absence of blue in the postcolonial agroindustrial world represents, thus, the forced disappearance of traditional cultural systems and the imposition of colonizing systems of knowledge.

In the Western context, the absence of blue, too, might be read as the loss of vital forces identified with water, sky, universe, and infinity. In his essay titled "Blue," Alexander Theroux reads blue as a polysemic sign in virtually all cultures: it is the "rarest of colors," connoting a range of human emotions and states, from melancholy to (royal) power; it is the color of infinite imagination and creativity as the Latin American modernistas claimed; it is the color of desire and "yearning"; and it is the color that the Maya used as body paint when offering human sacrifice to the gods (Theroux 1994, 1–67; see also Coe 2000).[14] Blue is also the color of the robes of the Christian Madonnas, with which the indigenous peoples of the Americas were conquered (Brusatin 1987, 50–54). Denied material ownership and traditional uses of indigo in their colonial peonage, the peoples of *Cuzcatlán* are made physically ill by indigo production, and they are made to suffer the physical and emotional scars of its extraction from the isthmus. Further, they are deprived of pleasure, beauty, and a sense of aesthetics symbolized by the color blue. Now bleached white, the peasants' clothes represent repression. Repeatedly, the novel reminds us that the original name of Cuzcatlán was "la tierra azul donde el venado cruza" (Argueta 1987, 37). For the indigenous people of Cuzcatlán, the colonialists' expropriation of indigo and control of the color blue implied the loss of a significant marker of Mesoamerican identity. Robbed of the sign of "blue" of pre-Conquest times, the land would now be transformed into the newly evangelized El Salvador. Sensing this deep loss, Argueta's novel sets a new course, bound for the final stages of revolution, or the recovery of "la tierra azul" without foreign intervention.

The novel *Cuzcatlán* thus registers the social transformation of various characters in different stages of their own demystification and politicization. The novel concedes that Emiliano, his daughter, Ticha, and his grandchildren by virtue of their status as peasants were already "inmersos en el conflicto. Lo adivinaban, lo olían desde su inocencia [immersed in the conflict. They perceived and smelled it despite their innocence]" (1987, 43). Ticha's son, Jacinto, reflects on his people coming into a historical consciousness:

> La guardia había hecho la guerra desde siempre. Desde que tenía memoria. Pero también se daba cuenta que de pronto la gente ya no aceptaba con resignación someterse a las autoridades. Y por eso habían entrado a hacer otro tipo de lucha. Un tipo de protesta que nunca antes había existido en Cuzcatlán. La guerra de liberación. Aunque no tuviera conciencia plena de lo que eso significaba. (253)
>
> [The guards have always made the war ever since he could remember. But he was also aware that all of a sudden the people were no longer willing to accept with resignation their submission to the authorities. And this is why they had decided upon a different type of struggle. A type of struggle that had never before existed in Cuzcatlán. The war for liberty. Even though they might not have full knowledge of what exactly it meant.]

Throughout the novel, the characters feel the impact of living in times of historical transformation, and yet only toward the end of the novel, with Lucía, do they acquire the formal critical (Marxist) language to analyze their pain, anger, frustration, and alienation in material terms. By refusing to work in the indigo mills, Emiliano initiates the resistance that culminates with the militant revolutionary practices of his great-granddaughter, Lucía.

In this transformation, Emiliano guides the reader into the experiential history and world knowledge of the peasants of *Cuzcatlán*. According to the novel, "La voz de Emiliano es un árbol de pájaros y flores [Emiliano's voice is a tree filled with birds and flowers]"; "la voz interior de Emiliano es exuberante como un volcán en erupción [Emiliano's interior voice is exuberant like an erupting volcano]"; and "su voz interior resuena como un eco [his interior voice resounds like an echo]" of the historic moments that he lives and describes (Argueta 1987, 52, 49, 43). At one point, in fact, Emiliano reflects on the massacre of more than thirty thousand Salvadoran peasants by authorities in 1932.

> [En] el año 32 tenía quizás unos treinta años. Capturaban al montón de gente y las ponían a abrir sus propias tumbas, grandes zanjones hacían. Luego formaban en filas a la gente y la ponían a la orilla de los zanjos. Ahí mismo los fusilaban: después venían los mismos soldados a echar paladas de tierra y a empujar con los pies a los que habían quedado con

los brazos o con parte del cuerpo fuera de la zanja. Cualquier pareja que se juntara en la casa o en los caminos ya era considerada una reunión comunista y eso significaba ser candidato a la muerte. Las autoridades no perdonaban nada, estaban salvando la nación, imponiendo el orden y el cristianismo, como afirmaban ellos. La civilización. (43)
[In the year 1932, I was perhaps thirty years old. They captured a lot of people and they had them open their own tombs; they made large trenches. Then they put people in line alongside the trenches. They shot them right there: later the same soldiers came to shovel dirt and push with their feet those whose arms or body parts had remained outside of the trenches. Any group that got together at home or on the roads was considered a communist meeting and that meant being a candidate for death. The authorities did not forgive anything; they were saving the nation, imposing order and Christianity, as they affirmed. Civilization.]

Through Emiliano's memories, the narrative exposes "las desgracias de nuestros pueblos" (the misfortunes of our people), recounting the long chain of misfortunes in the lives of Salvadoran peasants. As Emiliano explains, "Apenas había terminado la persecución del 32 y ya se nos venía otra desgracia [The persecution of 32 had barely passed before another misfortune fell upon us]" (53). In 1934, the eruptions of the volcano Chinchontepec destroyed homes, while in 1946, many Salvadoran small farmers lost their land to single-crop farming and their sons to military service. Suffering blow after blow, the people learned to simulate submission and resignation: "ahí la vamos pasando [we are just getting by]" (201). But as Emiliano explains:

Decir mi pobreza no es quejarme de cómo me tiene Dios, sino de hacer un poco de conciencia para no aceptarla. Para darse fuerzas y tener una luz de esperanzas. . . . Nada más es cosa de saberse adaptar a la vida dura para ir sobreviviendo, pero también buscar esas lucecitas que muchas veces a uno lo iluminan. (201)
[To talk about my poverty is not to complain about how God is treating me, but it is a way of being conscious of not accepting it (poverty). It is a way of giving oneself strength and hope. . . . It is a way of knowing how to adapt to a hard life in order to survive, and also to look for those little lights that many times illuminate us.]

Throughout the novel, the characters attempt to "buscar otras maneras de sobrevivir" (find other ways to survive) (244), and to speak out against the exploitation of the peasant class in El Salvador. Emiliano concludes, "Es cosa de decidirse y no quedarse con los brazos cruzados. Hay que tener esperanzas en Dios, pero tampoco vamos a estar esperando que nos caiga maná del cielo [It is a matter of deciding and not crossing our arms. We must have faith in God, but we are not going to sit here and wait until bread falls from the heavens]" (244).

Cuzcatlán opens and closes with the revolutionary moment in which political, economic, cultural, and social transformations are made possible. Up to this point, the novel constructs the history of Salvadoran peasants and workers as a process of (de)mystifications and self-revelations, through which the characters recognize themselves as subjects with historical agency. Generations of the Martínez family narrate a common narrative of survival in which they are subject to the external economic and neocolonial forces of indigo and coffee production. Their historical path leads them towards the struggle for "a better day," when "algún día va a cambiar la vida para todos nosotros" (one day life will change for everyone) (260). Through the voices of the characters, the novel registers the different meanings that survival takes on for the Martínez family.

For Lucía, the transformation or politicization of her peasant family is a historical process entailing three stages—living, surviving, and resisting. She explains:

> Vivir es una cosa: mantener el cuerpo libre de enfermedades, no morirse de hambre ni de diarrea. Más de la mitad de los cipotes de una familia mueren por esa causa. Quizás por eso queremos tener una familia grande. Para que no se termine la raza. Además, entre más manos hay en una familia, más posibilidades hay para ganarse la vida, la tortilla. También debemos sobrevivir. Esto es otra cosa. (11)
> [To live is one thing: maintaining the body free of illnesses, not dying of hunger, or of diarrhea. More than half of the children in a family die because of that. Perhaps that is why we want to have a large family. So that our people will not cease to be. Anyway, when there are more hands in a family, there are more possibilities of making a living, buying tortilla. Also we must survive. That is another thing.]

In the novel, to live means to resign and submit oneself to power and institutional order (the government, the church, the army), or to live by sheer luck and "la Gracia de Dios" (the grace of God). Survival signifies struggling or "getting by," despite all the obstacles. The peasants of

Cuzcatlán prolong their lives by inventing ways of surviving, adopting "otras maneras de sobrevivir," and adjusting themselves to declining living conditions (244). They eat less, have more children, produce grinding stones, sell pigs, cultivate maize, and become labor migrants—all practices that bring them closer as a family in their time of need. The Salvadorans of Argueta's novel use their "moral force" to overcome their lack of material resources: "Fuerza moral le llamaba el abuelo Emiliano a nuestras durezas frente al sol y las pobrezas. . . . Nosotros usamos la fuerza moral para no agotarnos, para seguir adelante, para que la esperanza no caiga [Grandfather Emiliano called our strength in the sun and poverty moral force. . . . We use our moral strength in order not to exhaust ourselves and to go on, and for our hope not to fall]" (260). The characters in *Cuzcatlán* thus survive in spite of their history: the exploitation of their labor in indigo production, the massacre of peasants in 1932, and the prolongation of a civil war that killed almost eighty thousand people throughout the 1980s. The novel, however, does not end with a celebration of peasant moral strength and survival but exposes how various sectors of Salvadoran society, peasants and women among them, begin to actively resist poverty, alienation, and exploitation.

Through a series of intercalated chapters titled "Microbús a San Salvador, Enero 9, 1981," the novel reveals Lucía's meta-reflection on the (his)story of the Martínez family and brings narrative resolution to the history of struggle in El Salvador. In these chapters, we learn of Lucía's participation in the leftist revolutionary movements, for as she explains, "Trato de resistir y por eso uso seudónimo [I try to resist, and that is why I use a pseudonym]" (14). At the end of the novel, Lucía is identified as part of a new generation of Salvadorans who in the 1980s took up arms to liberate their nation. She is a member of a war tribunal that will judge Cabo Martínez (her uncle), who is accused of war crimes against the Salvadoran people and his family. At the trial, she represents all those affected by political violence in El Salvador and articulates their demand for social justice. Lucía joins the revolution to gain for her people the right to life, land, and freedom. She hopes to fulfill her people's dream for "un pedazo de tierra, semillas para sembrar y abonos. . . . En fin que nos den un manera de vivir y no de morir como nos dan ahora [a piece of land, seeds to plant, fertilizer. . . . In the end, they must give us a way to live and not die like they give us today]" (215).

Cuzcatlán donde bate la mar del sur is undoubtedly informed by Argueta's transformational political agenda and Marxist ideology. The historical agency of Salvadoran society is played out in the political transformation of the Martínez family, who at the beginning of the novel are subject to the production of indigo and by the end are *almost* freed from the agrarian export economy that the revolution intended to abolish. At the end of the novel, Lucía takes up her call to armed insurrection, and, empowered by her reality, she seeks to put an end to exploitation and oppression in El Salvador. Enlightened and emboldened by historical meta-consciousness, Lucía takes up the struggle for a new Salvadoran society. As the revolutionary conscience of the novel, Lucía imagines the reconstruction of Cuzcatlán from the material and symbolic source of the Salvadoran people, explaining, "Los campesinos molemos el maíz con la fuerza de nuestros brazos [We peasants ground maize with the strength of our arms]" (9). In the end, the competing metaphors of maize and indigo represent the larger struggles for discursive power in the isthmus. More than representing a moment, a voice, a people, and a nation (in this case El Salvador), Argueta's novel can now be reread as a testimonial historiography of El Salvador and as a textual narrative of decolonization for the isthmus of Central America.

CHAPTER 4

K'atun Turning in Greater Guatemala:
Trauma, Impunity, and Diaspora

*To those who are sure that right is on one side, oppression and injustice on the
other, and that the fighting must go on, what matters is precisely who is killed
and by whom.*

—SUSAN SONTAG, *Regarding the Pain of Others*

The novel *Cuzcatlán donde bate la mar del sur* ends with an imaginary act of reparation, as Pedro Martínez, a soldier in the Salvadoran National Guard, is at last brought before a people's tribunal to face charges of war crimes against the Salvadoran people. Unbeknownst to Martínez, his niece, Lucía—a leftist revolutionary—is a member of the tribunal. Conscripted into the army as a boy and transformed into a "uniformed man," Martínez has terrorized and killed countless Salvadoran peasants for many years. Moreover, he is responsible for the death of his own grandfather, Emiliano, his mother, Beatriz, and members of his family's community (Argueta 1987, 246–285). In her interrogation, Lucía challenges Martínez to assume responsibility for his actions by asking him almost rhetorically: "Who will take vengeance against you for your twenty-five years as a soldier committing injustices with *impunity*?"(283; my translation and emphasis). Who will judge and punish the soldier when his superiors remain untouched and impunity is the rule of law? How will El Salvador and the rest of Central America deal with the enduring effects of violence and trauma under state imperatives of national reconciliation, forgetting, and impunity?

After jury deliberations, Lucía announces the people's verdict on Martínez's fate: "lo hemos condenado a que siga viviendo [we have condemned him to continue living]" (284). Essentially declaring him guilty of all charges in the production of violence and war in El Salvador, Lucía, however, leaves open-ended and ambiguous the question of social justice, reparation, and restitution in the context of postwar El Salvador and the isthmus. Although seemingly incommensurable with the soldier's horrendous past deeds, the sentence, as Lucia explains, can only be understood within the "profound history" of war, trauma, and recovery in her country, where victims, perpetrators, bystanders, and sympathetic and unsympathetic parties have all played significant intertwined roles in the production of violence. In such a context, it is difficult to differentiate victims and perpetrators and to apportion justice evenly and easily, although for the victim and the injured it will always matter who the perpetrator is, as Susan Sontag reminds us in the epigraph to this chapter. Indeed, with her pronouncement on Cabo Martínez's fate, Lucía acknowledges that decades of institutionalized violence in El Salvador and the rest of Central America have left gaping social wounds and deep psychic traumas in individuals and in societies as a whole. Indeed, the cultural critic Ileana Rodríguez does well to remind us that countries, like individuals, carry specific genealogies of violence,[1] which are rooted in larger global systems of power and control enforced through local forms of (neo)colonialism, imperialism, racism, war, genocide, and impunity. As it should be clear by now, impunity serves as the cultural logic that gives shape to postwar cultural memory in Central America and informs the production of a posttraumatic literature across the isthmus, even in those locations that did not experience war.

This chapter explores in the context of Guatemala the production of what Dominick LaCapra (in reference to the Holocaust) calls "posttraumatic narrative" or "traumatic realism" (2001, 179, 196). According to LaCapra, such narratives replay and perform collective experiences of posttraumatic stress disorders (PTSD) deeply embedded in the cultural and affective psyche of a people who have endured persecution, violence, and, in some cases, genocide, as is the recent case of the Maya in Guatemala. Perhaps before continuing, a brief description of PTSD and its relationship to the production of a posttraumatic literature is in order. In *Trauma: A Genealogy* (2000), Ruth Leys describes the clinical condition of PTSD as "fundamentally a disorder of memory":

The idea is that, owing to the emotions of terror and surprise caused by certain events, the mind is split or dissociated: it is unable to register the wound to the psyche because the ordinary mechanisms of awareness and cognition are destroyed. As a result, the victim is unable to recollect and integrate the hurtful experience in normal consciousness; instead, she is haunted or possessed by intrusive traumatic memories. The experience of the trauma, fixed or frozen in time, refuses to be represented as past, but is perpetually reexperienced in a painful, dissociated traumatic present. All the symptoms characteristics of PTSD— flash-backs, nightmares and other reexperiences, emotional numbing, depression, guilt, automatic arousal, explosive violence or tendency to hypervigilance—are thought to be the result of this fundamental dissociation. (2)

Posttraumatic memory and by extension posttraumatic literature can serve as a site to record, replay, and rewrite those "flash-backs, nightmares and other reexperiences" and PTSD psychic discharges for imaginary and real interlocutors. In the context of postwar Central America, a corpus of testimonial, documentary, ethnographic and autoethnographic, and fact-finding and truth-seeking texts produced in response to the violence of past decades has allowed ample room for the recall, recovery, and reproduction of war memories and experiences in written form. In *Writing History, Writing Trauma*, LaCapra suggests that a literature that metaphorically (and metonymically) repeats traumatic experience and works through collective trauma "can somehow get at trauma in a manner unavailable to theory—[in] that it writes (speaks or even cries) trauma in excess of theory" (2001, 183). Further, he proposes:

> Writing trauma would be one of those telling aftereffects in what I termed traumatic and post-traumatic writing (or signifying practices in general). It involves processes of acting out, working over, and to some extent working through in analyzing and "giving voice" to the past— processes of coming to terms with traumatic "experience," limit events, and their symptomatic effects that achieve articulation in different combination and hybridized forms (186).

Posttraumatic literature may function as a vehicle to articulate and deal with unresolved material such as the effects of violence in postwar Central American cultures. Following LaCapra's work on the performance of trauma through narrative, this chapter focuses on two postwar, post-traumatic, and diasporic reconstruction narratives of Guatemala.

Published just two years after the signing of the Guatemalan Peace Accords (December 29, 1996) and the same year of the publication of the Spanish version of *Guatemala, Never Again!* REMHI *(Recovery of His-*

torical Memory Project/The Official Report of Human Rights Office, Archdi-ocese of Guatemala) (1999; Spanish version, 1998), the novels *Return of the Maya (El retorno de los Mayas)* (1998) by the Maya Q'anjob'al writer Gas-par Pedro González and *The Tattooed Soldier* (1998, 2000) by the U.S. Guatemalan author Héctor Tobar address the complexities of postwar, posttraumatic society. Moreover, collectively, they elaborate a critique and indictment of the current state of impunity in Guatemala and Cen-tral America. Read together, these texts challenge the official histori-cal record, as they present factual and fictional evidence and testimony against entities still working under the guise of impunity, or what the REMHI defines as "a pervasive reality in which government agents oper-ated, and continue to operate, without fear of punishment. Impunity is presented as a cause of and a consequence of [state-generated] violence, as well as a central obstacle to justice and reconciliation" (xxxiii). The critique of impunity in these texts not only provides a textual account-ing of war crimes, actions, methods and means of violence, victims, per-petrators, and other involved parties but also articulates a call for social justice and long overdue forms of reparation in Guatemala, especially for the Maya, who were most affected by the repression. Looking into the heart of darkness and human depravity, these texts recall, replay, reli(e)ve, and represent the horrors of the recent past and, in doing so, confront the "repressed and buried reality" of Maya people and their way of life in Guatemala. Moreover, through a symbolic repetition of a *spiritual unconscious* associated with Maya cosmology, González and To-bar seem to suggest that full recovery from "cycles of violence" (Lovell 2000b) and civil war in Guatemala is only possible with the continuation of Maya life-ways and cosmology.

War and Displacement

The cycles of violence in Guatemala began long before the 1954 U.S.-sponsored military overthrow of President Jacob Arbenz, whose great-est legacy (and downfall) was perhaps to propose land reforms that en-croached on U.S. business holdings in Guatemala. Long before that fateful event, however, indigenous struggles in Guatemala began with the arrival of the Spanish conquistadors and intensified with the *criollo* nation-building projects of the nineteenth century, when the state ex-propriated indigenous communal lands and labor for the production of coffee and other export crops (Pérez Brignoli 1989, 49; REMHI 1998,

181). In the twentieth century, indigenous and popular struggles grew in direct response to vast historical inequities, including unequal distribution of lands; high levels of poverty, illiteracy, and mortality; lack of political representation; and ingrained practices of racism touching all aspects of Maya and Ladino life (Casaús Arzú 1998). In the 1970s and 1980s, Guatemala was thus ripe for popular and revolutionary uprisings against an entrenched elite ruling class, strong military presence, and foreign intervention. At the height of the repression, the Guatemalan government, in collusion with the country's military forces, intensified the violence through the work of paramilitary groups, death squads, Civilian Self-Defense Patrols (PACs), and other mechanisms of war that relentlessly made Maya people their prime target.

In the 1980s, over 150,000 people were killed or disappeared, over 440 villages were destroyed, over one million people were internally displaced, and up to 500,000 people were forced into exile in Mexico and other countries (*REMHI* 55, 61). By December 29, 1996, when the Guatemalan Peace Accords were signed, there would be over 30,000 widows, 90,000 children without a parent, and 38,000 orphans (Dunkerley 1994, 79). In its copious accounting of the Guatemalan civil war, the *REMHI* attributed 89.7 percent of human rights violations to the Guatemalan government and 4.8 percent to leftist guerrillas and confirmed that those most affected by the violence were the Maya people (xv–xvii). In addition to compiling statistics on human rights violations committed against Guatemalans, the *REMHI* gathered and recorded *testimonios* from victims, perpetrators, and others who were interviewed after the cease-fire, all describing in graphic detail the form and extent of state-generated violence against the Guatemalan people. The report told how, in addition to killing, disappearing, displacing, torturing, raping, and grievously injuring people, the Guatemalan military destroyed homes and property and, in sum, "damaged basic means of survival and their symbols of life," especially those of the Maya. Underscoring the loss of Maya homes, household goods, animals, clothing, and ritual objects (41, 49), the *REMHI* explained that destruction of the most basic elements of Maya culture was especially dramatic and profound:

> When crops were destroyed, part of the seed supply that communities had inherited and preserved for generations was also lost. This interfered with the production cycle and reduced the quality of corn and other crops. And lost was the wisdom and genetic inputs contained in the seeds that had been selected and tended for generations. The diverse

and depraved strategies used to destroy communities also damaged their basic means of survival and their symbols of life. (41)

Cultural genocide was ensured with the killing of elders, the traditional bearers of memory, language, knowledge, aesthetics, cosmology, calendar counting, and other social practices in Maya communities (48). Each lost seed of corn, like each lost human life, thus represented massive and enduring losses for the Maya and the world as a whole. These losses are recorded and recovered in posttraumatic narratives such as those by Gaspar Pedro González.

González's novel of trauma, *Return of the Maya*, published in Spanish in 1998, the same year of the Spanish publication of the REMHI and the assassination of Archbishop Juan Girardi, describes the impact of the Guatemalan civil war on one Q'anjob'al community and one boy left an orphan amid the violence. A fictional account based on the experiences of many Maya people in Guatemala, *Return of the Maya* is more than a testimonial novel, a genre by now much discredited by David Stoll's interventions and the ensuing "Rigoberta Menchú controversy."[2] González's text provides a fictional accounting of deeds almost too horrendous to be believed as historical truths, yet based on the experiences of the author and other Mayas. Strategically, the novel uses what LaCapra calls traumatic realism to represent the extreme realities experienced by the Maya in Guatemala during the civil war period, if not before and after. In this fashion, the novel painfully revisits, recalls, and re-presents the recent period of violence from what could be identified as Maya posttraumatic recovery. It pushes the limits of posttraumatic recall and recovers Maya philosophical thought and historical and spiritual consciousness, situating the civil war within larger "cycles of conquest" endured by indigenous peoples in the Americas (Lovell 2000b) and offering an imaginary and practical plan of reconstruction for Yichkan, as Guatemala is called in the novel.

The Maya in Yichkan

Structured as repetitious memories and flashbacks, *Return of the Maya* tells the story of the destruction of an entire Maya village, the exodus and exile of surviving community members to the "other country," and the return of *one* survivor to Guatemala. In the first-person collective voice of *testimonio*, the Maya of the novel tells of his personal return and that of the Maya nation to Yichkan. In the words of the narrator:

Yichkan (Ixcán in Spanish) is that place of profound contrasts, a place where many people come as if to a promised land. Yichkan is where two dimensions of nature converge: *yich*, 'base, root, at the foot of'; *kan*, 'heaven, sky, firmament, infinite space.' It is a compound Q'anjob'al word that means 'where the sky begins' or 'the root of heaven.'
(G. González 1998, 3)

Symbolically and physically located at the crossing of land and sky, Yichkan is the liminal place in the middle, equally rooted in the earth and the sky, which hold special value for the Maya. It is an intermediary space, where the Maya have lived for thousands of years, making and remaking the world amid waves of violence. Indeed, the narrator tells us that "Yichkan [is the] scene of pain and blood" (4). But Yichkan is also a site of creation, where "an immense blue curtain rises . . . at whose base lies a green carpet of vegetation" (6). Yichkan represents the center of the earth located in the hearth of every Maya home, community, and village and connecting every Maya person with the wider Maya cosmology and world. In Yichkan, the Maya play a central role in re-creating their lives, traditions, and cosmology. Having survived over five hundred years of Western conquest, colonialism, and continued repression, the Maya of Yichkan carry the great responsibility of maintaining the Maya world in its place, mediating between the earth and the sky, the past and present, and seemingly incommensurable knowledge systems. Yichkan, thus, reminds us of Nepantla, as the Aztecs called their postconquest state of being and condition of neocolonialism. Yichkan, like Nepantla, is the reference and subjective point where the past and the future are held in balance, or imbalance, and the space-in-between where different forms of knowledge and practices of time, life, and beliefs and modes of cultural survival coexist. From this cultural and cosmological divide, the Maya speak through González's novel of trauma.

Testimonio of a Maya Orphan

At the very beginning of *Return of the Maya*, the narrator declares that his intention is to give testimony of his experiences and his truthful account of them. Identifying himself only as "the orphan" (the Meb'ixh), the narrator remains anonymous throughout the text. It is imperative that his identity not be revealed, for he will give evidence of the horrendous crimes committed against his people by perpetrators who still pose danger, and, thus, they, too, must not be identified. He warns the reader that he will give "the testimony of *a* reality, of *a* living truth like that of thousands of other brothers and sisters of mine, who are now multiplying in the garbage dumps of my fatherland, a fatherland that is not ours . . . [and] where a few hoard the goods of the world for themselves" (5; my emphasis). There is no claim to represent the totality of Maya reality, as the 1980s *testimonio* might have implied, but rather *a* reality that may have been experienced differently by other Mayas. The Meb'ixh can only tell his story, which may or may not be corroborated by others living in the aftermath of the civil war in Guatemala. His testimonial narrative is only as reliable as his posttraumatic memory, which by virtue of its very constitution is filled with gaps, distortions, and disassociations, as Leys (2005) explains. Far from telling the whole testimonial truth in Menchú fashion, González's *Return of the Maya* is a post-*testimonio* testimonial novel offering a highly reflexive and subjective account of a life recovered from partial and fragmented memories. Its truth is subject and open to questioning and retelling. A pastiche of partial memories, *Return of the Maya* engages in larger debates on the genre of testimonial literature but concerns itself largely with recalling a past from multiple indigenous subjective positions. One of these perspectives is that of Gaspar Pedro González—a Maya writer and cultural activist working in the postwar Guatemalan cultural ministry and Pan-Maya revitalization programs (Arias 2005). *Return of the Maya* and González's other works are directed toward a postwar cultural reconstruction project in Guatemala that is inclusive of Maya participation and mindful of a government that still claims impunity in its repression of Maya peoples.

The orphan's testimony in *Return of the Maya*, then, is just as relevant today as it was during the Guatemalan civil war, for crimes against the Maya continue to take place and the guilty continue to enjoy positions of prestige. Toward the end of the text, the orphan declares, "Privilege and impunity for a small group must end" (137), acknowledging that within the current neoliberal regime of Guatemala the same military, political, and economic elite sectors continue to be "protected by the impunity they have always enjoyed" (138). The reader is called to take a position in regard to the historical and present predicament of the Maya in Guatemala. Lest the reader be one of the many who "left the Maya to [our] fate without anyone to help us," as the novel puts it, the reader, too, is made complicit in the fate of the Maya people. *Return of the Maya* calls for an affectively engaged reader, one who allows herself to feel as she reads and analyzes the text and to occupy a critical position akin to what LaCapra calls an "empathic bystander" in the field of history and what Ruth Behar identifies as a "vulnerable observer" in anthropology.[3] When talking about Guatemala, the cultural geographer George W. Lovell describes Guatemala as possessing a "beauty that hurts" (2000a) and that drew many academics like him to support the Maya cause during the most critical periods of the civil war and thereafter.

González's *Return of the Maya* represents a trauma that hurts and engages the reader in active and attentive listening, processing, and assessing of the testimonial evidence presented by the orphan, who declares, from the start:

> I must speak of what I have seen, what I have heard and what they have done to me, so that a record will be kept behind and its memory continues. I must testify to the attempts of some to exterminate a race, a culture and a people—my people. And my testimony is the truth, a truth denied by others, a truth engraved on my martyred skin, where you can observe the still fresh scars of what they have done to me. (G. González 1998, 2)

Without fully identifying the perpetuators of violent acts carried out against him and his people, the orphan draws the reader into hearing, seeing, and reli(e)ving the great trauma of his life. In LaCapra's terms, the orphan narrator-writer is "writing trauma . . . in terms of enacting it, which may at times be equated with acting (or playing) it out in performing discourse or artistic practice" (2001, 186–187). Readers are reminded in the preface, written by the translator, Susan G. Rascón, that *Return of the Maya* is a testimonial novel: "Throughout the novel, the author weaves a tapestry of Maya symbolism as he tells the story of the Orphan, which is also the story of his people" (1998, iii). The novel represents what LaCapra alludes to as "extreme realities," events that are unfathomable within the standard scope of Western reception. The killing of the orphan's family, the massacre of his community, and the suffocation of crying babies are extreme material experiences and events that form the basis of such an extreme realism. The REMHI, in fact, documents de facto methods of killing, raping, and torture, which appear as if taken from the pages of González's novel, while at the same time, the novel uncannily evokes victim *testimonios* like those recorded in the report. One *testimonio*, for example, describes the unintentional killing of babies in their mothers' arms: "And the children could not cry; we had to cover their mouths. We stuffed handkerchiefs in their mouths so they wouldn't cry. Case 3804, Cotzal, Quiché, 1976" (*REMHI* 36). In like fashion, the orphan in *Return of the Maya* describes how his mother and others unintentionally suffocated their children at their breasts in an attempt to stifle their cries. From personal memory, the narrator recalls episodes of extreme human suffering and human rights violations similar to those documented and enumerated in the *REMHI*. Thirty years old when he tells his retrospective story, the narrator presents his life span as a condensation of the thirty-year war in Guatemala and the collective experiences of the Maya people as a whole. Of his life, the narrator says, "Now I am a product . . . reflecting a whole history of cruelty" (1998, 3). In getting to the trauma, recovering buried memories, and telling of extreme acts of violence, *Return of the Maya* plays out its function as a posttraumatic narrative and partial *testimonio*.

Reli(e)ving the Trauma: Exodus (I) from Yichkan

In the first part of *Return of the Maya*, titled "Exodus From Yichkan," the orphan recalls his parents' and community's participation in a fateful march, where everyone protested against "the abuses and arbitrary actions of the authorities and other powerful people who were against us" (1998, 7). He describes the immediate and long-term repression of the Maya by the "uniformed men" who massacred and tortured entire communities, relocated survivors to "model villages," raped men and women, conscripted Maya men into the Civil Defense Patrols, outlawed traditional practices, killed, disappeared, or otherwise "removed" elders from their positions of authority, and drove people into exile. Little by little, with each replay of violent acts, the orphan documents the creation of "a generation of beings hanging by a thread from terror, of a generation of people who walked between anxiety and fear, a generation of the fearful" (90). Literally left an orphan after his father is killed and his mother dies escaping from the Guatemalan army, the narrator becomes the voice of a generation of Maya suffering from PTSD, many of whom were persecuted and stripped of their culture by the political and military forces of Guatemala.

In the day-by-day account of the Maya flight from Yichkan in the first part of the novel, the orphan relives the relentless trauma of loss. He witnesses soldiers killing his brother, father, and neighbors. He flees with his community by night and wanders with them through mountains, ravines, and caves. He loses his mother, who dies in the jungle, and is separated from his sister, who is carried away in the arms of another woman. With each step of the exodus, the Maya boy leads readers through a landscape of horrors. Jungles, mountains, ravines, and particularly caves that are sacred to the Maya regain their function as portals to the Maya spiritual substrata, where underworld deities reside and rule (Bassie-Sweet 1996). At a crucial point in the novel, the orphan and his community during their escape literally and symbolically enter death as they seek refuge in a dark and wet cave. In the cave, many die of exhaustion and cold; the orphan emerges alone, nearly catatonic, and subject to supernatural forces that control his death and life. Losing his *nawal*—his protective spirit—the orphan, along with others in flight, enters his own Xibalba underworld, or posttraumatic condition, eventually becoming a man in "a faraway place with no name[,] . . . no papers, no identity, no country, no people, no family, no parents, brothers or sisters." "They were all left behind on the road at different places and times," he says, "as I struggled ahead, when I left here, this place called Yichkan, where everything began" (1). Furthermore, the narrator's orphaned condition represents the extended condition of displacement of the Maya, as they are forced to leave their homeland and resettle in a land to which they have no ritualistic connection.

In their flight northward, the orphan and his community travel toward the place of their origin, which the *Popol Vuh*, the Sacred Book of the Maya, identifies as Tulan. They travel in step with the days of the Maya calendar and cycle of time, each day connected with past days and future days, prophesy and reality meeting with each step of the orphan's exodus. Once on this cycle, Maya cosmological forces assume control and direct the progress of the narrative of exile, even though it does not become apparent to the narrator until the end of his journey. The guiding imperative of the *Popol Vuh* becomes apparent as analogous figures surface in the novel. Just as One Hunahpu and Seven Hunahpu—the first set of twin brothers in the *Popol Vuh*—were summoned to the underworld Xibalba to play ball, that is, to confront the cosmic forces governing their lives, the orphan is called to fulfill his special destiny in and outside Yichkan. In Xibalba, the first twins were put through a series of trials, which led to their sacrifice and burial in the Pulverizing Ball Court. The spit of One Hunahpu's head, which merges with a calabash tree bearing fruit, impregnates Lady Blood, the daughter of one of the lords of Xibalba. This impregnation produces the second set of twins of the *Popol Vuh*, named Hunahpu and Xbalanque, thus fulfilling the promise made by the first set of brothers to return to their mother(land).[4] Hunahpu and Xbalanque, too, are put through a series of trials and tests by their grandmother, until they prove to be the true sons of the earth, cultivating corn and taking up their father's ball game once again but finally defeating the forces of Xibalba, when summoned to the ball game like their fathers (Christenson 2000, 93–126). Orphans of a kind, the first and second sets of brothers challenge the Xibalba gods who wreak havoc in the lives of people in the upper world. In return for vanquishing the Xibalba gods, the second set of twins loosen the powerful hold of Xibalba over the human world, for as the *Popul Vuh* declares:

> No longer will clean blood be yours. . . . Only the sinner and the offender, the wretch and the molester whose sins are well established, will be given to you. No longer will you be able to seize suddenly any person. . . . Thus their [the Xibalba overlords'] greatness and glory were destroyed. Never again would their dominion become great. This was the great accomplishment of Xhunahpu and Xbalanque. (124–125)

Xhunahpu and Xbalanque curb the Xibalba lords' power over the Maya people. As Allen Christenson explains in a footnote to his free translation of the *Popol Vuh*, the Xibalba lords hold power "over those who have truly committed punishable offenses and have thus submitted themselves to the powers of the underworld" (Christenson 2000, 124n297). I would like to suggest here that, in modern times (from the Spanish conquest to today), people carrying out the work of Spanish colonial and Guatemalan neocolonial regimes may be seen by the Maya as analogous incarnations of the underworld forces of Xibalba. (This will become more apparent in the reading of Héctor Tobar's novel *The Tattooed Soldier* in the second section of this chapter.) Within Maya beliefs, these forces will be vanquished, as the twin brothers vanquished the lords of Xibalba in their own time, and thus bring about a new era, a *k'atun* turning for the Maya people. Gaspar Pedro González's *Return of the Maya* intertextually recalls and reenacts the narrative of the twin brothers' vanquishing of the lords of Xibalba, this time through the actions of the orphan. The potential to interpolate the *Popol Vuh* narrative into the novel functions as a strategy of release from the containment narrative of posttrauma. Whereas repetition entraps the orphan Maya of the novel in a perpetual cycle of pain and suffering, the Maya cosmic cycle, recalling the liberating potential of the *Popol Vuh*, offers a narrative of continuity, release, and regeneration to readers of *Return of the Maya*.

Healing the Wounds: Exile (II) and Return (III)

While Part I of the *Return of the Maya* presents the initial trauma of the orphan and his community's escape from Guatemala, Part II, titled "The Torment of Exile," describes the posttraumatic condition of the Maya exiled from their families, villages, communal lands, and traditions. The orphan, a member of the moribund community, explains:

> During the time I was in exile, I visited several camps where they were just warehousing a great number of people, and saw the same attitude: introverted, broken spirits, taciturn, distrustful, defensive, not hungry, sleepless, without dreams, capable of withstanding cold, heat, beatings and mistreatment. It was as if they no longer had any feelings, or cared whether life was good or bad. When pain has stifled feeling, an insensibility is created toward that which ordinary people consider a novelty. But for a population like ours, the limits of the humanly bearable had already been exceeded. They had already experienced the excesses of the trauma of pain, both physical and spiritual. People told me about many of the experiences they had suffered through, which had scarred both their bodies and their souls. (G. González 1998, 90)

To heal himself and his people from trauma (*susto*), the orphan and refugees must return to the Maya homeland, to the family hearth, to the central point of existence, which is Yichkan. Healing can be found only there. Fittingly, the novel begins and ends with the repetition of the first lines of the novel and the orphan's realization that he must return to "Yichkan, where everything began" (1). His return to Guatemala in Part III, which is titled "The Road Back," brings closure and *continuity* to the cycle of life that is so central to Maya cosmology. Here the orphan tells of "beginning to awaken from a long sleep, so long that it goes back more than twenty years: a dark and gloomy night, full of nightmares and fright, of black clouds and cold wins" (121).

Conquering the darkness of Xibalba, the twins Xhunahpu and Xbalanque return from that death with renewed and creative energy, as does the orphan of the novel. Like the fatherless twins, the orphan returns to Yichkan, "the starting point in my homeland, . . . the land of my ancestors that belongs to me by historical right" (121). Empowered by his recuperation from the trauma of war and exile and possessing a newly recentered historical and spiritual consciousness, the orphan of the last part of the novel recognizes that he is living a *k'atun* turning period, wherein darkness will give way to light and life, according to the Maya calendar. In the last part of the novel, the orphan comes to the conclusion that "the recent armed conflict is nothing more than the continuation of the same war which was declared against us some twenty k'atun ago" (122). Following the narrative of the twin brothers, the novel proposes that the Maya people, too, will defeat modern forces that continue to repress them through an organized political agenda and action plan, which the orphan identifies as the *Accords on the Identity and Rights of Indigenous People* (156).

In order to heal Maya wounds, reconstruct Yichkan, and bring peace to Guatemala, the orphan insists, the Maya people must be integral actors in the reconstruction effort. For the orphan, peace will come when the Maya return to Guatemala from their exile, that is, "after the rescue of thousands of meb'ixh, orphans, and thousands of widows, who wander the roads of the world with their little children on their backs, seeking their daily tortilla" (139). Peacemaking, says the orphan, must include all those "left behind, where all can rise, where all are called. With a kernel from each of us, an ear of corn will be made" (139). Peace will come to Guatemala only when the Maya are involved in what he calls the "task of resurrection" (155) and when the Maya fully practice and transmit their cultural values and traditions, contribute to the "material and spiritual rebuilding of their people," and prepare themselves for the future through "an authentic indigenous education" (155). In the orphan's discourse, the plan for peace in Guatemala is infused with Maya thought, philosophy, collectivity, and activism, for, as he says, "It means a fair distribution of goods and services" (140). González's novel is not merely a retrospective testimonial account and description of what happened to the Maya during Guatemala's civil war. Rather, it is a call to remember, recall, and reinstate Maya peoples and their cultures in the historical record of Guatemala so as to challenge the imperative of impunity. A fictional and testimonial record of past and present misdeeds, González's text envisions Yichkan as a material and symbolic location of justice and engages the larger debates on the role of testimonial literature in postwar truth-finding discursive practices.

From Testimonial to Historical Record in the Age of Impunity

Return of the Maya and testimonial novels such as Manlio Argueta's texts examined in the previous chapter not only have the potential to record local histories and to become historiographic sources in the process but also have the power to document through fiction the evidence of war crimes, genocidal acts, and mass violence inflicted on civilian populations. As John Beverley claims in "The Margin at the Center," the *testimonio* articulates "a story that *needs* to be told—involving a problem of repression, poverty, subalternity, exploitation, or simply survival that is implicated in the act of narration itself" (1993, 73; original emphasis). That holds true for texts such as *Return of the Maya* in the current struggle against impunity and other forms of social and economic violence in Central America, which are examined in later chapters. Although *testimonio* may have lost its immediacy, urgency, and perhaps relevancy with the demise of leftist revolutionary programs in the isthmus, it remains a significant expressive form in works by indigenous writers such as Gaspar Pedro González, Victor Montejo, Maya Cu, and Calixta Gabriel Xiquín.[5]

Producing in multiple languages and cultural locations, Maya writers challenge and decenter the hegemonic interference, or mediation, of Western critics and writers who in the 1970s and 1980s promoted testimonial texts as the next subaltern voice of struggle. Testimonial texts seemed to necessitate and justify the mediation of second-party editors, compilers, transcribers, translators, solidarity workers, and ethnographers. They were read in Western academic circles sometimes as celebrated exchanges between First World scholars and Third World peoples, and much of the criticism focused not on the struggles themselves but on the role of the editor and reader. The critical literature on *testimonio* focused more on the reading practices of Western readers and less on the content expressed in the text (Martínez Echazábal 1991, 57). Stoll's verification of the data presented in Rigoberta Menchú's *testimonio* and his subsequent questioning of their representation as "scientific fact" and testimonial truth shattered the faith (and pact) that readers had hereto invested in testimonial literature. Stoll's intervention would give way to a reevaluation of the genre of *testimonio* and the representation of war crimes committed throughout the Guatemalan civil war. Stoll's and Arturo Arias's ongoing debate over Rigoberta Menchú's text seems to confirm Beverley's claim that "the links between testimonio, liberation struggle and academic pedagogy" continue to be important topics today, especially now that indigenous writers are contesting the historical record of the Guatemalan civil war (Beverley 1993, 87). Despite the post-Menchú disqualification of the *testimonio* as a valid and "truthful" genre, or because of it, *Return of the Maya* and other Maya texts are important contributions to the creation of a modern Maya historical record and the critique of the current state of impunity in postwar Central America and elsewhere.

In the case of postwar Central America and other countries recovering from collective trauma (South Africa, Rwanda, Argentina, Chile, and Uruguay, to name a few), truth commission reports and other such fact-finding and information-recuperation documents create a public forum to discuss issues of historical trauma, social justice, and impunity (Minow 1998; Rotberg and Thompson 2000). These, too, draw from testimonial discourse to recount and document the variety and extremity of the acts of violence perpetrated on many people in Latin America and elsewhere during periods of crises. As the editors of the REMHI put it, "The compiled testimonies are imbued with the virtue of the victims' own words. . . . [T]he report is an attempt to piece together, in their own words, the many complex and divergent experiences of the populations touched by the war" (xxxii). Conscious of the discursive turn whereby texts, irrespective of disciplines, are understood to be constructed narratives, the preface to the REMHI states that the document "can be read as a book, . . . can be heard as a story, but above all it can be learned from as a collective memory" (xxxii). In a foreword to the same report, the commentator identifies truth commission reports as "an outstanding example of a literary genre that, given the horrors of this century, has become increasingly widespread." [6]

Although the Maya and other marginalized subjects in Guatemala have played significant sociopolitical, historical, and economic roles, rarely do they figure as subject-producers of knowledge and subject-actors of national history, that is, in their own right. The official historical record is bleak with regard to its inclusion and representation of Maya people. In this context of misinformation, the work of Maya writers such as Gaspar Pedro González, the testimonial literature on and by indigenous people such as Rigoberta Menchú, and documentary texts such as those produced by truth commissions and human rights organizations fill a significant void in Guatemalan historiography. In these texts, the Maya people recollect traumatic memories and make a call for justice, retribution, and reparation. As the orphan of the *Return of the Maya* makes clear, the interpolation of Maya cosmology in historical and social justice narratives is imperative for the reconstruction of Maya communities as Guatemala and the Americas enter future *k'atun*s.

Violence and Diaspora in *The Tattooed Soldier*

Like González's *Return of the Maya*, Héctor Tobar's *The Tattooed Soldier* revisits and reconstructs the Guatemalan civil war from other diasporic locations while challenging the present condition of impunity in the isthmus. Although rarely discussed as such, Central American exiles, refugees, and immigrants forced to flee from their homelands are yet another product of the wars in Central America. In the case of Guatemala, statistics show that in the 1980s as many as 200,000 people (especially Maya) found refuge in Mexico and about the same number reached the United States. Still others resettled throughout the isthmus (Dunkerley 1994, 47; Jonas 2000, 24). In 1997, the United Nations High Commission for Refugees (UNHCR) designated Guatemalans one of the "major refugee populations worldwide." By the end of the civil war, many refugees returned to Guatemala, but others remained indefinitely in Mexico and the United States in dispersed sites such as California, Florida, Texas, North Carolina, Delaware, and Maryland's Eastern Shore.[7] Deploying what Robert S. Carlsen has identified as an enormous "adaptive capacity," the Maya in particular have shown great resiliency, carrying forth "the continuity of ideas, religious or otherwise, [that] is essential to cultural stability and continuity" (Carlsen 1997, 19, 48, 66). Despite their history, or because of it, the Maya have survived ongoing cycles of violence, beginning with the Spanish conquest and continuing today (Lovell and Lutz 1996, 401–407; Lovell 2000a, 2000b). The continuity of Maya traditions, practices, and cosmology is manifested in Tobar's *The Tattooed Soldier*, as the Maya world travels from Guatemala and takes root in Los Angeles, California.

In jarring episodes, the novel shifts between scenes of torture and death in Guatemala in the 1980s, violence in the streets of Los Angeles on the eve of the 1990s popular uprising, and alternate forms of justice in the Americas in 2000, as survivors of violence increasingly take justice into their own hands. It tells the entwined stories of Antonio Bernal, a former Guatemalan university student-turned-homeless refugee, who flees his country after his family is killed by paramilitary forces, and Guillermo Longoria, the soldier behind the killings. Unbeknownst to one another, both men leave Guatemala for Los Angeles, where they quickly join the ranks of undocumented immigrant laborers. As the revenge narrative unravels, Bernal is increasingly haunted by the memory of his wife and child's assassin and drawn into the path of a soldier with a jaguar tattoo on his forearm. It is only a matter of time before Bernal and Longoria encounter one another on the streets of Los Angeles, for as the novel poses it, "Antonio spun in the flux between decades and countries, time and space distorted. He was in a park in Guatemala, a park in Los Angeles. The present, the past, somewhere in between" (Tobar 2000, 79). When the paths of the jaguar man and the homeless refugee finally clash, the reader is forced to confront the local/global narrative of violence in the Americas and the role of the United States in the production of violence in the world. As Sontag, in *Regarding the Pain of Others*, suggests for other texts, *The Tattooed Soldier* takes the Guatemalan civil war "out of its immediate constituency" (2003, 35) and traces its origins to the United States, showing violence to be a cornerstone in the building of the American Empire. Perhaps its focus on the production of violence in the Americas is what gives *The Tattooed Soldier* social relevancy and currency in light of posttraumatic accounts of neocolonialism, imperialism, empire, war, and immigration across the Americas.

A thriller of sorts, *The Tattooed Soldier* compels the reader to uncover the crime of a war waged against a civilian population and to identify Guatemala and the United States as guilty of war crimes. Indeed, the Central American wars were funded by U.S. economic and military aid. In Guatemala in 1989, economic aid peaked at $146.2 million and military aid reached $9.4 million, still a smaller aid package by far than what El Salvador and even Honduras received during the same period.[8] During that period, the United States dealt a heavy and long-lasting blow to Central America, as it trained national armies in the art of war against local civilian populations.[9] Tobar's tattooed soldier, representing U.S. intervention, graduates from that School of the Americas, carrying its badge of horror on his forearm. The one-of-a-kind U.S.-made jaguar tattoo on his arm links Longoria to Guatemalan Special Forces secretly trained in Panama Canal Zone bases, Fort Bragg, the John F. Kennedy Center for Special Warfare, and the School of the Americas (2000, 29). As the text reveals:

> It was an American tattoo, expertly administered by a man called Jake . . . in a place called Tattoo Fayetteville: a jaguar with sleek yellow pelt and fierce eyes, sharp and resplendent, its mouth open, exposing a pink tongue rendered with such skill that you could almost see the saliva glistening. (240–241)

The premier sign of violence in the novel, the jaguar tattoo provides material evidence of U.S. military intervention in Guatemala since it is a product of Longoria's stay in North Carolina and his visit to Fayette-ville, where he receives special training and branding (the tattoo).

The Jaguar Returns

In Tobar's narrative of two embattled Guatemalan sons, Guillermo Longoria and Antonio Bernal are brought together by the forces of the jaguar. As the novel tells us, "The tattoo [of the jaguar] was key to ev-erything" (164). Repeatedly throughout the novel, the jaguar appears in various symbolic valences. The jacket cover depicts the "tattoo of the jaguar . . . yellow pelt, black spots, moist red mouth" (21), fresh as when Longoria had it imprinted on his skin during his School of the Ameri-cas days. Successively, the jaguar tattoo identifies Longoria as a mem-ber of the Jaguar Battalion of the Guatemalan army, for the image was "synonymous with the terror the army spread through the countryside" (163), where "the Jaguars had carried out the holocaust in the moun-tains" (164). Associated with all things military, the jaguar tattoo im-bues Longoria with a heightened sense of masculinity and aggression, sharpened by U.S. military training. Living in Los Angeles, Longoria still carries that "soldier's gaze, his *cara de matón*, the look that said he was one of the serious ones, the type to grin after he hit you over the head with his rifle butt. Anyone from Central America recognized this look" (25). His boss at the Pulgarcito Express courier service hires him for that strong-man look that would surely keep customers in check and in fear, especially when confronted by the menacing jaguar, ready to spring at them.

The jaguar tattoo, acquired at a U.S. tattoo parlor for nearly the price of two of Longoria's paychecks, represents his hyper-heteromasculine trappings—his military training, his violent and destructive behavior, his "matón" look, and his performance of machismo. All of these signs of masculinity are not inherent features of Longoria's identity but rather learned and internalized. The jaguar "tattoo announced the new spe-cies of man Longoria had become, the warrior who had been born with him" (241). The fear and envy that the jaguar instills in his cohort of soldiers and the terror it produces in the general populations embolden Longoria with a heightened sense of power, especially over the less pow-erful. Longoria becomes the jaguar; he assumes its qualities and preys on weakness. On discovering at the end of the novel that Longoria is ethnically Maya, readers may come to understand that his identification with the jaguar and its power is an attempt to deny his Maya identity and heritage, which he associates with inferiority, weakness, fear, and emasculation. Indeed, Longoria has long since internalized the dominant racist Ladino ideology and commonplace neocolonial historicism that reject, demean, and reduce all things Mayan to caricatured national symbols—quetzals, typical costumes, and archaeological ruins of lost civilizations. Longoria acknowledges that while the Maya had been admirable warriors who worshiped the jaguar and built temples to jaguar gods (242), they and other civilians had become "cancer," "infection," and "moving targets" (64, 250), which he had to destroy.

It is only toward the end of the novel—in Longoria's death trance after being shot by Bernal in a fateful encounter in the streets of Los Angeles—that the reader's suspicion about Longoria's Maya origins are confirmed. Through a series of latent flashbacks, or posttraumatic memories, Longoria is revealed to be Maya, "the son of a peasant woman who grew corn on two acres of hillside. His life revolved around the soil, the cycle of rain and harvest" (33). After being conscripted by force into the Guatemalan army at the age of seventeen, he had been "made a man" after doing "terrible, violent things" to men, women, and children (63, 65). He was "never the same again" (64). As he lays dying at the end of the novel, Longoria is finally and conclusively taken back to the cornfield of his youth, where he wears *traje*, "rainbow-color trousers" made at his mother's loom and sandals of wire and twine (301). We are told that he felt "so strange and happy, after all these years, to be wearing his peasant clothes again" (301), the Mayan marker of indigenous ethnic identity (Hendrickson 1996). It is only near death that Longoria seems to remember and reclaim his Maya identity, the culture of maize, the land that gave him life, and his mother, who calls him back to his homeland and roots. Longoria sees "a burst of light":

> Glowing golden in the darkness of the tunnel is a cornfield. Stalks rise
> from the black mud and push against the cement walls, fleshy leaves
> shining, tiny husks bursting like green embryos. A dark woman stooped
> between the rows of plants. She cuts into the earth with a hoe, grunting
> in a quiet and familiar way, then turns to look at him. Stretching out her
> hand, she gestures for him to rise. Stand up, quickly, there is work to be
> done. (301)

The spirit of his dead mother then calls out to him in a language that he has nearly forgotten: " 'Balam' "—a word and appellation, which in Mayan languages means "jaguar" (Benson 1998, 69). Hence in death and rebirth, the jaguar image, now resignified in Maya terms, connects Longoria to a greater cosmology, heritage, and identity embedded in him, which in his colonized mind he has tried to destroy in others and himself.

As Mayanist historians, archaeologists, and epigraphers tell us, the jaguar is one of the principal gods of the Maya pantheon, transformed many times over as anthropomorphic, zoomorphic, and shamanic, regal, and warrior figures.[10] The jaguar is the Sun God, who in his daily trajectory enters the underworld as the sun sets to the west. In Xibalba, the jaguar god commands presence over humans. The jaguar is also transfigured into one of the four hearthstones of the world, one of the cardinal directions that holds the universe in place. He is the god of the number seven, the god of day but also the night of the setting sun in the underworld. The jaguar is one of the paddler gods that transports gods, warriors, and humans between the upper and the lower world. In Maya cosmology, the liminal jaguar, as all things, is night and day, darkness and light, life and death (Thompson 1970, 292–294). As gleaned from the murals at Bonampak in Chiapas and archaeological sites throughout the Maya world, kings and warriors dedicated themselves to the jaguar cult, wearing jaguar pelts, headdresses, and other symbols of the feline (Benson 1972, 1998). Archaeological artifacts often show human, god, and jaguar figures in transformation. Spotted jaguarlike body markings and scarring on archaeological figures invoke the jaguar and the cult of the jaguar. The image of the jaguar has had long-lasting symbolic and spiritual value for the Maya because, as the supreme mammal, the jaguar has been venerated and associated with hunters, warriors, gods, kings, and shamans, as well as the forces of the underworld, night, darkness, war, duality, destruction, and regeneration (Thompson 1970, 292–294). Nicholas Saunders explains that in the Americas "the contexts of jaguar imagery reveal a density associated with aggression, the qualities of strength and fierceness, supernatural protection, and pre-eminent social status" (1998, 25), all of which the tattooed soldier valued and sought to acquire through his jaguar image.

Although not speaking about the Maya, Jane Caplan, in *Written on the Body*, explains that tattooing was a generalized practice in ancient cultures. For many, the tattoo was used "as a marker of difference, an index of inclusion and exclusion" (xiv) in communities with certain values, belief systems, practices, and social relations. In many ancient and modern cultures, tattooing is, moreover, a marker of physical, emotional, and spiritual "belonging" to a group or spiritual force, manifesting this association through some visible form or image that may entail ritual acts of bodily inscription (Rush 2005, 75, 226). In *Spiritual Tattoo*, John Rush mentions that the ancient Maya, particularly nobles and kings, practiced a range of bloodletting rituals, among them, bodily scarification and tattooing, "to keep the universe alive" (40). Ancient Maya tooth implants and inlays (jade fillings, skull ornaments), forehead flattening, piercing, and other forms of scarification such as tattoos may be associated with the all-powerful and sacred ritual of bloodletting (Schele and Miller 1986). Archaeological evidence on stelae, murals, vases, and other artifacts found throughout the Maya world, which encompasses southern Mexico, Guatemala, Belize, and parts of Honduras and El Salvador, shows that bloodletting was a regular practice. In particular, nobles practiced bloodletting on various occasions, for specific trance-inducing spiritual ends, and on body parts such as the earlobe, lips, tongue, and penis, using special tools, such as ropes with thorns, stingray spines, obsidian blades, bark paper, cloth, and bowls (Schele and Miller 1986; Schele and Freidel 1990). Both men and women let blood in vision quests to achieve direct communication with gods and ancestors, and "personal bloodletting took place not only in the temples of the mighty but at the altars of the humble village as well" (Schele and Freidel 1990, 89). In *The Tattooed Soldier*, tattooing, torture, and war may be read as modern-day practices of bloodletting.

Read in light of Maya cosmology, the jaguar tattooed on Longoria's forearm not only links him to Maya jaguar cosmology, symbology, and identification but also draws attention to Longoria's aggression, power, and predatory form of masculinity (codified in modern military terms). It ties him to the cult of the jaguar and signals the presence of deep secrets cryptically associated with the power and prowess of the jaguar, which are precisely the attributes that Longoria, as shaped by the Guatemalan army since his adolescence, seeks to embody as a soldier and man. Like the jaguar amulets carried in ancient and recent times by many people, Longoria's jaguar tattoo ensures a symbolic transference of potency, force, strength, stealth, and other jaguarlike physical and supernatural powers to the wearer (Tobar 2000, 25). Aligning himself with the men of the Jaguar Battalion, Longoria produces a twisted symbolic genealogical link between the new military order and the ancient Maya warrior tradition:

Jaguars were feared even way back in Guatemala's history, during the Mayan empire. The Mayans built temples to the jaguar gods. Jaguars had spots that were like the camouflage uniforms the battalion wore. The jaguar stood for the new Guatemala the army wanted to build, a country of warriors and strong men, an empire like the one the Mayans had, except now they would carry submachine guns instead of spears. (Tobar 2000, 242)

In his reading of Maya warrior culture, Longoria strips the jaguar of its spiritual and cosmological attributes, which are so central to ancient and living Maya. Though possessing Maya ancestry, he has alienated himself from his Maya heritage, spirituality, and ethnic identity and aligned himself with the destructive forces of the Jaguar entering Xibalba, thus committing acts of bloodletting against his own people. Longoria's jaguar tattoo can be reread as an ambivalent sign of his racial, ethnic, and spiritual identity as a Guatemalan Maya.

Longoria is and is not Maya. Although he may have been born within a Maya community, he has long since transformed himself into a "uniformed man," refusing the heritage and gift handed down to him. It is significant to reiterate that Longoria, though indigenous, has long ago forgone the wearing of Mayan traditional clothing, or *traje*, associated with ethnic indigenous identification in the Maya world.[11] The more Westernized a person is, the less likely it is that she or he will wear full *traje*. It has been noted that Maya men and boys who adopt more public roles do not wear, or wear partially, traditional clothing. In Maya traditional culture, *traje*, like tattoos in certain contexts, represent cultural, community, and ethnic identity (Hendrickson 1996, 39). Longoria's rejection of Maya dress for military dress carries special significance in the reading of *The Tattooed Soldier*. In the end, Longoria does not wear indigenous clothing and he seems not to speak a Mayan language, yet he tattoos his body with the image of the jaguar.

Appealing to the jaguar and participating in a form of bloodletting, Longoria summons the most important underworld god, for according to the text, "as it [the tattoo] breathed in the tropical air it became a real Guatemalan jaguar" (Tobar 2000, 242). Read in this light, Longoria— the jaguar man—is neither evil nor good: he is Balam rising, returning, and regenerating the forces of life and death that have reigned in Yichkan-Guatemala with the Maya deities who, as we know, have never disappeared. Longoria is capable of such great aggression, violence, and destruction that, in the end, he also channels regenerative and life-giving Maya forces. In Maya belief, for a new day to rise, an old one must wane, and there must be bloodletting. For maize to grow, an ear of corn (also associated with drops of blood) must enter the soil and be re-born. In practice, as Linda Schele and Mary Ellen Miller explain in *The Blood of Kings*, a king's letting of his own blood "served both to nourish and sustain the gods and to communicate with them. In this role, the king was a nourisher of the gods, of maize and of his people (1986, 301). Equally, the vision quest leading to contact with the gods necessitated bloodletting by kings, subjects, and war captives. Further, Schele and Miller write, "The Maya believed that bloodletting brought the gods as well as their ancestors into physical existence in human space and time. . . . It appears that the king was conceived to be a vessel of sorts and that through ritual, a god was brought into his body" (183). So, too, in the novel, Longoria figures as the bloodletter, the killer of many sac-rificial people, including the family of Antonio Bernal. By the end of the novel, he, too, gives his blood as Bernal avenges the assassination of his family, killing and abandoning Longoria in a tunnel in the heat of the Los Angeles Uprising of 1992. In an apocalyptic encounter, Bernal kills the Balam (Longoria) in a freeway tunnel (cave) to make way for a new period, or *k'atun*, to turn for himself and other war survivors in Los An-geles and the Americas. Bernal's final act of bloodletting of the captive jaguar suggests that there has been a reversal in the power hierarchy: this time the victim will sacrifice the victimizer. While Longoria may have had impunity for his actions in Guatemala, in Los Angeles Bernal takes justice into his own hands and reinstates an ancient cosmological order in the Americas.

By the end of the novel, the jaguar becomes a symbol of justice, for as Bernal sees it, "Each moment that the soldier lived was a crime against nature, against the laws that made the planet spin and babies grow. The soldier's life, his living steps in Los Angeles, were a violation. They were *a stain* on the earth as indelible as the pigment etched into his skin, the jaguar on his forearm" (Tobar 2000, 184). When Bernal kills the jag-uar, taking justice into his own hands, he closes a cycle of war and im-punity. In the end, it is Bernal who closes in on the perpetrator (the jaguar man), as he seeks restitution for the killing of his family and oth-ers in Guatemala for which Longoria had gone unpunished. As Bernal knows it to be true, "The responsibility of bringing him to justice had fallen to him [Bernal] because there was no one else to do it" (229). Only the bloodletting of Longoria (and other government soldiers and death squad members) could put an end to the rule of impunity and bring a new day to Guatemala and Guatemalans, still carrying the scars of the civil war. Ensuring the continuity of the Maya world and other world orders, "Now Antonio [a Guatemaln immigrant, no less] could act for them. He could act for the massacred who had been left without fathers, husbands, or brothers to avenge them" (198). And he could act for the Meb'ixh and the refugees suffering from posttraumatic stress disorders in González's *Return of the Maya*.

In the end, *The Tattooed Soldier* works through the posttraumatic narrative of war from both the victim's and the perpetrator's subject positions and interpolates it with the cosmic narrative of the hero twins' vanquishing of the lords of Xibalba through the killing of the jaguar. This time Maya cosmological forces are brought to life again by Longoria's invocation of the jaguar god inscribed on his tattoo. A metamorphosis of One Hunahpu and Seven Hunahpu, Bernal and Longoria are subject to the forces and cycles of the Maya gods and deities. Student and soldier, like the hero twins, are mirror images of one another, fulfilling the prophecy that godlike sons must confront the underworld forces governing their lives in a game of death. As the first and second set of twins played the ball game of death, Bernal and Longoria play a game of "predator and prey" in the streets of Los Angeles. Like the two sets of twins, Bernal and Longoria are called to fulfill a special destiny in Yichkan: Bernal vanquishes the jaguar god represented by Longoria, and Longoria enters the underworld as the jaguar returning home to Xibalba, the underworld, where he may yet be redeemed. A new day rises in Los Angeles in the wake of Longoria's death, and a cease-fire between local and global forces begins. Justice is served in Bernal's final act of retribution against the soldier, and the prophecy of the *Popul Vuh*, as restated here, holds true:

> No longer will clean blood be yours. . . . Only the sinner and the offender, the wretch and the molester whose sins are well established, will be given to you. No longer will you be able to seize suddenly any person. . . . Thus their [the Xibalba overlords'] greatness and glory were destroyed. Never again would their dominion become great. This was the great accomplishment of Xhunahpu and Xbalanque. (Christenson 2000, 124–125)

In defeating the lords of the Xibalba (the Guatemalan military) and reenacting the narrative of Xhunahpu and Xbalanque, Bernal and the jaguar man fulfill their mythic and historic roles, ending a cycle of violence and beginning a cycle of life (or the potential of one, for Bernal is regenerated as a diasporic subject in Los Angeles). Set in 1992, the Five-

Hundredth Anniversary of the Encounter, the International Year of Indigenous People, and the Los Angeles Uprisings, *The Tattooed Soldier* thus recovers the narrative of past violations into a modern narrative of reparation. In its invocation of Maya cosmology, the novel suggests that although posttraumatic subjects may not break completely with the haunting narratives that travel within them, other life narratives are always possible.

Return of the Maya and *The Tattooed Soldier* show that the struggle for cultural survival continues among Central Americans in and outside the isthmus. These texts recall the past and bring impunity to the attention of the present, triggering historical insight on the part of readers. Within these posttraumatic narratives, evidence of past wrongs is inscribed in the memories and bodies of many Central Americans in diaspora. As the orphan of *Return of the Maya* and Bernal of *The Tattooed Soldier* remind us, the recent past cannot be forgotten for it will return in some shape, form, and fashion. The past must be recalled, reli(e)ved, recovered, and recorded in order to overcome the lagging traumatic effects carried by many, especially when they have been silenced and hidden for so long. Indeed, the orphan in *Return of the Maya* says, "There are no written documents, because the guerrillas [and military] burned down most of the town halls in this region" (G. González 1998, 155). In lieu of absent documents on war crimes and impunity, texts such as *Return of the Maya* and *The Tattooed Soldier* may be read as fictional evidence written under the duress of extreme trauma. In their own right, these and other posttraumatic texts of Central America provide significant fictional evidence of past wrongs and continuing acts of impunity across the Americas.

CHAPTER 5

The War at Home: Latina/o Solidarity
and Central American Immigration

*Don't put your pictures away . . . Let them tell the story . . . Of the life we
shared. The day the army came, tried to kill our friends, and the night they
shot at us from everywhere . . . Don't put your pictures away . . . Let the
memories be shared.*
—FRANCISCO JAVIER HERRERA, MADELINE RÍOS, AND THE SALVADORAN
COMMUNITIES, "Don't Put Your Pictures Away," in *Lucha y Esperanza*

D uring the 1980s, the so-called Lost Decade of Latin America,
also known as the Decade of the Hispanic in the United States,[1]
U.S. military and economic aid to Central America reached an
annual average of $612 million and $130.2 million, respectively, at the
height of the civil wars (Dunkerley 1994, 145). James Dunkerley states,
"The 1980s were miserably harsh years for Central America. Precise
and reliable figures will never be available for measuring the human cost
of the region's three civil wars. A fair but conservative estimate would
be 160,000 people killed and two million displaced during the decade; it
is the scale, not the precision, that impresses" (1994, 3).[2] Many of those
who were displaced in the 1980s, especially Salvadorans, Guatemalans,
and Nicaraguans, sought refuge in the United States, and a number of
laws made provisions for the new immigrants. The 1980 Refugee Act
set up official classifications to identify refugees and political asylum
seekers, and the Immigration Reform and Control Act of 1986 (IRCA)
granted legal resident status to Central American immigrants showing
evidence of having lived in the United States prior to January 1, 1982.
The arrival of an increasing number of undocumented immigrants in
the 1980s put into effect new legislation, such as Temporary Protected

Status (TPS), Deferred Enforced Departure (DED), and the American Baptist Churches (ABC) ruling, which sought to gain permission for temporary and extended stays for immigrants. By 1990, well over one million Central Americans had immigrated to the United States (Pinderhughes, Córdova, and del Pinal 2002), making Central Americans (after Mexicans) one of the fastest growing subgroups of foreign-born Latinos/as in the United States. Of this number, the three Central American countries at war generated the greatest number of immigrants in the United States (Pinderhughes, Córdova, and del Pinal 2002).[3]

A product of cold war geopolitics in the isthmus, Central American immigrants, exiles, and refugees experienced directly much of the violence across the southern hemisphere. Migrants gave testimony to the atrocities committed against them in their own countries and made an explicit call for more effective resistance, collaboration, and political mobilization on many fronts. During that period of war, U.S. Latinos/as (especially Chicanos) began increasingly to support antiwar efforts and to participate in underground networks assisting Central American refugees and immigrants. In "Chicano Politics and U.S. Policy in Central America, 1979–1990," Antonio González writes that "Chicano politicians and community organizations played a key but unexplored part in defeating Reagan's interventionist policy" (1990, 155). He explains that Chicanos/as protested economic and military aid to Central America, although Chicano organizations and institutions, most notably the Mexican American Legal Defense and Education Fund (MALDEF), the National Council of La Raza (NCLR), and the League of United Latin American Citizens (LULAC) remained virtually uninvolved in the Central American conflict debate until late into the decade (166). In the late 1980s, Chicano/a political leaders, community activists, and the general public, however, became more openly critical of U.S. intervention in Central America and U.S. immigration policy in regard to Central American refugees.[4] In March 1986, the governor of New Mexico, Toney Anaya, declared his state "a sanctuary for Central American refugees," and some Chicanos/as reached a consensus, ultimately opposing further U.S. economic and military aid to the Nicaraguan counterrevolutionaries and supporting the Central American Peace Plan (González 1990, 162–164).

During this period, Chicano/a and Latino/a solidarity with Central America was forged, as many U.S. Latinos/as identified themselves with a common hemispheric struggle for "self-determination, social justice, human rights, and democracy" and recognized "[U.S.] foreign and domestic policy as interconnected" (González 1990, 169–170). A discursive shift toward solidarity, sanctuary, and collaborative political work among U.S. Latinos/as was documented in a body of literary, musical, and cinematic texts. This chapter focuses on the production of a vanguard transnational solidarity culture and literature by Latinos/as and Central Americans in the United States, which challenged the occluded history of U.S. imperialism and U.S. Latino/a sociopolitical activism in the hemisphere. In particular, the countries in Central America that experienced the most intensive intervention—Nicaragua, El Salvador, and Guatemala—would draw Latino/a support. The Contra War against the Sandinista government proved a "staging ground" of cold war conflict, as well as a catalyst for solidarity and peace mobilization in the 1980s.

Central American Solidarity Networks

In response to the escalating violence in Central America and the increase in immigration of Central American refugees to the United States, a number of solidarity, sanctuary, and peace movements gained momentum.[5] With the intent to bring U.S. military intervention in Central America to public attention, three organizations—Sanctuary, Witness for Peace, and Pledge of Resistance—became especially visible. Sanctuary, which originally grew out of the Tucsonian Jim Corbett's desire to assist Central Americans crossing the Arizona border, quickly expanded throughout the United States as churches formed a covenant, or partnership of religious entities. Members of the covenant publicly declared their sanctuary status, aided refugees in their border crossings, and transported them to safehouses throughout the United States. Early Sanctuary workers personally posted bail for those migrants who were arrested and welcomed them into their homes and churches. Beginning with individuals who provided humanitarian aid to Central American refugees, primarily from El Salvador and Guatemala but increasingly from Nicaragua as the Contra War grew more intense, Sanctuary "grew into a political movement that sought to end the human oppression by U.S.-sponsored war of Central America" (C. Smith 1996, 69). By the mid-1980s, Sanctuary workers not only guided refugees through the borders and to destinations in the United States and represented them in the legal system but also put their lives on the line by continuing to challenge the U.S. legal system. In February 1984 and January 1985, Sanctuary workers were arrested and indicted in Texas and Arizona, bringing greater exposure to Central American refugees and the wars they were fleeing. The city of Los Angeles, in addition to the state of New Mexico, also home to large numbers of Latinos/as, declared itself a sanctuary for Central American refugees (C. Smith 1996, 70); other cities adopted sister towns throughout Central America.

Witness for Peace focused a great part of its attention on Nicaragua, to which the group sent U.S. citizen volunteers on fact-finding tours and long-term and short-term delegations. Volunteers traveled to Nicaragua, witnessed the disastrous effects of the U.S.-funded Contra War (1983–1987) on the general population, and reported their findings to the public in the United States. In *Resisting Reagan*, Christian Smith states that "Witness for Peace had hit upon a tactic, it seemed, that transformed people, that disturbed and electrified U.S. citizens into fervent political action against their own government" (1996, 78). In the United States, participants' testimonies were used to inform the public about U.S. involvement in the Contra War in Nicaragua and show the effects of the war on the Nicaraguan people.

The third peace activist group, Pledge of Resistance, was perhaps the most vocal of the Central America antiwar movements, also mobilizing especially against the Contra War in Nicaragua. The group staged nonviolent acts of resistance in public spaces, organized demonstrations, held civil disobedience events, and gathered signatures in ongoing petition drives. Remaining vigilant to a possible all-out U.S. invasion of Nicaragua, Pledge of Resistance monitored arms shipments to Central America and U.S military maneuvers in the region and served as a clearinghouse of counterinformation for a receptive public nurtured by the peace movement and its organizations. These antiwar, peacekeeping groups presented a challenge to the Reagan administration, for which Central America was the "proving ground" and "test case" for the enforcement of U.S. hegemony in the western hemisphere, even as U.S. power was being challenged throughout the world. By the 1980s, the United States had pulled out of Vietnam, but the memory of that war lingered in the political imaginary, as the cold war continued in Central America and the Sandinista revolution ousted the Somoza dictatorship, which had held power in Nicaragua since 1936. The Reagan administration identified the Sandinista government as a Communist regime that threatened the stability of the isthmus (C. Smith 1996, 20–21). Time and time again, Reagan and his spokespeople (foremost among them, Jeane Kirkpatrick, U.S. ambassador to the United Nations) lashed out against Nicaragua, portraying the country as a cauldron of communism overflowing into the region as a whole. Throughout his presidency, Ronald Reagan expounded on the threat posed by Central America, starting with Nicaragua. Among his many pronouncements on Central America was the following: "The national security of all the Americas is at stake in Central America. If we cannot defend ourselves there . . . the safety of our homeland would be put at jeopardy" (quoted in C. Smith 1996, 18). The United States attempted to show its might in the wars it supported throughout Central America in the 1980s, for as one of Reagan's key advisers told him, "Mr. President, this is one you can win" (Alexander Haig, quoted in C. Smith 1996, 22).

A host of solidarity, sanctuary, peace, antiwar, and immigrant-aid groups challenged the Reagan administration's war in Central America. In *The Culture of Protest* (1993), Susan Coutin argues that while sanctuary workers saw themselves as saving the lives of refugees, they also recognized themselves as an important "challenge to institutional imperialism" (176). Christian Smith, in fact, estimates that in its first three years, Sanctuary counted on more than 70,000 individuals and numerous covenant churches in the United States; Witness for Peace sent over 4,000 people in its delegations to Nicaragua; and Pledge of Resistance had almost 80,000 supporters ready to participate in civil disobedience, especially if the United States invaded Nicaragua (C. Smith 1996, 374–375). According to Smith, "Without the movement's opposition, the administration's policy actions would have been much more overt, intense, and unrelenting, and the human misery and loss of life in Central America would have been greater" (368). The Central America peace movements of the 1980s thus were a force to be reckoned with.

Although, as C. Smith shows, most of the participants in these movements were white, middle-class, educated lay and religious workers, participation by Latinos/as and Central Americans was significant at the more informal and grassroots levels. Many Central American families aided relatives and others in their migration to the United States by sending money, contracting border smugglers, providing housing, finding jobs, helping refugees adjust to their new lives, and establishing social networks, though at certain costs, as Cecilia Menjívar shows in her book *Fragmented Ties* (2000). Many Central Americans and their Latino/a allies worked in local immigrant and refugee-aid organizations, identifying and allocating resources, providing legal services, filling out paperwork, and representing immigrants in the U.S. court system. On their arrival, Central American refugees also worked in solidarity organizations, lending credibility to the peace movement as a whole with their *testimonios* and firsthand narratives of war experiences and human rights violations. They infused the solidarity and peace movements not only with their *testimonios* but also with their zeal for liberation theology, revolutionary action, and organizing at the community level (*comunidades de base*). Indeed, solidarity and peace activists and Central American refugees empowered one another during that period. Although domestic Latinos/as (those born, raised, and/or acculturated in the United States) provided significant aid to Central American refugees, much research still remains to be done in the area of Latino peace activism during that period. I explore here a literature and a culture of solidarity produced by Latinos/as and Central Americans in the United States, both of which provide insight into significant intra-Latino affiliations forged during the 1980s.

Central American and Latino/a Cultural Alliances

In the 1980s, a cohort of Central American revolutionary youths and others who were displaced by the wars infused Latino/a communities in the United States with a sense of urgency to participate in political organizing and solidarity work. This ideologically transfused Central American and Latino/a community grew into organized political entities in the United States as people mobilized around human and refugee rights, participated in solidarity groups, disseminated information, sent material aid to Central America, and provided services for immigrants. In *Legalizing Moves* (2000), Coutin explains that various Salvadoran-focused immigrant-aid organizations in Los Angeles

> grew out of the political struggle in El Salvador, and . . . pursued
> political change in the United States as well. El Rescate and CARECEN
> [Central American Refugee/Resource Center] were founded in the early
> 1980s by activists associated with different popular organizations in El
> Salvador. ASOSAL [Association of Salvadorans in Los Angeles], which
> grew out of CARECEN, was founded much more recently, in the early
> 1990s, as part of the campaign to extend TPS for Salvadorans. Though
> organizations' strategies and philosophies have differed somewhat
> over the years, each of these groups strives to improve the situation of
> Salvadorans in the United States as well as to promote human rights and
> economic development in El Salvador. (2000, 20)

Parallel to these organizations, solidarity artistic and cultural movements were formed in cities like San Francisco, Los Angeles, New York, and Washington, D.C.—which together received the bulk of Central American immigrants in the 1980s. Cultural brigades, organization fund-raisers, community activists, writers, artists, and musicians formed an extended network of solidarity activist workers who may not have been directly linked but who nonetheless mobilized themselves in an antiwar effort throughout the United States that would continue as long as the civil wars raged in Central America. In *Dimensions of the Americas* (1994), Shifra M. Goldman points out that the Central American armed struggles of the 1980s inspired many artists in the United States, some of whom joined organizations such as Artists Call Against U.S. Intervention in Central America. Founded in New York in 1983, Artists Call "spread to twenty-six cities in the United States, and to Mexico, Canada, and France" (1994, 34). It organized events, performances, and exhibits to draw attention to the state-sponsored violence in Central America and to raise funds for refugee-aid organizations.

At the local level, Central Americans and Latinos/as established and participated in cultural centers such as CODICES (Cultural Documentation and Investigation Center of El Salvador) in San Francisco and INALSE (Institute of the Arts and Letters of El Salvador) in New York, as well as cultural programs within the existing organizations of CARECEN and ASOSAL and others that developed attendant cultural programs throughout the United States and Central America.[6] The Salvadoran poet, painter, and cultural critic Martivón Galindo explains "that the 1980s for Salvadorians were like the 1960s for North Americans, when the 'compañerismo' was vital and a warm energy flourished" (Galindo 2000, 4). According to Galindo:

> The United States was the country where the greatest number of Salvadorians arrived during the 1980s. Many of them were political exiles or undocumented refugees. Washington and California—Los Angeles and San Francisco—were the sites where the greater cultural activity existed. In Washington, a group of writers published the literary review *El Tropezón;* in Los Angeles, another group of artists and writers worked in different projects of music, dance, poetry and theatre. (2000, 1)

Indeed, Salvadorans and other Central Americans joined Chicanos/as and Latinos/as in antiwar efforts and local organizations such as CODICES

MANLIO ARGUETA, El Salvador, 1935. En 1956, junto con Roque Dalton, Otto René Castillo y otros, fue fundador del *Círculo Literario Universitario*. Estudió Derecho; fue director de la Editorial Universitaria de su país, y luego de la Editorial Universitaria Centroamericana (EDUCA). En poesía ha publicado: *En el costado de la luz* (1968); *Las bellas armas reales* (1979), y es autor de la antología *Poesía de El Salvador* (1983). En novela: *El valle de las hamacas* (1970); *Caperucita en la zona roja* (Premio Casa de las Américas 1977) y *Un día en la vida* (1981). Esta última novela ha sido traducida a una decena de idiomas.

C☉DICES

Y
EL CENTRO CULTURAL DE LA MISION

PRESENTAN

UN

TALLER LITERARIO
CON
Manlio Argueta

Escritor salvadoreño autor de UN DIA EN LA VIDA

Contenido del Curso:
I- LITERATURA CENTROAMERICANA: Principales escritores del area, influencias, tendencias, principales obras. Como el proceso literario y la Estructura Social en la region han influenciado uno al otro.
II- TALLER: Tecnicas para escribir, proceso, discusion y analisis del trabajo de los participantes.

DURACION: 6 Semanas (Nov. 6 - Dic. 16)

DIAS: Martes y Jueves

HORA: 7:00 - 9:30 pm.

LUGAR: Centro Cultural de la Mision
2868 Mission Street, San Francisco
El inicio del Curso sera una recepcion para el escritor y los participantes del taller.

VALOR DEL CURSO $25.00 Favor registrarse al Telef. 821-1155

CODICES—Un Taller Literario con Manlio Argueta. Courtesy of Martivón Galindo.

and the Mission Cultural Center in San Francisco, which according to Galindo was founded by Salvadorans and "other members of the Chicano and Latino community" (2).

The "collective spirit" of the 1980s resulted in various cultural projects and fund-raising events: art exhibits, musical concerts, poetry readings, performances, lectures, literary workshops, student events, literary journals, cultural magazines, and the 1989 founding of Editorial Solaris, which published Spanish-language works. According to Galindo, Solaris is "devoted to the Salvadorian and Latino/a writers who don't have the support of any other publishing house" (2000, 2). The San Francisco-based Latino cultural journal *Voces*, grounded in early solidarity work, began to publish works in Spanish by Central Americans in the United States. And in 2000, CARECEN of Los Angeles and Pacific News Service of San Francisco copublished *Izote Vos: A Collection of Salvadoran American Writing and Visual Art*, the product of creative and

"Contributing to Peace through Culture"

C⬤DICES

CENTRO DE DOCUMENTACION E INVESTIGACION CULTURAL DE EL SALVADOR
CULTURAL DOCUMENTATION AND INVESTIGATION CENTER OF EL SALVADOR

96 Balmy Alley   San Francisco   California   94110   (415)6485510

CODICES—Contributing to Peace through Culture. Courtesy of Martivón Galindo.

educational workshops conducted with Salvadoran immigrant youths of those two cities (Cowy Kim et al. 2000).

Martivón Galindo recalls that the 1980s "were permeated with a sense of collective work and solidarity" (2000, 4), as manifested in student organizing and activism at San Francisco State University (SFSU). In the 1980s, when Galindo attended SFSU and Alejandro Murguía and Carlos Córdova taught in the La Raza Studies Program there, a number of classes on Central American history, literature and culture, politics, and immigration responded to the needs and interests of a highly diverse Latino population in the San Francisco Bay Area that was becoming politicized by the wars in Central America. A product of the 1968 Third World student movements at SFSU, the Ethnic Studies Department and La Raza Studies Program in particular supported the political work of a new generation of students through student recruitment, community outreach programs, political activism, and community-based research. During that period, scholar and student activists in La Raza Studies produced various publications, foremost among them *Cipactli* and *Journal of La Raza Studies*, both of which focused on Latino/a communities at large while also presenting Central American topics of interest.

In his editorial comment in *Cipactli*, Carlos Córdova (then acting chair of La Raza Studies) wrote that the journal's mission was "to demonstrate the high quality of work being produced by Raza students and faculty" and that the program's goal was "to develop highly qualified professionals who will go back to our communities to improve social, economic, and political realities of La Raza people in Latin America and the United States." According to Córdova, La Raza students would be in a position "to create a La Raza political base at the neighborhood, municipal, state, and national levels."[7] Combining Chicano Movement and U.S. Third World ethnic identity politics with Central American revolutionary sensibilities and community-based practices, La Raza Studies shaped generations of U.S. Latino/a scholar-activists such as Ricardo Salinas of the Latino performance troupe Culture Clash, the Salvadoran poet Martivón Galindo, the Chicano film scholar Sergio de la Mora, and a number of filmmakers, artists, and educators working throughout the United States. Throughout the 1980s, the program supported a number of student research projects and publications in Central American studies. The first issue of *Cipactli*, which appeared in fall 1988, contained poems by the Nicaraguan writer and Sandinista minister of culture, Ernesto Cardenal, as well as student writings on Central American literature and immigration, interviews, and photographs representing the Latino diversity of the San Francisco Bay Area. During those years in San Francisco, Latino/a communities were infused with a renewed sense of solidarity that coincided with the cultural work being done in other regions of the United States, especially Los Angeles—the home of the largest Central American communities in the nation.

In February 1980, the Los Angeles–based Chicano cultural journal *XhismeArte* dedicated a pathbreaking issue to Latin American revolutionary struggles, including those in Central America. In the editorial comment, the staff explained:

> Our focus in this issue of *XhismeArte* is distinctly Latin American. While this new year appears to return us to the cold war, with every possibility of world war, the leadership responsibility of Latin America and the developing world becomes greater and greater. The attention given by our national media, shifting from tacit neglect to nearsighted close-ups, sensational headlines of newly discovered countries, gives us the image of the Third World as one governed by chaos, irrationality and backwardness. There is an informational void that needs to be filled by some sense of historical perspective, whether in the case of Iran or El Salvador. (1980, 5)[8]

Joined in solidarity, artists and writers, mainly Chicanos/as, published in this journal's issue an array of short stories, *testimonios*, photographs, cartoons, drawings, and poetry, including pieces by Roberto Vargas, whom the editors of *XhismeArte* described as "a molding force in his highly political poetry" (1980, 31). Born in Nicaragua and raised in San Francisco, Vargas was part of the San Francisco Beat and Haight-Ashbury alternative cultural scenes in the 1960s. In the 1970s, he participated in the Chicano Civil Rights movement, writing poems that were published in leading Chicano anthologies such as *Aztlán* and *Flor y canto*. And, in the 1980s, Vargas promoted the Sandinista cause in the United States and joined the Nicaragua Revolution as a Sandinista combatant at the southern front (the border of Nicaragua and Costa Rica). Out of this experience, he wrote *Nicaragua, yo te canto, besos, balas y sueños de libertad* (Nicaragua, I Sing to You, Kisses, Bullets, and Dreams of Liberty) (1980).[9] The solidarity volume of *XhismeArte* featured Vargas's poem "UNIDAD" (Unity), in which the poet calls people to action:

YA ES TIEMPO QUE NOS PONGAMOS / MAS SERIOS / SI
ESTAMOS MAS SERIOS YA ES HORA / QUE NOS PONGAMOS

MAS BRAVOS / SI ESTAMOS MAS BRAVOS YA ES / TIEMPO
QUE NOS PONGAMOS MAS / FUERTES SI ESTAMOS TAN
FUERTES / YA ES HORA QUE NOS UNAMOS / SI ESTAMOS
UNIDOS / YA ES HORA QUE ESTEMOS LUCHANDO / SI ES-
TAMOS LUCHANDO / SERIOS / BRAVOS / FUERTES Y UNI-
DOS ¡VENCEREMOS! (Vargas 1980, 31)
[IT IS TIME THAT WE BECOME / MORE SERIOUS / IF WE
ARE MORE SERIOUS IT IS TIME / THAT WE BECOME AN-
GRIER / IF WE ARE MORE ANGRY IT IS / TIME THAT WE
BECOME STRONGER / IF WE ARE THAT STRONG / THEN
IT IS TIME THAT WE UNITE / IF WE ARE UNITED / IT IS
TIME THAT WE STRUGGLE / IF WE ARE STRUGGLING /
SERIOS / ANGRY / STRONG AND UNITED / WE WILL
WIN!] (My translation)

The capital letters and irregular line breaks express the urgency of calling people to action during the era of U.S. interventionism, armed conflict in Central America, and U.S. domestic policies that adversely affect
people of color. In a strident voice, the poem further addresses a dis-
united U.S. Latino population and urges Latinos/as to join a common
struggle to end the war at home against minority, ethnic communities.
Solidarity was key to forging local and international alliances.

As part of their solidarity practice, some Latino/a writers, artists, and
critics participated in the sanctuary, solidarity, or peace movements in
the United States. Some traveled on peacekeeping and fact-finding missions to Central America. The Chicana novelist Graciela Limón joined
a 1990 delegation that investigated the 1989 military-directed assassination of six Jesuit priests and their housekeeper and her daughter in
San Salvador, an experience out of which she developed her novel *In
Search for Bernabé* (1993). In the 1980s, the Chicana journalist and writer
Demetria Martínez participated in the Sanctuary movement assisting
Central American refugees in New Mexico. In 1987, she was arrested
and indicted for aiding and abetting "illegal aliens." Although she was
later acquitted, the trial against Martínez was widely known, especially
since her solidarity poems were used as evidence against her in court.[10]
Throughout the 1980s, the Chicano musician and solidarity activist Francisco Javier Herrera (whose song lyrics open this chapter) performed at fund-raising benefits for Central America, recorded his music
of solidarity, and traveled to El Salvador on various occasions. During
the late 1970s, the Chicano scholar, writer, and solidarity activist Ale-

jandro Murguía worked "full time organizing solidarity committees in support of the Nicaraguan people" (Murguía 1990, 7) and traveled numerous times to Central America in that capacity. In June 1979, he went to the border of Costa Rica and Nicaragua as an enlisted internationalist volunteer to "join in the Final Offensive" (7) of the Sandinista National Liberation Front (FSLN). Murguía's experience in the war in Nicaragua became the focus of his book, *Southern Front* (1990), which I examine below.

Collaborating with the Enemy: Chicano Solidarity with Nicaragua

In an unpublished paper, "Concordia: The San Francisco Bay Area in Central American Literature" (1999), Alejandro Murguía examines the cultural networks and production of Central American writers in the Bay Area before and during the 1980s. An active member of the solidarity movements there, Murguía taught Central American and Chicano literature in La Raza Studies at San Francisco State University, where he also coedited the journal *Cipactli*. During the 1970s and 1980s, he translated Central American literature, participated in cultural programs with Latino/a activist writers, and wrote creative and critical works in solidarity with the Central American struggles. In "Concordia" (one of the few bibliographic essays to date to document the solidarity cultural production of that period), Murguía describes the Bay Area, in particular, San Francisco's Mission District, "as a greenhouse for many Central American writers during their periods of exile, most notably the decades from the 1970s to the present" (Murguía 1999, 1). Charting important ground in U.S. Central American diasporic studies, Murguía identifies Central American writers who lived and wrote in the Bay Area before the 1970s. According to Murguía, the Nicaraguan poet José Coronel Urtecho wrote *Rápido Tránsito (Al ritmo de Norteamérica)* (Rapid Transit [The Rhythm of North America]) (1985) during his sojourn in San Francisco in the 1920s. Murguía explains:

> In his autobiographical essay, José Coronel Urtecho describes the life
> of a young Nicaraguan living with his family on Van Ness Avenue, near
> Vallejo Street, and attending Commerce High School to learn English.
> In many ways, Urtecho's essay is the precursor of Central American
> writing in the Bay Area: he touches on themes that will occupy future
> generations—the rapid pace of a big city; the glamour of its nightlife;

alienation, racism, solitude; he also grafts English words and phrases to his Spanish to more fully capture his experience as a Central American in the United States. (1999, 2)

In his literary account of the San Francisco Bay Area, Murguía describes Latino/a writers who, like the Nicaraguan-born, San Francisco-raised poet Roberto Vargas, were politicized in the Chicano Movement, the armed struggles in Central America, and the antiwar, solidarity movements in the United States. Murguía suggests that the permanent settlement of Central American artists and the temporary exile of writers such as Manlio Argueta invigorated the cultural work of many Latino/a and Chicano/a artists. During that period, Salvadoran immigrant writers like Galindo, Armando Mauricio Molina, and Jorge Argueta were key figures in the cultural antiwar effort in the Bay Area (J. Argueta 1989, 1990, 1991a, 1991b, 1996, 1997; Galindo and Molina 1995; Galindo 1996; Molina 1996), while Chicano writers and artists such as Murguía, Francisco J. Herrera, and Cherríe Moraga advanced the cause of the Central American civil wars among U.S. Latino/a communities of color. According to Murguía, the Roque Dalton Cultural Brigade, named after the Salvadoran revolutionary poet, formed "a collective of Bay Area writers, poets, and translators who [took] up the task of promoting Central American literature and poetry" (Murguía 1999, 5). The brigade published books in solidarity with Central America, including English translations of Otto Rene Castillo's *Tomorrow Triumphant* (1984) and Roque Dalton's *Clandestine Poems* (1984), and the anthology, *Volcán: Poems from Central America* (1983), also coedited by Murguía.

In *Southern Front* (1990), Murguía takes up the revolutionary cause in a series of war vignettes based on his own experiences in the Nicaraguan Revolution (1978–1979) as an enlisted internationalist volunteer.[11] In that capacity, as Murguía explains in the foreword, he unloaded planes, trained personnel, and entered active combat in the last days of the Sandinista insurrection, from which "every member of [his] squad came out alive" (Murguía 1990, 7). The main character of Murguía's composite novel is Ulises, a Chicano internationalist volunteer who travels to the Nicaragua–Costa Rica border to join the Sandinista National Liberation Front (FSLN) (1990, 5–8). Along with "over half a dozen Chicanos [who] participated in the Southern Front" (6) and other volunteers from Europe, the Caribbean, and North, Central, and South America, Ulises not only confronts U.S. intervention in Nicaragua but also, with his narrative of international solidarity, seeks to deconstruct hegemonic cold war rhetoric and geopolitics in Central America.[12]

Identifying personally with the Sandinista struggle as a Chicano Vietnam veteran, [13] Ulises aligns himself with an international struggle against U.S. imperialism. From the start, he challenges the "Vietnam [War] syndrome" employed by the Reagan administration to propose Nicaragua as "another Vietnam." [14] Remembering his own experience in Vietnam, Ulises transforms the war in Nicaragua into his own personal struggle and vindication and into a collective rebellion on behalf of Chicano/Latino people. For Ulises, Nicaragua signifies yet another link in the long chain of U.S. imperialist aggressions, which included the Mexican American War of 1848 and the Vietnam War to which a larger number of young Chicano soldiers were deployed. With each successive U.S. war, enlisted and drafted Chicano soldiers were sent to Europe, Asia, and Latin America. Wearing the "brown beret" of Chicano militancy to the Nicaraguan front lines, Ulises seeks, thus, not only to topple a dictator but also to wage battle against U.S. imperialism in its international and national affronts. He sees the wars in Nicaragua and Vietnam and the violence in Latino barrios as U.S. aggression. The text explains that "Ulises, along with a half-dozen other Chicanos from the Valley and from Los [Angeles], had come to the front, to salvage the honor of a whole generation who didn't make it" (Murguía 1990, 13). While Ulises might have fought for the United States in Vietnam, in Nicaragua he allies himself with Third World anti-imperialist struggles after undergoing a revolutionary conversion. He reasons that "Chicano, Mejicano, Nicoya . . . [were] the same ancient Nahuatl culture and language, the same struggle from Cuauhtemoc to Carlos Fonseca—even if others didn't understand it now, they'd understand it later" (18). Ulises thus positions himself in the international revolutionary drama of the 1980s, for "this was for him, a clear-cut, well-defined little war" (13). Nicaragua, which had been invaded and occupied by the United States numerous times in the nineteenth and twentieth centuries, would come to signify for many Latinos/as the worst of U.S. imperialism in Latin America. [15]

Interpolating himself into the long-standing tradition of international solidarity in Nicaragua, Ulises assumes a revolutionary (heroic) identity. He chooses "Ulises" as his nom de guerre, not to commemorate the Ulysses of Greek legends, but "in honor of one who, armed with a rifle and a grenade, had faced off with a rank in the barrio of Monimbó during the insurrection of September. That Ulises from Masaya had been a warrior-hero" (Murguía 1990, 12). Murguía's *Southern Front* is thus an antiepic about an everyday antihero liberating Nicaragua. By taking the name of a fallen Sandinista combatant, Ulises casts himself in the revolutionary narrative of Nicaragua and the Americas, figuratively joining the ranks of the classic heroes of the Sandinista Revolution, beginning with General Augusto César Sandino and followed by his revolutionary descendants, including Carlos Fonseca, Tomás Borge, Omar Cabezas, Doris Tijerino, Dora María Tellez, and Gioconda Belli. In Nicaragua, Ulises "was without a country, without a passport, under another name and there was no turning back. This was his land now, his people, paid with skin, like they say. Che would have said, 'Wherever there is a struggle, they're my people'" (Murguía 1990, 20). Divesting himself of his U.S. nationality and collaborating with "the enemy" (as the Sandinistas were identified by the Reagan and Bush administrations), Ulises finds revolutionary agency in Nicaragua.

In the course of the narrative, Nicaragua becomes the playing field of revolutionary action and agency for Ulises. The would-be Chicano internationalist revolutionary desires "to be like Che," or in this case to be like the Nicaraguan Sandinista Omar Cabezas, who inspired a generation of Central American guerrilla fighters in the 1980s. In his *testimonio, Fire from the Mountain: The Making of a Sandinista* (1985; *La montaña es algo más que una inmensa estepa verde* 1982), Cabezas embodied the revolutionary ideal that was within reach of male fighters willing to enter "the mountain" and to assume "historical responsibility, a commitment to others[,] . . . to raise up others out of poverty and exploitation, and to rise to a higher level on the revolutionary scale" (Cabezas 1985, 11–12). Read intertextually, Cabezas's *Fire from the Mountain* and Murguía's *Southern Front* show uncanny resemblances, right down to a heterosexist and misogynist preoccupation with Nicaraguan women, whom the protagonists resent for leaving and driving them into combat: for Cabezas, it is Claudia; for Ulises, Miriam. Both texts represent the homoerotic construction of the "new man," already patented in the figure of Che and reproduced in the formation of a platoon of "new men" in the revolutionary forces of Central America. According to Cabezas, the new man, "began to be born with fungus infections and with his feet oozing worms. . . . [T]he new man was being born with the freshness of the mountains. . . . The new man was born in the mountains, as others were born in the underground in the city, as the guerrilla was born in the brush" (87). Murguía's Ulises shows (male) Chicano and Latino solidarity workers to possess the hypermasculinity to enter the revolutionary ranks of the Americas. Echoing Che Guevara's and Cabezas's guerrilla manuals, Murguía's war sketches represent the revolutionary fantasy of transforming everyday men into revolutionary agents in the killing fields of Central America.

After the Earthquake: Picking Up the Pieces and Moving On

Exposing U.S. intervention in Nicaragua while challenging the masculinist revolutionary master narrative through a *transfronterista* (border-
crossing) feminist narrative of affinity and alliance, the Latina filmmakers Lourdes Portillo and Nina Serrano, in their short film *Después del
Terremoto (After the Earthquake)* (1979), depict the life of a young Nicaraguan immigrant named Irene (Vilma Coronado). The film, produced
in 1979 just as the Sandinista government was coming into power in
Nicaragua, is situated in the midst of the coming-of-age(ncy) of two social bodies—Sandinista Nicaragua and the Nicaraguan diaspora. The
year is 1976, when Nicaraguan refugees are continuing to flee a devastating earthquake that occurred on December 23, 1972, destroying
the capital city of Managua and killing almost twenty thousand people.
Precisely at that moment, the U.S.-supported dictator, Anastasio Debayle Somoza, intensified his repression of the Nicaraguan people, and
the Nicaraguan Revolution entered into its final phase. On November
10, 1976, Carlos Amador Fonseca (1936–1976), the cofounder of modern Sandinista thought and militancy, was ambushed and assassinated
by the U.S.-trained Nicaraguan National Guard, pushing the country
into a full-blown civil war.[16]

In the context of the film narrative, 1976 not only refers to the rise
of the Sandinista Revolution, but also to a turning point in the life of
the protagonist, Irene. It is in 1976 that Irene finally decides to make a
life for herself in the United States and to leave behind her past, which
reappears in the form of her Sandinista fiancé, who immigrates to San
Francisco as well. Reliving the trauma of her life in Nicaragua under
Somoza rule and during the Sandinista Revolution, Irene tells her story
to her friend, Luisa Amanda. Irene explains, "There was hunger, misery,
thirst, my house was only rubble. . . . That's the reason why I am here."
The title of the film situates the viewer in the aftermath of the historical
forces that produce Irene's diasporic condition. In order to rebuild her
life, Irene must rise from the ruins of her past and free herself of the
destructive (masculinist) narrative of nation, war, and revolution as represented in Alejandro Murguía's expatriate novel, *Southern Front*, and
Omar Cabezas's classic revolutionary *testimonio*, *Fire From the Mountain*.
In the *liminal* year of the U.S. bicentennial anniversary, San Francisco's
centennial, and the umpire strike in baseball, Irene sets out to construct
a more woman-centered liberation narrative for herself.

In San Francisco, Irene works as a house cleaner, earning money to
send to her family in Nicaragua. She lives with her unmarried aunts,

who pray to San Antonio (Saint Anthony) to grant Irene a good husband. Theirs is a feminine household, governed by conservative Catholic traditions, especially in regard to female sexuality and family values. Catholic symbols like the Virgin of Guadalupe and Saint Anthony seem to represent the gendered tensions conditioning the lives of the women in the household. While Guadalupe—Queen of the Américas—long recovered by Chicana feminists as an empowering female deity, invokes feminine forces, *facultades* (sensibilities), and transcendental hybrid spiritualities, San Antonio stands guard over the female household, which lacks father, husband, and sons. As Catholic tradition would have it, Anthony is the patron saint of lost hopes; women pray to him for husbands. In his reincarnation in the household, Saint Anthony seems to fill the void of male absence and to lay down the law of the father, at least for the aunts, who follow the ritual of praying to him for a husband for Irene.

In a key scene in the film, while the aunts make tamales and gossip in their apartment kitchen, Irene receives a visit from her liberated modern-day (pants-wearing) girlfriend, Luisa Amanda, who encourages her to become more independent and self-reliant. As they prepare for a party later in the day, they talk about their lives and the unexpected arrival of Irene's former boyfriend, Julio. As if torn between her friend and her aunts, and what they signify, Irene hesitantly responds to her aunt's call in the kitchen. On her way back to her bedroom, she passes by her aunts' homemade altar in the darkened apartment hallway, stopping only momentarily to set aright the statue of San Antonio, which one of the aunts had put on his head as a petition for Irene's finding a "responsible" husband. In the bedroom, Luisa Amanda advises Irene to get an education (a life?), and, on their way out, she shouts out within the aunts' hearing range: "¡Qué viva la Independencia! ¡Qué los hombres hagan los tamales" (subtitled as, "Liberate the women from the kitchen! Let the men make the tamales!"). The aunts respond with visible disapproval: one does the sign of the cross as if to ward off evil, and the other calls attention to Luisa Amanda's *unnatural* wearing of pants, or her way of "vestir ridícula" (dressing ridiculously) and acting "pesada" (unfeminine). As Irene and her friend leave, the hall resonates with the young women's laughter, the laugh of Medusa punctuating the household and awakening Irene to other feminine possibilities, as I discuss below.

The image of the spinster aunts, the religious iconography, and the enclosed darkened quarters of the apartment are set in direct contrast to Irene's light-filled bedroom, Luisa Amanda's disruptive shout and laughter, and the complicit conversation engaged in by the two friends in Irene's room. Caught between contradictory forces—her past and present, her old homeland and new country, her obligations and desires, her subjection and emancipation—Irene desires to break out of the constraints that govern her life. She seeks a *revolution* in her life. However, she is torn between her memories of a Nicaragua in chaos, pulling her back to the woman she was/is, and her fascination with the action-filled streets of San Francisco, pushing her forward to the woman she is becoming. Representing her own psychic upheaval, the static images of Nicaragua in photographs in her room contrast deeply with the "moving pictures" of Irene in her daily life in San Francisco.

In the establishing scene, for example, Irene is observed in motion—walking, speaking, thinking, remembering, and making choices. As the film critic Rosa Linda Fregoso explains, "Irene is a woman who works outside the home, a woman who moves between cultures, languages, the public and the private, possessing the ability to act on multiple levels" (1993, 98). In contrast, her aunts and the other women in the film are rarely seen outside the protective walls of their apartments, as if controlled by their conditions and traditions. With the exception of Luisa Amanda, whose name references the fallen Sandinista militant, Luisa Amanda Espinoza (1948–1970), all the women wear dresses, seemingly subscribing to traditional gender roles and scripts. Only Irene and Luisa Amanda seem to escape the constraints of their symbolic and real walls and to defy the public image of *mujeres de la calle*—women of/in the streets—by walking, meeting, sitting in, working in, and thus appropriating the open spaces of the Mission District. In the film, the Mission District and its outlying streets represent a hybrid contact zone, a third space of contradictions, or as Gloria Anzaldúa would have it, a "third country" (1999), where diverse peoples, cultures, histories, and traditions intersect and where that contact produces differential and deeply situated social identities. For Fregoso, Irene's excursions into the streets represent, in part, "the liberation of a Latina immigrant in the United States, shifting toward the attitude of 'differential consciousness' that Chela Sandoval speaks of" (1993, 96). Indeed, Irene in San Francisco is not the same Irene trapped in the ruins (*escombros*) of Managua, for in San Francisco Irene is reshaped by diasporic experiences that permit her "a Latina emancipation" of sorts (96).

Following the lead of her mentor and sister, Luisa Amanda, Irene thus begins to take control of her life and to enact other scripts. Even before he appears, Irene has already decided not to marry Julio, her Nicaraguan Sandinista fiancé. Her decision signifies not only an emancipation from the history that pulls her back to Nicaragua but also a rejection of the feminine patriarchal subjection that awaits her if she marries him. In regard to the life that she has fled, Irene ambivalently states early in the film: "¿y qué hay de nuevo?" (So what's new?). Breaking her ties to her absent parents, surrogate family, would-be-husband, war-torn nation, and patriarchal subjection, Irene realizes that her new city offers her the opportunity to reinvent and transform herself. The film is thus about new beginnings for the Nicaraguan diaspora and for Irene, who in 1979, the year of the triumph of the Sandinista Revolution, takes control of her life and story in the context of San Francisco, California, and subsequently rejects Sandinista revolutionary society. In the film, however, Irene cannot seem to reconcile (bridge) her Central American Nicaraguan and "Central American–American" (Arias 2007) woman-centered selves, and thus the film highlights her coming into a Latina "differential consciousness." At the same time, however, she is shown choosing the United States over Nicaragua, her future over her past, her independence over marriage, and her self over all those still suffering political repression in Nicaragua. For Irene, there is no going back to Nicaragua or to her preimmigrant self. The film seems to posit that she must become less nationalistic and less Nicaraguan to become more "American" and more feminist. Appropriately, then, the film opens and closes with the same subtitled lines: "and so it began . . . y empezó así."

Indeed, as the film begins, Irene gathers and counts her money to make the first lay-away payment on a television set. She keeps her money in a top drawer of her dresser, hidden in the pages of a premarital sex self-help book. The sex book, the money, and the television set signify for Irene a "slippage of desires between sexual freedom and freedom to consume," as Fregoso suggests (1993, 96, 103). Irene's television purchase is key to reading the film as a site of desire for narratives other than those predesignated for most Central American women in their countries of origin. In prerevolutionary and revolutionary Nicaragua, Irene might have been expected to fulfill traditional patriarchal roles such as those of mother, daughter, and wife. As a Sandinista militant, she might have been expected to give her life to the revolution, as did other Sandinista revolutionary heroes. Her models might have included the revolutionary guerrilla fighter Lavinia in Gioconda Belli's novel, *The Inhabited Woman* (1994), or one of the Sandinista women whose story is told in Margaret Randall's *Todas estamos despiertas* (We Are All Awake) (1980) or *Sandino's Daughters* (1981).[17] But Irene is not in Nicaragua. In fact, several times in the film she insists, "But I am here!" And in the United States, she sets out to buy a television set of her own, representing the nexus of multiple yet competing gendered national imaginaries, ideologies, and subjective positions intersecting in her life. Depending on the subjective positionings of characters and spectators, the TV set might signify U.S. (cultural) imperialism in Central America, immigrant socialization in the United States, or an act of feminist emancipation, as Fregoso suggests (1993, 102–103). By the end of the film, for better or for worse, Irene has become a woman with a television set of her own, exhibiting feminine liberation in the form of personal consumption. Although fraught with contradictions, Irene's declaration of independence through a singular act of consumerism should be read within the ambivalent space of female immigrant agency.

While in Nicaragua, Irene would never have spent $300 on a television set. In the United States, however, she has the opportunity to make that decision and purchase. For Irene, the TV set does not merely signify an object. Instead, it represents an act of volition. Irene will buy the television, despite the fact that it will cost her $300, or 5,400 cordobas, money that could easily feed two families for a year in Nicaragua, as her ex-fiancé Julio reminds her during their conflict-filled encounter. The TV set is invested with the emotional and economic agency that Irene seems to think she has gained in her new country and in her search for new prospects. While the collection of family photographs and newspaper clippings stacked on her dresser anchor Irene to war-torn and earthquake-struck Nicaragua, the TV set will generate new American images, dreams, and desires, serving as a vehicle of acculturation for Irene in the United States. Irene rejects the culture of war that Julio represents and vehemently chooses her life in the United States, asserting yet again, "But I am here now!" The willful purchase of the television set with *her own* hard-earned money signals for Irene a break with the past and a rejection of masculinist revolutionary Nicaragua, memorialized in the still-life photographs of Nicaragua, wherein everything is forever trapped in the *escombros*.

Through Irene's TV purchase, the film thus seems to reject the gender ideologies, patriarchal traditions, and women's lives under Sandinista masculinist rule. Rather than try her luck with her Sandinista sisters in wartime Nicaragua, Irene, like her mythological namesake (Eirene, goddess of peace, wealth, and springtime), makes peace with her (diasporic) condition and seeks her fortune in her new homeland. Like one of her aunts, who objects to the images of hunger, poverty, dictatorship, and war in Nicaragua in the slide show Julio presents at the party, Irene, too, desires more positive images, "algo más alegre." Irene supplants her history in war-torn Nicaragua with her immigrant experiences, desires, and nostalgic memories. Portillo and Serrano's film thus writes beyond the political revolutionary narrative and gives Irene an upper hand in the gender wars that she now takes up in the United States. In contrast to Nicaragua, women can wear the pants in the United States and achieve their independence.

By the end of the film, Irene is fully read into and through the lens of Chicana/Latina "Third World" feminisms (Fregoso 1993, 96). Irene seems to reject the formal narrative of armed struggle and revolution and opts for a feminist "differential consciousness" in her goal to reach "Latina emancipation." She reaches this higher plateau, however, by breaking with her Nicaraguan history and occluding the nuances of her Central American and Nicaraguan identity, heritage, and diasporic condition. Not surprisingly, the film elicited contentious responses from the exile Nicaraguan Sandinista community. As expected, "Sandinistas living in the Bay Area who first viewed the film did not appreciate its emphasis on gender, and refused to be associated with the film" (Fregoso 1993, 153). Because *Después del terremoto* was not produced from *within* the Sandinista Revolution but rather represented the "informal" conflict over gender politics and offered Third World feminist (re)solutions, Sandinistas were critical of the film when it was first released. It did not speak to them, and they appear to have rejected it as a representation of Sandinista struggles on the northern front.

While Central American revolutionary organizations such as the FSLN and the FMLN invariably reproduced Marxist masculinist gender ideologies and rarely interrogated internal(ized) gender hierarchies within their revolutions, the film's apparent rejection of a Central American/Nicaraguan ethnic identity for a cross-border Latina feminist positionality is troubling in the end. As a U.S. Central American, a Salvadoran American growing up in the San Francisco Bay Area in the 1980s, I am torn by Irene's final (re)solution to adopt "differential consciousness" and "transfronterista feminism" from what I consider an "undifferentiated" ethnic Latina position. For all purposes, she seems to break with her past as signified by the masculinist Nicaraguan Revolution and to move on in her life as a Latina immigrant seeking feminist transformation. Like her aunts who refuse to see and hear images of war-torn Nicaragua, Irene seems to break with her Central American/Nicaraguan identifications, histories, traditions, and struggles. Alternately, she seems to adopt a differential consciousness as proposed by Chicana feminists in lieu of other feminist Latinidades that might fully incorporate her Central American legacy of struggles, resistances, and resilience. Does the film, in the end, deny Irene her Nicaraguan/Central American Latinidades and propose that Central American women drop what is "central" from their American identities?[18] How would Irene re-tell her story outside of the solidarity operative lens provided by Latina feminism? In the next section, I continue to explore the construction of a transisthmian and transnational solidarity imaginary by return-ing to the work of cross-border feminists who through their solidarity work intervened nonetheless in U.S. foreign policy in regard to Central America, constructed narratives of and for the isthmus, and along the way made possible the production of a transnational Central American–American cultural field in the United States.

U.S. Chicana/Latina Transnational Interventions in Central America

The groundbreaking works of Latina cross-border feminists and activ-ists such as Martivón Galindo, Maya Chinchilla, Lourdes Portillo, Nina Serrano, Gloria Anzaldúa, Ana Castillo, Rosa Linda Fregoso, Deme-tria Martínez, Cherríe Moraga, Gloria Saldívar-Hull, and Chela San-doval, to name only a few, set the course for the production of Central America–identified literature by Chicanas and Latinas. Following their lead, a corpus of Chicana/Latina cross-border and transnational texts allied with Central America struggles emerged in the 1980s and 1990s. At the height of the U.S.-funded civil wars in Central America, a first-wave, vanguard U.S. Latina/o Central American–allied literature en-listed the following works: Helena María Viramontes's "The Cariboo Cafe" (1985), Alma Villanueva's *The Ultraviolet Sky* (1988), Ana Castillo's *Sapogonia* (1990), Carole Fernández's *Sleep of the Innocents* (1991), Graciela Limón's *In Search of Bernabé* (1993), and Demetria Martínez's collection of sanctuary poems titled "Border Wars: 1985" and "Turning" in *Three Times a Woman* (1989) and her novel *Mother Tongue* (1994). Filmic texts included Gregory Nava and Anna Thomas's *El Norte* (1983) and Lourdes Portillo and Nina Serrano's *Después del terremoto (After the Earthquake)* (1979) and various documentaries, mock-documentaries, and narrative films. These texts were among the first produced by U.S. Chicanas/Latinas to express a growing concern among Latinas/os about the civil wars in Central America. They dramatized the plight of Central Americans within the wider narratives of the Latin American diaspora, the disenfranchisement of local immigrant populations, and the history of U.S. imperialism and manifest destiny in relation to Central America at the end of the twentieth century. Such texts produced significant points of affinity for an audience critical of U.S. intervention in Central America and elsewhere.

In a speech delivered in 1990 at California State University, Long Beach, and later published as "Art in América con Acento," Cherríe Moraga urged Latinas/os to ask themselves, "How can I, as a Latina, identify with those who would invade Latin American land?" (1995, 212). She elaborated that while Mexico was invaded in 1848, "today, nearly a century and a half later, the Anglo invasion of Latin America has extended well beyond the Mexican/American border" (1995, 213). She also recognized that more than any other region of the world, Central America has endured repeated episodes of U.S. interventionism. Moraga insisted, "One of the deepest wounds Chicanos suffer is separation from our Southern relatives" (1995, 210). Like Anzaldúa, in *Borderlands/ La Frontera*, Moraga identified the U.S.-Mexico border as a wound that severs Latinas/os in the United States from those in Latin America. Appealing to Latinas/os on both sides of the border to learn about each other's struggles and to build a "communal ground" of affinity, Anzaldúa writes:

> To the immigrant *mexicano* and the recent arrivals we must teach our history. The 80 million *mexicanos* and the Latinos from Central and South America must know of our struggles. Each one of us must know basic facts about Nicaragua, Chile and the rest of Latin America. The Latinoist movement (Chicanos, Puerto Ricans, Cubans, and other Spanish-speaking people working together to combat racial discrimination in the marketplace) is good but it is not enough. Other than a common culture we will have nothing to hold us together. We need to meet on a broader communal ground. (1999, 109)

In "Art in América con Acento," Moraga also called for building alliances, especially in regard to the Latina/o diaspora and the Sandinista Revolution. Further, she decried the demise of the Sandinistas in Nicaragua, who were voted out of power in March 1990. Moraga blamed the Reagan and Bush administrations for financing the Contra War and for co-opting the Sandinista Revolution through a foreign policy of military intervention and economic blockade. In an illuminating moment, she recognized that U.S. intervention and Latin American immigration are, in fact, linked, for "every place the United States has been involved militarily has brought its offspring, its orphans, and its casualties to this country: Viet Nam, Guatemala, Cambodia, the Philippines" (1995, 213). Taking the next critical step, she linked U.S. intervention in Central America with massive Central American immigrations that continue to this day. For Moraga, "What was once largely a Chicano/mexicano population in California is now guatemalteco, salvadoreño, nicaragüense" (1995, 213). What was once a U.S.-based, Chicano-centered, anticolonial struggle would have to transform itself into hemispheric transnational, *transfronterista* Latina/o alliances, embracing Central America in its imaginary (A. Rodríguez 2001). Like Anzaldúa, who made an appeal for Latinas/os to meet "on a broader communal ground" (Anzaldúa 1999, 109), Moraga argued that Latinas/os and Chicanas/os had to close the "separation from our Southern relatives" and "emerge as a mass movement of people to redefine what an 'American' is" (Moraga 1995, 219). Through her writing and political activism, Moraga delineated a plan for bridging hemispheric differences, separations, and divides produced by wider imperialist and global forces within U.S. Latina/o communities.

The Limits of Solidarity

In her essay, "Host and Guest in the 'Latino Contact Zone,'" Dalia Kandiyoti does well to remind us that solidarity discourses and practices are problematic at best because they are shaped by structures of power that often elide or blur "specific context and differences" (2004, 424). In her analysis of Martínez's novel of solidarity, *Mother Tongue*, which I examine below, Kandiyoti proposes the "formulation of 'asymmetrical reciprocity,' in which subjects practice mutuality, recognition and care, fully aware of the asymmetricity of their positions and the partialness of their knowledge of others" (425). In other words, while Chicana/Latina feminists attempt to build affinities, alliances, and "communal ground" across borders, we must also recognize that solidarity is problematic and not transparent and that it is critically shaped by borders, differences, and unequal hierarchical relationships, even within Latina/o communities. Moreover, the subject that extends solidarity to another also takes agency away from that other who is subjected to acts of solidarity. Hence, in the remainder of this chapter, I examine critically the Chicana/Latina solidarity of fiction and the fiction of solidarity.

As I have argued elsewhere (A. Rodríguez 2001), Central Americans have been read by many Chicanas/os, Latinas/os, and others as part of a larger hemispheric "familia" and as "relatives" in need of a helping hand. In a few literary and cinematic texts, Chicanas/os symbolically absorb Central Americans into the larger political and cultural imaginary of the Latino family.[19] For example, in Gregory Nava's film, *Mi Familia/My Family* (1994), the character of Jimmy marries the Salvadoreña refugee Isabel Magaña, saving her from deportation. In *Born in East LA* (1987), Rudy (Cheech Marin) helps his girlfriend, Dolores, a Salvadoreña working in Tijuana, to cross the border and join him in East Los Angeles—the home of Chicano nationalist culture. In *El Norte* (Nava and Thomas 1983), the indigenous Maya sister, Rosita, dies from an infected rat bite received while crossing the border; tellingly, there is no Chicano/Latino husband or knight in solidarity to rescue Rosita from her sure death. In these Latino (family) romances, the Central American woman is cast as the feminized figure of displacement, whose historical referent is the vast population of single-parent, female-headed families displaced by the wars in Central America and the aftermath of economic devastation exacerbated by the postwar neoliberalization of Central American economies. Indeed, the image of the hardworking immigrant woman with no man and family ties of her own, much like Irene in Portillo and Serrano's film, becomes the premier sign of Central American refugee populations in the United States.

Although the Chicana/o "familia discourse" clearly and powerfully denounced U.S. intervention in Central America and declared affinity and solidarity with Central Americans in the 1980s, many Chicano and some Chicana texts placed Chicana/o histories, subjects, and protagonists at the center of solidarity fiction. Central American struggles served as a stage for the larger narrative of Chicana/o resistance, often occluding or preempting Central American histories, cultures, and subjectivities. Solidarity fiction, like more hegemonic, conservative anti-immigrant narratives, also often represented Central Americans as stereotypes of the guerrilla fighter, refugee, victim, and, in many cases, the heroic but dead revolutionary figure. Chicana/o solidarity narratives invoked the heroic strength of Salvadorans, Guatemalans, and Nicaraguans, yet filtered it through Chicana/o struggles, histories, and imaginaries. For example, Helena María Viramontes's undifferentiated Central American washerwoman in the story "The Cariboo Café" (1985) and Graciela Limón's Salvadoran domestic worker Luz Delcano in *In Search of Bernabé* (1993) were both cast in the light of Mesoamerican Llorona women. Both characters lose their sons to civil wars in Central America; both mourn the loss of their sons and people; both flee to the United States seeking refuge. In both texts, Chicana writers and subjects, however, are the true protagonists, for *they* expose the cause and plight of Central Americans through discursive acts of solidarity. These writers engage in what I have called the "solidarity of fiction" and the "fiction of solidarity." Cutting both ways, this literature, although clearly representing the plight of Central Americans during the civil wars in the 1980s and in its diasporic aftermath, foregrounds Chicana/o agencies, subjectivities, histories, and cultural mythologies (e.g., La Llorona and La Malinche, as opposed to La Siguanaba, La Segua, and Los Cadejos of Central American traditions).[20] In this solidarity fiction, Central Americans, I maintain, often recede into the historical backdrop, the emotional plot, and the personal drama of Chicana/o protagonists, while their histories are made subject to the telling of the larger narrative of Chicana/o protest, resistance, and resilience.

In works by Ana Castillo, Graciela Limón, Demetria Martínez, Helena María Viramontes, and others, Chicanas are often represented as protagonists harboring, transporting, assisting, and saving Central Americans, asserting thus their solidarity agency. For example, in Castillo's novel, *Sapogonia*, Pastora joins the new underground railroad movement and shepherds Central American refugees to safe houses in the U.S. Midwest and Canada. In Martínez's novel, *Mother Tongue*, the young Chicana Mary assists, houses, feeds, translates for, and attempts to heal the wounds of her Salvadoran refugee lover, José Luis—a tortured political asylum seeker who has fled the nightmare of his country into the safety of Mary's love and arms. In this Chicana solidarity novel, Mary best exemplifies the not so transparent yet discursively elaborated romantic fiction of solidarity that shaped the reception of El Salvador among North American sanctuary and solidarity workers in the 1980s.

On March 24, 1982, on the anniversary of the government-ordered assassination of Salvadoran Archbishop Oscar A. Romero, a number of congregations and churches across the United States "declared themselves sanctuaries for Central American refugees" (Coutin 1995, 552). These sanctuary workers (comprising many races and ethnicities) were moved to action, which they called humanitarian "civil initiative" (1995, 553), by the plight of Salvadorans fleeing state-sponsored violence in their country. Sanctuary workers joined forces to transport, host, and protect the refugees, whom the U.S. government refused to recognize as "refugees," despite the stipulations of the 1980 Refugee Act. In response, sanctuary workers, including the journalist Demetria Martínez who was working in Tucson at the time,[21] "began bringing Central Americans into the United States and sheltering them at various locations around the country" (1995, 553), reactivating through their actions a new underground movement. Under U.S. court orders, sanctuary workers would face surveillance, criminal charges, and, in some cases, convictions for "aiding and abetting" and "smuggling alien" Salvadoran refugees.

In "Smugglers or Samaritans in Tucson, Arizona," Coutin shows how discourses—legal, media, biblical, moral, human rights, testimonial, autobiographical, anecdotal—were strategically negotiated in the construction of "official truth" in the Central American Sanctuary Movement. U.S. government officials, the legal system, and sanctuary workers battled not only over the fate of Salvadoran political asylum seekers but also for American citizens' First Amendment rights to free speech, assembly, and civil disobedience, or "civil initiative." Moreover, Coutin examines how sanctuary workers, too, defined and constructed themselves discursively in a highly conflictive, repressive context. While she points out that "Sanctuary activists manipulated [legal] proceedings to define themselves as law-abiding" (1995, 550), I would like to discuss how Martínez's *Mother Tongue* gives insights into the *affective* self-construction of one fictional sanctuary worker, taking readers deep into what I call the "heart of kindness."

In a telling moment, Mary (a New Mexican Chicana new to Sanctuary work) reveals herself and her intentions in regard to José Luis:

> The feelings of his poetry engendered in me were like nothing I had experienced before. His words and those of the poets he admired made me want to sell my belongings, smuggle refugees across borders, protest government policies by chaining myself to the White House gate—romantic dreams, yes, but the kind that dwell side by side with resistance. (Martínez 1994, 69)

José Luis, who benefits from Mary's refugee idealization, recognizes that Mary "really loves the idea of me. A refugee, a dissident, spokesman for a cause she knows little about, ignorance she seems to have made peace with" (1994, 84). By loving him and loving the war out of him, she wants above all to *reinvent* him and make him forget the Salvadoran history that has violated and expelled him. As evinced by Mary and José Luis's relationship in the novel, Mary's act of solidarity is really an act of making fiction, that is, of (re)constructing the other and each other according to Sanctuary symbolic tropes and narratives (Lev. 19:33: "When a stranger sojourns with you in your land, you shall not do him wrong"; as quoted in Coutin 1995, 566). Mary houses the sojourner José Luis and attempts with all good intentions, kindness, and dedication to do him good. Perhaps less explicitly and consciously, she also uses José Luis's story vicariously to work out personal trauma. A victim of sexual abuse as a child, Mary has a need to heal her and others' wounds. She recovers the memory of her violation by an adult man only when José Luis, suffering from an episode of PTSD, hits her and forces her to remember her past injury. Mary has a heart of kindness willing to absorb another's pain, but, as Sontag reminds us in *Regarding the Pain of Others*, pain cannot be fully shared without the subject in pain being appropriated (consumed) by the other.

Warning against the potential of sympathy to appropriate the pain of others and to mask complicity in the production of other's pain and suffering, Sontag writes:

> So far as we feel sympathy, we feel we are not accomplices to what caused the suffering. Our sympathy proclaims our innocence as well as our impotence. To that extent, it can be (for all our good intentions) an impertinent—if not inappropriate—response. To set aside sympathy we extend to others beset by war and murderous politics for a reflection on how our privileges are located on the same map as their suffering, and may—in ways we might prefer not to imagine—be linked to their suffering, as the wealth of some may imply the destitution of others, is a task for which the painful, stirring images supply only an initial spark. (2003, 102–103)

In their act of solidarity, Mary and José Luis blur and cross the lines between empathy and appropriation, self and other, and subject and object, only to hurt one another once again. Ultimately, *Mother Tongue* shows that, although we may attempt to build communal ground or solidarity based on identifying with others' pain and injury, in the end we must recognize the limits of those forms of identification. The subject in pain must be allowed to tell her or his story and to exercise her or his agency, and we must permit that narrative to unravel even if it lies unpredictably outside of preset models. The act of solidarity begins in letting others produce their own narratives out of their pain, injury, and situations, an act that Mary is not capable of carrying through because of her sympathetic identification with José Luis. Hence, Mary drives José Luis away and is left alone to deal with her own pain.

Bringing Down the Walls:
Chicana Anti-Imperialist Novels of Solidarity

In their solidarity literature, Chicana writers such as Martínez, Castillo, and Villanueva indict the United States for its interventionist politics and policies in Central America in the twentieth century. The protagonist of *The Ultraviolet Sky*, for example, associates a brand of U.S. nativist patriotism with the war machine, which destroyed entire populations, tortured people, and dismembered pregnant women in Central America in the 1980s. The Chicana protagonist, pregnant herself during most of the novel, identifies with the women of Central America and expresses her frustration and anger with the destructive role the United States has played in the region (Villanueva 1988, 161). In Castillo's feminist critique, Sapogonia is cast as the contact/border zone where mestizo Latino/a Americans cross paths: "Sapogonia is a distinct place in the Americas where all mestizos reside, regardless of nationality, individual racial composition, or legal residential status—or, perhaps, because of all these" (1990, 5). According to Castillo, "The Sapogón is besieged by a history of slavery, genocide, immigration, and civil uprisings, all of which have left their marks on the genetic make-up of the generation following such periods as well as the border outline of its territory" (5). Sapogonia, hence, represents the Americas, which share a history of neocolonialism, imperialism, and alliances. It is the location of military action and resistances in Central America and other places undergoing civil crises (including the United States). In particular, the refugees of *Sapogonia* "risked their lives in hopes of improving their chances of survival, who separated themselves from family and homeland" (185). The Central American washerwoman in Viramontes's "The Cariboo Café," the housekeeper Rosario in Fernández's *Sleep of the Innocents* (1991), and the cleaning woman Luz Delcano in Limón's *In Search of Bernabé* join the ranks of Sapogón refugees in the United States.[22]

Although signs in Castillo's novel situate Sapogonia somewhere in the United States, where much of the plot unravels, the novel makes clear that there is also a Sapogonia in the South. Its referent is a country (in Central America) where there have been "civil wars over the centuries, over the decades" (Castillo 1990, 218), carried out in assassinations, disappearances, and displacements. In Sapogonia, "signs of the military were everywhere" (218). Pastora, the Chicana artist and singer of social protest music at solidarity events, becomes involved in an underground railroad sanctuary movement. She transports newly arrived Central American refugees from a clandestine safe house in Michigan to Chicago. Eventually she is apprehended by INS agents, tried for the crime of harboring illegal aliens, and imprisoned. Pastora pays the price for her solidarity work, much like Demetria Martínez did in the late 1980s, when she was arrested, tried, and later indicted for her work in the Sanctuary Movement. The text explains:

> [Pastora] had never brought any of the undocumented workers/refugees to her place, but because of her reputation of singing protest music and the public positions she took during her performances, she knew the federal government could very well be suspicious as to what degree she was willing to fight policies she objected to. (178)

When she is interrogated by INS agents, Pastora insists that "people from Sapogonia, like the refugees from other countries who were given political asylum, were here in search of refuge" (179). But to the INS agents, the would-be refugees were criminals, "murderers, in fact. They're wanted for killing American citizens in their country" (179). Anyone assisting the refugees was also considered a criminal.

In Martínez's solidarity romance, *Mother Tongue*, Mary, like Pastora, works in the underground solidarity movement and lives in fear of surveillance, detection, and criminalization. Through her godmother, who is highly critical of the role of the United States in Central America, Mary becomes involved not only with the Sanctuary Movement but also with her first sanctuary charge, the Salvadoran José Luis. Sympathizing with his personal/national history, she acts according to a politics of affinity and solidarity, whereby she presumably transcends the borders of class, nationality, and privilege granted to her by her U.S. citizenship. Indeed, as Coutin explains in *The Culture of Protest*, "Volunteers [in the Sanctuary Movement] defined solidarity as a relationship in which North Americans abandoned their privileged positions in order to support the struggles of Salvadoran and Guatemalan refugees" (1993, 184). Joining this struggle, Mary dedicates her days and limited income to giving refuge to José Luis in her apartment and to helping him heal his wounds. Still, Mary as a U.S.-born citizen may cross, straddle, and live on the border, while José Luis as an undocumented refugee is "disappeared" even within its confines, hiding behind a red bandana when he gives testimony of his experiences and in the refuge that Mary offers him.

Through the lens of sympathy, subjection, and solidarity, Mary transfers onto José Luis her own pain caused by past sexual violation and personal trauma, making her incapable of seeing him as anything but the tortured refugee from El Salvador. Fraught with cultural differences, linguistic miscommunications, and historical impasses, Mary and José Luis represent the (im)possibilities of solidarity as a level and equal field. As an American citizen, Mary finds herself, although not of her free will, complicit with the foreign politics, policies, and actions of the United States in Central America. Solidarity serves as a means to channel sympathy and empathy into action. Indeed, as Sontag explains, "Compassion is an unstable emotion. It needs to be translated into action, or it withers. The question is what to do with the feelings that have been aroused, the knowledge that has been communicated" (2003, 101).

For Mary and José Luis, the knowledge of the internal workings of the neocolonial and imperialist order that bring them together in their provisional contact/border zone proves to be their breaking point, as José Luis, in a posttraumatic disassociated state, confuses Mary for his torturer and injures her. The romance of solidarity proves thus to be less than ideal, and José Luis disappears once again to some clandestine place beyond Mary's reach, memory, and narrative plot. Through their broken relationship and narrative, solidarity is shown to be a fragile ideal, fraught with unsustainable contradictions and barriers. As José Luis flees Mary, the Latina/o family is divided once again.

In the course of the story, after José Luis's departure, Mary reflects on her loss and her gains, for she is pregnant with his child. The separation gives way to the writing of a text configuring *Mother Tongue* in which Mary attempts to tell José Luis's story to her son and to understand the greater geopolitical forces affecting their lives. Mary makes the following revelation:

> El Salvador is rising from the dead, but my folder of newspaper clippings tells the story of the years when union members disappeared and nuns were ordered off buses at gunpoint, a country with its hands tied behind its back, crying, *stop, stop*. These and a few journal entries are all I have left to fasten my story to reality. Everything else is remembering. Or dismembering. Either way, I am ready to go back. To create a man out of blanks that can never wound me. (Martínez 1994, 12; emphasis in original)

In an attempt to understand her relationship with José Luis, Mary confronts the imperialist and neocolonial history of the United States. His story and the story of El Salvador, however, become Mary's Chicana story. Symbolic reconciliation is found only at the end of the novel, when in a meta-reflexive act Mary writes, from her point of view, of her years of involvement in the Sanctuary Movement. In that narrative, José Luis is a central character that gives personal and national testimony: his story is the story of many Salvadorans in the 1980s. But when Mary retells his story, it is her Chicana subjectivity that gives shape to every part of the narrative. For Mary, "His was a face I'd seen in a dream. A face with no borders: Tibetan eyelids, Spanish hazel irises, Maya cheekbones dovetailing delicately as matchsticks. I don't know why I had expected Olmec" (2–3). From the start, Mary reconstructs José Luis from her hybrid borderland/borderless/cross-border gaze, and he resists that gaze all along, painfully asserting his subjective differences. Whose story, then, is *Mother Tongue*? For whom is it written? As in the case of the Sandinista reception of Portillo and Serrano's *Después del terremoto (After the Earthquake)*, how does the Salvadoran diaspora identify with this fiction of solidarity? Indeed, how could the story be told otherwise from other subjective positions?

In writing about her relationship with a Salvadoran refugee man, Mary sets out to write a solidarity fiction, only to discover the fiction of her own solidarity. José Luis, the subject of his revolutionary narrative, becomes the object of Mary's affection, as well as her story of compassion, empathy, and solidarity. The empathizer always requires an empathee for transference to take place. In solidarity, Mary appropriates José Luis's pain and attempts to fill the gaps of his incomplete story, but, in doing so, she exposes the limits, transgressions, and mishaps of solidarity. In her meta-fictional act, moreover, Mary exposes the unexplored limitations of solidarity narrative: Can the solidarity subject really tell the "inside" story of her or his community, whether the communities of solidarity and sanctuary workers or others?

The crisis of testimonial literature at the turn of the twentieth century reminds us that there can never be one singular representative voice but many voices in cacophony telling the many fractured sides of any narrative. Thus, *Mother Tongue* shows that torture survivors, political asylum seekers, and solidarity workers have only partial stories to tell. Which ones do we listen to, especially as U.S. Central Americans begin to tell their own stories and histories? In their literary interventions of the 1980s and '90s, Chicana/o writers such as Demetria Martínez, Ana Castillo, Gloria Anzaldúa, and Alejandro Murguía who were critical of

U.S. imperialism in Central America engaged in the production of solidarity fiction. These writers registered the deaths, displacements, and border crossings of Central Americans to the United States, thus bringing to the fore the effects of the crises in Central America and Central American diasporic communities. Their work (pre)cedes the telling of Central American stories by Central American–Americans, to whom I turn next.

In Their Own Words: Central Americans in the United States

In his chapter titled "Central American–Americans: Latino and Latin American Subjectivities" (in *Taking Their Word*), Arturo Arias uses the term "Central American–American" (originally coined by the spoken-word and visual artist Maya Chinchilla in her poem, "Central American American") to make visible Central American Latinidades in the United States. Arias argues:

> A Latino identity is often constructed through the abjection and erasure of the Central American-American. Members of this group are doubly marginalized and thereby invisiblized, to coin a neologism. For this population, already large and multiplying at a faster pace than most other so-called minorities within the United States, their invisible status, their nonrecognition, generates a sense of nonbelonging, of nonbeing, a cruel invisibility that was first imposed on them in their countries of origin and has carried over to these latitudes. (2007, 186)

In his discussion of the marginalization, excision, and occlusion of Central Americans from the cultural sphere of the Americas as a whole, Arias suggests that U.S. Central Americans must make themselves visible, as the increasing production of U.S. Central American texts attests. The state of U.S. Central American cultural production is such that writers, critics, and readers are not only actively producing texts and markets but also constructing new Latina/o identities, imaginaries, and narratives that might be more inclusive of Central Americans. To answer the question of whether there is a Central American literature, a question posed to Arias by a colleague, we can only point to the diverse and rich production of Central American and U.S. Central American texts examined in this book and others.

As we have seen, Central American cultural production in the United

States is not an entirely recent or stand-alone phenomenon but one built on historical collaborations, solidarity networks, and transnational dialogues established among artists, scholars, and activists. The last decades of the twentieth century were watershed years not only for Central American immigration but also for the production of texts by and about Central Americans in the United States. In the early twenty-first century, a growing corpus of Latino/a literature registers the presence of Central Americans in the United States. To date, a growing corpus of U.S. Central American–themed and authored literature includes Maya Chinchilla and Karina Oliva-Alvarado's poetry anthology, *Desde el Epicentro* (2007); Francisco Goldman's *The Art of Political Murder* (2007), *The Divine Husband* (2004), *The Ordinary Seaman* (1997), and *The Long Night of White Chickens* (1992); Mario Escobar's *Gritos interiores* (Interior Cries) (2005); Mario Bencastro's *Viaje a la tierra del abuelo* (A Promise to Keep) (2004), *Odyssey to the North* (1999), *A Shot in the Cathedral* (1996), and *The Tree of Life* (1997); Quique Avilés's *The Immigrant Museum* (2003); Leticia Hernández-Linares's *Razor Edges of My Tongue* (2002); Roberto Quesada's *Never through Miami* (2002) and *The Big Banana* (1999); Tanya María Barrientos's *Frontera Street* (2002); Marcos McPeek Villatoro's *HomeKillings: A Romilia Chacón Mystery* (2001), *Minos* (2003), *A Venom beneath the Skin* (2005), and *A Fire in the Earth* (1996); Héctor Tobar's *The Tattooed Soldier* (2000); Sandra Benítez's *The Weight of Things* (2000) and *Bitter Grounds* (1997); Cowy Kim et al.'s *Izote Vos* (2000); Manuel Olmos's *Caminantes de maíz* (Maize Walkers) (1998); Martivón Galindo's *Retazos* (1996); and Victor Perera's *Rites: A Guatemalan Boyhood* (1985).

U.S. Central American authors are bringing to the fore Central American identities, imaginaries, and bodies of knowledge from other subjective locations and engaging issues of their marginality along the coordinates of geopolitics, race, class, gender, sexuality, and migration, among other things. As Arias would have it, U.S. Central Americans are speaking out of their silence, disenfranchisement, violence, near-ethnogenocide, self-annihilation, and identicide (discussed in chapter 7), residual trauma, victimization, migrancy, and dislocation—all subjects that make U.S. Central American narratives distinct and recognizable rather than invisible. Thus, it is through textual narrative that a new configuration of the isthmus is once again brought into being in the cultural locations and "latitudes" that Arias alludes to.

In her poem "Solidarity Baby," Maya Chinchilla attempts to find and define a place for herself as a Central American–American born and raised in the 1980s and 1990s, amid Central American revolutions, solidarity movements, and immigration waves. She writes, "I'm just looking for my place / Am I a CENTRAL American? Si, pues, soy el epicentro" (2007, 19). Rather than blend into the homogenizing narrative of Latinos in the United States, without distinct antecedents, precedents, or makers of difference, Chinchilla asserts the centrality of her Central American heritage, even though she was born in the United States. As such, she assumes a cultural location (an epicenter) from which to claim her Central American and more specifically Guatemalan Latinidad, as I would claim my Salvadoran American Latinidad. The poem speaks to her particular Central American "solidarity baby" identifications, experiences, histories, heritages, and desires in mixed U.S. Central American idioms: "Si, pues, soy el epicentro [Sure, I'm the epicenter]." She situates herself in the culture of solidarity into which she was born as a "solidarity baby" whose parents took her to grassroots organizing meetings, marches, and demonstrations, whose house served as a "Central American Underground Railroad" for refugees and undocumented immigrants fleeing their homelands, and whose early childhood lessons included "the names of dictators and leaders . . . Somoza and Sandino? Rios Montt and Otto Rene Castillo? A-B-CIA-GIC-FMSLN-URGNG-UFW-XYZ" (19), and whose heroes included a "proud maya woman, mujer de maíz," giving testimony (19). She goes on to tell of her U.S.-bred struggles amid the Central American conflicts like "just trying to keep [her] head up" while the revolutions in Central America were aborted by U.S. conspiracies, covert operations, and overt interventions. Chinchilla speaks about having to "survive race riots in high school," being told by high school counselors that college "couldn't be done," yet persevering toward her "secret plans" to do it all in "documentary días, radio nights, printed palabras" (20). Finally, Chinchilla admits to her calling, given her Central American history of resistance and resilience: "Holding the door open for the little ones who are coming thru" and "Risking reporting truths untold" (20).

Part of a group of Central American–American writers, performers, poets, artists, and visionaries self-named "The Epicentros," Chinchilla shows us that U.S. Central Americans need not drop the identifications, histories, idioms, and practices that make them "Central Americans." Irene need not choose her Latina feminisms over her Nicaraguan ethnicity, as my willful (mis)reading of *After the Earthquake* (Portillo and Serrano 1979) shows. Instead, Chinchilla, a "solidarity baby," entreats Central American–Americans to claim, assume, and make visible what is central to their Latinidades. She ends her poem by encouraging U.S. Central Americans to rise out of their invisibility:

Unless we document ourselves we are invisible!
There is so much left to do.
I'm taking on telling the truth.
I'm just a revolutionary mama, solidarity, baby. (20)

In signing off her spoken-word poem as a "solidarity baby," Chinchilla recognizes solidarity as central to the construction of her Central American Latinidad and claims her place alongside other artists, writers, poets, and activists for whom "solidarity" is a constructive field of political, philosophical, moral, and cultural engagement.

New Endings and Beginnings

Since the 1980s, a U.S. Latino/a literature identified with Central American causes and issues has articulated an important critique of U.S. interventionism in Central America, cold war rhetoric and geopolitics, U.S. immigration policies, and the militarization of the U.S.-Mexico border, all of which were terribly imbricated in the 1980s but covered up by hegemonic political discourse.[23] A critique of U.S. imperialism in the isthmus informs and shapes the early solidarity work of artists such as Roberto Vargas, Alejandro Murguía, and Martivón Galindo who, in the 1980s, participated in artistic collectives in San Francisco, Washington, D.C., New York, Los Angeles, and other U.S. cities. In the 1990s, U.S. Latino/a writers such as María Helena Viramontes, Carole Fernández, Demetria Martínez, and Graciela Limón produced texts of solidarity identification, communication, cultural exchange, and political engagement as U.S. Latinos/as struggled to present a unified front in the United States of the Americas. At the same time, these writers positioned U.S. Latino/a literature within the larger debates of postcolonialism, transnationalism, globalization, cultural, subaltern, and diasporic studies and U.S. cultures of imperialism.

Moreover, U.S. Latino/a literature served as a forum for the discussion of the effects of massive immigration reforms such as the Immigration Reform and Control Act of 1986, the Immigration Reform and Immigrant Responsibility Act of 1996, and the USA Patriot Act of 2001, all of which have imposed stricter sanctions on Latino/a immigrants in the United States and increasingly supported the militarization of the U.S.-Mexico border. At the apex of U.S. interventionism in Central America and the militarization of the U.S.-Mexico border, many U.S. Latinas/os and Chicanas/os allied themselves with Central American causes, thus engaging in transnational solidarities and dialogue with Central Americans, as well as the production of texts concerned with Central America that crossed borders and exceeded the territorial isthmus. These textual solidarities and dialogues of the 1980s and 1990s not only made possible the production of Central American transnational cultural production but also made Central Americans less invisible in the United States.

CHAPTER 6

"Departamento 15":
Salvadoran Transnational Migration and Narration

The political, economic, and demographic crises in the isthmus during the 1980s and 1990s forced many Central Americans to relocate permanently throughout the Americas, Europe, Australia, Canada, and elsewhere. Many people never returned to the isthmus but became part of an expansive Central American diaspora. It is estimated that "between 1820 and 1993, over one million immigrants from Central America legally resettle[d] in the United States" (Pinderhughes, Córdova, and del Pinal 2002), without counting an even larger number of undocumented Central Americans who also made their way to the United States in those years.[1] Sarah Mahler predicts that in the future Central American "regional migration to certain poles of opportunity . . . will persist and evolve as a consequence of myriad factors including disparities in prosperity as well as political and environmental stability between countries" (2000). Regional economic, political, social, and environmental crises will continue to be determining factors in people's decisions to emigrate from the Central American isthmus and resettle in specific locations in the United States and elsewhere. This chapter focuses on Salvadoran transnational migration and cultural production in the Washington, D.C., metropolitan area, examining the construction of an expansive Salvadoran diasporic imaginary now configured across the world.

Coming to America: Salvadoran Transnational Migration

The history of Salvadoran transnational migration to the United States does not begin with the Salvadoran civil war in the 1980s but dates to the nineteenth century, when Salvadoran émigrés began to travel to U.S. industrial centers tied to agricultural production in Central America. In *The Salvadoran Americans* (2005), Carlos Córdova identifies at least six waves of Salvadoran migration to the United States (2005, 60–68). First, in the late nineteenth century, members of the Central American elite classes, political dissidents, workers in transnational companies (fruit, coffee, railroads, and the Panama Canal), and others resettled in port cities such as San Francisco, New Orleans, and New York (Córdova 2005, 60–62; see also Pinderhughes, Córdova, and del Pinal 2002). Coffee-processing plants owned by MJB, Hills Brothers, and Folgers in San Francisco attracted émigrés already linked to the international coffee industry. In the 1930s and 1940s, a second wave of Central American immigrants included "men and women from the urban middle and upper classes who had relatively high levels of education—intellectuals, teachers, labor organizers, political dissidents, and exiled military officers who were not in agreement with their national governments," as well as others who were part of the dominant class, yet sought their luck elsewhere (Córdova 2005, 61–62; see also Pinderhughes, Córdova, and del Pinal 2002). In the 1940s, in the midst of a third migration wave, many found work in local "shipyards and other industries suffering from shortage of laborers," which was especially acute during World War II (Córdova 1987, 22). Along gendered lines of labor division, Central American women migrants began to work in textile factories and men in construction and shipping (Córdova 2005, 62). At the end of the war, with the return of U.S. GIs, some Central Americans also returned to their countries, leaving behind family and other social networks that would assist future migrants and build ties with other Latino ethnic groups (63). It was to these social networks that the fourth Central American migration wave of the 1960s and 1970s gravitated.

With the political crises and civil wars intensifying in Central America in the late 1970s and 1980s, a fifth wave of refugees and exiles arrived in the United States, where they were for the most part denied political asylum and documented status due to U.S. economic, military, and ideological support of right-wing governments (see chapter 5). It is estimated that half of the Central American population currently living in the United States arrived as of the 1980s. Many immigrants who came to the United States as of the 1980s remained undocumented or were granted TPS, or Temporary Protected Status, which gave renewable temporary stay permits for immigrants fleeing economic, political, and environmental crises in Central America.

By the late 1990s, over 800,000 Salvadorans were living in Los Angeles alone; more than 400,000 lived in the San Francisco Bay Area; and 150,000 Salvadorans lived in the Washington, D.C., metropolitan area.[2] In 2006, the total population of El Salvador, a country of barely 21,000 square kilometers, was estimated at approximately six million. Comprising almost three million Salvadorans living across the world, the Salvadoran diaspora represents a great economic resource for El Salvador. The Alianza Republicana Nacionalista (ARENA; Nationalist Republican Alliance) government of El Salvador has recognized the Salvadoran diaspora as the country's most valuable commodity (PNUD 2005). The Salvadoran government, business sector, and various interested parties have begun "to cultivate ties with their expatriates and to advocate on their behalf with politicians in the North" (Mahler 2000). In March 2001, following a round of deadly earthquakes in El Salvador, former President Francisco Flores, for example, called on the Salvadoran immigrant community to come to the aid of their country. He and his cabinet members personally visited Washington, D.C., and other cities to seek emergency relief assistance from the U.S. Congress, to petition for an extension of TPS for undocumented Salvadorans, and to meet with leaders of Salvadoran grassroots organizations. In one of his speeches quoted in the *Washington Post*, Flores explained "that if 100,000 Salvadorans legalize their immigration status, they could produce an additional $300 million a year in remittances to their families. Already, Salvadorans send home $1.7 billion annually" (Murphy 2001, A8).

To the sum of billions of dollars in remittances, the Salvadoran state is invested in Salvadorans gaining permanent and legal immigrant status in the United States and remaining loyal cultural if not voting political citizens of El Salvador. Salvadoran government agencies, finance organizations, media corporations, and operators of transnational markets cater to Salvadoran communities abroad, which, in addition to sending remittances, are also potential investors in the country. Salvadoran immigrants often travel to El Salvador as tourists and send remittances to their relatives, which represents a consumer market that may have influence over U.S. policy making in the isthmus. Like other transnational migrants, Salvadorans maintain strong material, affective, and symbolic connections to their homeland and produce significant social networks, cultures, and identities in their new homes. Mahler (2000) argues that as of the 1990s, Salvadoran "migrants began to conduct their lives across borders or 'transnationally'": "People, who travel back and forth or at least maintain close contact with family and friends in two or more nations through phone calls, letters and even the Internet, serve to knit together both individuals and nations in ways that have only begun to be explored" (2000).

In his studies of the Haitian diaspora, Michel S. Laguerre (1998) corroborates Mahler's account of transnational migration. He explains that key features of transnational migration include migrants' attachment to the homeland, in whose affairs they continue to be active and with which they claim some political affiliation and degrees of personal identification. The connection of transnational migrants to their homeland, he writes,

> is made possible by a constant flow of border-crossing people through international migration, with the availability of cheap and fast air travel, information technology (telephone, fax, e-mail, radio and video cassettes) and transnational financial circuits, including money wiring and fast-courier operations; all these sustain the diaspora-homeland web of relationships. (Laguerre 1998, 177)

Recalling Haiti's "extra-territorial Tenth Department" (Laguerre 1998), media experts in El Salvador have invented the term "Departamento 15" (after the fourteen political departments or provinces in El Salvador) to identify the totality of Salvadoran transnational communities residing across the world.[3] The more familiar and colloquial term—*los hermanos lejanos* (the distant relatives)—is also used in El Salvador to refer to an emigrant population of almost three million. Transnational Salvadoran cultures are an aggregate of various immigrant waves, generations, and identities, ranging from most recent arrivals to long-standing communities in major cities and locations across the world.

Transnational Economic and Cultural Remittances

The Salvadoran national government, media, and banking systems are cognizant of the economic, political, and social significance of Salvadoran transnational migrants, who, besides generating remittances and assisting their country in other ways, are willing international investors. Regularly traveling to El Salvador as national tourists, Salvadoran immigrants buy property and spend large sums of money there, contributing capital to a consumer market that caters to their nostalgic desires and tastes. In turn, the Salvadoran state, the financial sector, and other vested parties attempt to do "outreach" to immigrants still tied to the country by familial obligation and affective ties. These entities strategically turn to the transnational culture industry—the homeland image-making and nostalgia-tugging machine—to promote ties with diasporic communities through the marketing of Salvadoran food, music, literature, newspapers, and other cultural products abroad. Factory-made and imported frozen *pupusas* (the trademark Salvadoran corn tortillas stuffed with cheese, beans, and/or pork) are now a staple in every city where Salvadorans reside. In Langley Park, Maryland, Latino grocery stores carry *garrobo* (an iguana-like reptile) for the Salvadoran palate, while Pollo Campero inaugurated its first franchise in the state on November 22, 2004, after opening in the same year two restaurants in Bailey's Crossroads and Herndon, Virginia. In its first six weeks, the Bailey's Crossroads site made over $1 million in sales (Redacción, *El Tiempo Latino* 2004, B4). In addition, every Saturday morning throughout the D.C. area the El Salvador–focused television program, *Orgullosamente Salvadoreño*, airs images of Salvadoran tourist spots, events, festivals, musical acts, folkloric traditions, and food, thus projecting images, messages, and values from the homeland.

By transforming immigrants into distant relatives (*los hermanos lejanos*)—always tuned in to the latest developments in the country, always concerned about the crises back home, always desiring a taste of the homeland—media experts and politicians in El Salvador have duly capitalized on the personal struggles of Salvadoran immigrants (A. Rodríguez 2000). They have used immigrants' stories as publicity narratives to represent immigration as a source of hope, survival, and opportunities outside the purview of the state. Read in this light, immigrants also represent a valuable commodity in the symbolic economy of El Salvador, not only because they produce remittances, but also because they generate crucial immigrant narratives that circulate among potential migrants, who, in turn, become new sources of capital for El Salvador (Zilberg 1997; Baker-Cristales 2004). The transnational movement of human capital is fueled thus by the hard-pressed stories of migration of *los hermanos lejanos*, who have been mythologized in monuments, songs, and other public displays. Beth Baker-Cristales (2004) discusses at length the debates regarding the construction of the monument "El hermano lejano" in San Salvador in 1994 and the subsequent attempt to rename it in 2002. According to Baker-Cristales, "the monument was meant to encapsulate and to render in a public fashion the government's attitude toward Salvadorans living abroad—you are part of the national family, yet different" (2004, 99). At all levels, the notion and image of the *hermano lejano* are inflected by extranational location, immigrant class status, and gender stratification: "migrants as males, reinforcing notions of the male as breadwinner, the male as adventurer, the male as the architect of the national imaginary" (99). Thus, Baker-Cristales analyzes the production of a highly gendered "homeland nationalism" that in the case of Salvadoran immigrants reinforces exclusive national affiliations with El Salvador and with others of the Salvadoran diaspora at large (125–132).[4] (Salvadoran women are rarely recognized in this national mythology, although they are central to the narrative of Salvadoran transnational migration.) It is the immigrant stories of *los hermanos lejanos*, regularly transmitted through letters, phone calls, electronic communications, media (newspaper, TV, radio, film, video), music, literature, and other print and nonprint materials, that support the imaginary of Departamento 15.

The immigrant narratives of Departamento 15, however ambivalent, are used to justify migration patterns, to present migration as a viable economic valve, and to release the state from systemically addressing the economic needs of a great majority of Salvadoran nationals, many of whom are forced into migration. The mythology of *los hermanos lejanos*, however, often masks the socioeconomic inequities that produce emigration from Central America, as well as the contradictions of life on the transnational divide. Roland Barthes, in *Mythologies* (1975), examines the ways in which cultural narratives and mass media products such as magazines both naturalize and neutralize unequal socioeconomic relations in bourgeois consumer culture. He identifies these not so transparent narratives as mythologies. The mythology of *los hermanos lejanos*, promoted by the media, the financial sector, the Salvadoran government, and the transmigrants themselves tends to highlight the success-despite-hard-luck stories of immigration while obfuscating the less than noble financial interest in Departamento 15 on the part of Salvadoran transnational actors (Robinson 2003, 270–277). This mythology, moreover, glosses over the fact that the Salvadoran government values the diaspora for its economic and political force in the United States (PNUD 2005).

As Benedict Anderson (1998) has suggested for the nation-building projects of nineteenth-century Europe, national identity is a discursive and imaginary production, mediated by print culture such as newspapers, journals, and literature. Given the new technologies of the twenty-first century, imagined communities are solidified not only by the print materials that Anderson analyzes but also by transnational television, film, radio, musical recordings, Internet, and other new (and not so new) media.[5] In creating the image of *los hermanos lejanos* and promoting the idea of Departamento 15, the Salvadoran and Latino transnational media have played a significant role in reconstructing the image of El Salvador in a postwar era, often in compliance with the agendas of the Salvadoran government and transnational financial agencies. A case in point is *La Prensa Gráfica*'s daily section, "Departamento 15," which appears in print form and on the newspaper's Web site.

Focusing exclusively on the Salvadoran diaspora, "Departamento 15" features human interest stories on Salvadorans living abroad, announcements of events, services and products catering to Salvadoran interests and needs, news reports on El Salvador, and e-mails and editorials from Salvadorans around the world seeking to reconnect with their homeland. On February 13, 2003, for example, one immigrant wrote from Houston, Texas, looking for her father, whom she had not seen since childhood; another wrote from Rogers, Arkansas, searching for his sisters in

"Departamento 15." Courtesy of La Prensa Gráfica.

Santa Ana, El Salvador; and still another wrote from Querétaro, Mexico, hoping to contact a "linda salvadoreña" (a pretty Salvadoran) whom he had met once in Mexico.[6] Activities advertised on the Web site for that same day included a presentation on "Viviendas para el Pueblo" in Falls Church, Virginia; the screening of the film *1932, cicatriz de la memoria* (1932, Scars of Memory) (dirs. Consalvi and Gould) at the Latin American Film Festival in New York City, and the "la reina infantil" (the child beauty queen) contest sponsored by La Asociación de Salvadoreños en Illinois (ASI) in Chicago. The feature article for February 13, 2003, focused on Arlington, Virginia's elected county board member, Walter Tejada, a Salvadoran immigrant who came to the United States at the age of thirteen and worked as a business consultant and aide to Virginia congressman Jim Moran. The leading democratic candidate for the Arlington County Board in the elections of March 11, 2003, Tejada won with a vote of 11,801 to 9,787, becoming the first Salvadoran to be elected to public office in Virginia. On a regular basis, "Departamento 15" provides updates on the demographics of the Salvadoran diaspora, as well as information on remittances, laws, visas, grassroots organizations, and other news bites. Through the virtual screen and the printed page, *La Prensa Gráfica* has partly shaped the transnational image and discourse of Departamento 15 and promoted the notion of a transnational imagined community linking Salvadorans in and outside the country. Today, "Departamento 15" is a familiar term in and outside El Salvador, while in cyberspace it has various Web sites both affiliated and not with *La Prensa Gráfica*, such as one that claims to be "el departamento virtual de los Salvadoreños alrededor del mundo [the virtual department of Salvadorans around the world]."[7] In what follows, I examine cultural texts produced by what I call the cultural artisans of Departamento 15 in Washington, D.C., many of whom challenge the mythologized status of *los hermanos lejanos* while representing the tensions and contradictions of transnational life in the United States.

Cultural Landscaping: Distant Relatives, Pupusas, and the Transformation of Washington, D.C.

Central American migration to Washington, D.C., dates to the late nineteenth century, when government business brought diplomatic émigrés and sojourners to the U.S. capital. By the early twentieth century, embassy personnel began to settle in the District of Columbia, "near present-day Adams Morgan and Mt. Pleasant" (Cadaval 1998, 56). The bulk of Central American immigrants, however, came to Washington during the height of the civil wars in the isthmus in the 1980s (Ferris 1987, 121; Repak 1995; Cadaval 1998), as refugee centers and solidarity networks opened offices in the accessible locations to which newly arrived immigrants gravitated. David E. Pedersen (1995) explains that robust job markets in the Washington, D.C., metropolitan area, including the ever-expanding U.S. military industrial complex, attracted to the region a number of high-tech industries engaged in research and development, telecommunications, transportation, defense, and international finance, as well as legal, governmental, and diplomatic services. After September 11, 2001, Homeland Security activities and industries also created new jobs for many directly or peripherally attached to this sector. Entwined and offshoot industries continued to generate employment for a "growing population of young attorneys, high-tech engineers, architects, and bureaucrats," which, in turn, require services such as "landscaping, construction and service work" (Pedersen 1995, 428–431), as well as housekeeping and child care (Repak 1995). Local African American, Latino, and immigrant communities have historically supplied laborers for these job markets in the region.

In *Waiting on Washington* (1995), Terry A. Repak explains that diplomats, government employees, and international agency personnel sponsored Central American, especially Salvadoran, female domestic workers and child care providers. It is these women who "pioneered the migration in the 1960s and 1970s" to the Washington, D.C., metropolitan area (2), although the construction, hospitality, and service industries soon opened new jobs for immigrant men and women in the 1980s and 1990s (59–60). Focusing on gender-based migration, labor recruitment, and social networks, Repak further describes the establishment of a primarily Salvadoran enclave in the Latino neighborhoods of Mount Pleasant and Columbia Heights. In the 1970s and 1980s, somewhat affordable housing, immigrant service agencies, and the relatively easy commute to jobs in the District of Columbia and the nearby suburbs in Maryland and Virginia drew still more Salvadorans to the Adams Morgan and Mount Pleasant area. Newly arrived immigrants often moved into already economically depressed and racially stratified neighborhoods, consequently exacerbating tensions that culminated in 1991 with the so-called Salvadoran-led Mount Pleasant Riots (Jennings and Lusane 1994; Council of Latino Agencies 2002). In the 1990s, throughout the metropolitan area, the Salvadoran population increased steadily,[8] manifesting its presence in neighborhoods, businesses, churches, community centers, public clinics, service providers, and even an annual Latino festival (Repak 1995, 61–71; Cadaval 1998) and producing the local imaginary of *los hermanos lejanos*.

In El Salvador, in addition to the monument mentioned above, *los hermanos lejanos* are honored with an eponymous song produced and performed by the internationally known orchestra Los Hermanos Flores on their CD, *Super Fiesta 99* (1998). In the song, the narrator, an immigrant Salvadoran, reminisces about his "beautiful land, while dying of sadness and loneliness . . . yearning for the warmth of his parents [and] . . . hoping to overcome the distance in order to work for those he left behind" (my translation). The song hits the nostalgic chord of Salvadoran immigrants, who regularly consume products such as the famous pupusa, perhaps one of the most reproduced symbols of Salvadoran cultural identity in and outside El Salvador. It is no coincidence, then, that on the same *Super Fiesta 99* CD, Los Hermanos Flores sing the praise of the "Pupusas de Olocuilta"—"the delicious rice pupusas of El Salvador"— as invoked by the refrain of the song. Located along the highway leading to and from the Comalapa International Airport, Olocuilta serves as a pupusa pit stop for many transnational immigrant tourists.

In recent years throughout the greater Washington, D.C., metropolitan area, pupusas have become a news item, and local news broadcasts have reported that Salvadoran pupusas are quickly becoming a favorite fast food among Washingtonians. The pupusa is a postcolonial product of transculturation integrating the ingredients of the New and Old Worlds in one corn shell and signifying Salvadoran mestizo identity. While corn has been the dietary staple of the Mesoamerican corn-based peoples, European conquistadors introduced dairy products and pork to the Americas, producing the *pupusa mestiza*, which has traveled to the United States with Salvadoran immigrants and market forces. Pupusa eateries not only feed a new American ethnic craving but also service the nostalgic market of Salvadoran immigrants seeking to consume home goods and purchase a little cultural memory. Businesses such as international couriers, financial organizations, telephone services, and exporters of goods have been quick to respond to the appetites, desires, and consumption needs of nostalgic immigrants. In Mahler's words, "Transnational businesses thrive off of meeting the needs and desires of a migrant clientele, often aided by Central American governments who have also become transnational actors" (2000).

Latino-owned and run stores in U.S. cities regularly sell imported Salvadoran products such as red beans, *masa harina* (corn flour for tortillas), *horchata* (a rice-based drink), *queso y crema* (cheese and cream), and other specialty items that appeal to Salvadoran nostalgia and nationalism while producing immigrant capital for El Salvador. A 2002 article in the business section of *La Prensa Gráfica* reported on the initial export and marketing of "loroco" in the United States. According to the article, "loroco," a flavorful wild plant used as an ingredient in pupusas that is inexpensive to grow and requires little labor may be sold for local and international consumption, making it a viable export crop and a nontraditional product of high commercial value (Redacción de Departamentos 2000, 41). In 1999, ten thousand kilograms of Salvadoran loroco were shipped in paste form to the United States, yielding about $50,000 in profit. The article suggests that the demand for loroco will increase as the number of Salvadoran immigrant consumers increases in the United States.

Along the same lines, a Salvadoran-based company named La Casa de las Pupusas, run by a married entrepreneurial couple in El Salvador, put the pupusa on the international market and on the Internet.[9] In the early phases of marketing frozen pupusas for international export, Sidney and Denia de Masey developed a process for freezing, patented their invention, and invested in a factory with the capacity to produce twenty-five thousand pupusas in an eight-hour shift (Inglés 2000, 32). The de Maseys, one an industrial engineer and the other a specialist in nutrition and corn technologies, conducted market research and were convinced of the market niche for their product in Salvadoran communities. The most "typical" Salvadoran foods can be found in the frozen food section of Latino grocery stores throughout the metropolitan area. As Denia de Masey claimed, there are *"hermanos lejanos* in Washington, New York, and Miami interested in selling pupusas to the Salvadoran community" (Inglés 2000, 32; my translation). De Masey assured the public that her pupusas were made with the best local ingredients ("el quesillo, la masa, los frijoles o el chicharrón"), in a hygienic and controlled environment, combining traditional cooking techniques with high technology. Aware that she was selling *sabor salvadoreño* (a taste of El Salvador), de Masey capitalized on the affective signification of her pupusas, which are stuffed with the nostalgia and desire for authenticity and local color of the homeland. (The logo of de Masey's company is a smiling pupusa.) At the time of her interview with *La Prensa Gráfica*, de Masey was launching the production of Salvadoran frozen tamales and contemplating the production of other Salvadoran delicacies such as "pasteles de carne, de vegetales y las empanadas."

The popularity of pupusas and the rise in Salvadoran-run restaurants (*pupuserías*) in the area suggest that Salvadorans are not only becoming more visible in the nation's demographics and labor force but also transforming social and cultural space and contributing to the economy of the region. Cultural products such as Salvadoran-identified music, art, and print material are also making their way into the public sphere in geographic sites that have a sizable Central American population. The 2000 U.S. Census results showed that Prince George's County in Maryland is home to the second largest number of Latinos (57,000), after Montgomery County (100,600) (Aizenman 2001, T8). In an interview published in the *Washington Post*, William Stagg, director of the Prince George's Hispanic Resource Center, stated that "he has seen many grocery stores, restaurants, construction companies, and janitorial and landscaping services open up, catering mostly to the Spanish-speaking community" (Goo 2001b, T5).

As Salvadoran immigrants and businesses stake their claims in areas such as Prince George's County, the signs of Salvadoran cultures become even more visible. Salvadoran images, motifs, and cultures are projected in various public arenas through multimedia arts such as murals in the Mount Pleasant and Columbia Heights areas of northwest Washington, D.C. Latino festivals and Hispanic Heritage Month events now extend beyond the District of Columbia: Langley Park celebrates an annual Langley Park Day, organized by a coalition of residents, activists, business owners, and University of Maryland students. In a growing U.S. Salvadoran production of novels, poems, *testimonios*, music, visual pieces, and performance art, *los hermanos lejanos* are actively producing hybrid cultural spaces amid wider transnational market forces intersecting in the metropolitan area.

The Hispanic Belt: "Wachintonian" Salvadorans

For years, the Latino population in Washington, D.C., has been increasing steadily, "from 7,370 in 1990 to 12,732 in 2000" (Fernández 2001, T3). In 2000, the U.S. Census reported that out of more than 400,000 Latinos living in the Washington, D.C., metropolitan area, 45,000 people reside in the District itself, with more than a quarter of them concentrated in the Mount Pleasant and Columbia Heights area. Straddling both sides of the Sixteenth Street northwest corridor, the Columbia Heights and Mount Pleasant area lies "between the city's largely white neighborhood to the west and largely black neighborhood to the east" (Cohn and Fernández 2001, A1). A border space of sorts, the Columbia Heights and Mount Pleasant area enfolds apartment complexes, houses, businesses, restaurants, shops, offices, clinics, schools, and centers, where Spanish with a Salvadoran accent is spoken and diverse Latino cultural practices are commonplace.

While scholars of social and discursive space might see in this D.C. contact zone the construction of vibrant, multidimensional Latino communities and others would applaud the neighborhood's reclaiming of space and cultural citizenship rights for Latinos (Flores and Benmayor 1997; Davis 2000; Valle and Torres 2000; Villa 2000), more conservative observers of the city detect the creation of a segregated enclave, or "a belt of Hispanics," as reported by the media (Cohen and Cohn 2001, A1). Indeed, a *Washington Post* article claimed that "for Hispanics, increasing segregation is largely related to a huge influx of immigrants in segregated neighborhoods, where it is often possible to get through the day without speaking English" (Cohen and Cohn 2001, A1). The article neglects to mention that the area has historically provided somewhat affordable housing, formal and informal social networks and services, and a sense of place and community for many groups, not just Latinos, whose paths intersect daily in one of the most multiethnic neighborhoods of the District. By 2005, however, this area was undergoing massive gentrification. This Hispanic belt, or cross-section of Washington, D.C., is still home to more than 12,000 Latinos (Fernández 2001, T3), whose experiences often run counter to the media-created mythology of *los hermanos lejanos*. A feature article titled "Breaking Through," in the local magazine *Washingtonian,* for example, described the lives of Central American and Salvadoran families in the Mount Pleasant and Columbia Heights neighborhoods (Foster 2001, 76–84, 108–109). One young Salvadoran, José Rosales, summed up the experience of his peers, "And it's frustrating because I work so hard" (78), in a community where Latino adults earn on average less than $20,000 annually (80). As Foster puts it, "But if life in El Salvador was a struggle, their life here proved even more tumultuous" (78). Demythologizing the image of the *hermanos lejanos* (those who make it, although barely, in the Mount Pleasant area), the mother of one youth says, "'I hate the phrase that people use, *el sueño americano*, the American dream. . . . To hear it makes me cringe. For us, it has been the American nightmare'" (80).

Counternarratives: Quique Avilés Is in the House

The Salvadoran-born poet, performance artist, and community activist Quique Avilés immigrated to Washington, D.C., as a child and grew up in Mount Pleasant during the critical years of civil unrest in El Salvador and Washington, D.C. In the late 1980s, Avilés cofounded and directed the theatre collective LatiNegro, which recruited local Latino and African American youths to perform in theatres, schools, prisons, universities, and communities (Avilés 2003). In 1999, he cofounded Sol & Soul, a nonprofit arts organization, which continues the work of LatiNegro in conducting workshops with young performers in the District of Columbia, collaborating with community groups, and organizing theater events in the District for local and visiting artists. Avilés continues to perform his mixed-media work on- and offstage and to be active in community-based projects. His performance pieces and poetry often incorporate ethnographic accounts of immigrants and everyday folks from the local neighborhoods of Washington, D.C.

In his poem titled "Barrio" (1999), Avilés alludes to the unspoken struggles of Latinos in the District. He tells of his attempt to find the words and the poetic form to describe life in the neighborhood. Avilés grapples with the spoken word, "Trying to write things / without naming names / not pointing the finger / not saying what the throat wants to / say / in these arrogant times / in this arrogant place." This "arrogant place" is, of course, the nation's capital, where foreign and domestic policies are unequivocally made, where the city and its monuments obfuscate the inequities experienced by many of its residents, and where Latinos—especially Salvadorans—have little political representation and voice. Avilés highlights the contradictions of life in the nation's capital. He begins almost every stanza of the poem with the line, "trying to write things," as if representing the impossibility of language, or perhaps, more precisely of the English language, to translate the anguish, sadness, suffering, and life experiences of many Latino residents in D.C.

Indeed, Avilés grapples with the anxiety of "trying to write about things that do / not belong in poems," as in "this air that / hangs around the place / whistling / chewing time / blowing bubbles." Mount Pleasant is that place of "drunken days / of 'here's some money mama' / of 'we're out of beers' / of 'you all take care.'" Without the precise words to express the sensibilities of Mount Pleasant and its people, Avilés attempts "to say it right / to put it down," producing in the end a poem that says nothing concrete about his neighborhood but which expresses the weight of life anchored in linguistic and economic barriers. In the end, Avilés's poem expresses the unstated needs and the underestimated sensibilities of everyday folks who want to say "we want attention / . . . we'd like some honesty." Through the dialogic spaces and colloquialisms of the poem seep the neglected voices of Mount Pleasant and Columbia Heights, the unheeded protests of D.C.'s Departamento 15, where old occupants meet new (im)migrants, creating "this place of slanted eyes / corn rows / this place of last call ripe avocados." Avilés ventures thus into the tenuous in-between, in-flux crevices of Departamento 15, where identities are produced out of transcultural materials and transnational social practices.

In his poems published in *Paper, Fabric, String and Poetry* (1999) and his anthology, *The Immigrant Museum* (2003), Avilés distances himself from essentialist notions of Salvadoran national identity. In one poem he insists that his "tongue is divided into two" (1999) by his diasporic condition and explores his transplanted and expanded Salvadoran identity. In another poem, "El Salvador at a Glance" (1999), he (re)turns to the country that he left as a child, producing for his readers a lesson in cultural geography, from his side of Departamento 15. The poem begins with a stanza that reads like a country profile, listing the major anecdotal features by which El Salvador is best known:

Area: the size of Massachusetts
Population: Not much left
Language: War, blood, broken English, Spanish
Customs: Survival, dances, birthdays, parties, funerals
Major Exports: Coffee, sugar, city builders, busboys, waiters, poets

Parodying the discourse of statistical analysis and quantitative data collection that converts countries and communities into numbers, Avilés's portrait privileges an insider's anecdotal knowledge of the country. This insider knows, for example, that labor migrants are indeed the country's main export. The poem highlights the fact that despite recent war and massive migrations, Salvadorans resourcefully reterritorialize and reconstruct themselves across sites of their diaspora:

El Salvador's major cities:
San Salvador
San Miguel
Los Angeles
Wachinton, D.C.

In reconceptualizing the Salvadoran nation across these transnational and translocal sites where migrants have relocated, Avilés makes San Salvador (the originating source of the nation) just another translocation, or permutation of the Salvadoran extended transnational community. Writing from the perspective of a Salvadoreño in "Wachinton," Avilés's diasporic subject speaks ambivalently without a trace of nostalgia or sentimentality about his displaced condition. The persona of the poem testifies "that pain has the ability to / travel," for s/he has endured "that pain [that] does not know / how to pose for a green card picture." There is no room for nostalgia in Avilés's poems of immigrant life in Washington, D.C.

Avilés's lyric profile of El Salvador hence is as much about the country he left behind ("the belly button of the world") as it is about its transmigrants—the busboys, waiters, and poets who have been expelled from the nation. Attempting to understand his homeland from a physical and cultural distance, the persona screens El Salvador through a series of questions: "El Salvador / there are questions in the air about your / character / they say you've dared to do the impossible / you've challenged the tiger to a wrestling / match / you've decided that bullets hold / the answers." El Salvador unsettles the narrator with questions that cannot be dismissed: "El Salvador / little question mark . . . little question mark that begins to itch." In the end, the poem provides a meta-reflection on Salvadoran transnational identity: "El Salvador in Washington / little question mark / little east of the border / migrant earthquake / wet back volcano / banana eating / tortilla making / mustache holder / funny dressing." Here, Avilés alludes to Roque Dalton's "Poema de amor" (1974/2000), in which the Salvadoran revolutionary poet enumerates the efforts of Salvadoran labor migrants ("los eternos indocumentados, los hacelotodo, los vendelotodo, los comelotodo [the eternally undocumented, the do-everything, the sell-everything, the eat-anything]"), from those who participated in the building of the Panama Canal to those who continue to cross multiple borders to work in the United States. While Dalton in his poem reclaims the Salvadoran spirit to do everything, Avilés, in "El Salvador at a Glance," calls attention to labor migrants in Washington, D.C., and speaks from the subjective space of transnational migration, "in the strangest cities / under the strangest circumstances." At the end of the poem, the diasporic subject claims to be "forever happy / forever sad / forever wachintonian salvadorean," remaining forever ambivalent about his own displacement (Bhabha 1990b, 1994). Avilés's "El Salvador at a Glance" thus provides a lyrical meta-reflection on the reconstruction of Salvadoran identities in sites where Salvadorans have resettled.

From this vantage point, Avilés surveys his respective Salvadoran city in the United States. "El Salvador at a Glance" represents the diasporic experiences of *los hermanos lejanos* across the United States and the world. Such narratives textually reproduce the locally inflected cultural imaginary of Departamento 15, drawing from Salvadoran popular idioms, legends, and folklore to express the relocations of Salvadoran culture. Read as narratives of transnational migration, Avilés's texts are empowering, hybrid narratives that challenge the mythology of *los hermanos lejanos* by gendering, racializing, localizing, and recasting Salvadoran migrants in the context of Washington, D.C.

Mario Bencastro's Transnational *Cuentos de Camino*

In his novel *Odyssey to the North* (1998), Mario Bencastro tells yet another story of the migration of Salvadorans to the greater Washington, D.C., metropolitan area. In an appropriation of the travel narrative, which has traditionally been the domain of European and U.S. adventurers in Latin America (à la Alexander von Humboldt and John L. Stephens),[10] Bencastro follows a few characters on their border-crossing journey to the United States through El Salvador, Guatemala, and Mexico. The novel presents a meta-reflection on the Salvadoran diaspora, as it purports to focus on the

> countless dramatic stories of the great Latin American exodus, the stories of millions of human beings who were fleeing from the misery and violence of their countries, in search for the promised land. Each traveler left a drop of suffering etched on the floor of that labyrinth as a living testimony of the painful odyssey toward the vast lands of the North. (Bencastro 1998, 87)

The novel recounts the journey of Calixto and his fellow migrants as they escape death in El Salvador. In their trajectory, they contract border smugglers, who lead them to the north; cross multiple hazardous borders through Guatemala, Mexico, and the United States; face many dangers along the way; and, on arriving in the United States, constantly risk their lives at home and at work and in the streets. The obvious trope of the odyssey makes clear that, like Ulysses in Homer's *Iliad*, Calixto and his fellow migrants must endure many trials before completing their perilous journey. The journey is a metaphor for self-exploration and the reconstruction of identities in an era of diaspora. Many of the characters are destined never to return to El Salvador; if they were to do so, they would meet certain death at the hands of the death squads. Still, even fewer migrants will find a home in exile.

Calixto's personal odyssey begins in El Salvador, where he is accused of being "an enemy of the government" (11). The death squads search for him at his house, and he is forced to flee. Some of Calixto's travel companions make it through El Salvador only to be taken by the Guatemalan or Mexican "Migra" (immigration authorities); some of the women are raped; some migrants are left for dead in the Arizona desert; some are captured and held in detention centers; and some are deported to El Salvador, only to be later found dead. Those who reach Washington, D.C., sleep twenty to a room and suffer the persecution of the Migra. Washington, D.C., is shown to be a hostile place, where the migrants earn $3.65 an hour, still an improvement over life in El Salvador, where their daily wage may be $1.00 a day. Calixto's relationship to his new home is thus filled with the contradictions faced by many Salvadoran immigrants.

A collective testimony representing Salvadoran migrants, the novel tells about "going hungry, of constantly looking and never finding even one damn job" (9), and of living in constant fear of death and deportation, which in the novel are almost synonymous. In Bencastro's first novel to focus on Salvadorans in the United States, or for that matter Latinos in Washington, D.C., we see the city confronting a rapidly changing demography and an influx of Salvadorans in need of resources, amid deteriorating social and racial relations in the poorest neighborhoods. Four chapters of the novel are devoted to covering the 1991 "Mount Pleasant Riots," in which Latinos battled the D.C. Metropolitan police after a migrant was shot in a barrio street. What followed were several days of looting, destruction, and violent confrontations between Latinos and African Americans and the police forces of the city. As one character states, "It's like being in El Salvador. . . . This is like the battles we have all the time over there. Like when the government forces attack the political demonstrations to break them up, and the people respond throwing rocks and battle to defend themselves" (93). The uprising on the streets of Washington, D.C., made the international news, as did the Los Angeles Uprisings of 1992 during that year of national discontent, eerily commemorating five hundred years of neocolonialism in the Americas. While federal and local leaders virtually ignored the demands of Latinos after the riots, Bencastro uses his novel as a platform to present the conditions that gave rise to the street protests. According to the novel, "The official report, nevertheless, failed to document the fundamental reasons which generated, and fueled, the two nights of violence" (132). A newspaper citation interpolated in the narrative explains that the shooting of the immigrant was "only the spark, which set off the time bomb that had been waiting to explode in the community due to frustration and discontent for various reasons. One of them being the police mistreatment that our community has suffered repeatedly. . . . To this, one must add the lack of work training programs" and the general disregard for the needs of the Latino community in Washington, D.C. (132). In its description of the Mount Pleasant Riots, Bencastro's novel presents the protest of Latinos who continue to struggle for political representation and power in the District.

A travel narrative from below, the novel produces a literary autoethnography of Salvadoran migrants by compiling and interpolating various texts—memories represented as flashbacks, monologues, conversations, and indirect discourse written as script; and letters, newspaper articles, deportation hearing proceedings, and song lyrics. The protagonist, Calixto, carries the memory not only of his private war in El Salvador but also of the collective history of his D.C. barrio, which rarely has been documented. Calixto would "remember everything he could with great passion and detail, as if his very existence depended on that memory" (50). The novel opens on a "perfect spring day" in Washington, D.C., as Calixto and his friend clean windows on the exterior of a building near the National Zoo. A terrible accident occurs when the rope holding his friend breaks, and his friend plunges to his death. Unwilling to face probable deportation, Calixto joins the crowd that huddles around his dead friend. The first chapter of the novel, which describes Calixto's final days in the United States, opens into a series of flashbacks that tell the collective story of Calixto and his friends in Washington, D.C. At the beginning of the novel (the end of the narrative), Calixto is again jobless and in search of new prospects in the city. The novel's circular structure seems to suggest that Calixto is trapped in a vicious cycle of violence, poverty, and hardship, whether in El Salvador or in the United States. No "American Dream," Calixto's story represents millions of Latino narratives in the United States, which do not end as the mythology of *los hermanos lejanos* would have it. But, in the end, Calixto reminds himself, "At least I'm alive. . . . That's good enough for me" (4).

Bencastro's *Odyssey to the North* represents the making of a Salvadoran community in Washington, D.C., using the form of the immigrant travel narrative and the popular genre *cuentos de camino*, or stories of the road, which colonial subjects appropriated from Spanish *letrados* and converted into popular oral histories of everyday subjects. Many legends in Central America originate in *cuentos de camino*.[11] As a *cuento de camino*, or travel narrative from below, *Odyssey to the North* reveals migration as experienced by everyday folks like Calixto and his friends and uses Salvadoran idiomatic expressions and personal, often humorous, anecdotes while at the same time expressing the values of a people looking for work, home, and human bonds. Read as a travel narrative of everyday folks, the novel merges two literary forms—the hegemonic, imperial literary form "travel narrative" and the popular *cuentos de camino*—to produce an empowering narrative through which migrants tell of their own migration experiences. While in *Imperial Eyes* Mary Louise Pratt examines texts that emerge from the contact of "colonizer and colonized, or travelers and 'travelees,'" the autoethnographic texts of Salvadoran transnational migration represent the "very widespread phenomenon of the contact zone" (1992, 7, 9) of migration and diaspora.

Passage to Washington, D.C.: The Paintings of Karla Rodas

Whereas Mario Bencastro and Quique Avilés produce masculine figurative narratives of migration to Washington, D.C., Karla Rodas (Karlísima) represents the liminal, in-between space occupied by many Salvadorans in the diaspora. Like Avilés, Rodas immigrated to the United States as a child. She graduated with a degree in art from Washington University in St. Louis and lives in the Mount Pleasant–Columbia Heights neighborhood. Rodas paints a distinct picture of the District. She grafts themes and images associated with Mesoamerica into her Washingtonian cityscapes. Often, she produces unexpected magical realist moments as pre-Columbian and modern worlds comingle, and she plays with spectators' nostalgia for organic, homegrown connections, which can only symbolically materialize in her paintings. In her paintings, pre-Columbian figures bathe in the crystal waters of D.C.'s Rock Creek Park, while *mestiza*-looking women with Rodas's own facial features blend into the all-too-familiar D.C. monuments and buildings. Rodas's paintings and murals have been exhibited in local galleries, cafés, restaurants, clinics, and playgrounds, and some of her images have been used on posters promoting various services in the District. Interpolating Central American imagery into the canvas of the nation's capital, she produces a picture of intervention, this time El Salvador intervening in the United States.

Invoking primitivist art forms, in the tradition of the artisan work from La Palma, El Salvador, which was produced and sold in great quantities during and after the civil war, Rodas's paintings seem to reproduce the expected tropicalized and *costumbrista* image of Central America. Volcanoes, temples, tropical fruits, glowing suns, and brown bodies abound. Vertical side panels or border strips simulating pre-Columbian inscriptions or modern images almost always frame her paintings. Painted on the canvas itself, these frames produce the effect of a self-contained gaze—conscious meta-reflections on how Salvadorans are seen and how they see themselves, at least through Rodas's lens, in the United States. One such representation can be seen in Rodas's series of oil paintings, *Lamento Indígena* I and II (1999, 2005), which were inspired by a poem of the same title written by her mother—the Washington, D.C.-based Salvadoran poet Mayamérica Cortez.

Lamento Indígena II, by Karla Rodas (Karlísima), 2005. Courtesy of Karla Rodas.

In *Lamento Indígena*, Rodas depicts the passage of a woman from a pre-Columbian world into the late modernity of Washington, D.C. The painting is divided into two parts. On one side, the isthmian world shines in its greenery (the cardinal color of creation and regeneration in Maya cosmology); on the other, Washington, D.C., blurs in bureaucratic grayness. The painting is a horizontal spatialization of the Americas, with the Washington Monument and a mestiza woman in midstride slicing the hemisphere. Straddling that divide, the woman seems to embody a new borderland (Anzaldúa 1999), or an isthmian space of friction, conflict, separation, displacement, and diaspora. Eternally suspended in movement, the woman leans forward into migration, wearing on one foot a sandal and on the other a high-heeled shoe, perhaps signifying the suspended and ambivalent TPS migratory condition of many Salvadorans in the United States, which "'inscribes ambiguity' on the body of undocumented immigrants" and the "condition of 'permanent temporariness'" in their immigration status (Mountz et al. 2002, 340, 343). In "Lives in Limbo," Mountz and colleagues suggest:

> Compared with relatives who fled to other countries, the Salvadoran experience of asylum in the United States has been one of spatial displacement and confinement. Temporary programmes confine asylum applicants to a limbo of spatial, temporal, economic, social, and political dimensions. This prolonged experience of psychological imprisonment makes closure on the past and passage into the next stages of life difficult. (2002, 349–350).

Rodas's border-crossing woman represents that state of extended yet unresolved migrancy of undocumented Salvadorans awaiting resolution of their cases after various changes in immigration law through the years—from IRCA to Homeland Security. In Rodas's image, the isthmus-crosser is the Salvadoreña who forges new ground in the United States across time and space. Caught in midstep, or in the third space of lived contradictions (Soja 1998b), the woman in the painting looks back at an idealized tropical space of luscious fruits and greenery but moves forward into Washington, D.C. The grimace on her face may be read as feminist ambivalence rather than immigrant nostalgia, for as she laments her passing from an idyllic arcadia (that never was), overzealously represented with glowing bananas, mangoes, suns, and volcanoes, she steps away from that scene of the past. This border woman does not dwell on nostalgia—the desire for the past and for a nation that casts her out—but moves toward an undetermined future awash in the gray not of despair but ambiguity. Far from a picture of nostalgia, *Lamento Indígena* represents the tenuous position of many undocumented Salvadoran immigrants, living in the physical, material, and symbolic space of TPS, or "'permanent temporariness'" (Mountz et al. 2002).

In her work, Rodas brings to the fore *las hermanas lejanas*—the women who have been at the vanguard of Salvadoran migration to Washington, D.C., as Repak writes in *Waiting on Washington*. In the seed text of the paintings, a poem also titled "Lamento indígena," Rodas's mother, Mayamérica Cortez, lyrically retraces the passage of immigrant women to the United States (Cortez 1995). Cortez begins with a discussion of the pain of being uprooted ("Cuando me duelen mis hondas raíces [when my deep roots hurt]") and works through the experience of nostalgia for the homeland ("Cuando la huella de las carretas / y el susurro de la milpa . . . son un torrente de lamento indígena [When the wagon tracks / and the whisper of the corn field . . . are a torrential indigenous lament]") and the disorientation of translocating in a new land ("Cuando extranjera en tierra de nórdicos orígenes [When I find myself a stranger in Nordic lands]"). In its final lines, the poem describes a woman's struggle to resituate and reconstitute herself amid the modern machines of her daily routine: highways, subways, canned soups, washing machines ("super autopistas / trenes subterráneos / sopas enlatadas / máquina lavatodo . . . traga-todo").

By gendering Roque Dalton's Salvadoran labor migrants in his "Poema de amor" as female, Cortez and Rodas represent the transnational migration narratives of Salvadoran women. The immigrant woman grapples with her migratory experience, embodying her highly gendered narrative of migration. At the end of the poem, the female persona declares, "Entonces dejo que mis raíces de polvo / y el grito de mis ancestros / sea un llanto quedo y lento . . . por el instinto de supervivencia / por la constante asimilación de cambios" (And then I let my dirt roots / and my ancestors' scream become a muffled and drawn out cry . . . for the instinct of survival / for the assimilation of change). The Salvadoran woman of the poem resolves, it seems, to adapt to her new condition, allowing the yearnings for her homeland to subside in order to reroot herself in a new context. Like Rodas's *Lamento Indígena* I and II, Cortez's poem represents the contradictions of women's transnational migration and her dwelling in migration, or in travel, as James

Clifford has suggested (1992, 96–116). Cortez's and Karlísima's verbal and visual "Lamento indígena" represent the agency of Salvadoran immigrant women as they take their leap of faith into the United States.

Lilo González Making Music in Mount Pleasant

Finally, the Salvadoran-Washingtonian musical group Lilo González y los de la Mount Pleasant take migrant narratives into the Salvadoran heart(land) of Washington, D.C., as they compose and perform songs that chronicle the lives of people in the Mount Pleasant neighborhood. Born in Armenia, El Salvador, González immigrated to the United States in 1981, arriving in the Columbia Heights and Mount Pleasant neighborhoods, after which the group is named. Since founding his group, González has worked with the Latino community in Washington, D.C., taking his music (a remix of folk music, *cumbia*, salsa, tango, and reggae) to local fund-raising events, on cross-country tours in the United States and El Salvador, and to President Bill Clinton's 1997 inaugural celebration. González has won the WAMMIES Award for "Best Latino Vocalist," and the group has been recognized through the years. González has also composed music for educational documentaries and Quique Avilés's performance piece "Latinhood" and collaborated on various projects with Salvadoran, Latino, and other artists throughout the metropolitan area (González, pers. com., April 5, 1999).

In his CD, *A quien corresponda* (To Whom It May Concern, 1994), González sings about Salvadorans and others living in Washington, D.C. Tracks on the CD offer critiques of immigration policies, as in the songs "Amor sin papeles" (Love without Papers) and "Ningún humano es illegal" (No Human Being Is Illegal); race relations between African Americans and Salvadorans, as chronicled in the "Historias prohibidas de Pedro y Tyrone" (Forbidden Tales of Pedro and Tyrone); and the U.S. imperialist legacy dividing Mexican Americans and Salvadorans in "Lamento de la Nana-Tierra" (The Border Crossed My Land). Other tracks include the love songs "Patita Chueca" (Crooked Leg) and "Te quiero" (I Love You); a salsa version of "El carbonero" (The Charcoal Maker); and a Latin(o) Americanist manifesto in "Forjando un solo pueblo" (Constructing One Nation)—all invoking the transnational experiences of Salvadorans in the Washington, D.C., metropolitan area.

In the song "La Mount Pleasant," González reconstructs the tale of an *hermano lejano*. As the song tells it, don Manuel

ya la dieron la amnistía, / y para acabar de joder, / le pegó a la lotería. /
Ya no quiere comer queso, / ya no quiere comer pan, / hoy solo quiere
pupusas, / pero que sean made in the USA.
[just got his amnesty, / and to top it all off, / he won the lottery. / He
won't eat cheese / and he won't eat bread, / now he only wants pupusas, /
but made in the USA.]

"The infamous don Manuel" has fled to the suburb, green card in hand,
abandoning his friends, customs, and traditions, "pues la Mount Pleasant no sabe igual" (since Mount Pleasant is not the same). By the end of
the song, don Manuel provides the listener with a lesson in transmigrant
living: Although he has moved out of the barrio, he cannot disconnect
himself from the narratives and stereotypes associated with Salvadorans
in D.C. that eventually catch up with him, when he is arrested in the
street for drinking rum in broad daylight ("por andar tomando ron, / en
la calle a pleno día"). The song demystifies the image of the apparently
successful *hermano lejano*, for the refrain interrupts don Manuel's narrative of assimilation with stories of other "hermanos salvadoreños"—
the people who clean offices, the drunks on the corner, the kids from
Lincoln School, those who go to the Wilson Center, and those who return from the local clinic ("los que limpian oficinas, / los bolitos de la
esquina, / los cipotes de la Lincoln, / los que van al Centro Wilson, /
los que juegan capirucho, los que vienen de la clínica"). González thus
sings of transnational immigrant América, precisely to represent urban
migrant laborers—the bakers, cooks, artisans, carpenters, and laborers
trying to make ends meet ("porque ellos son, / panaderos, cocineros, /
artesanos, carpinteros, / los arrechos pa'l trabajo, / como le suben al
cuarto, / el part-time no me da abasto, pa' la olla de frijoles"). In sum,
like the work of Dalton, Avilés, Bencastro, Rodas, and Cortez, the song
gives testimony to the everyday Salvadoran folks of Departamento 15,
who keep Washington, D.C., San Salvador, and other sites economically
afloat.

Particularly poignant and relevant to the context of Washington,
D.C., González and his group chronicle race relations in the District
through the telling of the "Historias prohibidas de Pedro y Tyrone,"
or the stories of African American Tyrone and Salvadoran Pedro, both
of whom are young, male, and poor in Washington, D.C. In 1991, this
lethal combination sparked the Mount Pleasant Riots. As in many U.S.
cities, African American and Latino youths in the District of Columbia live in neighborhoods divided by urbanization and gentrification

projects, unemployment or underemployment, and urban crime, which often set these populations against one another (Jennings and Lusane 1994). González's song, which is set to reggae, begins with the lines "Negro matando a negro, / negro matando a Latino, / Latino matando a negro, / Latino matando a Latino" (Black killing Black, / Black killing Latino, / Latino killing Black, / Latino killing Latino). The song would seem to suggest that it is only a matter of time before Tyrone and Pedro clash.

A product of the 1980s immigration of Salvadorans to the area, the lyrical Pedro is orphaned, homeless, and addicted to crack. At six years of age, he emigrates from his war-torn country, but in D.C. he grows prematurely old and hopeless: "Llegó buscando a estas tierras, / la estatua de la libertad, / pero ella estaba muy alta, / me dijo, no la pude yo alcanzar" (He came to this land in search of, / the Statue of Liberty, / but she was much too high, / he told me, I wasn't able to reach her). The Statue of Liberty, symbolizing opportunity, freedom, and justice, does not extend her hand to these new migrants from Central America. Instead, the statue represents the denial of (inalienable) refugee rights to a population that was assaulted in its own land by the economic and military forces of the United States. Do they not have the right to seek refuge in the United States? the song seems to ask. Caught in the middle of two cultures without the material and creative means to use his cultural capital, Pedro learns to think and live in the present: "Siempre piensa en el presente / suspira por el pasado, / conociendo nuestra historia, / Pedro, el futuro es tu regalo" (He always thinks in the present, / he always longs for the past, / but if you know your own history, / Pedro, the future shall be your reward). Pedro's counterpart, Tyrone, also lives in the margins, in the shadow of the White House, overshadowed by power, poverty, and oppression.

Underscoring the parallels in these lives, González's song prompts listeners to reach the conclusion that Pedro and Tyrone equally lack access to education, employment, personal security, and affirmation of their human potential. Both are overcome and overwhelmed by a sense of entrapment, alienation, and disenfranchisement. Both youths, the song suggests, believe in the capitalist imperative "que ser y tener, es igual," that what you have is what you are. And if you have nothing, you are nothing. The lyrics comment on the materialist American narrative, asserting to Pedro and Tyrone, "You are . . . no matter what car you drive." In its final lines, the song calls the youths to creative intervention in their lives, despite their experiences of civil and urban war. In an indictment of Tyrone's and Pedro's disempowerment by economic and material forces, González's song imagines the possibility of solidarity among ethnic, racial, and diasporic communities: "¿Por qué no se ponen en onda, / luchando por el pueblo de Sudáfrica, / ¿por qué no se ponen en onda, / luchando por la paz en América" (Why don't you get high, / supporting the people of South Africa, / why don't you get high, / struggling for peace in America?).

Ultimately, Lilo González y los de la Mount Pleasant produce a discourse that is highly critical of the racial, ethnic, and class hierarchies that structure the barrios and neighborhoods of many U.S. cities and that divide Latinos, African Americans, and other ethnic groups from one another. Moreover, González and los de la Mount Pleasant disarticulate the grand narrative of *los hermanos lejanos*, as Pedro struggles to survive in the streets of Washington, D.C., without memories, dreams, and prospects.

Against Pedro's immigration *cuento de camino*, the last track of the CD, titled "Forjando un sólo pueblo," calls on Salvadorans, Central Americans, Latinos, and others to forge a Latino American nation from the cultural materials and practices that have traveled and translocated with them. The song suggests that as members of the transnational community, Central Americans have the power to "construir mi patria, / con madera u hojalata" (construct my nation, / with wood and traditional materials). Transplanted in a new location and creating a *transnation*, Salvadorans are called to produce multidimensional, heterogeneous, and interlinked communities. The Americanist fiesta at the end of the song serves as a metaphor for constructing self-sustaining transnational communities linked by a common project of economic, political, and cultural solidarity and revitalization, producing in the end "una gran fiesta, / con taquitos mejicanos, / con pupusas de mi patria, / con arepas de Carácas, un lechoncito dorado" (a big party, / with Mexican tacos, / with pupusas from my country, / arepas from Caracas, / and a roasted pig). The construction of an imaginary transnational homeland in the United States incorporating different Latino diasporic groups and linked by alliances and solidarities, as González suggests, "es tarea de todos" (is the task of everyone).

A transnational cultural anthem, "Forjando un sólo pueblo" thus interpolates the stories of Salvadorans in Washington, D.C., in the wider Latino American transnational and diasporic narrative. In the end, the song seems to suggest that, regardless of their points of departure and entry, Latinas/os continue to be linked to their countries of origin by material, affective, and symbolic obligations. Once in the United States, the migration experience incorporates subjects into the larger narrative of displacement and diaspora. González thus ends his song with a rallying call for Latinos/as in the United States to unite in a common diasporic front spread unevenly across different sites but remaining connected to disenfranchised communities from below. In "Forjando un sólo pueblo," González reminds his listeners, "Y cuando vengas aquí, / no te olvides de allá abajo, / porque todo lo que sube, / siempre se viene pa' abajo" (But when you come here, / don't forget what's down there, / because all that goes up, / must always come back down). The Haitian Department 10 and the Salvadoran Departamento 15 comprise such extended extranational spaces of diasporas intersecting in the United States, each still tied to the conditions of the South that sent them away in the first place.

The cultural texts examined in this chapter present the experiences of transnational migrants, who make the Mount Pleasant and Columbia Heights neighborhoods their physical and imaginary home in the United States. Following the work of theorists of third space, Edward Soja foremost among them, Salvadorans not only reconfigure social space and produce changes in their immediate material conditions but also produce reterritorialized Salvadoreñidades that challenge hegemonic versions of history and deconstruct national mythologies such as those of "los hermanos lejanos." This recasting of people and their stories in a cultural landscape as distinct as Washington, D.C., permits the identification of subjects that usually go underrepresented and elicits the acknowledgment of the presence of "a range of other dissonant, even dissident histories and voices" (Bhabha 1994, 5). In "Locations of Culture," Bhabha describes diaspora as that constructive "in-between space" and "in-between moment," where and when different, dissonant, and dissident identities, histories, and subjectivities are elaborated. While creatively inserting themselves into the cultural spaces opened by their own migration, Salvadoran transnational immigrants challenge the dominant narratives of casualty of war, economic drainage, and invisible labor migration, which generally erase them from the national imaginaries of El Salvador and the United States. Instead Salvadoran immigrants reemerge as vibrant transisthmian communities extending beyond Central America.

CHAPTER 7

Wasted Opportunities:
Central America after the Revolutions

We do not know where we are going. We only know that history has brought us to this point and—if readers share the argument of this book—why. However, one thing is plain. If humanity is to have a recognizable future, it cannot be by prolonging the past and or the present. If we try to build the third millennium on that basis, we shall fail. And the price of failure, that is to say, the alternative to a changed society is darkness.
—ERIC HOBSBAWM, *The Age of Extremes*

The passing of the twentieth century provided Central Americans in and outside the geographic isthmus with the opportunity not only to examine their condition after decades of armed conflict and destruction but also to begin a political, economic, and social reconstruction of their societies. Fast on the heels of the signing of the Peace Accords in El Salvador in 1992, a number of books on the construction of peacetime civil societies were published. These books included *América Central hacia el 2000* (Central America toward 2000) (Torres Rivas 1989), *Forjando la paz* (Constructing Peace) (Fagen 1988), *De la locura a la esperanza* (From Madness to Hope) (Comisión de la Verdad 1993), *Esquipulas, diez años después* (Esquipulas, Ten Years After) (Ordoñez and Gamboa 1997), and *Traspatio florecido* (Regenerated Backyard) (Cuevas Molina 1993). These texts not only assessed the period of civil unrest in the region but also provided a prognosis for Central America in the twenty-first century. Invoking a violent past indelibly etched into the isthmus, these publications foreshadowed the critical challenges that Central America, as a whole, would face as it entered the neoliberal era and resituated itself within the economic and political realignments of a globalized world.

In *Traspatio florecido*, Rafael Cuevas Molina explains that at the turn of the millennium there was an urgent need to examine the state of postrevolutionary cultural realities in Central America, as well as a need to forge a regional Central American cultural imaginary. For Cuevas Molina, the imperative was to bring to the fore connections between the peoples, histories, and societies of the isthmus and to underscore the differences among them (1993, 14). In his view, the wars of the last decades generated new heterogeneous cultural forms that offer sites for critical study. In Central America, where cultural exchange and communication among Central Americans themselves have been limited, transisthmian cultural linkages become increasingly necessary in order to offset homogenizing cultural trends brought on by economic globalization. Cuevas Molina explains:

> Tal descuido permite que, incluso en círculos de intelectuales preocupados por la temática de la identidad cultural, prevalezca el desconocimiento mutuo de lo que ocurre en países vecinos del istmo, de lo que en ellos se produce, se publica, etc. y se reproduzcan, en formas bastante acrílica, estereotipos, mitos, prejuicios provenientes del sentido común respecto a los otros países de la región. (13)
> [Such neglect, even among intellectuals who are concerned with the issue of cultural identity, permits a lack of mutual awareness of what goes on in neighboring countries of the isthmus, of what is produced there, of what is published there, to prevail. It also foments the reproduction of uncritical stereotypes, myths, commonsense prejudices against the other countries in the region.]

To offset these biases, the construction of postwar cultures in the region requires the promotion of mutual recognition among Central Americans and the production of an extended Central American imaginary, a project in which cultural texts are indispensable. The integration of Central American cultures into a regional imaginary might serve as a defense against further cultural memory loss and as a front against cultural homogenization induced by the expansion of global (cultural and economic) capital in the region. As Cuevas Molina suggests, Central American communities would benefit from composing a transisthmian cultural field,[1] which promotes awareness of a common history and the coexistence of cultural differences, histories, and identities throughout the region (16–17).

Indeed, at the turn of the millennium, Central American cultures are not the national cultures *imagined* by nineteenth-century liberals and federalists, nor are they the revolutionary cultures projected in the late twentieth century. Furthermore, they are no longer strictly located within national geographic boundaries, as we have seen in the previous chapters. Central American cultures, in fact, have spilled over their national confines into other spaces throughout the world. According to Cuevas Molina, regional and comparative studies of Central American cultures are necessary, as Central Americans share both a geographic region and similar historical developments. He suggests, however, that there is a near-void in full-length studies of Central American isthmian cultures, with the exception of two significant works by Sergio Ramírez Mercado: *Balcanes y volcanes y otros ensayos y trabajos* (1985), an overview of Central American cultural production from pre-Columbian times to the 1970s; and *Hatful of Tigers* (1995), which examines the direct and subtle impact of revolutionary cultures in the region. Cuevas Molina's *Traspatio Florecido* and Magda Zavala and Seidy Araya's *La historiografía literaria en América Central (1957–1987)* (Literary Historiography in Central America [1957–1987]) (1995) have been also important contributions to the field of comparative/regional Central American cultural studies. Occasioned by the opportunity to reenvision a transisthmian imaginary for Central America, this chapter examines the reconstruction, or recycling, of narratives in the context of postwar and free-traded Central America.

Postwar Cultural Production in Central America

Contemporary Central American cultural production, which follows the noted apex of the *testimonio* and a critical break with the Marxist-Leninist revolutionary narrative of the 1980s (Camacho 1993, 36–58),[2] is located at the crossroads of discourses on Central American regional cultures. Postwar and reconstruction literature shows the signs of recent historical and discursive transformations. As it grapples with the legacy of armed conflict, postwar literature in Central America is in the process of constructing peacetime narratives. Major strategies of this literature include, as Cuevas Molina's study suggests, the invention of a Central American imaginary across texts that propose both utopic and dystopic visions of the future and that seek to disrupt official peacetime narratives of the region, as represented by the postwar and posttraumatic literature of Central America. Many recent literary texts also interrogate the effects of neoliberal politics and economies on the specific and diverse populations of the isthmus and offer critiques of the general devastation of the South, including Central America. Often, these texts engage in a rethinking of alliances forged among Central Americans and their displaced refugee/immigrant populations.

Under neoliberal regimes, all the countries of Central America show the impact of similar economic, political, social, and cultural programs, which are implemented throughout the South. The imaginary of Central America as the South is not limited to the confines of individual nation-states but covers a wide expanse of sites across the world ruled by neo-liberal regimes that implement violent domestic policies and reforms. In this construction of a southern Central American imaginary, individual countries identify themselves as part of a larger Central American entity and as part of the even larger economic composite of the South. Located in particular sites across the globe, the South might be understood as a location of cultures[3] produced under the heavy strain of the expropria-tion and accumulation of capital in the northern regions of the world. Jonathan R. Barton, in *A Political Geography of Latin America*, offers a working definition of the region and the conditions of the South:

> The South is a geographical reference within which the *majority* of countries share *similar* environmental, social, cultural, political and economic development contexts and conditions. . . . The South defini-tion is neither precise, inclusive nor exclusive, and as such it reflects the heterogeneity of Latin American circumstances. Rather than attempt-ing to justify the term, it is better to point out that there are many and various contradictions and ambiguities within this universalisation. The definition should continue that a recognition of the difference within the South is as important as a recognition of the difference between the North and the South. (1997, 6; emphasis in original)

Spanning a vast terrain across national territories, the South comprises two-thirds of the earth's surface, where 3.5 billion people, or three quarters of humanity, live in extreme degrees of impoverishment.[4] With the exception of Costa Rica, Central American countries rank among the poorest in the world. According to researchers at the Facultad Lati-noamericana de Ciencias Sociales (FLACSO), over 68 percent of the to-tal population in Central America lives in degrees of poverty, with that percentage growing every day. In 1990, extreme poverty rates reached 52 percent in Guatemala and El Salvador, 63 percent in Honduras, 42 percent in Nicaragua, 25 percent in Panama, and 11 percent in Costa

Rica.[5] These percentages have since widened: Nicaragua and Honduras now figure among the four poorest countries in the western hemisphere. In general, Central America is greatly affected by large population growth, unequal distribution of wealth, repeated foreign political and economic intervention, declining literacy and basic needs attainment, and extremely low annual income earnings per capita. The most impoverished citizens in Central America earn between $200 and $400 per year. John A. Booth and Thomas W. Walker, in *Understanding Central America*, explain that as a whole Central America has suffered from "the long-term, grinding deprivation of poverty" and continually "declining living conditions," which now make it part of the economic South (1993, 9–16).

The new South, to which the Central American isthmus belongs, encompasses the sites formerly and recently known as the Third World, the developing countries, and the peripheries. Currently, Central Americans engage in a common struggle against the violent economic forces of the North. In the arena of the globalized state, as Barton points out, it is the financial agencies and organizations such as the World Bank and the International Monetary Fund (IMF) that determine domestic policies in specific countries. The Free Trade Area of the Americas, which followed the approval of the Dominican Republic–Central American Free Trade Agreement on October 7, 2007, is further reshaping the socioeconomic, political, and cultural landscape of the isthmus. Barton notes, "Within the globalised context of neocolonialism, the manipulation of armed forces is being replaced gradually by the manipulation of market force" (1997, 3). Under such conditions, Central America has gained a place among the impoverished states of the South, of which Latin America is a "key region" (3).

In much literature, media representation, and photojournalism (Asociación Equipo Maíz 1995, 1999; Towell 1997; Saxgren 2000), Central America is imagined as a site undergoing great socioeconomic and ecological devastation (the general condition of the South). The image of *garbage* or *waste* surfaces as the metaphor of Central American nations attempting to rebuild themselves from the rubble of armed conflict while at the same time confronting the disruptive fallout of global capital. Waste also serves as the sign of the uncertain future of the isthmus, requiring critical readings of the devastation of the region throughout its long history of imperialism and intervention. Throughout the history of Central America, structures of power and attendant systems of thought have converted the region into raw material and terrain for (mis)use by the North. In an act of reification, the same devastating effects produced in the South by the North come to represent Central America as a natural(ized) site of decomposition and underdevelopment, which requires regeneration by outside forces. Regeneration from the North comes to Central America in the form of imperialism, (neo)colonialism, and now neoliberalism.

In "Through the Tropical Looking Glass," Stephen Benz explains that the isthmus has been repeatedly imagined as a "deadly, diseased, disorderly, dissolute, and decadent" region, which must be brought to order by outside forces (1997, 69). According to Benz, tropicalism or tropicalization (the southern version of Edward Said's orientalism) is the underlying logic that informs many projects of imperialism, (neo)colonialism, and neoliberalism that take root in Central America. Responding to this legacy of decomposition, the texts analyzed here pick at the waste left behind by those structures imposed on Central America and attempt to reconstruct narratives for the region out of the remains. These texts, moreover, trace the devastation of Central America directly to the North. Waste, in these Central American texts, is the premier sign of the degradation of the South, as produced by northern agents. In Carmen Naranjo's story "And We Sold the Rain" (1989), Fernando Contreras Castro's *Única mirando al mar* (1994), Manlio Argueta's *Milagro de la Paz* (1994), and Gioconda Belli's *Waslala: Memorial del futuro* (1996), I examine the representation of communities living in the virtually wasted lands of Central America. Part of a wider network of postrevolutionary cultural politics and cultural production, these texts represent a general scene of devastation, which sets the ground for the construction of peace in Central America. The survival of Central America into the next millennium depends on the reconstruction of its societies and the reimagining of more equitable narratives of development and progress in the region. What follows, then, is a discussion of the construction of a Central American transisthmian imaginary in postwar literature, where waste is a prime signifier of the contradictions of peacetime conditions and where the ambivalent f(r)iction of peace casts subjects into internal and external holding spaces of economic, material, and human expropriation.

Central America: A Place Called *Milagro de la Paz*

As formal peace agreements were institutionalized in subsequent policies over the past decades, the narrative of peace in Central America began to show its contradictions. At a most basic level, *peace* is defined by the *Oxford English Dictionary* as freedom from or cessation of hostilities and war; as a state of security, concord, and amity within a determined group or location; and as freedom from civil disorder, disturbance or perturbation, and dissension between parties. Peacetime is defined, moreover, as "a period when a country is not at war." After the signing of peace accords across Central America, a narrative of peace was constructed for the region by political leaders, nongovernmental organizations, the media, and others. This fiction required the disarming of revolutionary sectors in order for countries to begin a multifaceted process of national socioeconomic reconstruction and recovery. Although the signing of the initial peace accords of Esquipulas II on August 7, 1987, and the Salvadoran peace accords on January 16, 1992, promised new practices of peace in the region, these efforts often congealed into documents on peace, discourses of peace, and institutions of peace.[6] (The Universidad para la Paz, with campuses in Ciudad Colón, Costa Rica, and Managua, Nicaragua, is one such institution generated by regional peace processes.)[7]

In "Un plan de paz para Centroamérica" (1991), Marlen Retana Guido sheds light on how the peace plans and accords of the past decades used the language of peace and drew from idealist master narratives to mask regional economic objectives. Peace, according to Retana Guido, was presented as concomitant with the ideals of democracy, progress, and liberty and served as a front for a market economy that until then had been deterred from expanding by the conflict in the isthmus. The production of peace would initiate the economic recovery of Central America. In this context, peace was constructed as a space of forced "interconnections" produced by North-South relations: peace provides the conditions that make it possible for neoliberal economies to take hold and thrive in the region. The imperative of peace thus begins to blur the line between fact and fiction, war and peace, and the rule and the exception in Central America.

A culture of peace that advocated development, progress, and capital growth under the tutelage of neoliberal programs was almost immediately inscribed in the Central American imaginary after the 1980s. In the 1990s, Central America dealt not only with the lagging effects of the previous conflicts but also with new crises produced in an ambivalent time of peace. At the beginning of the twenty-first century, many Central Americans experienced peace as a continuation of previous crises. They found that peace did not immediately and necessarily translate into democracy, liberty, and development. For many, peacetime Central America translated into what I call the f(r)ictions that continue to tear families apart; push people into deeper levels of poverty, illiteracy, and hunger; foster drug trafficking and criminal activity; induce migrations and scatter individuals throughout Central America and elsewhere; and, finally, generate higher levels and new forms of violence. The wars of the 1980s may have ended in most areas of Central America, but violence and declining socioeconomic conditions continued to spread: *El Diario de Hoy*, in El Salvador, for example, reported eight hundred kidnappings between January and August 1995; *La Nación*, in San José, noted on June 2, 1995, the sparking of political and economic tensions throughout Central America. Such news reports from the region projected an image of "alta tensión" (Redacción, "Crispación en Centroamérica" 1995, 18A), or high voltage, surging with continued human rights violations in Guatemala, catastrophic natural disasters in Honduras, institutional crisis in Nicaragua, contradictory peace processes in El Salvador, crippling programs of economic structural adjustment in Costa Rica, and escalating levels of poverty and "ungovernability" throughout the isthmus.[8] As we enter the third millennium, unemployment, poverty, and lack of opportunities are contributing to escalating levels of quotidian violence, especially among the youth of Central America.[9] The rift between the narrative of peace and the practice of peace becomes wider, and the f(r)ictions and contradictions of peace in the region become more apparent.

A critical intervention into the hegemonic narrative of peace building and national reconstruction, Manlio Argueta's *Milagro de la Paz* depicts conditions of life in a country struggling with the effects of its recent wars. The novel grapples with the contradictions of peace as they are lived in a marginal community that has been abandoned by the state and left to resume its course in history. The novel, moreover, offers a gendered history that focuses on female subjects who live out crises of peacetime in various dimensions and locations. William Rowe and Vivian Schelling, in *Memory and Modernity* (1991), note that popular sectors register and remember their versions of history through alternative modes that might include, in the case of El Salvador, *testimonios*, letters, artisan work, and finally, novels by authors such as Argueta. Produced under the pressure of hegemonic narratives—the institutional fictions of peace—these texts assume hybrid forms such as the testimonial novel to which Argueta repeatedly returns. Beyond recording the voices of marginal subjects, Central American testimonial novels and documentary fiction (of which *Milagro de la Paz* is a late exponent) register the social contradictions produced out of the frictions and fictions of peace in the isthmus. Argueta's text participates in the struggles with and over the verbal fiction of history,[10] which has worked to erase histories and subject.

Argueta's postwar novel is ironically yet appropriately titled *Miracle of Peace;* it alludes to the long-awaited and deferred miracle of peace in El Salvador. This is the story of a family of women who have survived the civil war in El Salvador, during which at least eighty thousand Salvadorans lost their lives. The mother, Latina, as her name implies, is the allegorical figure of women across the Americas, a single mother who has kept her family together, despite the irresponsible paternity of the state, its institutions, and, in many cases, the male heads of household. She tells her daughter, "[Los hombres] se han inventado que son valientes, pero a la hora de la verdad son más cobardes que nosotras [(The men) have imagined they are courageous, but in the end they are more cowardly than us]" (Argueta 1994, 15). This family of women continues to live through and beyond the crisis, the militarism, and the phallocratic violence that have ravaged parts of Latin America, especially Central America and, more particularly, El Salvador during the past decades. Latina and her daughters, Magdalena and Crista, now live in a place called "Milagro de la Paz," which still awaits the miracle of peace. (The miracle, in this novel, is that the fictionalized Salvadorans have survived at all to tell their stories.) Although the war may have ended, the conflicts that gave rise to it are very much present in this peacetime community. Impoverished further in the aftermath of the war, the general population works harder to subsist during peacetime. Latina sews clothing, Magdalena sells it in the streets, and Crista takes care of the animals and the garden. The three live by the general law, "El que no trabaja no come [S/he who does not work does not eat]" (12).

In telling the story of the significant role of Salvadoran women in the history of their country, *Milagro de la Paz* picks up where Argueta's wartime novels, *Un día en la vida* (1980) and *Cuzcatlán donde bate la mar del sur* (1987), leave off. The wars have permeated the social fabric, disrupting traditional family and social structures. Women, in particular, have carried the weight of the prolonged war, and, as Argueta's novel seems to indicate, their struggle is no less difficult in peacetime.[11] Latina and her daughters, for example, suffer posttraumatic stress disorders. They are haunted by the *aullidos de los seres desconocidos* (the howls of unknown beings) who roam the night: "Andan muy cerca de nosotros y pueden atacar cualquier casa del barrio [They are very near us and they could attack any house in the neighborhood]" (13). The text does not disclose if these are the cries of the war dead or the signals of the prowlers who invade most areas of El Salvador. The reader, however, becomes aware of the acute levels of trauma and fear embedded in the characters after years of institutionalized violence against which there is little safeguard and protection.[12] The trauma of war crimes remains fresh in the minds of Salvadorans, as *Milagro de la Paz* indicates. In its critical intervention into the fiction of peace, the novel writes the particular history of Salvadoran women into a hegemonic discourse that tends to erase them throughout the vast regions of the South.

Neoliberal Regimes: The Exception and the Rule

While it was once the exception to the rule of unrest in Central America and it boasted the highest standards of living in the isthmus, Costa Rica in the 1990s joined the ranks of war-torn countries of Central America. Along with El Salvador, Nicaragua, Honduras, and Guatemala, Costa Rica is enmeshed in the narrative of "marginalization and impoverishment" and "a generalized public squalor that was already formidably wide" (Dunkerley 1994, 17), all of which are compounded by rising levels of exploitation of labor and appropriation of capital by the industrialized countries. Along with the rest of Central America, Costa Rica is part of the larger f(r)ictions of peace, development, and progress in the era of neoliberal reform.

In "And We Sold the Rain," the Costa Rican writer Carmen Naranjo produces an allegory of the neoliberal nation that Costa Rica and other Central American countries have become. In the story, a small developing nation has fallen into hard times of economic structural adjustments requiring a revamping of economic, social, and cultural systems. The story begins with the treasury minister summing up the predicament of his country: "This is a royal fuck-up" (1989, 149). The IMF has demanded payment on the interest of the small country's loans, "stubbornly insisting that the country could expect no more loans until the interest had been paid up, public spending curtailed, salaries frozen, domestic production increased, imports reduced, and social programs cut" (149). Under pressure from the IMF, the ministers and the president rehearse a list of last resorts: why not pray to the competing patron virgins of the country, La Negrita or the Virgin of Ujarrás? But even the Virgen de los Angeles, the patron mother of Costa Rica who blesses Catholic national

alliances, has stopped listening to the Costa Ricans. One by one, institutional icons are erased from popular memory, until even "the government had faded in the people's memory" (152). The country quickly falls
apart: the president "had to dismiss civil servants, suspend public works,
cut off services, close offices, and spread his legs somewhat to transna-
tionals" (152); "hunger and poverty could no longer be concealed" (150).
The poor could not even buy beans. Shantytowns spring up around the
capital, while Mercedes and BMWs cruise the city, which is rapidly falling into decay and disorder: "In the marketplace, robberies increased
to one per second, and homes were burgled at the rate of one per half
hour" (150). Capitalizing on an idea, the export minister agrees to sell
the country's oversupply of rain to an unnamed country in the Middle
East, which, with the help of French technicians, builds an aqueduct
that siphons the water. The Central American country is depleted of
natural resources, economic means, and spiritual hope. Eventually, the
people are forced to emigrate to the Arab nation to which their government sold the rain.[13] Equally indebted to the IMF (when petroleum prices
fall), the Middle Eastern nation privatizes and relinquishes control of its
water supply, and it, too, eventually runs dry.

An allegory of North-South relations, Naranjo's satiric story foretells the role of multinational organizations in the depletion of weak
economies, which are highly vulnerable to external forces and uneven
flows of capital. The story also represents the deterritorialization of national subjects, even within the borders of their own country, once they
are dislodged from the social pact and the ideals of the model Central
American republic (Costa Rica). These subjects have few options for
survival. Either they join the ranks of shantytown dwellers or become
migrant laborers in distant lands, tending to "coffee, sugar cane, cotton,
fruit trees, and gardens" in other locations (156).

As their country falls into social dis/ease, people are forced to live
in abject conditions of poverty, waste, and disorder. Falling out of the
order of hegemonic society, they are (to follow Julia Kristeva's notion
of the abject) quite meaningless, "fading away of all meaning" (Kristeva
1982, 18). They become human degenerates, living in the putrid state
of the decomposing nation. The human by-products and wasted bodies
churned out by the neoliberal economy in the country, they are, to push
Kristeva's terms further, the "inassimilable alien" and "jettisoned object" that have lost their place in the order of society (1982, 11,2). Likewise, they have lost the capacity to produce meaning in the logocentric
chain of the narratives of development and progress. Failing to generate

exploitable human capital or labor, they are cast out or discarded by the nation, which runs on the production (and the logic) of late capitalism. Transformed into the most abject of materials, wasted bodies, the poor people in Naranjo's story are "what human life and culture exclude in order to sustain themselves."[14] Because waste and filth are among the most degraded and rejected products in the material and symbolic economy of the West and are considered offensive and repulsive in many cultures, subjects living in such conditions disturb the sensibilities and order of a healthy body politic.[15] These garbage societies and shantytown dwellers in Naranjo's story disrupt the orderly progression of development in the southern country. The first paragraph of the story, in fact, shows the nation to be a mess and the narrative of progress to be a myth:

> "This is a royal fuck-up," was all the treasury minister could say a few days ago as he got out of the jeep after seventy kilometers of jouncing over dusty rutted roads and muddy trails. His advisor agreed: there wasn't a cent in the treasury, the line for foreign exchange wound four times around the capital, and the IMF was stubbornly insisting that the country could expect no more loans until the interest had been paid up, public spending curtailed, salaries frozen, domestic production increased, imports reduced, and social programs cut. (Naranjo 1989, 149)

Amid the wreckage left in the wake of the country's impoverishment and exploitation by industrialized nations, the people of this Central American country are left to fend for themselves and to look for alternatives outside of their religious, juridical, and political institutions. They are "people living in leaky houses, without a change of shoes for when they're shipwrecked" (151). In a critique of the narratives of state, development, and progress, the ending of Naranjo's story begs for an alternative to the fiction of progress in Central America and for a projection of different modes of development and modernization that rely on local resources, knowledge, or sustainable methods based on "a development strategy that combines human development, growth, equity and technological change with a wiser and more creative use of local resources and knowledge" (Wignaraja 1993, 4). In its use of the metaphor of the selling of the rain, the story suggests that the ecological devastation in the isthmian region is irreversible. The prognosis of eminent economic and natural disasters in the Costa Rica of Naranjo's story serves as a warning call to the region, which, like the rest of the South, is quickly destroying its rain forests and natural resources, perilously increasing in population, and on the brink of ecological disaster. These un/natural disasters, as manifested in Naranjo's story, are a product of inequitable exchanges of capital and unequal relations of power, yet naturalized by the myths of neoliberal progress in the region.[16] In "And We Sold the Rain," Naranjo makes the case for a mode of sustainable development that would meet the greater needs of the poorest and most excluded people in Central America.[17] According to Naranjo's story, a society that sells its resources and its people as labor force seals their fate and sells their future.

The novel *Única mirando al mar* by the Costa Rican writer Fernando Contreras Castro continues Carmen Naranjo's narrative of the wasting away of Costa Rican society. Contreras Castro's text comments on the sociohistoric implications of a society that throws its citizens away into *el basurero*, the dump site or wasteland, once their productivity is spent. According to Margarita Rojas and Flora Ovares, in *100 años de literatura costarricense* (One Hundred Years of Costa Rican Literature), *Única mirando al mar* is informed by the recent production of literature in Costa Rica that reinstates the communicative value of literary discourse and proposes that the literary text may still serve as a vehicle for denouncing social abuses (Rojas and Ovares 1995, 244). As represented in "And We Sold the Rain" and *Única mirando al mar*, the social reality of Costa Rica has undergone great alterations and degradations over the past decades: the state has failed the nation and abandoned the founding principles, ideals, and values of the Costa Rican republic. Rojas and Ovares suggest that *Única mirando al mar* does not offer solutions to a "mundo [que] está condenado al fracaso [a world condemned to failure]" (244). Hence, at the end of the novel, the protagonist is left gazing into the sea of her despair and homelessness. The text, however, destabilizes the illusive principles, ideals, and values on which Costa Rican exceptionalism are based: "El mundo armónico y familiar, propio del estereotipo costarricense, la representación del espacio nacional como lugar íntimo y conocido, sin conflictos, aparecen profundamente cuestionados en *Única mirando al mar* [The harmonious and familiar world belonging to the stereotype of Costa Rica and the representation of the nation as an intimate and known space without conflicts are profoundly interrogated in *Única mirando al mar*]" (244). Read as an allegory of the demythologized republic of Costa Rica, the novel designates *el basurero* as an alternate imaginary space located within the ever-deteriorating social conditions of the nation-state. While the dump site regenerates a community, the country at large rapidly decomposes, as Naranjo's story also shows.

Contreras Castro's novel represents a contemporary moment in Costa

Rican and Central American history. It follows the tradition of the social realist text, the thesis novel, and (along with Naranjo's story) the
popular genre of social satire, which have been prime discursive vehicles
of social criticism in Central American literature. This is a novel with
recognizable referents, attempting to communicate a message about
Central American realities in the late twentieth and early twenty-first
centuries. It is part of a literature written to initiate a highly polemical
discussion about the problem of the garbage from the perspectives of
those who are dispossessed and disposed of in the general context of
the decomposing nation-state. The site of enunciation in these novels
is the dump site, from which those subjects most affected by the socioeconomic fallout speak. Contemporary Central American literary
texts such as those examined here meet the new challenges of representing Central American realities within the conditions of the South and
address the discursive needs of Central American subjects that remain
grounded in local realities.

In "Seis falsos golpes contra la literatura centroamericana" (Six False
Blows against Central American Literature), Sergio Ramírez Mercado
succinctly tackles the main critique of Central American literature (1985,
117–128). Ramírez proposes that Central American literature, contrary
to literature written elsewhere, (1) engages with referents and social realities; (2) produces rich imaginaries based on those referents and references; (3) thrives as an artistic enterprise, despite the high levels of
illiteracy in the region; (4) speaks out of Central American contexts using local vernacular sign systems; (5) shows literary texts to have a discursive, communicative, and thus material function in society; and (6)
claims that literature still has plenty to denounce in Central America.[18]

The narratives of waste that are discussed in this chapter seem to respond to Ramírez's admonitions and theses on Central American literature with a brand of texts addressing local social realities and composing
a contemporary imaginary for the region. In representing a postrevolutionary, peacetime moment in Central America, these texts offer highly
contradictory, volatile images of transisthmian social realities, which
are encoded in the prevailing sign of waste and neglect.

The Decomposed and Recomposed Nation

A composite of the larger debates in and about Central American literature, the novel *Única mirando al mar* is based on a series of prolonged
discussions about the (re)location of a new dump site for the capital's

solid waste, which actually took place in the Costa Rican media between 1994 and 1995. In these public debates, the former president of Costa Rica and Nobel Peace Prize recipient Oscar Arias critiqued the administration of then-President José María Figueres (1994–1998) for not quickly resolving the local problem of garbage disposal in order to attend to issues such as the fiscal deficit and the privatization of pubic institutions. The two problems were insurmountably and intractably linked, of course. In *La Nación*, Arias commented on his own role "en un momento crucial, donde se luchaba por la paz y la igualdad de la mujer, y no 'por buscar donde botar la basura' [at a crucial moment, when we fought for peace and equality of women, and not 'where to throw away the garbage']" (*La Nación*, June 2, 1995). This debate over waste management informs Contreras Castro's novel.

At the level of plot, *Única mirando al mar* is the story of Única Oconitrillo, her son, El Bacán, and his stepfather, Momboñombo Moñagallo. The threesome symbolically constitutes the Costa Rican family unit, now living in and off the garbage produced by San José. They literally make their residence in Río Azul, the massive dump site for the garbage of the Costa Rican capital. Every day, eight hundred tons of waste are deposited on these grounds, which the dump dwellers scout for recyclable goods, including their daily meals, clothing, and other necessities and accessories. The text describes the *basurero* as the place where everything is turned upside down, where people eat garbage and dress in ripped clothing: "donde todo se vuelve al revés, donde la gente come basura y se viste con lo roto" (38). This is "el país de los buzos" (the country of the garbage surfers) (76), where people living on the wasted margins of society *bucean* (surf) the waves of garbage for their subsistence. Everyone living in the *basurero* has suffered a fall from society: Única, a former teacher, was forced to retire at the age of forty, "por esa costumbre que tiene la gente de botar lo que aún podría servir largo tiempo [because of that custom that people have of throwing away what could still be useful for a long time]" (14). Her meager pension forces her to retire to the newly opened dump, where she finds amid the rejected material a four-year-old-boy, whom she adopts. She finds subsequently another social outcast in the garbage, a fired security guard who, attempting to commit (as he calls it) "identicidio" (identicide) (24), throws himself into the garbage truck: "a la hora que pasa el camión recolector, tomé la determinación de botarme a la basura [at the hour that the garbage truck came, I decided to throw myself into the garbage]" (17).

Upon finding himself resurrected in *el basurero* and rescued by Única, the former guard renames himself Momboñombo Moñagallo, taking on other social and personal identities and defacing his original family name, as his new appellation seems to imply. Throughout the novel, Moñagallo does not disclose his original name but rather fabricates for himself an excessively repetitive syllabic name. Indeed, "the man elaborated a strange and grotesque name," one analogous to his extraneous status in society (17). His newly invented mumbo-jumbo name reads like a tongue twister, surely drawing a chuckle from any reader attempting to pronounce *Mom-bo-ñom-bo Mo-ña-ga-llo*. The onomastic wordplay is significant. In the first and second names, a total of five letters from the Spanish alphabet are repeated: 6 *o*'s, 4 *m*'s, 2 *ñ*'s, 2 *b*'s, and 2 *a*'s, a repetition of letters that perhaps simulates the guard's recycled status in the dump. While the *g* and *ll* each appear only once in his new last name, Moñagallo, the *ll* stands out as a marker of linguistic and cultural difference, as there is no letter like it outside of the Spanish language. The *ll* in Moñagallo, or rather in the word *gallo*, serves as a double phallic symbol, perhaps signifying the emasculation of the old guard as he falls from grace and rank into the dump site, where he virtually has no power. Indeed, the word *gallo* (rooster, cock) coupled with the prefix *moña/o* (woman's hair ribbon) that make up his new name would seem to signal a defaced masculinity by the standards of dominant forms of masculinity within the patriarchal order in the Hispanic world. In renaming himself, Moñagallo seems to ridicule the patriarchal national order that once defined yet rejected him.

Pushed to commit identicide, Moñagallo rejects his former social identifications and reinvents himself in the dump site as Moñagallo—a *gallo* with a *moña/moño*—in the inverted carnivalesque world of the *basurero*. At the beginning of the novel, Moñagallo

> había matado su identidad, se había desecho de su nombre, de la casa donde vivió solo años de años, de su cédula de identidad, de sus recuerdos, de todo: porque el día que se botó a la basura fue el último día que sus prestaciones le permitieron simular una vida de ciudadano. (24)
> [had killed his identity, had gotten rid of his name, the home he had lived in for years, his identity card, his memories, everything, because the day he threw himself into the garbage was the last day that his income allowed him to simulate his life as a citizen.]

On losing his job, or the sign of his material worth and subjective value, he loses all social standing as a Costa Rican citizen. Like Única, Moñagallo is relegated to the margins of society, where he festers amid the rejected material of the nation. It is in Río Azul, however, that Única rescues him. He becomes *un humano reciclado*, a recycled human being (33), as well as a member of the community of dump dwellers, who form alternative families and organizations with their own logic, politics, and daily rituals. The *basurero* becomes the habitus of what Moñagallo calls a life in decomposition (23), running on its own organic momentum rather than on the logic of consumer society. The dump citizens make their home in a rehabilitated and sustainable (dump) site, a new location of culture for the impoverished, abject masses of the South. This marginal community, as the text shows, lives a sustainable existence, using, rather than producing, waste. They establish family bonds and are loyal in their recycled love (86). Moñagallo marries Única in a wedding ceremony conducted by a preacher invested by a Bible and other religious paraphernalia found in the dump and attended by everyone in their community of *buzos*. In its ironic reassessment of hegemonic society, the novel shows that "todo el país se estaba convirtiendo en un basurero [the whole nation was turning into a dump site]" (116).

In the novel, Costa Rica—the former "Switzerland of Central America"—is represented as contaminated, degraded, and made violent by the forces of the neoliberal regime. The novel reaches its climactic point as violence breaks out over the relocation of the dump: eight hundred riot policemen attack the citizens of Esparza when they protest against their city housing the newly privatized dump site. The armed police force represses a demonstration organized by the *buzos*, who will be turned out of their homes with the closure of Río Azul. One of the *buzos* takes stock of the situation, stating, "Hasta ahora nunca habíamos visto la policía utilizar esos métodos para dispersar la gente [Until now we had never seen the police use those methods to disperse the people]" (105).

Moñagallo cannot but be shocked by the overall decomposition and violent turn of Costa Rica, which takes pride in its history of demilitarization and promotion of social welfare programs for its citizens since at least 1949. In the dump site, he witnesses the rise of a new Costa Rica from the rubble of economic structural adjustments such as those already seen in Carmen Naranjo's "And We Sold the Rain." In the new Costa Rica, even the garbage will be appropriated by private industry (121), and the *buzos* will be excluded from the new site/nation. Where will the displaced people of Moñagallo's wasted land go? Who will protect them? Providing no answers, the novel ends with Momboñombo and Única—now completely homeless—sitting on a bench at the shores

of Puntarenas, their adopted son, El Bacán, now dead from asthma com-
plications produced by years of living in the dump site and exacerbated
by the water used by the antiriot police force to flush out the *buzos'* social movement. In a catatonic state, Única sits at the shore *mirando al
mar*, looking into the vast sea and horizon of Central America.

Wasted Opportunities for Peace

In these texts of wasted Central American nations, the isthmus is represented as the dumping ground of globalization. Costa Rica's city dump
becomes overwhelmed by its own consumer waste while El Salvador
and Guatemala recover from an era of armament dumping that wasted
the lives of thousands of people. In her study of the image of waste in
what she calls the "postnatural novel" of the 1980s in the United States,
Cynthia Deitering has suggested that in the North waste may serve as
a "cultural metaphor for a society's most general fears about its collective future and as expression of an ontological rupture in its perception
of the Real" (1996, 197). Waste as a metaphor for First World dystopia
abounds in many northern narratives, especially in neo-noir science fiction novels such as Octavia Butler's *Parable of the Sower* (2000) and *Parable of the Talents* (2001) and Alejandro Morales's *The Rag Doll Plagues*
(1991), and a vast number of posthuman novels and films such as *Blade
Runner* (Scott 1982) and *Soldier* (Anderson 1998). On the flipside, the
case might be made that garbage, in the southern texts analyzed here,
expresses a collective fear of the uncertain yet devastating future faced
by many Central Americans at the turn of the millennium. Indeed in
The Age of Extremes, Hobsbawm describes the turn of the twenty-first
century as an era of deep social uncertainties, uncalculated human
losses, extreme acts of violence, and accelerated ecological devastation
of global proportion that "must be measured in decades rather than centuries" (1994, 569).

Although the sign of waste prevails in *Única mirando al mar*, "And
We Sold the Rain," *Milagro de la Paz*, and other Central American texts
produced at the turn of the twenty-first century, these same texts are
open to more regenerative, sustainable readings, resolutions, and interpretations of the problem of the wasting away of Central America at
its human, material, and symbolic levels. These texts, I suggest, project
the possibility of resolutions onto the space of reader reception as Rojas
and Ovares suggest in their analysis of the novel in *100 años de literatura*

costarricense. Readers are called to ponder the aggravated conditions of globalization across the isthmus and to offer more sustainable solutions to the problem of the garbage and social neglect that politicians have been unable to proffer, as, for example, in the case of the garbage debacle in Costa Rica, where the relocation of the Río Azul dump site still remained in question in late 2006. *Recycled Life* (Iwerks and Glad 2006), an award-winning documentary about a little-known secret outside of Guatemala City, introduces viewers to the communities of garbage dwellers (Guajeros) who have lived and worked in the massive landfill of Guatemala City for over sixty years. Highly toxic yet populated by thousands of people, the dump was ravaged by a methane-induced fire on January 24, 2005, which forced dwellers out and brought new state-sanctioned restrictions on access to it, threatening the main source of livelihood and community for many displaced people. Like *Recycled Life*, the texts examined here leave their characters and readers suspended, in an interstitial, *unhomely* space, neither here nor there, with no definitive answers and resolutions to the problem of the garbage, or to the worsening conditions of life for the poor across the isthmus. In the end, readers are invited to propose resolutions for Única who sits and waits at the shore, for the women in *Milagro de la Paz* who struggle bravely and eternally to survive, and for the labor migrants who like those in "And They Sold the Rain" must leave their homes, time and time again, in search of other prospects.

With problems left unresolved and providing no narrative closure, the texts discussed here open a discussion on the socioeconomic and political problems signified by the garbage. At the end of *Milagro de la Paz*, Latina and her daughters remind readers that at least they still have each other to face the next day of hardship: "Mañana será otro día común y corriente. Las cosas no habían mejorado pero estamos vivos [Tomorrow will be another ordinary day. Things have not changed, but we are alive]" (Argueta 1994, 188). The displaced people in Naranjo's "And We Sold the Rain" find temporary shelter in their diaspora, where "in a short time we were happy and felt as if these things too were ours, or at the very least, that the rain still belonged to us" (1989, 156). Finally, Única sits on a bench in Puntarenas, facing the sea of Central America's discontent, a living testament to displacement and disposability in a global consumer society. But, as Sergio Ramírez would remind us in his essay, "Seis falsos golpes contra la literatura centroamericana," Central American literature may not only mimetically represent local contexts but also meta-critically engage with social issues and realities, hence, the discursive, communicative, and material function of literature in Central American society. Literature. I believe, retains a critical denunciating function. Why else, then, would a novel like *Unica mirando al mar* mobilize an entire country to find a solution to the problem of the garbage site and the larger crisis of neoliberalism in the isthmus? When I lived in Costa Rica in 1993–1995, I witnessed the mass mobilization against the privatization of state-run agencies, the effects of globalization in the country, and the general discontent of the people with their government. Contreras Castro's novel aptly captures the moment of a country heading into greater socio-economic disarray and crisis and calls on the public to take action while there is still time. While fearing the worst, Contreras Castro, Naranjo, Argueta, and others, however, also propose that garbage may be reread as organic material that regenerates life. Manlio Argueta's novel about despoiled peace in postwar countries and Carmen Naranjo's and Fernando Contreras Castro's texts about the generalized decomposing state of Central American societies equally show the need to imagine other narrative endings if not alternatives for Central America. Indeed, all is not lost or wasted in Central America, as Gioconda Belli's futuristic novel, *Waslala: Memorial del futuro* (1996) suggests.[19]

Regenerating *Waslala:* Central America in the Third Millennium

In her 1996 novel, *Waslala: Memorial del futuro*, the Nicaraguan writer Gioconda Belli returns to Faguas, the location of her first novel, *La mujer habitada* (1989; *The Inhabited Woman*, 1995).[20] In *La mujer habitada*, Faguas depicts a late-twentieth-century Central American country where leftist guerrillas and the military dictatorship fight a revolution. Faguas is a developing country showing the signs of superficial progress and uneven economic development and modernization. Its landscape is a distorted pastiche of elements reflecting the various competing forces there. In Faguas can be found "volcanic, seismic, opulent nature, the lust of the trees piercing the asphalt" and "artifices to convey modernity," such as two-story department stores with elevators and shopping centers that displace poor residents and produce shantytowns overflowing with slum dwellers. In the late twentieth century, Faguas "was trying at all costs to become modern, using any outlandish method possible" (Belli 1995, 14), but by the time the novel *Waslala* begins, in the third millennium, Faguas has lost its struggle for modernity.

In *Waslala*, Belli returns to Faguas in the third millennium, after all revolutions have been fought and lost and it lies in fantastic, futuristic abandonment. Quarantined from the rest of the world, Faguas festers in the corruption of warring internal factions and the contamination that is deposited there by the North. The region is ruled by los Espadas, two sibling dictators who oversee the trafficking of armaments and the export of *filina*, a genetically manufactured drug cocktail of marijuana and cocaine, which sells at a high price in the world market. Faguas's economy runs on the exchange of contraband, the production of air (trees are preserved to generate oxygen for the world), and the incineration of global waste, which is shipped to Faguas on highly toxic barges. Faguas is cut off from the rest of the world; no one visits, except for renegade smugglers, journalists, and individuals doing illegal or clandestine business there. No one leaves Faguas either, for immigration to the North has been completely shut down: "Ahora era muy peligroso emigrar. Era muy difícil. Casi nadie lograba cruzar la muralla [Now it was very dangerous to emigrate. It was very difficult. Almost no one could cross the wall]" (1996, 44).

In its isolation, Faguas had long ago reached a maximum state of deevolution, or what the novel calls *involution*, an in-growth and decline so great that Faguas loses touch with time and other parts of the world. Sometime in its history,

Faguas empezó a involucionar y el país inició su retorno a la Edad
Media, perdiendo sus contornos de nación y pasando a ser, en los mapas,
una simple masa geográfica como lo eran antes las selvas del Amazonas
y ahora vastas regiones en África, Asia, la América del Sur, el Caribe:
manchas verdes sin rasgos, sin indicación de ciudades: regiones aisladas,
cortadas del desarrollo, la civilización, la técnica; reducidas a selvas,
reservas forestales, a función de pulmón y basurero del mundo desa-
rrollado que las explotó para sumirlas después en el olvido, en la mis-
eria, condenándolas al ostracismo, a la categoría de *tierras incognitas*,
malditas, tierras de guerra y epidemias donde nadie llegaba más que los
contrabandistas." (18)
[Faguas had begun to grow inward (in-volve) and the country had begun
its return to the Middle Ages, losing its national configurations and
becoming on the map a simple geographic mass just like the Amazon
jungle had been, and Africa, Asia, South America, and the Caribbean
now are: green blotches without signs of cities; isolated regions, cut off
from development, civilization, technology; reduced to jungle, natural

reserves, a function of lungs and a dump site of the developed world, which exploited them only to abandon them to forgetfulness, misery, ostracism, and to categorize them as inhospitable *terra incognita*, land of wars and epidemics to which no one except for traffickers traveled.]

Fagüenses live in Amazon-like jungle overgrowths, or in wasted cities like Cineria, an extensive incinerator that receives the garbage from the North. Once Faguas had been on the path to development and progress, but now it is a place abandoned to the forces of nature and the most powerful in the natural, social, and economic Darwinist ladder: war, epidemics, and garbage are all that remain of the competitive socioeconomic forces introduced early in its history. Along with Africa, Asia, South America, and other former developing nations, Faguas has become a great green blotch on the map and an extensive undifferentiated region in the South whose cities and civilizations have receded into oblivion.

By the time the novel begins, Faguas has fallen out of the circuit of progress and development and has very few ties to the outside world, except for the illicit and informal economies controlled by a few powerful caudillos who rule over local populations, regions, and private industries. In Faguas, los Espadas control the drug and arms trade, while the *generala* (general) Engracia controls the canal zone through which pass barges filled with garbage. Engracia also rules Cineria, the seat of her garbage empire and mass-scale incinerator, where the discarded items of the civilized world ("descarte del mundo civilizado") are deposited (58). In Cineria, Engracia and her team of recyclers scavenge, repair, and rehabilitate "el desperdicio cotidiano de las sociedades de la abundancia [the daily waste of societies of excess]" (143) for Faguas. Radios, irons, toasters, mixers, lawn mowers, microwave ovens, and other strange and obsolete objects are brought to Cineria, along with dirty diapers, bottles, and toxic waste, all of which are the remains of consumer societies driven by the desire for novelty, "por lo nuevo, por lo último" (159). Deposited in the isthmus, these waste products allow Cineria to read its own position in the world: Cineria is "una ciudad del pasado, habitada por seres del presente [a city of the past, inhabited by people of the present]" (103). One of the few characters visiting from the North comments that Cinerians know very well "en qué época estaban, sólo que no lograban que sus vidas se entendieran con el tiempo [in what age they lived, only that they were unable to integrate their lives into the present time]" (103). Lacking the technology to compete in the post-development economy, Cineria and the rest of Faguas function as recipients and recyclers of cast-off consumer goods. Cinerians thus receive (for pay) barges filled with toxic waste from the North.

Fantastic though it may seem, the exporting of waste to Central America has a real precedent, as the environmentalists Dana Alston and Nicole Brown explain in "Global Threats to People of Color."[21] According to Alston and Brown, Central America and other regions of the South have become dumping grounds for an international waste trade that "seeks alternative dump sites overseas" and exports waste products such as "asbestos, incinerator ash, municipal wastes and sewage, and industrial chemical toxics" (1993, 183). Read in this context, Cineria is the metaphoric phoenix of Central America. It is in the garbage that Cinerians come to know directly and intimately "the underside of consumer capitalism" (Deitering 1996, 197), interpreting the excesses of the North as the widespread effects of the globalization of capital on the South. One of the garbage pickers in Belli's novel explains the logic of garbage in Cineria: "Esa basura, esa acumulación de objetos, eran como las huellas que un asesino deja tras de sí. . . . Así es el sistema; cobra su precio. No hay desarrollo sin desperdicio [That accumulation of objects was like the prints left behind by an assassin. . . . That is how the system is; it has a price. There is no development without waste]" (1996, 165–166). In a mirroring effect, Cinerians recognize that their degradation is the North's gain. The waste they import is the sign of massive production, consumerism, and excess generated elsewhere. Overtaken by its own nature, contamination and violence, and its dystopic future, Faguas is the site and symbol of the complete devastation and possible regeneration of Central America.

But for every dystopia there is a utopia, and somewhere within the interior of Faguas also lies the illusive and enigmatic city of Waslala—"un sitio fantástico, la última utopía [a fantastic place, the last utopia]" (33). Waslala, hidden in the folds of the fictional country of Faguas, alludes to a town with the same name located in north central Nicaragua, which was a Sandinista stronghold and site of a communitarian project in the 1970s and 1980s. In the novel, however, Waslala is more than a point on the map; it represents the southern tip of Utopia. The desire to reach Waslala represents the Fagüenses' desire for everything that Faguas is not: Fagüenses desire an end to the garbage, drug trafficking, and wars, and Waslala has none of these; Fagüenses seek peace, and Waslala offers harmony and tranquility; Fagüenses wish to return to pure essence, and Waslala lies in a prelapsarian state. Indeed, Waslala represents for the Fagüenses a lost paradise and time.[22] The novel's protagonist, Melisandra, who is the granddaughter of don José (one of the poet-founders of Waslala), embarks on a journey to find the utopic city, to which her mother and father are said to have retreated. Waslala, then, signifies the (lost) ideals of the Fagüenses.

In the beginning, even before the novel opens, a group of visionaries sought to build an alternative to declining Faguas—a communitarian society where there would be peace, justice, an equal distribution of goods, and an equitable division of labor among its inhabitants. Based on Thomas More's utopian experiment, as outlined in *Utopia* (1516), the visionaries, who were poets and people possessing the knowledge to generate a self-sustaining and sustainable community, looked for an ideal site that could be isolated and protected from the rest of Faguas and where a new generation of Fagüenses could be produced. Don José, one of two characters who has been to Waslala and returned (Engracia is the other), tells of the founding of Waslala, which was designed in principle on utopian literature:

Por ese entonces Faguas existía en los mapas como una nación con perspectiva. Las guerras no eran aún endémicas. Los tiranos eran sucedidos por gobernantes blandengues auspiciados por militares. Bajo estas administraciones benignas e intrascendentes se abrían espacios propios para que se juntaran intelectuales y políticos iluminados que, ni cortos, ni perezosos anunciaban poseer la fórmula mágica que daría estabilidad y progreso al país. Considerándolos deleznables y oportunistas, me uní a un grupo de poetas que, a partir de un método distinto; recurriendo a las posiblidades de la imaginación, de la mitología acumulada, de la experiencia colectiva, encontrado en la literatura humanista y en la poesía de todos los tiempos, se proponían crear un modelo de sociedad totalmente nuevo y revolucionario, basado en una ética que repudiaba el poder, la dominación y concedía a cada individuo la responsabilidad por la comunidad. (Belli 1996, 61)
[Faguas existed then on the map as a nation with perspective. The wars had not yet become endemic. Weak leaders favored by the military followed the tyrants. Under these benign and inconsequential administrations, far-reaching, rigorous, and luminous intellectuals and politicians met to announce magical formulas for the stability and progress of the country. Considering them flighty opportunists, I joined a group of poets, who adopted a different method. Turning to the possibilities of the imagination, mythology, collective experience, humanist literature,

and universal poetry, they proposed to create an entirely new and revolutionary society, based on an ethic that repudiated power and domination, and endowed each individual with communal responsibility.]

The project of Waslala was the production of a near-replica of More's Utopia: the ideal state, governed by wise elders and equitably run by all citizens according to their capacities. Everyone in Utopia/Waslala would contribute to the welfare and well-being of the community at large, sharing the work and the fruits of collective labor. As designated in the social plan of Utopia, capitalism (the source of economic and moral conflict among nations and peoples), violence, and war would be eradicated from Waslala, and everyone would live in peace and harmony. The founders of Waslala, like the Utopian leaders, firmly believed that "the one essential condition for a healthy society was equal distribution of goods— . . . impossible under capitalism" (More 1516/1985, 66).

Unlike More's Utopia, however, Waslala would not participate in slavery, colonialism, and surrogate armed conflict. (More's Utopians employed mercenaries to fight wars, whereby enemies would kill each other off. By a process of elimination of the enemy, the Utopians hoped to conquer the rest of the world.) Waslala, after all, is a replica of Utopia but with a *difference:* it rejected all practices associated with imperialism, neocolonialism, and armed conflict. The Waslalans sought to erase the socioeconomic structures of colonialism and capitalism from their project in order to transform Faguas. In Waslala, there would be a regeneration of values, ideals, and principles among its citizens, who would then transform the rest of Faguas (the isthmus?). The original visionaries felt that Fagüenses had lost the virtues of self-less communitarianism, which, like in Utopia, translates into a complete disavowal of private property and a practice of "communal ownership" (66). A subtext to Waslala, Thomas More's *Utopia* presents the blueprint for "wise social planning" (40) and serves as the prologue to Waslala's early demise, for Waslala, like Utopia, is "el lugar que no es [the place that does not exist]" (Belli 1996, 40). Waslala becomes the place that Fagüenses seek in their desire for alternatives to their contaminated and deteriorating social reality, as signified by the filth and garbage that arrive from the North. Belli writes, "Cómo no va a querer la gente creer en un lugar encantado, sin conflictos, sin contradicciones [Why wouldn't the people want to believe in an enchanted place, without conflict, without contradictions?]" (200).

At the end of the novel, Melisandra, whose mission had been to find

Waslala, arrives in the fabled city only to discover that it has long since fallen into decline because, as the novel makes clear through Engracia's critique, ideas and ideals cannot be isolated and separated from social practice. The failure of the visionaries of the utopian Waslala was that their ideal state was, in principle and practice, isolationist, where it should have been integrated and integral to the larger social dynamic of Faguas (i.e., the isthmus). Waslala should have served the social welfare of all Fagüenses ("el bienestar del más humilde de los seres humanos") (324). With this realization, Melisandra's own grandfather abandons Waslala to return to the world he had left behind, Engracia returns to Cineria in order to generate an alternative economy for the Fagüenses who were at the mercy of los Espadas, and Melisandra herself forgoes her mother's invitation to stay in Waslala, once she has found the illusive city. Along with the others who return to the social realities of Faguas, Melisandra takes up her role in the country's reconstruction. Utopic Waslala, as Melisandra perceives it, has nevertheless an important function in the imaginary of "lo que puede ser [what could be]" (376). Waslala is the signifier of alternatives that must be put into effect in some far-reaching context and capacity. As Belli's novel makes explicit:

> La razón de ser de Waslala era ser Waslala, una Utopía, el lugar que no era, que no podía ser el tiempo y el espacio habitual, sino otra cosa, el laboratorio, quizás, la luz tal vez, el ideal constantemente en movimiento, poblado, abandonado y vuelto a repoblar; creído, descreído y vuelto a creer. (372)
> [The reason for being of Waslala is to be Waslala, a Utopia, the place that does not exist, that could not exist in real time and space. It had to be another thing, perhaps the laboratory, the light, the ideal constantly in movement, populated, abandoned, repopulated, believed, disbelieved, and believed in once again.]

At the end of the novel, the only person left in Waslala is Melisandra's mother, who is entrusted with the Utopian dream. All the others have abandoned the utopian experiment, perished in the ingrown isolation of Waslala, or returned to practice the Waslalan ideal in Faguas.

Melisandra herself returns to Faguas carrying the manuscripts of the visionaries of Waslala, hoping to make some use of the Waslalan experiment in the reconstruction of Faguas, which lies in the divide of what can be and what is ("entre lo que puede ser y lo que es") (376). In that interstitial space, which signifies the postwar and peacetime condition of the isthmus, resides the message of the novel. Gioconda Belli, who participated in the construction of the revolutionary ideal of Sandinismo in Nicaragua during the 1970s and 1980s, would seem to suggest in *Waslala* that the reconstruction of Faguas (Central America) is still an inconclusive project. A postrevolutionary movement to reconstruct Faguas—the isthmus—requires a common imaginary (a Waslalan dream), a common project and practice (the regeneration of the Cinerian garbage cities), and a communitarian social agenda to forge Central America into *lo que puede ser*—what it could be.

As the texts examined here show, Central America is vital to understanding how global power and wealth are concentrated in the northern regions and expropriated from the South. The logic of tropicalism transforms Central America into a degraded and disorderly site requiring the aid, in this case, of agents skilled in the technologies of waste disposal. Following this imperative, the case is made that the isthmus does not possess the capital and technology to refurbish its societies and must remain dependent on those countries that do possess those means. The material and human potential of Central America is converted into expropriatable excess that can be recycled for profit. Read in this light, postrevolutionary, postwar, and postutopic Central American literature represents societies repeatedly robbed of their own productive and sustainable means and potential. What remain of Central American societies, then, are the impoverished shantytowns and depleted nations of Carmen Naranjo's story and Fernando Contreras Castro's novel, the conflictive peacetime villages of Manlio Argueta's *Milagro de la Paz*, and the quarantined regions of Gioconda Belli's *Waslala*, which have been abandoned by the state and left to the daily ingenuities and survival tactics of subjects shaped by the trauma of war.

In *Waslala* and the other Central American narratives of garbage analyzed here, waste circulates as the signifier of development and progress gained elsewhere but arriving in these locations in cruelly degraded forms: garbage, cheap products, stockpiled armaments, and other contaminants. The inhabitants of Central America, like the Cinerians, are inundated with the waste of highly industrialized regions, and they are pushed to the limits of a world that becomes more and more inhospitable and inhumane. In Carmen Naranjo's "And We Sold the Rain," a Central American nation undergoing neoliberal restructuring is turned into a massive shanty sprawl, its natural resources sold one by one and its populations pushed into labor migration. In Fernando Contreras Castro's *Única mirando al mar*, the discarded subjects of the nation commit acts of *identicide* by throwing themselves into a dump site where they live recycled lives. Manlio Argueta's *Milagro de la Paz*, a bleak prognosis for the wasted opportunity for peace in the region, imagines a place of impoverishment that survives only because of the miraculous effort of its people. Read together, these narratives produce a *transisthmian imaginary* that disarticulates the developmentalist myths and utopic narratives of Central America and challenges all those interested in the possibility that Central America can forge alternative narratives. Looking back from the dystopic future of Central America, Belli's *Waslala* warns readers of further economic, environmental, and human devastation in the region if action is not taken today.

EPILOGUE

Weathering the Storm:
Central America in the Twenty-first Century

La vida no se detenía, las voces siguieron corriendo hasta estrellarse contra los ruidos de una ciudad en movimiento en la que el muchacho seguía inerte, atascado a su esquina.
[Life did not stop, the voices continued flowing until crashing against the sounds of a city in motion in which the boy remained inert, stuck in his corner.]
—DANIEL JOYA, *Sueños de un callejero*

In the aftermath of the civil wars of the 1980s, the institutionalization of peace in the 1990s, and the ratification of the Dominican Republic–Central American Free Trade Agreement on July 28, 2005, by the U.S. Congress and its final approval by the Costa Rican government on October 7, 2007, Central American literary and cultural production remains key to the (discursive) reconstruction of the isthmus. As William I. Robinson has suggested for Central American anti-globalization movements and narratives, "The next round [of struggle] will have to be a transnational struggle involving regional and transnational social movements searching for viable formulas of social and economic democratization, political empowerment and the construction of a counter-hegemony under the new conditions of global capitalism" (2004, 20). While the scale of social and economic injustice has intensified in Central America and its transnational communities, cultural responses and critiques thus far have been less defined and more diffused but nonetheless quite copious and stringent at the beginning of the twenty-first century. At the newest cultural divide unraveling before our eyes, a new Central American transisthmian narrative textuality is struggling for economic, political, social, and cultural representation amid the onslaught of global forces. From this space of struggle and survival emerge location-specific cultural and literary texts, as pointed out by critics of neoliberal cultural politics and narration (Masiello 2001; García Canclini 2002; Yúdice 2003).

From the maelstrom of social reconstruction or engineering in Central America thus emerges a transisthmian neorealist textuality that is extremist, visceral, and at times so over the top as to appear surrealist, fantastic, and almost forensic. To name just a few texts: Franz Galich's *Managua Salsa City (¡Devórame otra vez!)* (Managua Salsa City: Devour Me Again) (2001) depicts the amoral, (dis)organized, and garish urbanity of Managua; Horacio Castellanos Moya's *El Asco* (The Disgust) (2000) eschatologically satirizes postwar Salvadoran society; and Lety Elvir writes razor sharp short stories of Honduran women's lives in *Sublimes y perversos* (Sublimes and Perverts) (2005). Even in Costa Rica, the proverbial exception to the rule, the city figures as an underworld of homelessness, despair, and survival, as depicted in texts by Fernando Contreras Castro (*Urbanoscopio* [Urbanscope] 1997), Sergio Muñoz Chacón (*Los Dorados* [The Golden] 2000; *Urbanos* [Urbanites] 2003), and Uriel Quesada (*Lejos, tan lejos* [Far, So Far] 2004). In his introduction to a collection of short stories titled *Cicatrices: Un retrato del cuento Centroamericano* (Scars: A Portrait of the Central American Short Story) (2004), Werner Mackenbach claims that the compiled stories in his book are about other wars: "la violencia de las ciudades, la lucha de géneros y los conflictos de los individuos [the violence of the cities, the struggle of genders, and the conflicts of individuals]" (2004, n.p.). As suggested by the title of the anthology, the stories emerge from the "cicatrices," the scars and lacerations, left by the violence of the past decades in Central America. The stories are populated by flightless wounded angels (Patricia Belli, Nicaragua, "Cicatrices"), twisted hit-men-for-hire (Eduardo Callejas, Honduras, "El francotirador" [The Hired Gun]), eating disorder victims (Roberto Castillo, Honduras, "Anita la cazadora de insectos" [Anita, Insect Catcher]), estranged and sexually frustrated couples, cynical prostitutes working the sex trade, PTSD sufferers, and other social outcasts of more recent wars. As a whole, the characters in these narratives attempt to move forward while still carrying the weight of the past, often wounded but never completely destroyed.

On the other hand, with the prolongation and end of the civil wars came the transnationalization of Central American cultures. Writers from the Central American diaspora in the United States also wrote back to the isthmus from transnational sites. From San Francisco, the Salvadoran Martivón Galindo compiled her exile poetry and short stories, in a collection titled *Retazos* (Pieces) (1996). In Los Angeles, young Salvis paired up with their counterparts in San Francisco to produce *Izote Vos: A Collection of Salvadoran American Writing and Visual Arts* (Cowy Kim et al. 2000), while rising performance artists such as Leticia Hernández-Linares and Maya Chinchilla collaborated in Epicentro and other art collectives in California (2007). In Washington, D.C., the home of a thriving Salvadoran community, Mario Bencastro produced several novels, including *Odyssey to the North* (1998) and *La tierra de mi abuelo* (translated as *A Promise to Keep*) (2004), documenting Salvadoran patterns of migration and return migration to the homeland. Also in D.C., the performer Quique Avilés cofounded and coordinated several community art collectives, first LatiNegro and then Sol & Soul. In his poetry, performances, and cultural activism, articulated especially in *The Immigrant Museum* (2003), Avilés chronicles the immigration and everyday struggles of Salvadorans and other Latinas/os in the greater Washington, D.C., metropolitan area. Other Central American Americans, as Arturo Arias (2007) would have it, also write about their diasporic experiences, some of which I have discussed in this book and elsewhere (A. Rodríguez 2003). These include Héctor Tobar's *The Tattooed Soldier* (1998/2000), Francisco Goldman's *The Long Night of White Chickens* (1992) and *The Ordinary Seaman* (1997), Roberto Quesada's *The Big Banana* (1999) and *Never through Miami* (2002), and Daniel Joya's *Sueños de un callejero* (2003), to name only a few.

Literary Forensics

Posing larger questions about the economic and social prospects of the region, many twenty-first-century Central American and U.S. Central American texts are steeped in a profound sense of uncertainty and residual trauma. While naming their condition, these texts also examine it closely in what I would call a practice of literary forensics. The prewar, war, and postwar longevity and staying power of the Salvadoran writer Manlio Argueta, for example, permitted him to publish a fictive memoir of personal and national reconstruction titled *Siglo de O(g)ro* (The Age of Gold/Ogre) (1997). Jacinta Escudos wrote *Cuentos Sucios* (Dirty Stories) (1997) and *A-B-Sudario* (A-B-Shroud) (2003), narratives of subjective and erotic desire from her self-imposed exile in Nicaragua. Otoniel Guevara, in his poems in *Despiadada ciudad* (Merciless City) (1999), explored the urban underworld of San Salvador and its inhabitants. In *Mediodía de frontera* (Midday Border/Frontier) (2002), Claudia Hernández produced a series of forensic stories dissecting the living and dead, zoomorphic and humanistic transfigurations, and rational and nonrational figures that appear in liminal zones—the midday, the border, the frontier of Central American societies, hence the title of her book. Her stories are strewn with cadavers and body parts reconstituted in the kitchens of the living, little girls and women enacting their own deaths, and animals and humans merging into the other. In "Carretera sin buey" (Road without an Ox), a man who has run over an ox on a road assumes his place, transforming himself through his own castration into that beast of burden.

In the title story of Hernández's collection, "Mediodía de frontera" (Midday Border), a dog accompanies a woman while she cuts off her tongue and commits suicide in the public bathroom of a border inspection site. Drawing from Salvadoran legends wherein animals like the Cadejo dogs mediate the passage of humans from one world to the next, the animals in Hernández's stories represent the alienation, dehumanization, disempowerment, and, in many cases, visceration of human characters. We are led to question the boundaries between animal and post–human life. In "Las molestias de tener un rinocerontes" (The Trouble with Having a Rhinoceros), Hernández, for example, writes about a young man who upon losing his arm (in a war?) acquires a playful rhinoceros that represents his condition of incompleteness. The narrator explains:

> Que a uno le haga falta un brazo es incómodo cuando se tiene un rinoceronte. Se vuelve más difícil si el rinoceronte es pequeño y jugetón, como el mío. Es fastidioso. La gente de estas ciudades bonitas y pacíficas no está acostumbrada a ver a un muchacho con un brazo de menos. La gente de estas ciudades bonitas y pacíficas no está acostumbrada a ver a un tipo con un brazo de menos y a un rinoceronte de más saltando a su alrededor. Un se vuelve un espectáculo en las ciudades aburridas como ésta y tiene que andar por las calles sorportando que la gente lo mire, le sonría y hasta se acerque para platicar de lo lindo que está su rinoceronte, señor, no lo compró acá, ¿verdad? (9)
>
> [It is uncomfortable to be *missing an arm when you have a rhinoceros*. It becomes even more difficult if the rhinoceros is small and playful, like

mine. It's a nuisance. The people of *these pretty and peaceful cities* are not used to seeing a guy with one less arm. The *people of these pretty and peaceful cities* are not used to seeing a guy with one less arm and one more rhinoceros jumping around him. You become *a spectacle in boring cities like this one* and you have to go through the city putting up with people looking at you, smiling at you, and coming up to you to talk about how beautiful your rhinoceros is. Sir, you didn't buy it here, did you? (2000, 9; my emphasis)

In the context of postwar El Salvador, the juxtaposed images, namely, the guy with "one less arm" and "one more rhinoceros," situate this story in the realm of extreme realities or the fantastically mundane—the inexplicable harbored in the everyday realities. While the missing arm might allude to unspoken traumas (was the arm lost in a past war?), the appearance of the rhinoceros signifies the magnified spectacle of living trauma in everyday contexts. Such contexts require heightened modes of representation such as the neorealism that has been identified with this literature (Mackenbach 2007). The people do not ask the young man about his missing arm, for they do not want to hear another testimonial, realist narrative, but they do ask about the rhinoceros: "Sir, you didn't buy here, did you?" (9). Hernández thus interrogates realist constructions of Central American societies, offering in their stead a heightened realism where talking animals, cadavers, and people commingle. It seems almost natural that in "these pretty and peaceful cities" armless men walk around with playful rhinos. After decades of wars leaving behind dismembered and tortured bodies, stranger things have been seen than rhinoceroses in the streets of these "pretty and peaceful cities," a phrase repeated twice for irony in the opening paragraph of the story.

Sueños de un callejero and DR-CAFTA Nightmares in Central America

In a forensic and supra-real vein similar to Claudia Hernández's short stories, *Sueños de un callejero* (Dreams of a Streat Boy) (2003) is the first novel published by Daniel Joya, a Salvadoran immigrant who fled El Salvador after the war. At the time the novel was published, Joya worked as coordinator of community services and employment at CASA de Maryland, a nonprofit organization in Takoma Park, Maryland, founded in the 1980s to provide legal, labor, health, and educational services to im-

migrants. As one of the job coordinators at CASA, Joya helped day laborers find paying jobs in the streets and lots near the labor center of
CASA. A *Washington Post* article, on December 17, 2001, notes that since
September 11, CASA de Maryland has seen "a steep increase in the number of people seeking day jobs. With that change have come new tensions as the day laborers who had considered the lot to be theirs find
that more people are showing up each day and competing for work" (Ly
2001). While working at CASA, Joya produced a series of sketches of his
immigrant clients, which were published in a local community newspaper, the *Takoma Voice* of Takoma Park,[1] as well as his novel, *Sueños de
un callejero*. This unassuming transnational novel, written in Maryland
and published by Editorial Nuevo Enfoque in San Salvador, presents the
plight of the dispossessed in El Salvador for a transnational readership.
It is about the "poor majority," or rather the multitude (Hardt and Negri
2000), which, according to Robinson in *Transnational Conflicts*, fills the
ranks of the ever-growing pool of national economic outcasts and global
reserve immigrant labor forces. Robinson explains, "As labor becomes
'free' in every corner of the globe, capital has vast new opportunities for
mobilizing labor power where and when required" (2003, 270).

In the larger context of hemispheric policies of CAFTA-DR, transnational migration, and emerging counterdiscourses critical of those policies, I read *Sueños de un callejero* as a tenuous response articulated by a
transmigrant in the United States. In my reading of the novel, I ponder
how Central American immigrants in diasporic sites fit into the larger
neoliberal transnational agenda and narrative. I further ask: How do the
most underprivileged sectors of transmigrants (those involved in the
circular flow of capital between their countries of origin and the United
States) produce a sense of "place" in relation to two nations—El Salvador, for example, and the United States—that value them only for their
immigrant labor power?[2] How can we better understand the nexus between local and global culture by way of a novel written by a Salvadoran
immigrant living and working in Langley Park, Maryland, who fled his
country due to (post)war conditions? How do the narratives of transnational migrancy and national dispossession critique the effects of neoliberal developmentalist policies in Central America and challenge the
regional publicity narratives of a transnational elite bent on selling their
resources to the lowest bidder?

In *Sueños de un callejero*, the forensic mirror held up to neoliberal
programs is the "heterotopic" image of the streets, which is foremost
symbolized by the imaginary and physical space of "streets" and street
corners in El Salvador. In "Different Spaces," Michel Foucault suggests

that heterotopic spaces are those spaces where a "set of relations . . . define emplacements of transit, streets, trains (a train is an extraordinary bundle of relations)" (1994, 178). Examples of such intersectional spaces include "cafés, movie theatres, and beaches" (178), but it is to the streets occupied by the homeless street people of San Salvador that I now turn.

The streets of San Salvador of Joya's novel are material and symbolic spaces where social, political, and economic forces coalesce into the lived realities of those dispossessed by hemispheric policies. Joya's novel is instrumental in representing the extreme conditions of contemporary public and private life in El Salvador, whose lines have blurred in a generalized state of homelessness and migrancy inside and outside of the country. Where once people from all socioeconomic classes could expect to have a modicum of private life—in the home, in the shack, and even in the refugee camps of the civil war—that space has ceded to homeless life in public spaces—the streets.

The Streets with People with No Names

In what follows, I survey the representation of transnational symbolic city-spaces, particularly the corners and streets of greater San Salvador, as shaped by the "new conditions of global capitalism" (Robinson 2003). In a mix of Central American urban literature written under the aegis of neoliberalism, the streets are as much, if not more than, the protagonists of transnational urban legends. As indicated, Joya's novel, *Sueños de un callejero*, serves as a discursive site representing not only the struggles of the dispossessed in El Salvador but also their material and symbolic homelessness in the streets. The novel tells the story of a young "huelepega" (glue-sniffer) and "esquinero" (street-corner guy) lost in the haze of his addiction and lying on the last corner of his life. The novel teems with cars, vendors, shoeshine boys, *pandilleros*, beggars, people rushing to and from work, and an assortment of "desperdicios humanos" (human waste) (Joya 2003, 96), in sum, the multitude and the riffraff, recalling my reading of waste as a premier metaphor of postwar Central America. According to the omniscient narrator who hovers at all times over "el huele pega de la esquina" (the corner glue-sniffer), the streets of San Salvador are home to

> los más débiles del orden liberal, los poco a poco corroídos en la
> dinámica de una vida que acelera la muerte, en esta nuestra "patria
> exacta." (15)

[the weakest of the liberal order, the slowly corroded by the dynamic of
a life that accelerates toward death, in this our "exact(ing) country."]

The narrator describes San Salvador as a monster swallowing up its
people:

Estas calles, esas y aquellas otras parecieran disfrutar viendo menguar
la vida[,] . . . avenidas que cual vértebras concretan la rutina de la gran
ciudad. (18)
[These streets, these and those others that appear to enjoy seeing the
diminishing of life[,] . . . avenues that are vertebras running through the
great city.]

In the novel, it is to those streets that a seven-year-old boy flees after
his mother fails to return home one evening from the market vegetable
stand where she works, because unbeknownst to her son, she has been
run over and killed by a speeding bus.

Most of the scenes in the novel take place on one particular
unidentified—and thus any—street corner of San Salvador, where "el
huele pega de la esquina" lives (32). Structured like a street in San Salvador, within which cars careen at all speeds and pedestrians run for
their lives, the novel follows the *huele-pega* on his daily quest to fulfill
his basic necessities—loose change, glue, food, sleep, and, if fortunate,
a show of sympathy. The streets are his caretaker and his predator, life
and death drives combined. Social and socializing agents in their own
right, the streets embody a cruel technology that maims and kills the
callejeros, who by virtue of living in the street have no names. No one
desires to know their names or to know their stories because they are
the cumulative human waste of the city, which shows the failings of a
social order and its web of socioeconomic and political relations. Thus,
as the novel progresses, the boy-turned-adolescent glue-sniffer becomes
a heap of inert bones and skin on the street corner that he calls home,
while the world whirls around him, bustling with vendors of newspapers, lottery tickets, fruits and vegetables, and other wares, and passersby, with someplace to go, fleeing the scene.

During the course of the novel, fatal automobile accidents abound.
The first to die is the *huele-pega*'s mother; then an eighty-year-old
woman who sells plastic bags in the Hula-Hula Park is killed. The narrator tells us that "fueron alrededor de diez vehículos los que pasaron
sobre su cuerpo" (over ten vehicles passed over her body) (16). The kill-

ing of a shoeshiner, whose pieces of flesh sprinkle the pavement like "chingaste" (glass pieces), follows this crash incident. The street carnage proceeds with the killing of a pregnant mother and her five-year-old daughter, a seller of newspapers, and finally the "esquinero," who throws himself into the oncoming traffic circling the Rotonda de El Salvador del Mundo—a site of condensed signification in the city. Located near the busy Zona Rosa (Pink Zone), the party haven of the Salvadoran transnational elite class and international tourists, the Rotonda is the glue-sniffer's final destination. It is telling that the *esquinero* kills himself under the watchful eye and hand-raised-in-blessing of the statue of the patron Christ of San Salvador, El Salvador del Mundo (the Savior of the World), after which the city and country is named. In the end, all institutions, including the state, religion, and family, have failed the *esquinero*, and he dies in a final act of self-immolation, as cars crush what remains of his spirit and body.

Flesh against steel, the "selva de concreto" (the jungle of concrete) exacts a heavy toll on those who live in the streets. With these scenes of carnage, *Sueños de un callejero* makes clear that the war can be found in every corner and that only the fittest can survive in an era of neoliberal reforms in San Salvador and the rest of Central America. As the novel progresses, the *huele-pega* becomes more addicted to glue and more attached to his corner, a heterotopia of sorts, a physical place of deviation "outside of all places," as Foucault explains in "Different Spaces." There in his corner the *huele-pega* finds temporary reprieve in the city, begs for coins, watches the flow of traffic and pedestrians, receives rebuffs from passersby, sniffs glue to oblivion, and dies with each day that passes.

> La pega, elixir que estimula sus células, dándoles sentido de locomoción; la esquina, su universo, espacio le apresaba, y; el oler, actividad conciente sobre la que gravitan todo sus esfuerzos, su lucha diaria, su actual razón de ser. (32–33)
> [The glue, the elixir that stimulates his cells, giving them movement; the corner, his universe, space that entraps him; and the smell, conscious activity around which all his efforts gravitate, his daily struggle, his actual reason for being.]

The boy who arrives in the streets around the age of seven, the text tells us, is known to others only by the name of his physical and subjective location, "el huele pega de la esquina" (94–95). Finally, his identity merges with the streets and with one particular corner that, as Foucault would have it, also serves as the mirror to the failed utopia of the post-war period. The *esquinero* embodies all that the postwar period did not bring to the majority of Salvadoreños, in other words, peace, security, jobs, and homes, which they must seek elsewhere, in migration.

As we have seen, *Sueños de un callejero* by Daniel Joya is a transnational novel written from the Salvadoran diaspora, in Maryland, to be precise, about the current plight of the dispossessed castaways of El Salvador. Like other Central American narratives mentioned here, *Sueños de un callejero* excavates the deepest social and material anxieties and insecurities of a society grappling with past and present crises and moving from one war to a more devastating one waged by global forces on the bodies and minds of the "poor majority." In this new war period, even the utopia of the day-after-the-war has vanished for the majority of El Salvador and Central America. The options are to die in place (in the streets of San Salvador), as the *esquinero* does, or to live in another place, as Daniel Joya, the author, opted, when he immigrated to Maryland. Joya's text is a diamond in the rough that gives us insight into greater socioeconomic inequities and transformations passed through the lens of a neorealist literary representation.

Into the Future

In this epilogue, I have analyzed Daniel Joya's novel, *Sueños de un callejero*, and surveyed a few other transisthmian texts produced under the symbolic membrane, as Edelberto Torres-Rivas would have it, of empire building and neoliberalism in Central America. I read these texts as a prognosis for the state of Central America, as experienced by the most dispossessed individuals—a *huele-pega* living in the streets, a man whose arms (and agency) were lost in a war, an angel without wings, and a people left picking at their own physical and emotional scars. The cultural critic Beatriz Cortez explains, in "Estética del cinismo" (Aesthetic of Cynicism), that postwar Central American literature, especially Salvadoran literature,

> carece de espíritu idealista que caracterizó a la literatura centroameri-
> cana durante la guerra civil. La posguerra, en cambio, trae consigo un
> espíritu de cinismo. En consecuencia, esta ficción retrata a las socie-

dades centroamericanas en estado de caos, corrupción y violencia. (Cortez 2000)
[lacks an idealistic spirit that characterized Central American literature during the civil war. The postwar (period), in turn, brought a spirit of cynicism. Consequently, this fiction portrays Central American societies in a state of chaos, corruption, and violence.]

For Cortez, postwar Central American literature is one of "desencanto" (disillusion), articulating cynicism as a social ethos and cultural aesthetic that informs and shapes the new century in Central America. This lack of narrative illusion can be discerned in the modes of narration in twenty-first-century cultural and literary production in the isthmus. Indeed, Cortez (2000) notes that the end of the wars called for the reconfiguration of Central American cultural production. The new narration is bound by libidinal drives—violence and sexuality—giving way to

> los deseos más oscuros del individuo, sus pasiones, su desencanto causado por la pérdida de los proyectos utópicos que antes dieron sentido a su vida y su interacción con un mundo de violencia y caos. (Cortez 2000)
> [The darkest desires of individuals, their passions, their disillusionment caused by a loss of utopic projects that once gave meaning to their lives and their interactions with a violent and chaotic world.]

The disillusionment and disarticulation of hegemonic and revolutionary narratives, thus, is also one of "desencuentros" (clashes) with notions of national and counternational identities on which many political and revolutionary projects had been based. Even testimonial literature, that literary bedrock of truth, was not left unturned. It thus can be said that with the end of the wars in Central America, there came an unhinging or coming apart of narratives that had provided solutions to important questions about the quality of life in the isthmus, especially for the dispossessed, an oxymoron worth exploring in future works.

Indeed, these new narratives of the isthmus critique the unrelenting violence of neoliberalism, especially as played out in the lives of the most vulnerable and poorest sectors of Central American society that surface as transmigrants in other places or as dispossessed women, children, and men within the market economy of the day. These texts, as

I see them, are part of a hemispheric literature being articulated from extreme spaces of labor migration and survival. Joya's novel is as much about El Salvador as it is about El Salvador in the United States, while the other texts referenced here are as much about the local as they are about the global. The publication of these texts suggests the construction of a transisthmian literature in the divide of neoliberal reforms curtailing the movement of migrants and others in and outside of the isthmus, hence the glue-sniffing *callejero*'s entrapment in the streets of El Salvador and the hermetic space of characters confined to national borders as global forces invade their territories. Attila is in the house. At ground zero the great majority of Central American society faces the onslaught of forces that would seek yet to consume and destroy it. As CAFTA-DR descends on Central America's most disenfranchised, Central Americans face little protection under the law, like Joya's *esquinero* in his corner. As I write these final lines, it is my hope, then, that readers will look past the economist rhetoric of globalization to the faces of hunger, desperation, and need, as represented in the transisthmian neorealist narratives of Central America.

Like my reading of Daniel Joya's novel, *Dividing the Isthmus* has been an exercise in reading the f(r)ictions of Central America. I have intended this book to be a fiction-finding mission in a place where fact seems always to meet fiction, and fiction often merges into fact through more venues than literature. I have examined Central America as an intermediary zone of crossings, at once trespassed by neocolonizing and globalizing forces and repeatedly reconstituted and reterritorialized by Central American cultural communities. Up to now, studies of Central American literature have failed to explain how fictionalized accounts of the isthmus are often consonant with the social production of culture. I have argued that, in the case of Central America, literary and cultural production have concomitantly shaped the imaginary of the isthmus and have been shaped by the material and historic conditions of the isthmus.

In specific chapters, I have examined successively f(r)ictions from the late nineteenth century through the early twenty-first century produced inside and outside Central America. I have shown Central American literature to be a transisthmian literature, setting in conversation texts across countries and continent or highlighting particular texts like Manlio Argueta's *Cuzcatlán donde bate la mar del sur* and cultural translocations like the stories of Salvadorans in Washington, D.C., which throw light on the neocolonial structures that still have an impact on the region and its people. I have divided Central America into various cultural and discursive zones in relation to shifting symbolic and material rubrics. Chapters of my book have paid special attention to regionally interlinked texts associated with the production of cacao, indigo, coffee, bananas, canals, waste, and labor (trans)migrants. At these discursive divides, or spaces of f(r)iction, economic and material interventions have produced the greatest fictions in and about the isthmus. It is at these cultural divides that the greatest contradictions of isthmian societies are manifested, thus making the divides productive sites of signification and interpretation.

By linking economic productions and cultural and literary formations across Central America, *Dividing the Isthmus* offers an intersectional reading of Central American cultural and literary spaces. Where else could we see the *esquinero* speak from his corner of the street? Or the mixed-race banana worker protest from her labor camp? Or even the turn-of-the-twentieth-century anti-imperialist coffee planter pre-echo the anti-imperialist rhetoric of the campesino family in the last civil war of Central America? Or from farther out, the transmigrant re-creating the isthmus in other nations? *Dividing the Isthmus* examines the anti-imperialist fiction of Central America that predicted and predicated U.S. hegemony in the region, the social realist protest literature that compensated for the lack of sovereignty in the isthmus, the testimonial and resistance narratives that cradled social and revolutionary movements, the dystopic narratives that announced the dawn of the neoliberal age, and the transnational autoethnographies of the Central American diaspora translocated across the United States and elsewhere, and finally the neorealist, neoliberal fictions dictating life in Central America in the twenty-first century. Most cultural and social historians of Central America recognize that beyond representing the larger social fabric, Central American cultural production has shaped and been shaped by the greater social, economic, political, and cultural contradictions of the isthmus.

Any constructive discussion of Central American cultural and literary production, I insist, entails reading where these contradictions are most pronounced, precisely at the divides that blur the line between fact and fiction, war and peace, nation and isthmus, and the rule and the exception. *Dividing the Isthmus* examines key discursive sites where the fractionalization or f(r)ictionalization, if I may coin a term for Central America, becomes more apparent from neocolonialism to neoliberalism and beyond. As I close this final chapter in *Dividing the Isthmus*, I would like to leave the reader with a final image salvaged from my Tica bus travels through the isthmus. On one particular trip, I crossed the land border from Nicaragua to Honduras, where children rushed to carry my bags for a few cordobas and lempiras under the unrelenting noonday heat and where a little girl, no more than four years old, sat on a bench while her mother sold hardened *bizcochos* and lukewarm sodas to disinterested and disgruntled isthmus-crossers. With one eye pussing from an untreated infection, the little girl stared blankly in no particular direction, as if looking into the horizon of Central America. Will we not look at this little girl, at the future of Central America, in the face? This book is dedicated to that little girl, wherever and whoever she may be, for like other Central Americans she carries the burden of her history and the hope of generations to come.

Notes

Introduction

1. Unless otherwise noted, in this chapter and throughout the book, all translations of materials in Spanish into English are mine. I have made an attempt to identify and use existing English translations when available, but translations of Central American literature and critical materials are still quite scarce.

2. In *Postmodernism, Or, The Cultural Logic of Late Capitalism* (1992), Fredric Jameson considers the periodization of texts a provisional task for organizing a range of discursive material. He rejects the notion of unitary principles for organizing texts according to classification such as temporality, world vision, style, movement, manifesto, generation, and epoch. Instead he argues for provisional categories, like what I offer here as the *transisthmus* based on shifting assemblages of cultural texts.

3. This is not to say, however, that *Dividing the Isthmus* argues for a deterministic relationship between nature and culture, or between Central America's geographic location as isthmus and cultural articulations traced and linked across the isthmus. Rather I propose to think of Central American cultural and literary production through spatial locations and temporalities.

4. This overview of Central American history draws from Hall 1985, 5–24; Pérez Brignoli 1989; Booth and Walker 1993; Carmack 1993, 15–59; Dunkerley 1994; Fonseca 1998; and Woodward 1999.

5. See the *Popol Vuh*, trans. and ed. Allen J. Christenson (2000, 144n62). Christenson explains that the K'iche' Maya of western highland Guatemala believe that the world is configured as "a great house, its walls or corners being the four cardinal points, its roof the sky, and its foundation the underworld." The cardinal axes (north, south, east, and west) converge at the center of the house (*na*), where "the powers of all creation are focused." The center of a structure, often signified by markers such as hearthstones in homes or deep holes in church buildings such as the one in the church in Santiago de Atitlán, recreates the sacred space from which grows the World Tree and staff of life—the source of maize culture. A Maya creation story has it that all life springs from

an original source—the World Tree—represented as the revered maize plant in some texts and as "the foliated cross" in one of the pyramids at Palenque, Chiapas. The center of the house serves not only as a portal to the underworld but also as the source of regenerative forces concentrated there. Since the center of the world is relative to each Maya group, every Maya home, village, and space of worship serves as an *axis mundi* connecting and holding in balance the forces of life and death, the world and the underworld, and the quotidian and the sacred. Each house, village, and community of the extended Maya World may be thought of as the center of the world. Thus I recognize that on these terms from pre-Columbian time onward, the Central American isthmus is the center of (re)creation.

6. It should be remembered that in the nineteenth and twentieth centuries the United States secured hegemony in Central America and the western hemisphere by claiming canal rights in Nicaragua. Up to the present, the symbol of the "doubtful strait" remains an active catalyst for foreign and domestic geopolitical ambitions in Central America.

7. Definition of *isthmus* from http://www.infoplease.com/ce6/sci/A0825658 .html (accessed January 16, 2008).

8. The Clayton-Bulwer Treaty states that neither the United States nor Great Britain could occupy, colonize, or control Nicaragua, Costa Rica, the Mosquito Coast, or any other part of Central America. It also stipulates that the United States and Great Britain could not build fortifications in the area or enter into alliances for canal-building and navigational purposes (Leiken and Rubin 1987, 73). In 1904 the Roosevelt Corollary to the Monroe Doctrine, nonetheless, authorized U.S. military and economic intervention in the region.

9. Approved by every Central American nation by the end of 2007 and ratified by the U.S. Congress on July 28, 2005, the Central American and Dominican Republic Free Trade Agreement (DR-CAFTA) ensures Central America a key place in the FTAA. In this economic reorganization of the western hemisphere, the Central American isthmus serves the expansion of the FTAA, eventually to encompass over thirty-four countries in the western hemisphere. The full text of CAFTA-DR is available at http://www.ustr.gov/Trade _Agreements/Bilateral/CAFTA-DR/CAFTA-DR_Draft_Revised_Texts/ Section_Index.html (accessed August 4, 2005). The Third Draft of the FTAA is available at http://www.ftaa-alca.org/FTAADraft03/Index_e.asp (accessed January 16, 2008).

10. I am indebted to the anonymous readers for the University of Texas Press for encouraging me to ponder more critically the relationship between nature and culture in my conceptualization of the isthmus.

11. For particular discussions of space as discursive, philosophical, political, economic, and cultural constructions, yet tied to geophysical space, see Barton 1997; Lefebvre 1998; Soja 1998a, 1998b; Randall and Mount 1998; Harvey 1999; Crang and Thrift 2000.

12. See Gabriel García Márquez's Nobel lecture, "The Solitude of Latin America," December 8, 1982, http://nobelprize.org/nobel_prizes/literature/ laureates/1982/marquez-lecture-e.html (accessed January 16, 2008).

Chapter 1

1. To raise funds for the construction of the National Theater, a coffee tax was levied, at twenty cents for every forty-six kilograms of exported coffee. See http://www.artstudiomagazine.com/arq_costa_rica_.html.

2. Most critics of Costa Rican literature tend to identify El Olimpo as the first generation of national writers.

3. For literacy levels in Costa Rica in the late nineteenth century, I draw from the research of Vega Jiménez (1992) and Molina Jiménez (1995), who discuss literacy levels in slightly different years—1858 and 1856, respectively.

4. A newspaper article dated July 2, 1893, announced José Martí's visit to San José: "En estas humildes regiones se le conoce, se le admira y se le ama [in these humble regions, he is known, admired and loved]" (quoted in Oliva Medina 1995, 36).

5. For his study of the coffee-producing elite class, Paige interviewed "members of leading coffee dynasties" in an effort to investigate their role in the 1980s crisis in Central America. Stone (1990) mapped out a genealogy of present-day elite classes and colonial aristocracies.

6. Jean Franco (1994) uses the term "literary nationalism" to refer to a range of romantic, political texts written throughout Latin America in the nineteenth century. Sommer redeploys Franco's concept to identify national romances, or foundational fictions, during the same period. In the context of South America, primary figures who contributed to the writing of national programs in Argentina and Chile, respectively, are Domingo Sarmiento and Andrés Bello, with their didactic, political, journalistic, and literary texts. In the context of Costa Rica, they are the Olimpo.

7. Vega Jiménez (1992) examined newspaper advertisements for import items on sale in San José at the turn of the century. These items included foods, liquors, furniture, clothing, textiles, accessories, and medicines imported primarily from Europe and, later, the United States (110), all of which were available for purchase in the city. She notes that the wealthy "agro-commercial bourgeoisie" (131) purchased luxury items such as lingerie and special household machines.

8. In "Nuestra América," Martí transfigured the Latin American ruling class, finely educated in Europe and espousing European values and ideals, into the figure of the *criollo exótico*. This figure represented Latin American nations in their neocolonial subjection. Disrobing the postcolonial predicament of Latin American criollos, Martí explained, "Eramos una máscara con los calzones de Inglaterra, el chaleco parisiense, el chaquetón de Norteamérica y la montera de España [We were a masquerader in English breeches, Parisian vest, North American jacket and Spanish cap]" (Martí 1987, 268; Schnookal and Muñiz 1999, 116). As Martí would have it, the *criollo exótico* wore foreign attire in local sites—the sign of a patented internalized colonialism exacerbated by the insertion of and competition for a modern economy in the region. In Central America, this agent of the ruling class subjugated other racial and gendered subjects (indigenous people, blacks, peasants, labor migrants, and women).

9. Most literary and cultural histories of Costa Rica address this debate, which determined the course of Costa Rican literature for at least the first three decades of the twentieth century. In 1894, two writers of Costa Rica's Olimpo published exchanges in local newspapers on the state of national literature in the country. Ricardo Fernández Guardia speculated that Costa Rica did not possess cultural materials sophisticated enough for the construction of a national literature even while participating in the building of the same. Carlos Gagini argued that a locally inflected literature (à la *costumbrista*) was the most appropriate form to express local themes and issues. Each defended his position in the public forum and wrote stories and novels to test his literary proposal. The critic Abelardo Bonilla has suggested that this debate was not prompted by the question of whether Costa Rica could produce a national literature or what local themes would serve as its content but rather by the quandary over *who* would control the image of Costa Rica. The *costumbristas* advocated for the transcription of regional speech, idiomatic expressions, realist representation, and the use of folkloric motifs (Bonilla 1981, 110–111, 120–121). On the cosmopolitan front, Fernández Guardia argued for a highly aestheticized and Europeanized *modernista* line of writing, which was open to foreign ideas and forms. Gagini's *costumbrista* and realist representations of national culture prevailed over Fernández Guardia's *modernista* vision of the nation, particularly because Gagini painted in his own novels and stories a frightening picture of foreign economic, political, and cultural intervention in Costa Rica. Gagini's and Fernández Guardia's positions on the construction of national literature, however, had a common agenda: selling an image of the nation to a reading public in search of a national identity.

10. All textual analysis and quotations of Carlos Gagini's *El árbol enfermo* are from the English translation of the novel.

11. According to Cecilia Barrantes de Bermejo (1997), *modernista* writers strongly opposed the constraints of the literary nationalism of the Olympian writers. The *modernistas* opposed regional *costumbrista* writing and sought to stimulate more cosmopolitan modes of representation (28).

12. I have conducted archival research on Máximo Soto Hall at the National Library in San José, Costa Rica; the University of Costa Rica; Stanford University; the library of *La Prensa* in Buenos Aires; and the Organization of American States (oas) in Washington, D.C. Soto Hall's work has not been translated into English.

13. Juan Durán Luzio (1985) reads Soto Hall's *El problema* as an anti-imperialist novel set in the context of U.S. intervention in the Caribbean in the late nineteenth century. Along with other *modernista* writers such as Martí (1891), Rodó (1900), and Darío (1904), Soto Hall situates his work within U.S. and Latin American geopolitics, consciously interrogating U.S. military, economic, and political intervention in the region.

14. Gagini's *El árbol enfermo* is the best example of Costa Rican genteel folklore.

15. Tennessee-born William Walker (1824–1860) attempted to build a private empire in Central America. From 1853 to 1860, he led at least five filibustering expeditions, first to Sonora, Mexico, and then to Central America,

all manned by mercenary recruits. He conquered and ruled Nicaragua as self-imposed president from 1855 to 1856.

16. In the next chapter, I analyze how proletarian-based, social realist literature represents popular labor struggles in Costa Rica and Central America.

17. Like other (anti-)empire-building novels of Central America, Soto Hall's *El problema* and Gagini's *El árbol enfermo* project the anxiety of conquest and imperialism onto its female characters. The Margaritas of these novels are embodiments of Central American nations—weak, impotent, sick (*enfermizas*), unintelligent, susceptible, seductive, and open to external influences. Julio repeatedly identifies his Margarita not only as "impotent" (a projection of his own male anxiety?) but also as imperfect, incapable, and incomplete (Soto Hall 1899, 116). This might not matter much if in the novel Margarita did not allegorically represent a larger entity—Costa Rica. When thinking about her, Julio also thinks about *los pueblos jóvenes* (the young nations) nurtured with sick blood and educated on false principles, now being devoured by a colossus or tricked by fantasy (96). The Margaritas thus are made scapegoats of the incapacity of male patriarchal leaders to protect the family house and nation. On the other hand, women like Emma, the half-U.S., half–Costa Rican cousin of Julio, are represented as *varonil* (male-like) "machas," independent, energetic, strong, and seductive, yet also prone to fall under the influence of U.S. men and to betray their nations. The male characters in these novels fear what they see as the feminization of their nation vis-à-vis the conquest of their women by male industrialists and imperialists. They displace this fear onto the misogynist discourse associated with the women of their class. Julio acknowledges his own emasculation and *impotence* (a word used repeatedly throughout the novel), when he says, "¡Qué diferencia entre ellos y él, entre ella y Margarita! El tenía el apasionamiento en la palabra y la impotencia en la acción. Era capaz de sentir, pero no de hacer [How different he and his American cousins were, and how different Emma was from Margarita! He was passionate in word but impotent in action. He was capable of feeling, but not of doing.]" (Soto Hall 1899, 116).

Chapter 2

1. I cite from the English translation of Carmen Lyra's "Bananos y hombres": "Bananas and Men," in Horan 2000, 47–61.

2. In *Las novelas de las compañías* (Company Novels) (1993), Angel T. Santiago Soto identifies "company novels" as those whose subject is the exploitation of sugar, coffee, cacao, bananas, indigo, rubber, *guano*, minerals, and other agroindustrial products of foreign companies in Latin America and the Central American and Caribbean Basin. Company novels provide a "representación y análisis de tal situación conflictiva [representation and analysis of such a conflictive situation]" (*Prefacio* vii). Santiago Soto identifies some of the novels that I examine in this chapter as "company novels."

3. The decline of social(ist) realist novels in Central America in the 1960s and 1970s signals the inception of other strategies of representation and struggle such as vanguard experimental literary and prototestimonial forms associ-

ated with Claribel Alegría's *Ashes of Izalco* (1966); Manlio Argueta's *El valle de las hamacas* (1970), and Roque Dalton's meta-satiric works.

4. Numerous texts have been published on the geopolitics and economy of banana production in Central America. See Ellis 1983; Bourgois 1989; Schlesinger and Kinzer 1990; Posa 1993; Dosal 1996; Euraque 1996; Viales Hurtado 1998.

5. For a history of banana production, U.S. economic and military intervention, and the rise to power of the United Fruit Company in Central America, see Kepner and Soothill 1935, 49; Woodward 1999, 177–202.

6. Bananas are not native to the Americas but originate in South Asia. In 1516, Spanish settlers began to transport and cultivate bananas on the island of Hispañola (Haiti/Dominican Republic) (Wilson 1947, 15). The "Gros Michel" Jamaican graft was first planted in Central America and Colombia in the late nineteenth century (15). Bananas were introduced to U.S. markets in the late 1870s and 1880s (Jenkins 2000). By 1884, over ten million bunches were being exported to the United States, mainly from Jamaica and Central America. New Orleans became "a year-round banana port," while Boston became the headquarters of the first companies engaging in the overseas production and export of the fruit (Wilson 1947, 15).

7. The Soto-Keith Concession (1884), signed by the government of Costa Rica and Minor Keith, set the "precedente para posteriores contratos que las compañías estadounidenses firmaron con algunos gobiernos de la región [precedent for later contracts that U.S. companies made with some governments in the region]" (cited in Ellis 1983, 36). See also May and Plaza 1958.

8. For a history of the companies and the eventual merging of the United Fruit Company and Cuyamel in 1933, see Langley and Schoonover 1995, 164; Jenkins 2000, 16–22.

9. See McCullough 1977, for a comprehensive history of the construction of the Panama Canal; and Lindsay-Poland 2003, for an updated study of the legacy of U.S. imperialism in Panama.

10. For a discussion of how the United States transformed the Caribbean, Central America, and northern South America into a "geopolitical entity," see Randall and Mount 1998.

11. In her prologue to "Bananas and Men," Lyra writes:

Pongo primero bananos que hombres porque en las fincas de banano, la fruta ocupa el primer lugar, o más bien el único. En realidad el hombre es una entidad que en esas regiones tiene un valor mínimo y no está en el segundo puesto, sino que en la punta de la cola de los valores que allí se cuentan. (González and Sáenz 1977, 105)
[I put bananas first, then men, because in the banana plantations, the fruit takes first place, or rather, the only place. In reality, man [humanity] is an entity that in those regions has minimal value and isn't in second place but instead is at the very tail end of the values that count there.] (Horan 2000, 48)

12. This biographical sketch of Carmen Lyra's life and work draws from Chase 1977; L. González 1989; Rojas and Ovares 1995; Palmer and Rojas Chaves 1998; Horan 2000; Molina Jiménez 2002.

13. As discussed in chapter 1, the Olympian image of Costa Rica was challenged by writers such as Manuel González Zeledón (Magón) (1864–1936) and Joaquín García Monge (1881–1958). Magón's "La propia" (1910) and Monge's *El moto* (1900) addressed the anxiety of change, displacement, and abandonment produced in the urban popular classes by the rapid modernization sought by national leaders.

14. See Rosa María de Britton's play, *Esa esquina del paraíso* (That Corner of Paradise) (1986), and her short story translated into English as "Love Is Spelled with a 'G,'" in Jaramillo Levi and Chambers 1994; as well as Gloria Guardia's novels, *El último juego* (1977) and *Lobos al anochecer* (2006); and Carlos Guillermo Wilson's ("Cubena") *Chombo* (1981).

15. For an analysis of black labor migration and the politics of the Gold and Silver Roll, see Lewis 1980; Coniff 1985.

16. For a discussion of Afro–Central Americans, see Martínez Montiel 1993.

17. See Gilroy 1993 and Martínez Echazábal 1997 for a critique of the omission of Latin America (and Panama in particular) from the Black Atlantic paradigm.

Chapter 3

1. Some notable fiction and nonfiction testimonial texts of the civil war period in Central America, besides those already mentioned, are Roque Dalton's *Miguel Mármol: Los sucesos de 1932 en El Salvador* (1982; *Miguel Mármol* 1982); Omar Cabezas's *La montaña es algo más que una inmensa estepa verde* (1982; *Fire from the Mountain: The Making of a Sandinista* 1985); Claribel Alegría's *No me agarrán viva: La mujer salvadoreña en la lucha* (1983; *They Won't Take Me Alive* 1987); Elvia Alvarado and Medea Benjamin's *Don't Be Afraid Gringo: A Honduran Woman Speaks from the Heart* (1989); Gioconda Belli's *La mujer habitada* (1989; *The Inhabited Woman* 1994); and Nidia Díaz's *Nunca estuve sola* (*I Was Never Alone*) (1989).

2. The first edition of *Cuzcatlán donde bate la mar del sur* was published in 1986, followed by a second edition published in Spanish in 1987. I cite from the 1987 Spanish edition. All translations into English from this text are mine.

3. A number of photography books depicting the war in El Salvador capture the sense of urgency and the horror of death written on the walls of buildings and on the banners of protesters. See Asociación Equipo Maíz, *No hay Guerra que dure cien años . . . El Salvador 1979–1992* (There Is No War That Lasts One Hundred Years . . . El Salvador, 1979–1992) (1995) and *El Salvador: Imágenes para no olvidar, 1900–1999* (El Salvador: Images in Order Not to Forget) (1999).

4. For accounts of the revolutionary media in the Salvadoran civil war, see Guadalupe Rodríguez, *Marianela, 1983–1994* (1994); and José Ignacio López Vigil, *Rebel Radio: The Story of El Salvador's Radio Venceremos* (1994).

5. See Thomas Anderson's much cited work on the Gran Matanza (1976).

6. Jim Sharpe (1992) and Michel de Certeau (1989) examine history written from alternate subject positions. The project of writing "history from below,"

which focuses on subaltern perspectives and draws from alternative sources, fostered new historical research, especially in the 1970s. Sharpe encourages historians to examine records associated with everyday lives and experiences in order to reconstruct marginal histories. The inclusion of the histories of "subjects from below" in the public record calls for the use of nonstandard methodologies and research tools (Sharpe 1992, 33), as well as other perspectives and knowledges (38). This reorientation of historical writing further validates what de Certeau calls other "subject-producers of history," such as women.

7. In a personal interview conducted at Universidad de El Salvador, San Salvador, on September 6, 1995, Argueta explained to me that his novel *Milagro de la paz* is autobiographical, based on his childhood memories of the women in his family. In another interview with Zulma Nelly Martínez, Argueta stated that *Un día en la vida* is based on oral texts and interviews conducted with a female Salvadoran peasant and combatant. Argueta defines his methodology as an incorporation of multiple voices into textual form ("incorporación de la voz colectiva en la obra individual"). He claims that his work transforms oral history into writing (Z. Martínez, 1985, 41–54).

8. The participation of women in the civil war generated a great deal of interest, and a large number of texts focused on the nature of women's struggles and women in the FMLN. For a comprehensive study of women in the war, see García and Gomáriz 1989.

9. Ileana Rodríguez states, "My hypothesis is that, in these narratives, women, children, and the elderly occupy the same space as people, masses, troops, and bases[;] . . . vanguard parties, political leaders, and engaged writers neglected, demeaned, and marginalized women, therefore disparaging and omitting all that was synonymous with Woman" (1996, xv).

10. In my summary of Salvadoran colonial history, I use Dalton's citation of Pedro de Alvarado's letter.

11. See Guevara 1975, 779. Rojas Rodríguez and Herrera Alfaro (1981) note that the indigo zones of El Salvador possessed favorable conditions for production: grainy soil; low, level lands; good drainage; and hot, humid climate. The available labor force and conditions of production made El Salvador an optimum site for the cultivation of indigo.

12. Pérez Brignoli (1989) and Palma Murga (1993, 308) bracket 1760 to 1790 as the height of indigo production in Central America.

13. In "Obra de Manlio Argueta," Argueta claims that he uses the peasant voice to express "la voz estremecedora y a la vez inclaudicable [que] trasmite una esperanza de la sociedad justa que se merece el pueblo salvadoreño [the moving and relentless voice that expresses the hope for a just society that Salvadorans deserve]" (11).

14. For studies of the production and signification of the color blue in the pre-Columbian Maya era, see Reyes-Valerio 1993; Coe 2000, 146. Coe states, "At some point in the Late Classic the lowland Maya invented a brilliant blue pigment which can often be seen on Jaina figures, on effigy incense burners, and in the murals of Bonampak'. This is the famous Maya Blue, now proven through physical and chemical analysis to have been produced by mixing indigo (a vegetable dye) with a special clay, and heating the combination. The resulting

pigment is extraordinarily stable, and—unlike modern blue pigments—highly resistant to the effects of light, acids, and time. Because this particular clay is found only at a place in Yucatan called Sakalum, it was probably there that the Maya artists made their extraordinary discovery. Maya Blue continued to be manufactured right through the Spanish Conquest, and has even been found in Colonial murals in central Mexico" (146).

Chapter 4

1. Personal conversation with Ileana Rodríguez, June 3, 2003, Columbus, Ohio.

2. In *Rigoberta Menchú and the Story of All Poor Guatemalans* (1999), the U.S. anthropologist David Stoll tackles the status of ethnography and the authority of historical evidence in social science research and the contemporary crises of "truth" in anthropology by questioning precisely what had been accepted as *key facts* in Menchú's account of her experiences during the Guatemalan civil war, as compiled in her *testimonio, Me llamo Rigoberta Menchú y así me nació la conciencia* (1983). In the aftermath of that interrogation, Stoll prompts what critics have called "the Rigoberta Menchú controversy," which is the title of Arturo Arias's anthology of essays (2001) by critics on both sides of the argument. In their attack on Menchú's testimonial veracity and voice, Stoll and his supporters unsettled the representation of the larger truths of an era in which the Maya suffered great repression and from which Menchú's *testimonio* emerged as a sole voice.

3. See Behar 1996 and LaCapra 2001, 211–213, for discussions of the "vulnerable observer" and the "empathic" bystander, respectively. LaCapra warns that "sympathetic" readers or receivers of a traumatic narrative have a tendency to identify with the victim and may engage in transference. The danger in identifying with the victim lies in appropriating her pain and/or making her "the object of pity, charity, or condescension" (2001, 212). On the other hand, empathy makes possible "an affective relation, rapport, or bond with the other recognized and respected as other" (212–213). Behar, too, in her discussion of the "vulnerable observer," allows for an empathic subject position for the ethnographer dealing with narratives of loss (1996, 80–81). She identifies an "ethnographic empathy" (167) that acknowledges the anthropologist's feelings in her or his research.

4. I have used the *Popol Vuh, the Mythic Sections—Tales of the First Beginning from the Ancient K'iche-Maya*, ed. and trans. Allen J. Christenson (2000, 70–92).

5. There is a growing body of Maya literature written in Mayan languages, Spanish, and English. Among these texts are Gonzalez's *Retorno de los Maya* and his other novels and books of poetry; Victor Montejo's *Voices from Exile: Violence and Survival in Modern Maya History* (1999), *El Q'anil: The Man of Lightning* (1999), *The Bird Who Cleans the World and Other Mayan Fables* (1991), *Brevísima relación testimonial de la continúa destrucción del Mayab' (Guatemala)* (Brief Narrative of the Continued Destruction of the Mayab' [Guatemala]) (1992), *Sculpted Stones: Poems* (1995); Maya Cu's *La rueda* (The Circle) (2001); and Calixta Ga-

briel Xiquín's *Tejiendo los sucesos en el tiempo / Weaving Events in Time* (2002). See Yax 'Te Publications, http://www.csuohio.edu/yaxte/.

6. See Thomas Quigley's foreword to the English edition of the REMHI (xv).

7. There is a growing body of literature on the Maya diaspora in the United States. See Burns 1993; Montejo 1999; Escobar and Sun 1999; Escobar 1999; Goodman 1999; Fink 2003. For an analysis of the Guatemalan diaspora, see Hamilton and Chinchilla 2001.

8. For more precise numbers on economic and military aid to Central America, see Dunkerley 1994, 145 (Appendixes 7, 8).

9. See Torres-Rivas 1993a, 6:11. Many social scientists, writers, representatives of organizations, Central Americans, and others have discussed the devastating impact of the wars in Central America in the 1980s. Studies have cited the numerous casualties and examined the displacement of people and their migration patterns. Statistics have tallied U.S. military and economic aid to regimes in the region. *Testimonios* have recounted the massacres, the terror, and the discontent of the general population. The period of the 1980s, as the historian Edelberto Torres-Rivas puts it, "has been critical to the destiny of the majority of Central Americans. Up to then, the region had not experienced such bloody civil wars, or such profound and prolonged economic crisis. Having become accustomed during those years to live amid the ominous sign of crisis—violence, fear, massive poverty—these adverse effects seem to be part of our daily lives now, although they constitute the greatest of our current problems" (my translation).

10. There is considerable literature on the Maya symbolism of the jaguar. A good place to start is Miller and Taube 1997, 102–104. I am indebted to George L. Scheper and Laraine Fletcher, project directors of the NEH-CCHA "Maya Worlds: Cultural Continuities and Change," summer 2002, in which I had the good fortune to participate, for referring me to bibliographic sources on jaguar iconography and symbology, including Benson 1972, 1998; Coe 1972, 1–18; Kubler 1972, 19–49; and Saunders 1998.

11. For a critical analysis of the uses of Maya dress, see Hendrickson 1996.

Chapter 5

1. See Marín and VanOss Marín 1991. "The Decade of the Hispanic" is a term promoted by the mass media and social scientists, "due in part to Hispanics' significant impact on the demography of the United States."

2. For discussions of Central American immigration in and outside of the isthmus, see Torres-Rivas 1993, 6: 11–33; Dunkerley 1994; Hamilton and Stoltz Chinchilla 1997, 2001; Mahler 2000.

3. The breakdown of Central American immigrants by country in 2002 was as follows: 565,081 from El Salvador; 268,779 from Guatemala; 202,658 from Nicaragua; 131,066 from Honduras; 92,013 from Panama; and 57,223 from Costa Rica (Pinderhughes, Córdova, and del Pinal 2002).

4. For a study of the classification of Central American refugees by country of origin, see Ferris 1987.

5. The literature of solidarity, sanctuary, and peace movements associated with the Central American civil wars is extensive. See MacEoin 1985; Golden and McConnell 1986; Tomsho 1987; Crittenden 1988; Coutin 1993; and C. Smith 1996.

6. More recently, the Salvadoran government has supported the opening of branches of Casa de la Cultura in U.S. cities. This initiative is sponsored by the Salvadoran state.

7. See Córdova's editorial comment in *Cipactli* 1988: 3.

8. I am indebted to Michelle Habell-Pallán for bringing to my attention the Chicano cultural journal *XhismeArte*, which was published periodically in the 1980s. The February 1980 issue was dedicated to Latin American struggles, representing a significant chapter in Chicano/Latino discursive solidarities.

9. For a brief biographical sketch of Roberto Vargas, see Murguía 1999.

10. See Martínez, "Turning," in Gaspar de Alba, Herrera-Sobek, and Martínez 1989, 101–156.

11. In his essay "El muchacho de Niquinohomo," Sergio Ramírez explains that Augusto César Sandino's revolutionary forces comprised Nicaraguan nationals and international volunteers from Latin America and elsewhere (1987, 3–38). International solidarity committees based in New York, Los Angeles, Chicago, Detroit, Latin America, and Europe supported Sandino's anti-imperialist struggle by holding fund-raising meetings, much like solidarity groups did in the 1980s (28). The Sandinista Revolution (1979–1989) was also an internationalist movement that gained support throughout the world. In the Contra War phase, U.S. Latino/a cultural activists such as Murguía joined the struggle for Nicaragua.

12. The United States has had a long presence in Nicaragua, dating to, if not before, 1855, when William Walker invaded Nicaragua, after being invited by Nicaraguan Liberals to help them defeat conservative political opponents. Although he was driven out of Nicaragua by unified Central American military forces, Walker attempted to return to Nicaragua several times before finally being captured and executed in Trujillo, Honduras, in 1860 (Woodward 1999). Throughout 1848 and 1849, gold miners and other adventurers traveled through Nicaragua and Panama to reach the California goldfields by means of Cornelius Vanderbilt's Accessory Transit Company (McGuinness 2008). By the early twentieth century, the United States already controlled the politics and economy of Nicaragua through military intervention and "Dollar Diplomacy." Under the pretense of protecting U.S. economic interests in the region, the U.S. Marines successively invaded and occupied Nicaragua in 1894, 1896, 1898, 1899, 1910, 1912–1925, and 1926–1933, until their retreat in 1933 after establishing and training the National Guard (Ramírez 1987, 5–7). Two generations of Somozas, including Anastasio Somoza García (1896–1956) and his sons, Luis Somoza Debayle (1922–1967) and Anastasio Somoza Debayle (1925–1980), ruled Nicaragua from 1936 until the Nicaragua Revolution came to an end on July 19, 1979 (Booth and Walker 1993). The Somoza dictatorship and U.S. imperialism in Nicaragua were challenged by the FSLN, the leftist guerrilla movement that overthrew the Somoza dictatorship in 1979 and rose to power in the 1980s.

13. See Mariscal 1999. Mariscal's anthology of literature written by Chicanas/os during the Vietnam War also provides introductory essays on the rep-

resentation of the war. Murguía's *Southern Front* is not mentioned in Mariscal's book.

14. According to Christian Smith, the "Vietnam Syndrome," or the allusion to another Vietnam, generated great unease in the public in the 1980s. While Reagan used the syndrome to gather economic and military aid for Central American countries, the peace movement used it to harness support for its antiwar actions (C. Smith 1996, 93).

15. On U.S. cultures of imperialism, see Pike 1992; Kaplan and Pease 1993; Kenworthy 1995; P. Smith 1996; Joseph, Legrand, and Salvadore 1998; Bouvier 2002.

16. For a full-length account of the life and death of Carlos Fonseca Amador, one of the leaders and founders of the Sandinista Movement, see Zimmermann 2000.

17. For classic Nicaraguan female revolutionary narratives, see Randall 1980, 1981; and Belli 1995.

18. Arturo Arias asks, "Why is there such a resistance to Central American, and Central American-American, culture?" (2007, 187). Elsewhere I, too, have interrogated the tendency to represent Central Americans as refugees without agency, thought, and purpose other than to join the greater Latino American family, whether in the United States or elsewhere (A. Rodríguez 2001).

19. Saldívar-Hull (2000, 27–57, 125–159) examines the ideology of "political familism" based on nationalist and paternalist values and argues for a more inclusive and critical practice of feminist solidarity.

20. Los Cadejos and La Siguanaba (also known as Segua) are legendary figures in Central American lore. Los Cadejos are dogs representing good and evil that appear to humans, especially at night; La Siguanaba, in life, was a beautiful Pipil woman named Sihuehuet, who had a male child, el Cipitio, with the rain god Tlaloc's son. She neglected her son and was called a bad mother. Tlaloc punished her by making her both beautiful and hideous. Legend has it that she appears as a seductress to men at night and by rivers and attacks them for straying from home. A water spirit representing fertility and life, she may be read also as a symbol of female desire, sexuality, strength, and resistance to patriarchy. Like La Llorona (the woman who mourns the loss of her children along waterways) and La Malinche (the cultural translator for Cortés during the Spanish conquest), La Siguanaba is being recuperated and resignified on feminist terms (Hernández-Linares 2002).

21. Martínez, a native of New Mexico, worked as a journalist for the *National Catholic Reporter* and the *Albuquerque Journal* in the 1980s. In December 1987, she was indicted on charges of aiding and abetting Salvadoran refugees and was acquitted of those charges in 1988. She writes about her experiences in the Sanctuary Movement in her poems published in *Three Times a Woman* (1989) and in her semiautobiographical novel, *Mother Tongue*. I read her work as testimonial and autoethnographic, for it tells the story of Sanctuary Movement workers, based on personal experiences. She writes in her poem, "Grand Jury Indicts 16 in Sanctuary Movement": "An embrace, a meal, a bed, / harboring, aiding, abetting, / the night we went dancing / will be used against us" (1989, 124).

22. These texts are analyzed in A. Rodríguez 2001.

23. Dunn (1996) argues that the low-intensity warfare tactics and high technology first tested by the U.S. military in Central America were implemented along the U.S.-Mexico border.

Chapter Six

1. See Córdova 1987, 2005; Mahler 1995a, 1995b, 2000; Repak 1995; Hamilton and Stoltz Chinchilla 1997, 2001; Cadaval 1998; Winschun 1999; Menjívar 2000; Baker-Cristales 2004.

2. These population estimates are taken from numbers tabulated by the Ministry of Exterior Relations in El Salvador in 2001 (http://www.rree.gob.sv/ website/index.html), but population counts for Salvadorans in the United States vary greatly. For a comparison, see U.S. Census tables PCT 19, Place of Birth for the Foreign-Born Population [126], Data Set Census 2000 Summary File 3 (SF3) (http://www.census.gov/).

3. Departamento 15 calls to mind the "extra-territorial Tenth Department" of Haiti, which Michel S. Laguerre describes as comprising "Haitian immigrants living in the U.S., Canada, France and some other countries." Laguerre explains that the Jean-Bertrand Aristide administration was responsible for conceptualizing the Haitian diaspora as "an extra-territorial unit of the republic." In 1994, the Ministry of Diasporic Affairs was established to coordinate and centralize relations between Haitians abroad and the government of Haiti (Laguerre 1998, 162–164). Unlike the Haitian Department 10, the Salvadoran Departamento 15 is not an official administrative unit to date, although the Salvadoran government actively works to maintain ties with Salvadoran immigrants for obvious reasons: to solicit remittances and garner political support.

4. For theorization on *los hermanos lejanos* and their relationship to the Salvadoran state, see Baker-Cristales 2004.

5. In the United States, the radio broadcaster Renán Almendárez Coello, "El Cucuy de la Mañana," has been successful in producing a transnational audience comprising Salvadorans and the larger Latino and Latin/Central American community. Honduran El Cucuy is widely recognized in El Salvador, especially after his earthquake relief efforts in 2001, which brought material and monetary assistance to earthquake survivors in the country (Schiantarelli 2002).

6. See the Web site for *La Prensa Gráfica*: https://www.laprensagrafica .com/dpt15/.

7. See the Web site http://www.departamento15.com/.

8. For updated population data for the Washington, D.C., region, see the U.S. Census Web site, http://factfinder.census.gov/home/en/pldata.html.

9. See "La casa de las pupusas," http://www.coexport.com/masey (accessed September 9, 2002).

10. See Stephens 1841/1969.

11. According to Sergio Ramírez, "Los cuentos de camino llegan a ser una de las venas más ricas de la narración centroamericana, y sobreviven con su carácter oral incluso durante el siglo XX [The road stories have become one

of the richest veins of Central American narrative and survive with their oral character even during the twentieth century]" (1984, 14).

Chapter Seven

1. Following Williams 1977, Cuevas Molina defines "campo cultural" (cultural field) as "el sistema de relaciones (que incluye artistas, editores, marchantes, críticos, agentes, funcionarios, público) que determina las condiciones específicas de producción y circulación de sus productos. Dos elementos constituyen un campo: la existencia de un capital común y la lucha por su apropiación [the system of relations (which includes artists, editors, merchants, critics, agents, functionaries, and the public) that determines specific conditions of production and circulation of products. Two elements constitute a cultural field: the existence of common capital and the struggle for its appropriation]" (1993, 14–15).

2. Daniel Camacho claims that, for the most part, "the change in revolutionary thought has occurred as a rupture with the authoritarian Hispanic or Caribbean culture and with the culture of a certain Marxism-Leninism (not simply Stalinism)" (1993, 39).

3. The term is borrowed from Bhabha 1994.

4. See Wignaraja 1993, xv–xviii. Here, Wignaraja cites extensively from the South Commission's Report, *The Challenge to the South*.

5. These statistics are from *Perfil estadístico centroamericano* (1992, 11).

6. *Una hora para la paz* (1987) is the published text of an initial document signed by the presidents of El Salvador, Guatemala, Honduras, and Costa Rica. *Los Acuerdos de Paz: En el camino de la paz* (1991) is the published book-length text of the Peace Accords of El Salvador, which were signed originally in Mexico City on January 16, 1992. In the 1980s, former president of Costa Rica, Oscar Arias, played an important role in Central American peace negotiations, which culminated in various peace process and accord meetings and documents, among them the Esquipulas Accords II (August 7, 1987), which was to serve as the foundation for formal peace agreements between the Salvadoran government and the FMLN. As mediator, Arias used a discourse of dialogue and negotiation.

7. See Habachi 1986 for a discussion of the philosophical tenets of the Universidad para la Paz and the role that the United Nations and other global organizations played in promoting peace through the institution.

8. See "Oscar Arias reprende a políticos" (Oscar Arias Reprimands Politicians) (June 2, 1995); and O. Arias, "Los Desafíos del siglo XXI desde América Latina" (The Challenges of the Twenty-first Century in Latin America), the text of the speech given by the former President of Costa Rica at the National Theater, San José, Costa Rica, on April 25, 1995.

9. See Cruz and Portillo Peña 1998; Darling 1999a, 20–21, 34–36; 1999b, A1; Montaigne 1999, 44–51.

10. Hayden White, in "The Historical Text as Literary Artifact" (1978), uses the term *verbal fiction* to examine how historical writing and fiction share "literary sensibilities," devices, and tropes.

11. García and Gomáriz (1989) note that Central American women were among the most affected by the wars in the 1980s. They argue that over half of the population of displaced and refugee Central Americans was female.

12. The Peace Accord document, signed in Chapultepec, Mexico City, on January 16, 1992, stipulated that the creation of the the National Civil Police (PNC) required the inclusion of former guerrilla combatants and soldiers. The Accords mandated the "purging" of the old police force to ensure the success of the PNC. The signing of the final document, in fact, hinged on three significant issues: the cessation of the armed conflict, the economic and social recuperation of the country, and the founding of the PNC to ensure "safeguarding of peace, tranquility, order and public security in urban and rural areas, under the control of civilian authorities." See *El Salvador Agreements: The Path to Peace* (UN 1992, 53).

13. Alston and Brown (1993) discuss the marketing and selling of "plant materials for highly profitable biotechnology enterprises without any compensation to the source country" (190). In Costa Rica, plants are sold and patented for "medicinal, industrial and agricultural use" by the pharmaceutical industry (191). The selling of natural resources is not as far-fetched an idea as it would seem.

14. See definition of *abjection* in Childers and Hentzi 1995, 1.

15. For discussions of defilement and disease in different social contexts, see Douglas 1978; and Trigo 2000. For the context of Central America, see Benz 1997.

16. For a discussion of impoverished urban and rural communities at-risk and most affected by natural disasters in El Salvador, see Lungo and Baires 1996.

17. Dengo Obregón (1992) discusses the need for sustainable development in Central America.

18. Ramirez asserts:

Política, ideología, represiones, heroísmos, masacres, fracasos, traiciones, luchas, frustraciones, esperanzas, son aún materia novelable en Latinoamérica y seguirán siéndolo porque la realidad no se agota; el novelista toma el papel de intérprete entre otros muchos que se arroga y quiere hablar en nombre de un inconsciente colectivo largamente silenciado y soterrado bajo un cúmulo de retórica falsa y pervertida. Y en esto, el escritor no puede dejar de cumplir un acto político, porque la realidad es política" (1985, 120).

[Politics, ideology, repressions, heroisms, massacres, failures, betrayals, struggles, frustrations, and hopes are the subjects of novels in Latin America, and they will continue to be so because reality does not diminish; the novelist takes on the role of interpreter among others and desires to speak in the name of a collective unconscious largely silenced and buried beneath an accumulation of false and perverted rhetoric. And thus, the writer must commit a political act, because reality is political.]

19. I cite from Gioconda Belli's 1996 edition of *Waslala: Memorial del futuro*, published by Amama Ediciones in Nicaragua. This early edition makes more explicit than her later edition (Seix Barral, 2006) Belli's critique of globalization.

20. All quotes are taken from the English translation.

21. According to Alston and Brown (1993, 179–194), Central America, particularly El Salvador, is "one of the most ecologically deteriorated countries in the Americas," as a result of decades of land scorching and bombings by military forces sponsored by the United States. The authors claim, "By 1989, the Salvadoran air force had dropped more than 3,000 tons of U.S.-made bombs on the countryside" (180). In Guatemala, the population that was displaced by war destroyed a great deal of vegetation in their effort to seek cover, while the government used destructive scorch-land tactics against them as well (181). They also discuss the global waste trade, which informs my own reading of Gioconda Belli's novel *Waslala*.

22. Waslala is "la ubicación del paraíso perdido, del tiempo perdido, de todo lo que la humanidad había perdido aún antes de aprender a nombrarlo [the location of lost paradise, lost time, of everything that humanity had lost before it knew how to name it]" (1996, 167).

Epilogue

1. See Daniel Joya's contributions to the *Takoma Voice*, http://www.takoma .com/archives/copy/2002/08/vozenglish0802.html (accessed January 19, 2008).

2. For a discussion of gendered labor migration to the Washington, D.C., region, see Repak 1995; Pedersen 1995, 415–442.

Works Cited

Acevedo, Ramón Luis. 1982. *La novela centroamericana desde el Popul-Vuh hasta los umbrales de la novela actual*. Río Piedras, PR: Editorial Universitaria.

———. 1991. "La violencia en la novela salvadoreña." In *Los senderos del volcán: Narrativa centroamericana contemporánea*, 121–138. Guatemala: Editorial Universitaria.

Aizenman, Nurith C. 2001. "Hispanic Population Nearly Doubles; County's Community Is Faster-Growing than Montgomery." *Washington Post*, Prince George's Extra, March 22, T8.

Alegría, Claribel. 1983. *No me agarrarán viva: La mujer salvadoreña en la lucha*. México: Era.

Allwood de Mata, Claudia. 1993. "Mensaje de la presidenta de CONCULTURA." *La Prensa Gráfica*, November 3, np.

Alonso, Carlos. 1990. *The Spanish American Regional Novel: Modernity and Autochthony*. Cambridge: Cambridge University Press.

Alston, Dana, and Nicole Brown. 1993. "Global Threats to People of Color." In *Confronting Environmental Racism: Voices from the Grassroots*, ed. Robert D. Bullard, 179–194. Boston: South End Press.

Alvarado, Evia, and Medea Benjamin. 1989. *Don't Be Afraid, Gringo: A Honduran Woman Speaks from the Heart. The Story of Elvia Alvarado*. Ed. and trans. Medea Benjamin. New York: Harper Perennial.

Amaya Amador, Ramón. 1950/1996. *Prisión verde*. Comayagüela, Honduras: Editorial Ramón Amaya Amador.

Anderson, Benedict. 1989. *Imagined Communities: Reflections on the Origin and Spread of Nationalism*. London: Verso.

Anderson, Thomas. 1976. *El Salvador 1932: Los sucesos políticos*. Trans. Juan Mario Castellanos. San José, CR: Editorial Universitaria Centroamericana.

Anzaldúa, Gloria. 1999. *Borderlands/La frontera: The New Mestiza*. San Francisco: Aunt Lute.

Archdiocese of Guatemala. 1998/1999. *Guatemala Never Again! Recovery of Historical Memory Project: The Official Report of the Human Rights Office, Archdiocese of Guatemala*. Trans. Gretta Tovar Siebentritt. Maryknoll, NY: Orbis Books.

Argueta, Jorge. 1989. *Del ocaso a la aborada/From Sundown to Dawn.* Berkeley, CA: Co Press.

———. 1990. *La puerta del diablo/The Devil's Gate.* San Francisco: Editores Unidos Salvadoreños.

———. 1991a. *Far from the Fire.* San Francisco: Editores Unidos Salvadoreños.

———. 1991b. *Love Street.* San Francisco: Tiki Bob Publishing.

———. 1996. *Litany of Love and Hate.* San Francisco: Luna's Press.

———. 1997. *Las frutas del centro y otros sabores/Fruit from the Center and Other Flavors.* Berkeley, CA: Canterbury Press.

Argueta, Manlio. 1980/1987. *Un día en la vida.* San Salvador, ES: Universidad Centroamericana José Simeón Cañas Editores.

———. 1982. War and the Writer in El Salvador. *Index on Censorship* 11.2: 3–5.

———. 1987/1998. *Cuzcatlán donde bate la mar del sur.* San Salvador, ES: Adelina Editores.

———. 1994. *Milagro de la Paz.* San Salvador, ES: Istmo Editores.

———. 1997. *Siglo de O(g)ro.* San Salvador, ES: Dirección de Publicaciones e Impresos, Consejo Nacional para la Cultura y el Arte.

Arias, Arturo. 1979. *Ideologías, literatura y sociedad durante la revolución guatemalteca.* Havana: Casa de las Americas.

———. 1998a. "De-Colonizing Knowledge, Reformulating Textuality: Rethinking the Role of Central American Narrative." In *New World [Dis]Orders and Peripheral Strains: Specifying Cultural Dimensions in Latin American and Latino Studies,* ed. Michael Piazza and Marc Zimmerman, 173–188. Chicago: March/Abrazo Press.

———. 1998b. *Gestos ceremoniales: Narrativa centroamericana 1960–1990.* Guatemala: Editorial Artemis & Edinter.

———. 1998c. *La identidad de la palabra: Narrativa guatemalteca a la luz del siglo XX.* Guatemala: Editorial Artemis & Edinter.

———, ed. 2001. *The Rigoberta Menchú Controversy.* Minneapolis: University of Minnesota Press.

———. 2003. "Central American Americans: Invisibility, Power and Representation in the U.S. Latino World." *Latino Studies* 1.1: 168–187.

———. 2005. "Conspiracy on the Sidelines: How the Maya Won the War." In *Cultural Agency in the Americas,* ed. Doris Sommer, 167–177. Durham, NC: Duke University Press.

———. 2007. *Taking Their Word: Literature and the Signs of Central America.* Minneapolis: University of Minnesota Press.

Arias, Oscar. 1995. "Los desafíos del siglo XXI desde América Latina." Speech given at the National Theater, San José, April 25.

Arreola, Daniel, ed. 2004. *Hispanic Spaces, Latino Places: Community and Cultural Diversity in Contemporary America.* Austin: University of Texas Press.

Asociación Equipo MAIZ. 1995. *No hay guerra que dure cien años . . . El Salvador 1979–1992.* Photographs by Iván C. Montecinos. San Salvador, ES: Equipo de Educación MAIZ.

———. 1999. *El Salvador: Imágenes para no olvidar, 1900–1999.* San Salvador, ES: Equipo de Educación MAIZ.

Asturias, Miguel Angel. 1946/2002. *El Señor Presidente*. Madrid: Ediciones Catédra.

———. 1950/1994. *Viento fuerte*. Guatemala: Editorial Piedra Santa.

———. 1954/1982. *El papa verde*. Madrid: Alianza Editorial.

———. 1960/1979. *Los ojos de los enterrados*. Buenos Aires: Editorial Losada.

Avilés, Quique. 1999. *Paper, Fabric, String and Poetry*. Washington, DC: n.p.

———. 2003. *The Immigrant Museum*. Mexico, DF: PinStudio y Raíces de Papel.

Baker-Cristales, Beth. 2004. *Salvadoran Migration to Southern California: Redefining El Hermano Lejano*. Gainesville: University Press of Florida.

Bakhtin, M. 1981. "Discourse in the Novel." In *The Dialogic Imagination: Four Essays by M. M. Bakhtin*, ed. Michael Holquist, trans. Caryl Emerson and Michael Holquist, 259–422. Austin: University of Texas Press.

Barrantes de Bermejo, Cecilia. 1997. *Buscando las raíces del Modernismo en Costa Rica: Cinco acercamientos*. Heredia, CR: Editorial de Universidad Nacional.

Barrientos, Tanya María. 2002. *Frontera Street*. New York: Penguin/New American Library.

Barthes, Roland. 1975. *Mythologies*. Trans. Annette Lavers. New York: Hill and Wang.

Barton, Jonathan R. 1997. *A Political Geography of Latin America*. London: Routledge.

Bassie-Sweet, Karen. 1996. *At the Edge of the World: Caves and Late Classic Maya World View*. Norman: University of Oklahoma Press.

Behar, Ruth. 1996. *The Vulnerable Observer: Anthropology That Breaks Your Heart*. Boston: Beacon Press.

Beleño C., Joaquín. 1951. *Luna verde*. Panama: Editora Panama América.

———. 1960. *Gamboa Road Gang: Los forzados de Gamboa*. Panama: Manfer.

———. 1962/1979. *Flor de banana*. Panama: Editores Librería Cultural Panameña.

———. 1963. *Curundú*. Panama: Imprenta Nacional.

Belli, Gioconda. 1989. *La mujer habitada*. Managua: Vanguardia.

———. 1995. *The Inhabited Woman*. Trans. Kathleen March. New York: Warner Brothers.

———. 1996. *Waslala: Memorial del futuro*. Managua: amamá Ediciones.

Bencastro, Mario. 1996. *A Shot in the Cathedral*. Houston: Arte Público Press.

———. 1997. *The Tree of Life: Stories of Civil War*. Houston: Arte Público Press.

———. 1999. *Odyssey to the North*. Houston: Arte Público Press.

———. 2004. *Viaje a la tierra del abuelo*. Houston: Arte Público Press.

———. 2005. *A Promise to Keep*. Trans. Susan Giersbach-Rascón. Houston: Arte Público Press.

Benítez, Sandra. 1997. *Bitter Grounds*. New York: Hyperion.

———. 2000. *The Weight of All Things*. New York: Hyperion.

Benson, Elizabeth P., ed. 1972. *The Cult of the Feline: A Conference in Pre-Columbian Iconography*. Washington, DC: Dumbarton Oaks Research Library and Collections.

————. 1998. "The Lord, The Ruler: Jaguar Symbolism in the Americas." In *Icons of Power: Feline Symbolism in the Americas*, ed. Nicholas J. Saunders, 53–76. London and New York: Routledge.

Benz, Stephen. 1997. "Through the Tropical Looking Glass: The Motif of Resistance in U.S. Literature on Central America." In *Tropicalizations: Transcultural Representations of Latinidad*, ed. Frances R. Aparicio and Susana Chávez-Silverman, 51–66. Hanover, NH: University Press of New England.

Beteta, Virgilio Rodríguez. 1949. "Biografía del poeta, literato y periodista Máximo Soto Hall, y prefacio a su obra *Pedro de San José Bethencourt*." In *Pedro de San José Bethencourt: El San Francisco de Asís Americano*, by Máximo Soto Hall, 13–86. Guatemala: Ediciones del Gobierno de Guatemala.

Beverley, John. 1993. *Against Literature*. Minneapolis: University of Minnesota Press.

————. 1999. *Subalternity and Representation: Arguments in Cultural Theory*. Durham, NC: Duke University Press.

Beverley, John, and Marc Zimmerman. 1990. *Literature and Politics in the Central American Revolutions*. Austin: University of Texas Press.

Bhabha, Homi K. 1990a. "DessemiNation: Time, Narrative, and the Margins of the Modern Nation." In *Nation and Narration*, ed. Homi K. Bhabha, 291–322. London: Routledge.

————. 1990b. "The Third Space: Interview with Homi Bhabha." In *Identity: Community, Culture, Difference*, ed. Jonathan Rutherford, 207–221. London: Lawrence and Wishart.

————. 1994. "Introduction: Locations of Culture." In *The Location of Culture*, 1–18. London: Routledge.

Blades, Rubén. 1996. "La rosa de los vientos." In *La rosa de los vientos*. Sony Music International. CDT-81992/485061-2.

Blanco, Patricia. 1983. "Holanda abrió las puertas a *Un día en la vida*." *Periódico Universidad*. UCR. San José, CR, August 19, 11.

Bolaños Varela, Ligia. 1988. "Discurso histórico e historiografía literaria: ¿Una alternativa en la construcción de un discurso explicativo de las producciones culturales en América Central?" *Káñina, Revista de Artes y Letras de la Universidad de Costa Rica* 12.1: 177–184.

Bolívar, Simón. 1987. "The Jamaica Letter." In *The Central American Crisis Reader: The Essential Guide to the Most Controversial Foreign Policy Issue Today*, ed. Robert S. Leiken and Barry Rubin, 63. New York: Summit Books.

Bonilla B., Abelardo. 1981. *Historia de la literatura costarricense*. San José, CR: Editorial STVDIVM.

Booth, John A., and Thomas W. Walker. 1993. *Understanding Central America*. Boulder, CO: Westview Press.

Booth, William. 2001. "California's Ethnic Diversity Grows; State Has the Most Multiracial People." *Washington Post*, March 30, A3.

Bourgois, Philippe I. 1989. *Ethnicity at Work: Divided Labor on a Central American Banana Plantation*. Baltimore, MD: Johns Hopkins University Press.

Bouvier, Virginia M., ed. 2002. *The Globalization of U.S.–Latin American Relations: Democracy, Intervention, and Human Rights*. Westport, CT: Praeger.

Britton, Rosa María. 1986. *Esa esquina del paraíso*. Panama: Editorial Mariano Arosemena (INAC).

———. 1994. "Love is Spelled with a 'G.' " In *Contemporary Short Stories from Central America*, ed. Enrique Jaramillo Levi and Leland H. Chambers, trans. Leland H. Chambers et al., 215–223. Austin: University of Texas Press.

Browning, David. 1982. *El Salvador: La tierra y el hombre*. Trans. Paloma Gastesi and Augusto Ramírez C. San Salvador, ES: Dirección de Publicaciones del Ministerio de Educación.

Brusatin, Manlio. 1987. *Historia de los colores*. Barcelona: Ediciones Paidós.

Brushwood, John S. 1975. *The Spanish American Novel: A Twentieth-Century Survey*. Austin: University of Texas Press.

———. 1981. *Genteel Barbarism: Experiments in Analysis of Nineteenth-Century Spanish-American Novels*. Lincoln: University of Nebraska Press.

Burns, Allan F. 1993. *Maya in Exile Guatemalans in Florida*. Philadelphia: Temple University Press.

Cabarrús, S.J., Carlos R. 1985. "El Salvador: De movimiento campesino a revolución popular." In *Movimientos populares en Centroamérica*, comp. Daniel Camacho and Rafael Menjívar, 344–372. San José, CR: Editorial Universitaria Centroamericana.

Cabezas, Omar. 1985. *Fire from the Mountain: The Making of a Sandinista*. Trans. Kathleen Weaver. New York: Penguin Books.

Cadaval, Olivia. 1998. *Creating a Latino Identity in the Nation's Capital: The Latino Festival*. New York: Garland Publishing.

CAFTA (Central American Free Trade Agreement). 2005, November 16. http://www.ustr.gov/Trade_Agreements/Bilateral/CAFTA/CAFTA_Draft _Revised_Texts/Section_Index.html (accessed August 4, 2005).

"CAFTA Does Not Measure Up!" http://www.afsc.org/trade/news/cafta/ measure-up.htm (accessed October 6, 2004).

Camacho, Daniel. 1993. "Latin America: A Society in Motion." In *New Social Movements in the South: Empowering the People*, ed. Ponna Wignaraja, 36–58. London: Zed Books.

Caplan, Jane. 2000. "Introduction." In *Written on the Body: The Tattoo in European and American History*, ed. Jane Caplan, xi–xxiii. Princeton: Princeton University Press.

Carlsen, Robert S. 1997. *The War for the Heart and Soul of a Highland Maya Town*. Austin: University of Texas Press.

Carmack, Robert. 1988. *Harvest of Violence: The Maya Indians and the Guatemalan Crisis*. Norman: University of Oklahoma Press.

———. 1993. "Introducción: Centroamérica aborigen en su contexto histórico y geográfico." In *Historia General de Centroamérica: Historia Antigua*, vol. 1, ed. Robert Carmack, 15–59. Madrid: Facultad Latinoamericana de Ciencias Sociales.

Carranza, Salvador. 1990. *Mártires de la UCA*. San Salvador, ES: Universidad Centroamericana José Simeón Cañas Editores.

Casaús Arzú, Marta Elena. 1998. *La metamorfosis del racismo en Guatemala*. Ciudad de Guatemala: Editorial CHOLSAMAJ.

Castellanos Moya, Horacio. 1997. *El Asco: Thomas Bernhard en San Salvador*. San Salvador, ES: Editorial Arcoiris.

Castillo, Ana. 1990. *Sapogonia (An Anti-romance in 3/8 Meter)*. Tempe: Bilingual Press/Editorial Bilingüe.

Centro de Estudios de la Mujer Norma Virginia Guirola de Herrera, comp. 1992. *Norma: Vida insurgente y feminista*. San Salvador, ES: CEMUJER.

Certeau, Michel de. 1989. *Heterologies: Discourse on the Other*. Trans. Brian Massumi. Minneapolis: University of Minnesota Press.

Chase, Alfonso, ed. 1977. *Relatos escogidos de Carmen Lyra*. San José, CR: Editorial Costa Rica.

Childers, Joseph, and Gary Hentzi, eds. 1995. *The Columbia Dictionary of Modern Literary and Cultural Criticism*. New York: Columbia University Press.

Chinchilla, Maya. 2007. "Solidarity Baby." In *Desde el EpiCentro: An Anthology of U.S. Central American Poetry*, ed. Maya Chinchilla and Karina Oliva-Alvarado, 18–20. Oakland, CA: n.p.

Chomsky, Aviva. 1996. *West Indian Workers and the United Fruit Company in Costa Rica, 1870–1940*. Baton Rouge: Louisiana State University Press.

Christenson, Allen J., ed. and trans. 2000. *Popol Vuh: The Mythic Sections—Tales of the First Beginnings From the Ancient K'iche-Maya*. Provo, UT: Foundation for Ancient Research and Mormon Studies (FARMS).

Clements, Charles. 1984. *Guazapa: Testimonio de guerra de un médico norteamericano*. San Salvador, ES: Universidad Centroamericana José Simeón Cañas Editores.

Clifford, James. 1992. "Traveling Cultures." In *Cultural Studies*, ed. Lawrence Grossberg et al., 96–116. London: Routledge.

———. 1997. *Routes: Travel and Translation in the Late Twentieth Century*. Cambridge, MA: Harvard University Press.

Coe, Michael. 1972. "Olmec Jaguars and Olmec Kings." In *Cult of the Feline*, ed. Elizabeth Benson, 1–18. Washington, DC: Dumbarton Oaks Research Library and Collections.

———. 2000. *The Maya*. New York: Thames and Hudson.

Coe, Sophie D., and Michael D. Coe. 2003. *The True History of Chocolate*. New York: Thames and Hudson.

Cohen, Sarah, and D'Vera Cohn. 2001. "Racial Integration's Shifting Patterns: Enclaves Persist, but Black-White Divide Shrinks." *Washington Post*, April 1, A1.

Cohn, D'Vera, and Manny Fernández. 2001. "Black Exodus Drove District's Population Loss." *Washington Post*, March 31, A1.

Comisión de la Verdad 1992–1993. 1993. *De la locura a la esperanza: La guerra de 12 años en El Salvador*. San José, CR: Editorial Departamento Ecuménico de Investigaciones.

CONCULTURA. 1991. Decreto 55. *Diario Oficial*, 313.206, November 4.

Conniff, Michael L. 1985. *Black Labor on a White Canal: Panama, 1904–1981*. Pittsburgh, PA: University of Pittsburgh Press.

Contreras Castro, Fernando. 1994. *Única mirando al mar*. San José, CR: Ediciones FARBEN.

———. 1997. *Urbanoscopio*. San José, CR: FARBEN.

Contreras Sánchez, Alicia del Carmen. 1996. *Capital comercial y colorantes en la Nueva España: Segunda mitad del siglo XVIII*. Zamora, México: El Colegio de Michoacán.

Córdova, Carlos B. 1987. "Undocumented El Salvadoreans in the San Francisco Bay Area: Migration and Adaptation Dynamics." *Journal of La Raza Studies* 1.1: 9–37.

———, ed. 1988. Editorial Comment. *Cipactli* (Fall): 3.

———. 2005. *The Salvadoran Americans*. Westport, CT: Greenwood Press.

Coronel Urtecho, José. 1985. *Rápido tránsito (al ritmo de Norteamérica)*. Managua: Editorial Nueva Nicaragua.

Cortez, Beatriz. 2000. "Estética del cinismo: La ficción centroamericana de posguerra." Paper delivered at V Congreso Centroamericano de Historia, UES, San Salvador, El Salvador, July 18–21. http://www.ues.edu.sv/congreso/Cortez,%20literatura.pdf (accessed May 13, 2005).

Cortez, Mayamérica. 1995. "Lamento indígena." In *Nostalgias y soledades*, 40–41. San Salvador, ES: Editorial Clásicos Roxsil.

Council of Latino Agencies (CLA). 2002. *The State of Latinos in the District of Columbia: Trends, Consequences and Recommendations*. Washington, DC: Council of Latino Agencies.

Coutin, Susan Bibler. 1993. *The Culture of Protest: Religious Activism and the U.S. Sanctuary Movement*. Boulder, CO: Westview Press.

———. 1995. "Smugglers or Samaritans in Tucson, Arizona: Producing and Contesting Legal Truth." *American Ethnologist* 22.3: 549–571.

———. 2000. *Legalizing Moves: Salvadoran Immigrants' Struggle for U.S. Residency*. Ann Arbor: University of Michigan Press.

Cowy Kim, Katherine, Alfonso Serrano F., Leda Ramos, and Rick Rocamora, eds. 2000. *Izote Vos: A Collection of Salvadoran American Writing and Visual Art*. San Francisco: Pacific News Service.

Craft, Linda J. 1997. *Novels of Testimony and Resistance from Central America*. Gainesville: University Press of Florida.

Crang, Mike, and Nigel Thrift, eds. 2000. *Thinking Space*. London: Routledge.

Crittenden, Ann. 1988. *Sanctuary: A Story of American Conscience and the Law in Collision*. New York: Weidenfeld and Nicholson.

Cruz, José Miguel, and Nelson Portillo Peña. 1998. *Solidaridad y violencia en las pandillas del gran San Salvador: Más allá de la vida loca*. San Salvador, ES: Universidad Centroamericana José Simeón Cañas Editores.

Cu, Maya. 2001. *La rueda*. Ciudad de Guatemala: Ministerio de Cultura y Deportes, Editorial Cultura.

Cuevas Molina. Rafael. 1993. *Traspatio Florecido: Tendencias de la dinámica de la cultura en Centroamérica (1979–1990)*. Heredia, CR: Editorial de la Universidad Nacional.

———. 2006. *Identidad y cultura en Centroamérica: Nación, integración y globalización a principios del siglo XXI*. San José, CR: Editoral Universidad de Costa Rica.

Dalton, Roque. 1974/2000. "Poema de amor." In *Las historias prohibidas del pulgarcito*, 199–200. San Salvador, ES: Universidad Centroamericana José Simeón Cañas Editores.

————. 1979. *El Salvador (Monografía)*. San Salvador, ES: Editorial Universitaria.

————. 1982. *Miguel Mármol: Los sucesos de 1932 en El Salvador*. San José, CR: Editorial Universitaria Centroamericana.

————. 1984. "La violencia aquí/The Violence Here." In *Poemas clandestinos/Clandestine Poems*, ed. Barbara Paschke and Eric Weaver, trans. Jack Hirschman, 140–143. San Francisco: Solidarity Educational Publications.

————. 1987. *Miguel Mármol*. Trans. Kathleen Ross and Richard Schaaf. Willimantic, CT: Curbstone Press.

Danner, Mark. 1994. *The Massacre at El Mozote: A Parable of the Cold War*. New York: Vintage Books.

Darling, Juanita. 1999a. "El Salvador's War Legacy: Teen Violence." *Los Angeles Times*, August 9, A1.

————. 1999b. "Mothers of the Banished." *Los Angeles Times Magazine*, November 21, 20–21, 34–36.

Davis, Mike. 2000. *Magical Urbanism: Latinos Reinvent the U.S. City*. London: Verso.

Deitering, Cynthia. 1996. "The Postnatural Novel: Toxic Consciousness in Fiction of the 1980s." In *The Ecocriticism Reader: Landmarks in Literary Ecology*, ed. Cheryll Glotfelty and Harold Fromm, 196–203. Athens: University of Georgia Press.

Deleuze, Gilles, and Michel Foucault. 1994. "Un diálogo sobre el poder." In *Un diálogo sobre el poder y otras conversaciones*, trans. Miguel Morrey. Madrid: Alianza Editorial.

Dengo Obregón, Jorge Manuel. 1992. "Presentación." In *Desarrollo sostenible y políticas económicas en América Latina*, comp. Olman Segura. San José, CR: Editorial Departamento Ecuménico de Investigaciones.

Departamento 15. 2008. *La Prensa Gráfica*. http://www.laprensa.com.sv/dpt15/ (accessed January 16, 2008).

Díaz, Nidia. 1990. *Nunca estuve sola: Testimonio de la comandante guerrillera salvadoreña*. Buenos Aires: Ediciones Dialéctica.

Dosal, Paul J. 1993. *Doing Business with the Dictators: A Political History of the United Fruit Company in Guatemala, 1899–1944*. Wilmington, DE: Scholarly Resources.

Douglas, Mary. 1978. *Purity and Danger: An Analysis of Concepts of Pollution and Taboo*. London: Routledge.

Dunkerley, James. 1988. *Power in the Isthmus: A Political History of Modern Central America*. London: Verso.

————. 1994. *The Pacification of Central America: Political Change in the Isthmus, 1987–1993*. London: Verso.

Dunn, Timothy J. 1996. *The Militarization of the U.S-Mexico Border, 1978–1992: Low-Intensity Conflict Doctrine Comes Home*. Austin: University of Texas Press.

Durán Luzio, Juan. 1985. "Estados Unidos versus Hispanoamérica: En torno a la novela del 98." *Casa de las Americas* 26.153: 121–127.

Ellis, Frank. 1983. *Las transnacionales del banano en Centroamérica*. Trans. Juan Mario Castellanos. San José, CR: Editorial Universitaria Centroamericana.

Elvir, Lety. 2001. *Mujer entre perro y lobo*. Tegucigalpa: Litografía Lopéz.

———. 2005. *Sublimes y perversos (cuentos)*. Tegucigalpa: Litografía Lopéz.

Escobar, Gabriel. 1999. "Immigration Transforms a Community: Influx of Latino Workers Creates Culture Clash in Delaware Town." *Washington Post*, November 29, A1, A8–9.

Escobar, Gabriel, and Lena H. Sun. 1999. "On Chicken's Front Line: High Volume and Repetition Test Workers' Endurance." *Washington Post*, November 28, A1, A24–25.

Escobar, Mario. 2005. *Gritos interiors*. Los Angeles: Cuzcatlán Press.

Escudos, Jacinta. 1997. *Cuentos sucios*. San Salvador, ES: Dirección de Publicaciones e Impresos, Consejo Nacional para la Cultura y el Arte.

———. 2003. *A-B-Sudario*. Guatemala: Editorial Santillana.

Euraque, Darío A. 1996. *Reinterpreting the Banana Republic: Region and State in Honduras, 1870–1972*. Chapel Hill: University of North Carolina Press.

Fagen, Richard. 1988. *Forjando la paz: El desafío de América Central*. Trans. Carine Malfait. San José, CR: Editorial Departamento Ecuménico de Investigaciones.

Fallas, Carlos Luis. 1941/1986. *Mamita Yunai*. San José, CR: Editorial Costa Rica.

Fernández, Carole. 1991. *Sleep of the Innocents*. Houston: Arte Público Press.

Fernández, Manny. 2001. "City Underwent Major Racial Shifts in '90s, Census Shows." *Washington Post*, DC Extra, April 5, T3.

Ferrero, Luis. 2004. *Sociedad y arte en la Costa Rica del siglo XIX*. San José, CR: Editorial Universidad Estatal a Distancia.

Ferris, Elizabeth G. 1987. *The Central American Refugees*. Westport, CT: Praeger.

Fink, Leon. 2003. *The Maya of Morganton: Work and Community in the Nuevo New South*. Chapel Hill: University of North Carolina Press.

Flores, William V., and Rina Benmayor, eds. 1997. *Latino Cultural Citizenship: Claiming Identity, Space, and Rights*. Boston: Beacon Press.

Flores Macal, Mario. 1980. "Semblanza del retorno." *Periódico Universidad. UCR*. San José, CR, March 7, 4.

Flores Zúñiga, Juan Carlos. 1980. "Premian en El Salvador a escritor exiliado." *Periódico Universidad. UCR*. San José, Costa Rica, October 24–30.

Fonseca, Elizabeth. 2001. *Centroamérica: Su historia*. San José, CR: Editorial Universitaria Centroamericana.

Foster, Brooke Lea. 2001. "Breaking Through." *Washingtonian* 36.8: 76–84, 108–109.

Foucault, Michel. 1967/1998. "Different Spaces." In *Michel Foucault: Aesthetics, Method, and Epistemology*, vol. 2, ed. James D. Faubion, trans. Robert Hurley et al., 175–185. New York: New Press.

———. 1979. *Discipline and Punish: The Birth of the Prison*. Trans. Alan Sheridan. New York: Vintage Books.

Franco, Jean. 1994. *An Introduction to Spanish-American Literature*. Cambridge, MA: Harvard University Press.

———. 1994. "What's Left of the Intelligentsia? The Uncertain Future of the Printed Word." *NACLA* 28.2: 16–21.

Fregoso, Rosa Linda. 1993. *The Bronze Screen: Chicana and Chicano Film Culture*. Minneapolis: University of Minnesota Press.

Freidel, David, Linda Schele, and Joy Parker. 1993. *Maya Cosmos: Three Thousand Years on the Shaman's Path.* New York: Quill/William Morrow.

Fumero, Patricia. 2002. "Este libro es una pequeña ofrenda que deposito en el altar sagrado de mi patria: History Textbooks in Costa Rica, Guatemala and El Salvador, 1884–1927." VI Congreso Centroamericano de Historia, Ciudad de Panama, 22–26 de julio 2002. *Istmo: Revista Virtual de Estudios Literarios y Culturales Centroamericanos.* http://www.denison.edu/collaborations/istmo/no4/proyectos/ofrenda.html (accessed January 16, 2008).

Gagini, Carlos. 1918/1985. *El árbol enfermo.* San José, CR: Ediciones Guayacán.

———. 1985. *Redemptions: A Costa Rican Novel.* Trans. E. Bradford Burns. San Diego, CA: San Diego State University Press.

Galich, Franz. 2001. *Managua Salsa City (¡Devórame otra vez!).* Managua: amamá Ediciones.

Galindo, Martivón. 1996. "SanFranciscanos." In *Retazos,* 81–84. San Francisco: Editorial Solaris.

———. 2000. "Dreaming a Nation: The Salvadoran Cultural Work in the San Francisco Bay Area." Paper presented at the conference Reconstructing Central America II: The Pueblos of Maize in the United States, University of Maryland, College Park, October 12–14.

———. 2004. *Whisper of Dead Leaves.* San Francisco: Black Note Publishing.

———. n.d. "Wounded Generation: Aftermath of Chaos in Central America." Unpublished paper.

Galindo, Martivón, and Armando Molina. 1995. *Imponiendo Presencias: Breve antología de otros narradores expatriados latinoamericanos.* San Francisco: Editorial Solaris.

García, Ana Isabel, and Enrique Gomáriz. 1989. *Mujeres centroamericanas: Efectos del conflicto,* vol. 2. San José, CR: Facultad Latinoamericana de Ciencias Sociales.

García Canclini, Néstor. 1992. "Cultural Reconversion." Trans. Holly Staver. In *On Edge: The Crisis of Contemporary Latin American Culture,* ed. George Yúdice, Jean Franco, and Juan Flores, 29–43. Minneapolis: University of Minnesota Press.

———. 2002. *Latinoamericanos buscando lugar en este siglo.* Buenos Aires: Paidós.

García Márquez, Gabriel. 1982. "The Solitude of Latin America." Nobel Lecture. http://nobelprize.org/nobel_prizes/literature/laureates/1982/marquez-lecture-e.html (accessed January 16, 2008).

Gargallo, Francesca. 1987. "La relación entre participación política y conciencia feminista en las militantes salvadoreñas." *Cuadernos Americanos* 2.2: 58–76.

Gaspar de Alba, Alicia, María Herrera-Sobek, and Demetria Martínez, eds. 1989. *Three Times a Woman: Chicana Poetry.* Tempe, AZ: Bilingual Review/Press.

Gilroy, Paul. 1993. *The Black Atlantic: Modernity and Double Consciousness.* Cambridge, MA: Harvard University Press.

Girot, Pascal O. 1995. ¿Tierra prometida o tierra patrimonial? Más allá de la frontera agrícola: Un ensayo sobre la formación del territorio nacional en Centroamérica. Mimeo. San José, CR.

Golden, Renny. 1991. *The Hour of the Poor, The Hour of Women: Salvadoran Women Speak*. New York: Crossroad.

Golden, Renny, and Michael McConnell. 1986. *Sanctuary: The New Underground Railroad*. Maryknoll, NY: Orbis Books.

Goldman, Francisco. 1992. *The Long Night of White Chickens*. New York: Atlantic Monthly Press.

———. 1997. *The Ordinary Seaman*. New York: Grove Press.

———. 2004. *The Divine Husband*. New York: Atlantic Monthly Press.

———. 2007. *The Art of Political Murder: Who Killed the Archbishop?* New York: Grove Press.

Goldman, Shifra M. 1994. *Dimensions of the Americas: Art and Social Change in Latin America and the United States*. Chicago: University of Chicago Press.

González, Antonio. 1999. "Chicano Politics and U.S. Policy in Central America, 1979–1990." In *Chicano Politics and Society in the Late Twentieth Century*, ed. David Montejano, 154–172. Austin: University of Texas Press.

González, Gaspar Pedro. 1998. *Return of the Maya*. Trans. Susan G. Rascón. Rancho Palos Verdes, CA: Yax Te' Foundation.

González, Lilo, y los de la Mt. Pleasant. 1994. *A quien corresponda . . .* CD. Washington, DC: LGP Records, LML-2741.

González, Luisa. 1989. *A ras del suelo*. San José, CR: Editorial Costa Rica.

González, Luisa, and Carlos Luis Sáenz, eds. 1977. *Carmen Lyra (Maria Isabel Carvajal)*. San José, CR: Ministerio de Cultura, Juventud y Deportes Departamento de Publicaciones.

Goo, Sara Kehaulani. 2001a. "Ownership Opportunities: Blacks, Hispanics Find Room for Their Businesses to Grow in the D.C. Area." *Washington Post*, April 9, E1.

———. 2001b. "Sharp Rise in Black-Owned Firms; Hispanics' Businesses Show Modest Growth." *Washington Post*, Prince George's Extra, April 12, T5.

Goodman, Peter S. 1999. "Eating Chicken Dust: In an Automated Industry, Catchers Still Must Grab Birds by Hand." *Washington Post*, November 28, A23.

Grandin, Greg. 2006. *Empire's Workshop: Latin America, the United States, and the Rise of the New Imperialism*. New York: Metropolitan Books.

Guardia, Gloria. 1977. *El último juego*. San José, CR: Editorial Universitaria Centroamericana.

———. 2006. *Lobos al anochecer*. San José, CR: Santillana.

Guevara, Concepción Clara de. 1975. "El añil de los 'indios cheles.'" *América Indígena* 35.4: 773–796.

Guevara, Otoniel. 1999. *Despiadada ciudad*. San Salvador, ES: Colección Intima.

Gugelberger, Georg M., ed. 1996. *The Real Thing: Testimonial Discourse and Latin America*. Durham, NC: Duke University Press.

Gutiérrez, Joaquín. 1950/1991. *Puerto Limón*. San José, CR: Editorial de la Universidad de Costa Rica.

Habachi, René. 1986. *Fundamentos filosóficos de una Universidad para la Paz*. San José, CR: Editorial Universidad para la Paz.

Hall, Carolyn. 1985. "América Central como región geográfica." *Anuario de Estudios Centroamericanos* 7.2: 5–24.

Hamilton, Nora, and Norma Stoltz Chinchilla. 1997. "Central American Migration: A Framework for Analysis." In *Challenging Fronteras: Structuring Latina and Latino Lives in the U.S.*, ed. Mary Romero, Pierrette Hondagneu-Sotelo, and Vilma Ortiz, 81–100. London: Routledge.

———. 2001. *Seeking Community in a Global City: Guatemalans and Salvadorans in Los Angeles*. Philadelphia: Temple University Press.

Hardt, Michael, and Antonio Negri. 2000. *Empire*. Cambridge, MA: Harvard University Press.

Harlow, Barbara. 1987. *Resistance Literature*. New York: Methuen.

Harvey, David. 1999. *Justice, Nature and the Geography of Difference*. Malden, MA: Blackwell.

———. 2005. *A Brief History of Neoliberalism*. Oxford: Oxford University Press.

Hendrickson, Carol. 1995. *Weaving Identities: Construction of Dress and Self in a Highland Guatemalan Town*. Austin: University of Texas Press.

Hernández, Claudia. 2002. *Mediodia de frontera*. San Salvador, ES: Dirección de Publicaciones e Impresos, Consejo Nacional para la Cultura y el Arte.

Hernández, David. 1995. "Novelística de Manlio Argueta." *ECA* 558: 400–403.

Hernández-Linares, Leticia. 2002. *Razor Edges of My Tongue*. San Diego, CA: Calaca Press.

Hernández Lozano, Judith Carolina, Fernando Dimitri Orellana Acevedo, and Carlos Roberto Pocasangra Landaverde. 1994. "La literatura testimonial en El Salvador (1970–1993)." Licentiate thesis, Universidad Centroamericana José Simeón Cañas, El Salvador.

Herrera, Francisco Javier, Madeline Ríos, and the Salvadoran Communities. 1990. "Don't Put Your Pictures Away." In *Lucha y Esperanza*. Cassette No. 32480.

Hobsbawm, Eric. 1994. *The Age of Extremes: A History of the World, 1914–1991*. New York: Pantheon Books.

Horan, Elizabeth Rosa, ed. and trans. 2000. *The Subversive Voice of Carmen Lyra: Selected Works*. Gainesville: University Press of Florida.

House Document 108–159. 2004. "Notification to Enter into a Free Trade Agreement with the Governments of Costa Rica, El Salvador, Honduras, Guatemala, and Nicaragua. February 20, 2004." http://frwebgate.access .gpo.gov/cgi-bin/getdoc.cgi?dbname=108_ . . . (accessed October 6, 2004).

Howarth, David. 1966. *The Golden Isthmus*. London: Collins.

Inglés, Dorys. 2000. "Las pupusas se volvieron industria." *Diario de Hoy*, August 2, 32.

Iwerks, Leslie, and Mike Gold. 2006. *Recycled Life*. Film. Leslie Iwerks Productions.

Jameson, Fredric. 1988. *The Political Unconscious: Narrative as a Socially Symbolic Act*. Ithaca, NY: Cornell University Press.

———. 1992. *Postmodernism, Or, The Cultural Logic of Late Capitalism*. Durham, NC: Duke University Press.

Jara, René, and Hernán Vidal, eds. 1986. *Testimonio y Literatura*. Minneapolis, MN: Institute for the Study of Ideologies and Literature.

Jenkins, Virginia Scott. 2000. *Bananas: An American History*. Washington, DC: Smithsonian Institution Press.

Jennings, Keith, and Clarence Lusane. 1994. "The State and Future of Black/ Latino Relations in Washington, D.C.: A Bridge in Need of Repair." In *Blacks, Latinos, and Asians in Urban America: Status and Prospects for Politics and Activism*, ed. James Jennings, 57–77. Westport, CT: Praeger.

Jiménez, Michael F. 1995. "'From Plantation to Cup': Coffee and Capitalism in the United States, 1830–1930." In *Coffee, Society, and Power in Latin America*, ed. William Roseberry, Lowell Gudmundson, and Mario Samper Kutsch-bach, 38–64. Baltimore, MD: Johns Hopkins University Press.

Jonas, Susanne. 2000. *Of Centaurs and Doves: Guatemala's Peace Process*. Boulder, CO: Westview Press.

Joseph, Gilbert M., Catherine C. Legrand, and Ricardo D. Salvatore, eds. 1998. *Close Encounters of Empire: Writing the Cultural History of U.S.-Latin American Relations*. Durham, NC: Duke University Press.

Joya, Daniel. 2002. "Painting the Day Laborer: A Tender Brush." http://www .takoma.com/archives/copy/2002/08/vozenglish0802.html (accessed January 16, 2008).

———. 2003. *Sueños de un callejero*. San Salvador, ES: Editorial Nuevo Enfoque.

Kandiyoti, Dalia. 2004. "Host and Guest in the 'Latino Contact Zone': Narrating Solidarity and Hospitality in *Mother Tongue*." *Comparative American Studies* 2.4: 421–446.

Kaplan, Amy, and Donald E. Pease, eds. 1993. *Cultures of United States Imperialism*. Durham, NC: Duke University Press.

Kenworthy, Eldon. 1995. *America/Américas: Myth in the Making of U.S. Policy toward Latin America*. University Park: Pennsylvania State University Press.

Kepner, Jr., Charles David, and Jay Henry Soothill. 1935. *The Banana Empire: A Case Study of Economic Imperialism*. New York: Russell and Russell.

Kit, Wade A. 1996. "Manuel Estrada Cabrera." In *Encyclopedia of Latin American History and Culture*, vol. 2, ed. Barbara A. Tenenbaum, 519–520. New York: Charles Scribner's Sons.

Kristeva, Julia. 1982. *The Powers of Horror: An Essay on Abjection*. New York: Columbia University Press.

Kubler, George. 1972. "Jaguars in the Valley of Mexico." In *Cult of the Feline*, ed. Elizabeth Benson, 19–49. Washington, DC: Dumbarton Oaks Research and Collections.

LaCapra, Dominick. 2001. *Writing History, Writing Trauma*. Baltimore, MD: Johns Hopkins University Press.

LaFeber, Walter. 1989. *The Panama Canal: The Crisis in Historical Perspective*. New York: Oxford University Press.

Laguerre, Michel S. 1998. *Diasporic Citizenship: Haitian Americans in Transnational America*. New York: St. Martin's Press.

Langley, Lester D., and Thomas Schoonover. 1995. *The Banana Men: American Mercenaries and Entrepreneurs in Central America, 1880–1930*. Lexington: University Press of Kentucky.

Las Casas, Bartolomé de. 1542/1989. *Brevísima relación de la destrucción de las Indias.* Ed. André Saint-Lu. Madrid: Ediciones Cátedra.

Lefebvre, Henri. 1998. *The Production of Space.* Trans. Donald Nicholson-Smith. London: Blackwell.

Leiken, Robert S., and Barry Rubin, eds. 1987. *The Central American Crisis Reader: The Essential Guide to the Most Controversial Foreign Policy Issue Today.* New York: Summit Books.

Levi, Enrique Jaramillo, and Leland H. Chambers, eds. 1994. *Contemporary Short Stories from Central America.* Trans. Leland H. Chambers et al. Austin: University of Texas Press.

Lewis, Lancelot S. 1980. *The West Indian in Panama: Black Labor in Panama, 1850–1914.* Washington, DC: University Press of America.

Leys, Ruth. 2000. *Trauma: A Genealogy.* Chicago: University of Chicago Press.

Leyva, Héctor. 2005. "Narrativa centroamericana post noventa: Una exploración preliminar." *Istmo: Revista Virtual de Estudios Literarios y Culturales Centroamericanos.* http://www.denison.edu/collaborations/istmo/n11/articulos/index.html (accessed June 27, 2006).

Limón, Graciela. 1993. *In Search of Bernabé.* Houston: Arte Público Press.

Lindsay-Poland, John. 2003. *Emperors in the Jungle: The Hidden History of the U.S. in Panama.* Durham, NC: Duke University Press.

López, Olinda. 2003. "Reflexiones sobre el libro: *Sueños de un callejero de Daniel Joya (Salvadoreño).*" November 23. http://www.libros.com.sv/edicion26/libro.html (accessed January 16, 2008).

López Vigil, José Ignacio. 1992. *Rebel Radio: The Story of El Salvador's Radio Venceremos.* Trans. Mark Fried. Willimantic, CT: Curbstone Press.

———. 1992. *Las mil y una historias de Radio Venceremos.* San Salvador, ES: Universidad Centroamericana José Simeón Cañas Editores.

López Vigil, María. 1987a. *Don Lito de El Salvador: Habla un campesino.* San Salvador, ES: Universidad Centroamericana José Simeón Cañas Editores.

———. 1987b. *Muerte y vida en Morazán: Testimonio de un sacerdote.* San Salvador, ES: Universidad Centroamericana José Simeón Cañas Editores.

Los Acuerdos de Paz: En el camino de la paz. 1991. San Salvador, ES: Editorial Arcoiris.

Los Hermanos Flores. 1998. "El hermano lejano." *Super Fiesta 99 con Los Hermanos Flores.* Hollywood, CA: Music Art Productions. CD MACD-2826.

Lovell, W. George. 2000a. *A Beauty That Hurts: Life and Death in Guatemala.* Austin: University of Texas Press.

———. 2000b. "The Highland Maya." In *The Cambridge History of the Native Peoples of the Americas,* vol. 2, *Mesoamerica,* pt. 2, ed. Richard E. W. Adams and Murdo J. Macleod. 392–444. Cambridge: Cambridge University Press.

Lovell, W. George, and Christopher H. Lutz. 1996. "'A Dark Obverse': Maya Survival in Guatemala, 1520–1994." *Geographical Review* 86: 401–407.

Low, Setha. 2000. *On the Plaza: The Politics of Public Space and Culture.* Austin: University of Texas Press.

Lungo, Mario, and Sonia Baires. 1996. *De terremotos, derrumbes e inundados: Los riesgos ambientales y el desarrollo urbano sostenible en El Salvador.* San Salvador, ES: Fundación Nacional para el Desarrollo.

Lungo Uclés, Mario. 1990. *El Salvador en los 80: Contrainsurgencia y revolución*. San José, CR: Editorial Universitaria Centroamericana–Facultad Latino-americana de Ciencias Sociales.

Ly, Phuong. 2001. "Newly Jobless Immigrants Swell Ranks of Day Laborers." *Washington Post*, December 17, B01. http://media.earthops.net/immigration/day-laborers1.html (accessed January 16, 2008).

Lyra, Carmen. 1931/1977. "Bananos y hombres." In *Relatos escogidos de Carmen Lyra*, ed. Alfonso Chase, 371–387. San José, CR: Editorial Costa Rica.

———. 1931/2000. "Bananas and Men." In *The Subversive Voice of Carmen Lyra: Selected Works*, ed. and trans. Elizabeth Rosa Horan, 47–61. Gainsville: University Press of Florida.

MacAdam, Alfred. 1987. *New York Times* book review (July 26). In *Spanish American Authors: The Twentieth Century*, ed. Angel Flores. 1992, 48. New York: H. W. Wilson.

MacEoin, Gary, ed. 1985. *Sanctuary: A Resource Guide for Understanding and Participating in the Central American Refugees' Struggle*. New York: Harper & Row.

Mackenbach, Werner, 2004. "Después de los pos-ismos: ¿desde qué categorías pensamos las literaturas centroamericanas contemporáneas?" *Istmo: Revista Virtual de Estudios Literarios y Culturales Centroamericanos*. http://www.denison.edu/collaborations/istmo/n08/articulos/pos_ismos.html (accessed January 16, 2008).

———. 2007. "¿Literatura light o escribir conscientemente? Entrevista a Fanz Galich." *Istmo: Revista Virtual de Estudios Literarios y Culturales Centroamericanos*. http://collaborations.denison.edu/istmo/articulos/mackenbach2.html (accessed March 20, 2008).

———. ed. 2004. *Cicatrices: Un retrato del cuento centroamericano*. Managua: amamá Ediciones.

Mahler, Sarah J. 1995a. *American Dreaming: Immigrant Life on the Margins*. Princeton, NJ: Princeton University Press.

———. 1995b. *Salvadorans in Suburbia: Symbiosis and Conflict*. Boston: Allyn and Bacon.

———. 2000. "Migration and Transnational Issues: Recent Trends and Prospects for 2020, Central America 2020." http://ca2020.fiu.edu/Themes/Sarah_Mahler/Mahler.htm (accessed July 30, 2005).

Marín, Gerardo, and Barbara VanOss Marín. 1991. *Research with Hispanic Populations*. London: Sage.

Mariscal, George, ed. 1999. *Aztlán and Viet Nam: Chicano and Chicana Experiences of the War*. Berkeley: University of California Press.

Martí, José. 1987. "Nuestra América." In *José Martí: Ideario*, comp. Cintio Vitier and Fina García Marruz, 261–272. Managua: Editorial Nueva Nicaragua.

———. 1999. "Nuestra América." In *José Martí Reader: Writings on the Americas*, ed. Deborah Shnookal and Mirta Muñiz. New York: Ocean Press.

Martínez, Ana Guadalupe. 1978. *Las cárceles clandestinas de El Salvador*. San Salvador, ES: Universidad Centroamericana José Simeón Cañas Editores.

Martínez, Demetria. 1989. "Turning." In *Three Times a Woman: Chicana Poetry*, ed. Alicia Gaspar de Alba, María Herrera-Sobek, and Demetria Martínez, 101–156. Tempe, AZ: Bilingual Review/Press.

———. 1994. *Mother Tongue*. New York: Ballantine Books.

Martínez, Zulma Nelly. 1985. "Entrevista con Manlio Argueta." *Hispamérica* 14.42: 41–54.

Martínez Echazábal, Lourdes. 1991. "Testimonial Narratives: Translating Culture While Narrowing the Genre Gap." *Translation Pespectives* 6: 57–65.

———. 1997. "Hybridity and Diasporization in the *'Black Atlantic'*: The Case of *Chombo*." *Palara* 1: 117–129.

Martínez Montiel, Luz María, comp. 1993. *Presencia africana en Centroamérica*. México: Consejo Nacional para la Cultura y las Artes.

Masiello, Francine. 2001. *The Art of Transition: Latin American Culture and Neoliberal Crisis*. Durham, NC: Duke University Press.

May, Stacy, and Galo Plaza. 1958. *The United Fruit Company in Latin America*. Washington, DC: National Planning Association.

McCullough, David. 1977. *The Path between the Seas: The Creation of the Panama Canal, 1870–1914*. New York: Simon and Schuster.

McGuinness, Aims. 2008. *Path of Empire: Panama and the California Gold Rush*. Ithaca, NY: Cornell University Press.

Melara Méndez, Efraín. 1998. *Mitología cuzcatleca: Los cuentos de mi infancia y otros*. Santa Tecla, ES: Editorial Clásicos Roxsil.

Meléndez, Carlos. 1981. *Historia de Costa Rica*. Heredia, CR: Editorial de la Universidad Nacional.

Menchú, Rigoberta, and Elizabeth Burgos Debray. 1983. *Me llamo Rigoberta Menchú y así me nació la conciencia*. Mexico, DF: Siglo XXI Editores.

Menjívar, Cecilia. 2000. *Fragmented Ties: Salvadoran Immigrant Networks in America*. Berkeley: University of California Press.

Menton, Seymour. 1985. *Historia crítica de la novela guatemalteca*. Guatemala: Editorial Universitaria de Guatemala.

Metzi, Francisco. 1988. *Por los caminos de Chalatenango: Con la salud en la mochila*. San Salvador, ES: Universidad Centroamericana José Simeón Cañas Editores.

Miller, Francesca. 1991. *Latin American Women and the Search for Social Justice*. Hanover, NH: University Press of New England.

Miller, Mary, and Karl Taube. 1997. *An Illustrated Dictionary of The Gods and Symbols of Ancient México and the Maya*. London: Thames and Hudson.

Minow, Martha. 1998. *Between Vengeance and Forgiveness: Facing History after Genocide and Mass Violence*. Boston: Beacon Press.

Molina, Armando. 1996. *Bajo el cielo del istmo*. San Francisco: Editorial Solaris.

Molina Jiménez, Ivan. 1992. "'Azul por Rubén Darío. El libro de moda': La cultura libresca del Valle Central de Costa Rica (1780–1890)." In *Heroes al gusto y libros de moda: Sociedad y cambio cultural en Costa Rica (1750/1900)*, ed. Iván Molina Jiménez and Steven Palmer, 137–167. San José, CR: Editorial Porvenir/Plumsock Mesoamerican Studies.

———. 1995. *El que quiera divertirse: Libros y sociedad en Costa Rica (1750–1914)*. San José, CR: Editorial de la Universidad de Costa Rica.

———. 2001. "La polémica de *El Problema* (1899), de Máximo Soto Hall." *Revista Mexicana del Caribe (RMC)* 12: 147–187. http://www.recaribe.uqroo.mx/recaribe/sitio/espanol/num12.html (accessed July 8, 2005).

———. 2002. "Un pasado comunista por recuperar: Carmen Lyra y Carlos Luis Fallas en la década de 1930." *Artikkelit Maaliskuu.* http:www.helsinki.fi/hum/ibero/xaman/articulos/2002_01/molina.html (accessed July 5, 2005).

Molina Jiménez, Iván, and Steven Palmer, eds. 1992. *Heroes al gusto y libros de moda: Sociedad y cambio cultural en Costa Rica (1750/1900).* San José, CR: Editorial Porvenir/Plumsock Mesoamerican Studies.

Molina Jiménez, Iván, and Verónica Ríos Quesada. 2002. "La primera polémica que provocó *El problema*, novela del escritor guatemalteco Máximo Soto Hall. Una contribución documental." *Istmo: Revista Virtual de Estudios Literarios y Culturales Centroamericanos.* http://www.denison.edu/collaborations/istmo/no3/proyectos/problema (accessed July 8, 2005).

Mondragón, Amelia, ed. 1994. *Cambios estéticos y nuevos proyectos culturales en Centroamérica: Testimonios, entrevistas y ensayos.* Washington, DC: Literal Books.

Montaigne, Fen. 1999. "Deporting America's Gang Culture." *Mother Jones* (July–August): 44–51.

Montejo, Victor. 1987. *Testimony: Death of a Guatemalan Village.* Trans. Victor Perera. Willimantic, CT: Curbstone Press.

———. 1991. *The Bird Who Cleans the World and Other Mayan Fables.* Willimantic, CT: Curbstone Press.

———. 1992. *Brevísima relación testimonial de la continúa destrucción del Mayab' (Guatemala).* Providence, RI.

———. 1995. *Sculpted Stones, Poems.* Willimantic, CT: Curbstone Press.

———. 1999. *El Q'anil: The Man of Lightning.* Rancho Palos Verdes, CA: Yax Te' Foundation.

———. 1999. *Voices from Exile: Violence and Survival in Modern Maya History.* Norman: University of Oklahoma Press.

Moraga, Cherríe. 1995. "Art in América con Acento." In *Latina: Women's Voices from the Borderlands,* ed. Lilliana Castillo-Speed, 211–220. New York: Touchstone Books.

More, Thomas. 1516/1985. *Utopia.* Trans. Paul Turner. New York: Viking Penguin.

Mountz, Alison, Richard Wright, Ines Miyares, and Adrian J. Bailey. 2002. "Lives in Limbo: Temporary Protected Status and Immigrant Identities." *Global Networks* 2.4: 335–356.

Muñoz Chacón, Sergio. 2000. *Los Dorados.* San José, CR: Editores Alambique.

———. 2003. *Urbanos.* San José, CR: Editorial Costa Rica.

Murguía, Alejandro. 1990. *Southern Front.* Tempe, AZ: Bilingual Press/Editorial Bilingüe.

———. 1999. "Concordia: The San Francisco Bay Area in Central American Literature." Paper presented at the First Annual Conference on Central American Literatures and Cultures, Arizona State University, Tempe, April 8–10.

Murillo Chaverri, Carmen. 1995. *Identidades de hierro y humo: La construcción del ferrocarril al Atlántico 1870–1980.* San José, CR: Editorial Porvenir.

Murphy, Caryle. 2001. "Gift to Salvadoran Community: Illegal Immigrants Granted Temporary Relief after Quakes." *Washington Post,* March 3, A8.

Naranjo, Carmen. 1989. "And We Sold the Rain." Trans. Jo Anne Engelbert. In *And We Sold the Rain: Contemporary Fiction from Central America*, ed. Rosario Santos, 149–156. Peterborough: Ryan Publishing.

Nouzeilles, Gabriela, ed. 2002. *La naturaleza en disputa: Retóricas del cuerpo y el paisaje en América Latina*. Buenos Aires: Paidós.

Office of the United States Trade Representative. *CAFTA Revised Draft Text*. http://www.ustr.gov/Trade_Agreements/Bilateral/CAFTA/CAFTA _Draft_Revised_Texts/Section_Index.html (accessed May 13, 2005).

Oliva Medina, Mario. 1995. *José Martí en la historia y la cultura costarricenses*. Heredia, CR: Editorial de la Universidad Nacional.

Olmos, Manuel. 1998. *Caminantes de maíz: Una historia guanaca*. Los Angeles: Ediciones M.O. Promotions.

Ordoñez, Jaime, and Nuria Gamboa, eds. 1997. *Esquipulas, diez años después ¿Hacia dónde va Centroamérica?* San José, CR: Editorial Universitaria Centroamericana.

Orozco, Manuel. 2004. "Rethinking Central America and Free Trade." Project Syndicate, University of California, Berkeley, June.

Ortiz, Fernando. 1947. *Cuban Counterpoint: Tobacco and Sugar*. Trans. Harriet de Onís. New York: Knopf.

Ortiz Wallner, Alexandra. 2005. "Historias de la literatura nacional en Centroamérica: Tendencias, continuidades y perspectivas." *Istmo: Revista Virtual de Estudios Literarios y Culturales Centroamericanos*. http://www.denison.edu/ collaborations/istmo/n11/proyectos/historias.html (accessed June 27, 2006).

Ovares, Flora. 1994. *Literatura de kiosko: Revistas literarias de Costa Rica (1890–1930)*. Heredia, CR: Editorial de Universidad Nacional.

Ovares, Flora et al. 1993. *La casa paterna: Escritura y nación en Costa Rica*. San José, CR: Editorial de la Universidad de Costa Rica.

Paige, Jefferey M. 1997. *Coffee and Power: Revolution and the Rise of Democracy in Central America*. Cambridge, MA: Harvard University Press.

Palma Murga, Gustavo. 1993. "Economía y sociedad en Centroamérica (1680–1750)." In *Historia General de Centroamérica*, vol. 2, ed. Julio Pinto Soria, 219–306. Madrid: Facultad Latinoamericana de Ciencias Sociales.

Palmer, Steven. 1992. "Sociedad Anónima, Cultura Oficial: Inventando Nación en Costa Rica (1848–1900)." In *Heroes al gusto y libros de moda: Sociedad y cambio cultural en Costa Rica (1750/1900)*, ed. Iván Molina Jiménez and Steven Palmer, 169–205. San José, CR: Editorial Porvenir/Plumsock Mesoamerican Studies.

Palmer, Steven, and Gladys Rojas Chaves. 1998. "Educating Señorita: Teacher Training, Social Mobility, and the Birth of Costa Rican Feminism, 1885–1925." *Hispanic American Historical Review* 78.1: 45–82.

Pedersen, David E. 1995. "States of Memory and Desire: The Meaning of City and Nation for Transnational Migrants in Washington, D.C., and El Salvador." *Amerikastudien/American Studies* 40.3: 415–442.

Perera, Victor. 1985. *Rites: A Guatemalan Boyhood*. San Francisco: Mercury House.

Pérez Brignoli, Héctor. 1989. *A Brief History of Central America*. Trans. Ricardo B. Sawrey A. and Susana Stettri de Sawrey. Berkeley: University of California Press.

Perfil estadístico centroamericano. 1992. San José, CR: Facultad Latinoamericana de Ciencias Sociales.

Pike, Fredrick B. 1992. *The United States and Latin America: Myths and Stereotypes of Civilization and Nature.* Austin: University of Texas Press.

Pinderhughes, Raquel, Carlos Córdova, and Jorge del Pinal. 2002. "Central and South Americans. Our Multicultural Heritage: A Guide to America's Principal Ethnic Groups," http://bss.sfsu.edu/raquelrp/pub/heritage_pub.html (accessed January 16, 2008).

Pinto Soria, Julio César. 1993. "La independencia y la federación (1810–1840)." In *Historia General de Centroamérica*, vol. 3, ed. Héctor Pérez Brignoli, 73–140. Madrid: Facultad Latinoamericana de Ciencias Sociales.

Portillo, Lourdes, and Nina Serrano. 1979. *Después del terremoto (After the Earthquake).* Film.

Posas, Mario. 1993. "La plantación bananera en Centroamérica (1870–1929)." In *Historia General de Centroamérica*, vol. 4, ed. Victor Hugo Acuña Ortega, 111–165. Madrid: Facultad Latinoamericano de Ciencias Sociales.

Pratt, Mary Louse. 1992. "Introduction: Criticism in the Contact Zone." In *Imperial Eyes: Travel Writing and Transculturation*, 1–11. London: Routledge.

Putnam, Lara. 2002. *The Company They Kept: Migrants and the Politics of Gender in Caribbean Costa Rica, 1870–1960.* Chapel Hill: The University of North Carolina Press.

Quesada, Roberto. 1999. *The Big Banana.* Trans. Walter Krochmal. Houston: Arte Público Press.

———. 2002. *Never through Miami.* Trans. Patricia J. Duncan. Houston: Arte Público Press.

Quesada, Uriel. 2004. *Lejos, tan lejos.* San José, CR: Editorial Costa Rica.

Quesada Soto, Álvaro. 1988. *La voz desgarrada: La crisis del discurso oligárquico y la narrativa costarricense (1917–1919).* San José, CR: Editorial de la Universidad de Costa Rica.

———. 1995. *La formación de la narrativa nacional costarricense (1890–1910): Enfoque histórico social.* San José, CR: Editorial de la Universidad de Costa Rica.

———. 1998. *Uno y los otros: Identidad y literatura en Costa Rica 1890–1940.* San José, CR: Editorial de la Universidad de Costa Rica.

Rama, Angel. 1996. *The Lettered City.* Trans. John Charles Chasteen. Durham, NC: Duke University Press.

Ramírez, Sergio. 1982. "Introducción: la narrativa centroamericana." *Antología del cuento centroamericano*, 9–63. San José. CR: Editorial Universitaria Centroamericana.

———. 1985. *Balcanes y volcanes y otros ensayos y trabajos.* Managua: Editorial Nueva Nicaragua.

———. 1987. "El muchacho de Niquinohomo." In *Las armas del futuro*, 3–38. Managua: Editorial Nueva Nicaragua.

———. 1995. *Hatful of Tigers: Reflections on Art, Culture and Politics.* Trans. D. J. Flakoll. Willimantic, CT: Curbstone Press.

Ramos, Julio. 1989. *Desencuentros de la modernidad en América Latina: Literatura y política en el siglo XIX.* México: Fondo de Cultura Económica.

Randall, Margaret. 1980. *Todas estamos despiertas: Testimonios de la mujer nicaragüense hoy.* México: Siglo XXI.

————. 1981. *Sandino's Daughters: Testimonies of Nicaraguan Women in Struggle.* Vancouver, BC: New Star Books.

Randall, Stephen J., and Graeme S. Mount with David Bright. 1998. *The Caribbean Basin: An International History.* London: Routledge.

Redacción. 1968. "Manlio Argueta ganó en certamen C.A. de Novela." *La República*, San José, Costa Rica, December 28.

————. 1981. "Obra de Manlio Argueta circula en Centroamérica." *Periódico Universidad. UCR.* San José, Costa Rica, June 12/18, 11.

————. 1995. "Crispación en Centroamérica." *La Nación.* San José, Costa Rica, June 2, 18A.

————. 1995. "Oscar Arias reprende a políticos." *La Nación*, San José, Costa Rica, June 2, 4A.

————. 2004. "Pollo Campero abre en Langley Park." *El Tiempo Latino*, November 19, B4.

Redacción de Departamentos. 2000. "El loroco se posesiona de importante mercado en el exterior." *La Prensa Gráfica*, August 1, 41.

REMHI. 1998/1999. *Guatemala Never Again! Recovery of Historical Memory Project.* Archdiocese of Guatemala.

Repak, Terry A. 1995. *Waiting on Washington: Central American Workers in the Nation's Capital.* Philadelphia: Temple University Press.

Retana Guido, Marlen. 1991. "Un plan de paz para Centroamérica." Licentiate thesis, Philology, Linguistics, and Literature, University of Costa Rica, San José, Costa Rica.

Review of *Poesía de El Salvador.* 1983. *Periódico Universidad. UCR.* San José, Costa Rica, August 5, 11.

Reyes-Valerio, Constantino. 1993. *De Bonampak al Templo Mayor: El azul maya en Mesoamérica.* México: Siglo XXI Editores.

Ríos Quesada, Verónica. 2002. "El impacto de la publicación de la novela *El problema* de Soto Hall en la Costa Rica de 1899." *Istmo: Revista virtual de estudios literarios y culturales centroamericanos.* VI Congreso Centroamericano de Historia, Mesa Historia y Literatura, Ciudad Panama, 22–26 de julio. http://www.denison.edu/collaborations/istmo/n04/proyectos/soto.html (accessed July 8, 2005).

Robbins, Jill. "Neocolonialism, Neoliberalism, and National Identities: The Spanish Publishing Crisis and the Marketing of Central America." *Istmo: Revista Virtual de Estudios Literarios y Culturales Centroamericanos.* http://www.denison.edu/collaborations/istmo/n08/articulos/neocolonialism.html (accessed July 8, 2005).

Robinson, William I. 2003. *Transnational Conflicts: Central America, Social Change, and Globalization.* London: Verso.

————. 2004. "The New Right and the End of National Liberation." *NACLA Report on the Americas: Beyond Revolution: Nicaragua and El Salvador in a New Era* 37.6 (May/June): 15–20.

Rodas, Karla (Karlísima). 1999/2005. *Lamento Indígena I and II.* Paintings. Washington, DC.

Rodríguez, Ana Patricia. 2001. "Refugees of the South: Central Americans in the U.S. Latino Imaginary." *American Literature* 73.2: 387–412.

———. 2002a. "Encrucijadas: Rubén Blades at the Transnational Crossroads." In *Latina/o Popular Culture*, ed. Michelle Habell-Pallán and Mary Romero, 85–101. New York: New York University Press.

———. 2002b. "Wasted Opportunities: Conflictive Peacetime Narratives of Central America." In *The Globalization of U.S.–Latin American Relations: Democracy, Intervention, and Human Rights*, ed. Virginia M. Bouvier, 227–247. Westport, CT: Praeger.

———. 2005. "'Departamento 15': Cultural Narratives of Salvadoran Transnational Migration." *Latino Studies* 3: 19–41.

———. 2006. "Mozote Homeland: Diasporic Memories of the Salvadoran Civil War in Testimonial and Filmic Narratives." *Istmo: Revista Virtual de Estudios Literarios y Culturales Centroamericanos.* Ed. Beatriz Cortez and Alexandra Ortiz Wallner. Producciones audiovisuals en Centroamérica. 13 (July–December). http://www.denison.edu/collaborations/istmo/n13/articulos/mozote.html (accessed January 16, 2008).

Rodríguez, Guadalupe. 1994. *Marianela, 1983–1994.* San Salvador, ES: Editorial Guayampopo.

Rodríguez, Ileana. 1996. *Women, Guerrillas, and Love: Understanding War in Central America.* Trans. Ileana Rodríguez with Robert Carr. Minneapolis: University of Minnesota Press.

———, ed. 2001. *The Latin American Subaltern Studies Reader.* Durham, NC: Duke University Press.

———. 2004. *Transatlantic Topographies: Islands, Highlands, Jungles.* Minneapolis: University of Minnesota Press.

Rojas, Margarita, and Flora Ovares. 1995. *100 años de la literatura costarricense.* San José, CR: Ediciones FARBEN.

Rojas Rodríguez, María Eugenia, and Flor de María Herrera Alfaro. 1981. "El añil de Centroamérica." Master's thesis, Universidad de Costa Rica.

Román-Lagunas, Jorge. 1994. *La literatura centroamericana: Visiones and revisiones.* Lewiston, PA: Edwin Mellen Press.

Roque, Consuelo. 1988. "La violación de los derechos humanos en El Salvador reflejada en cuentos escritos por Salvadoreños entre 1970 y 1985." Licentiate thesis, Universidad de El Salvador.

Roseberry, William, Lowell Gudmundson, and Mario Samper Kutschbach, eds. 1995. *Coffee, Society, and Power in Latin America.* Baltimore, MD: Johns Hopkins University Press.

Rotberg, Robert I., and Dennis Thompson, eds. 2000. *Truth v. Justice: The Morality of Truth Commissions.* Princeton, NJ: Princeton University Press.

Rowe, William, and Vivian Schelling. 1991. *Memory and Modernity: Popular Culture in Latin America.* London: Verso.

Rubio Sánchez, Manuel. 1976. *Historia del añil o xiquilite en Centro América.* Vol.1. San Salvador, ES: Ministerio de Educación.

Rush, John A. 2005. *Spiritual Tattoo: A Cultural History of Tattooing, Piercing, Scarification, Branding, and Implants.* Berkeley, CA: Frog, Ltd.

Saldívar-Hull, Sonia. 1991. "Feminism on the Border: From Gender Politics to Geopolitics." In *Criticism in the Borderlands: Studies in Chicano Literature,*

Culture, and Ideology, ed. Héctor Calderón and José David Saldívar, 201–220. Durham, NC: Duke University Press.

———. 2000. *Feminism on the Border: Chicana Gender Politics and Literature.* Berkeley: University of California Press.

Samper, Mario K. 1993. "Café, trabajo y sociedad en Centroamérica, (1870–1930): Una historia común y divergente." In *Historia General de Centroamérica*, vol. 4, ed. Víctor Hugo Acuña Ortega, 11–110. Madrid: Facultad Latinoamericana de Ciencias Sociales.

Sandoval, Chela. 1991. "U.S. Third World Feminism: The Theory and Method of Oppositional Consciousness in the Postmodern World." *Genders* 10: 1–24.

———. 2000. *Methodology of the Oppressed.* Minneapolis: University of Minnesota Press.

Santiago, Silviano. 2001. "Latin American Discourse: The Space In-Between." In *The Space In-Between: Essays on Latin American Culture*, 25–38. Trans. Tom Burns, et al. Durham, NC: Duke University Press.

Santiago Soto, Angel T. 1993. *Las novelas de las compañías: Textos polisémicos de la cuenca del Caribe.* New York: Peter Lang.

Saunders, Nicholas, ed. 1998. *Icons of Power: Feline Symbolism in the Americas.* London: Routledge.

Saxgren, Henrik. 2000. *Solomon's House: The Lost Children of Nicaragua.* Photographs and text Henrik Saxgren. New York: Aperture Foundation.

Schele, Linda, and David Freidel. 1990. *A Forest of Kings: The Untold Story of the Ancient Maya.* New York: Quill/William Morrow.

Schele, Linda, and Mary Ellen Miller. 1986. *The Blood of Kings: Dynasty and Ritual in Maya Art.* New York: George Braziller/Kimbell Art Museum.

Schiantarelli, Fernando, with Renán Almendárez Coello. 2002. *El Cucuy de la Mañana: En la cumbre de la pobreza.* New York: HarperCollins/Rayo.

Schlesinger, Stephen, and Stephen Kinzer. 1999. *Bitter Fruit: The Story of the American Coup in Guatemala.* Cambridge, MA: Harvard University Press.

Scott, Joan W. 1991. "The Evidence of Experience." *Critical Inquiry* 17.4: 773–797.

Segura Montero, Alberto, ed. 1995. *La polémica (1894–1902): El nacionalismo en literatura.* San José, CR: Editorial Universidad Estatal a Distancia.

Sepúlveda, Mélida Ruth. 1975. *El tema del canal en la novelística panameña.* Caracas: Universidad Católica Andrés Bello.

Sharpe, Jim. 1992. "History from Below." In *New Perspectives on Historical Writing*, ed. Peter Burke, 24–41. University Park: Pennsylvania State University Press.

Short, John Rennie. 2001. *Global Dimensions: Space, Place and the Contemporary World.* London: Reaktion Books.

Smith, Christian. 1996. *Resisting Reagan: The U.S. Central America Peace Movement.* Chicago: University of Chicago Press.

Smith, Peter H. 1996. *Talons of the Eagle: Dynamics of U.S.–Latin American Relations.* New York: Oxford University Press.

Sobrino, Jon, Ignacio Martín-Baró, and Roberto Cardenal. 1980. *La voz de los sin voz: La palabra viva de Monseñor Romero.* San Salvador, ES: Universidad Centroamericana José Simeón Cañas Editores.

Soja, Edward W. 1998a. *Postmodern Geographies: The Reassertion of Space in Critical Social Theory.* London: Verso.

———. 1998b. *Thirdspace: Journeys to Los Angeles and Other Real-and-Imagined Places.* Malden, MA: Blackwell Press.

Sommer, Doris. 1991. *Foundational Fictions: The National Romances of Latin America.* Berkeley: University of California Press.

Sontag, Susan. 2003. *Regarding the Pain of Others.* New York: Farrar, Straus and Giroux.

Soto Hall, Máximo. 1899/1992. *El problema.* San José, CR: Editorial de la Universidad de Costa Rica.

———. 1901. *Un vistazo sobre Costa Rica en el siglo XIX.* San José, Costa Rica: Tipografía Nacional.

———. 1927. *La sombra de la Casa Blanca.* Buenos Aires: Ateneo.

———. 1928. *Nicaragua y el imperialismo norteamericano.* Buenos Aires: Artes y Letras Editorial.

Spivak, Gayatri Chakravorty. 1988. "Can the Subaltern Speak?" In *Marxism and the Interpretation of Culture,* ed. Cary Nelson and Lawrence Grossberg, 271–313. Chicago: University of Illinois Press.

Stoll, David. 1999. *Rigoberta Menchú and the Story of All Poor Guatemalans.* Boulder, CO: Westview Press.

Stone, Samuel. 1990. *The Heritage of the Conquistadores: Ruling Classes in Central America from the Conquest to the Sandinistas.* Lincoln: University of Nebraska Press.

Suleiman, Susan Rubin. 1983. *Authoritarian Fictions: The Ideological Novel As a Literary Genre.* Princeton, NJ: Princeton University Press.

Szok, Peter. 2002. "Octavio Méndez Pereira and Panamanian Foundational Fiction." *Revista Mexicana del Caribe (RMC)* 14: 145–165. http://www.recaribe.uqroo.mx/recaribe/sitio/espanol/num12.html (accessed July 8, 2005).

Tábora, Rocío. 2001. *Guardarropa.* Tegucigalpa, Honduras: Editorial Iberoamericana.

Taracena Arriola, Arturo. 1993. "Liberalismo y poder político en Centroamérica (1870–1929)." In *Historia General de Centroamérica,* vol. 4, ed. Víctor Hugo Acuña Ortega, 167–253. Madrid: Facultad Latinoamericana de Ciencias Sociales.

Theroux, Alexander. 1994. "Blue." In *The Primary Colors,* 1–67. New York: Henry Holt.

Thompson, J. Eric S. 1970. *Maya History and Religion.* Norman: University of Oklahoma Press.

Tobar, Héctor. 1998/2000. *The Tattooed Soldier.* New York: Penguin.

Tomsho, Robert. 1987. *The American Sanctuary Movement.* Austin: Texas Monthly Press.

Topik, Steven C. 1998. "Coffee." In *The Second Conquest of Latin America: Coffee, Henequen, and Oil during the Export Boom, 1850–1930,* ed. Steven C. Topik and Allen Wells, 37–41. Austin: University of Texas Press.

Topik, Steven C., and Allen Wells, eds. 1998. *The Second Conquest of Latin America: Coffee, Henequen, and Oil during the Export Boom, 1850–1930.* Austin: University of Texas Press.

Torres-Rivas, Edelberto. 1980. *Interpretación del desarrollo social centroamericano:*

Proceso y estructuras de una sociedad dependiente. San José, CR: Editorial Universitaria Centroamericana.

———, comp. 1989. *América Central hacia el 2000: Desafíos y opciones.* Caracas: Editorial Nueva Sociedad.

———. 1993a. "Introducción a la década." In *Historia General de Centroamérica,* vol. 6, ed. Edelberto Torres-Rivas, 11–33. Madrid: Facultad Latinoamericana de Ciencias Sociales.

———. 1993b. "La sociedad: La dinámica poblacional, efectos sociales de la crisis, aspectos culturales y étnicos." In *Historia General de Centroamérica,* vol. 6, ed. Edelberto Torres-Rivas, 163–208. Madrid: Facultad Latinoamericana de Ciencias Sociales.

———. 2006. *La piel de Centroamérica (Una visión epidérmica de setenta y cinco años de su historia).* Guatemala: Facultad Latinoamericana de Ciencias Sociales.

Towell, Larry. 1997. *El Salvador.* Photographs by Larry Towell. New York: W. W. Norton.

Trigo, Benigno. 2000. *Subject of Crisis: Race and Gender as Disease in Latin America.* Hanover, NH: University Press of New England.

Una hora para la paz. 1987. San José, CR: Imprenta Nacional.

United Nations (UN). 1992. *El Salvador Agreements: The Path to Peace.* New York: UN Office of Public Information.

U.S. Census. 2000. *State Population Tables.* http://factfinder.census.gov/home/en/pldata.html (accessed January 16, 2008).

Universidad para la Paz/Universidad Nacional. 1987. *Los refugiados centroamericanos.* Heredia, CR: Editorial de la Universidad Nacional.

Ureña, Pedro Henriquez. 1974. *Las corrientes literarias en la América Hispánica.* Mexico, DF: Fondo de Cultura Económica.

Valle, Victor M., and Rodolfo D. Torres. 2000. *Latino Metropolis.* Minneapolis: University of Minnesota Press.

Vargas, Roberto. 1980. "UNIDAD (UNITY)." *XhismeArte* 6 (February): 31.

Vega Jiménez, Patricia. 1992. "De la banca al sofá: La diversificación de los patrones de consumo en Costa Rica (1857–1861)." In *Heroes al gusto y libros de moda: Sociedad y cambio cultural en Costa Rica (1750/1900),* ed. Iván Molina Jiménez and Steven Palmer, 109–135. San José, CR: Editorial Porvenir/Plumsock Mesoamerican Studies.

Viales Hurtado, Ronny José. 1998. *Después del enclave, 1927–1950: Un estudio de la Región Atlántica Costarricense.* San José, CR: Editorial de la Universidad de Costa Rica.

Villa, Raúl Homero. 2000. *Barrio-Logos: Space and Place in Urban Chicano Literature and Culture.* Austin: University of Texas Press.

Villanueva, Alma Luz. 1988. *The Ultraviolet Sky.* Tempe, AZ: Bilingual Press/Editorial Bilingüe.

Villatoro, Marcos McPeek. 1996. *A Fire in the Earth.* Houston: Arte Público Press.

———. 2001. *HomeKillings: A Romilia Chacón Mystery.* Houston: Arte Público Press.

Villegas, Juan Jacobo. 1991. "El testimonio en la producción literaria salvadoreña." *Taller de Letras* 10.42: 20.

Viramontes, Helena María. 1985. "The Cariboo Café." In *The Moths and Other Stories*, 59–75. Houston: Arte Público Press.

Vizentini, Paulo, and Marianne Wiesebron, eds. 2004. *Free Trade for the Americas? The United States' Push for the FTAA Agreement*. London: Zed Books.

Walker, William. 1860/1985. *The War in Nicaragua*. Tucson: University of Arizona Press.

"War and the Writer in El Salvador." 1992. *Index on Censorship* 11.2: 3–5.

Warpehoski, Charles. n.d. "Nicaragua: Dry Canals vs. Communities." In *Plan Puebla Panama: Battle over the Future of Southern Mexico and Central America*, 34–36. n.p.: Network Opposed to the Plan Puebla Panama.

Warren, Kay B. 1998. *Indigenous Movements and Their Critics: Pan-Maya Activism in Guatemala*. Princeton, NJ: Princeton University Press.

White, Hayden. 1978. "The Historical Text as Literary Artifact." In *Tropics of Discourse: Essays in Cultural Criticism*, 81–100. Baltimore, MD: Johns Hopkins University Press.

Wignaraja, Ponna. 1993. "Preface." In *New Social Movements in the South: Empowering the People*, ed. Ponna Wignaraja, xv–xviii. London: Zed Books.

Williams, Raymond. 1977. *Marxism and Literature*. New York: Oxford University Press.

Wilson, Carlos Guillermo (Cubena). 1981. *Chombo*. Miami, FL: Ediciones Universal.

Wilson, Charles Morrow. 1947. *Empire in Green and Gold: The Story of the American Banana Trade*. New York: Henry Holt.

Winschun, Thomas 1999. *¿Por qué se van? La emigración de salvadoreños a los Estados Unidos*. San Salvador, ES: Fundación Heinrich Böll.

Woodward, Jr., Ralph Lee. 1999. "Banana Republics." In *Central America: A Nation Divided*, 177–202. Oxford: Oxford University Press.

Xiquín, Calixta Gabriel. 2002. *Tejiendo los sucesos en el tiempo/Weaving Events in Time*. Rancho Palos Verdes, CA: Yax Te' Foundation.

Yúdice, George. 1985. "Letras de emergencia: Claribel Alegría." *Revista Iberoamericana* 51.132–133: 953–964.

———. 2003. *The Expediency of Culture: The Uses of Culture in the Global Era*. Durham, NC: Duke University Press.

Zavala, Magda, and Seidy Araya. 1995. *La historiografía literaria en América Central (1957–1987)*. Heredia, CR: Editorial Fundación Universidad Nacional.

Zilberg, Elana. 1997. "La relocalización de la cultura en la migración internacional salvadoreña." In *Migración internacional y desarrollo*, vol. 2, comp. Mario Lungo, 129–161. San Salvador, ES: Fundación Nacional para el Desarrollo.

Zimmerman, Marc. 1995. *Literature and Resistance in Guatemala: Textual Modes and Cultural Politics from El Señor President to Rigoberta Menchú*. 2 vols. Athens: Ohio Center for International Studies/Monographs in International Studies.

Zimmermann, Matilde. 2000. *Sandinista: Carlos Fonseca and the Nicaraguan Revolution*. Durham, NC: Duke University Press.

Index

dump dwellers, 213; in *Única mirando
al mar*, 208–210
Dunkerley, James, 129
Durán Luzio, Juan, 39

Editorial Nuevo Enfoque, 228
Editorial Solaris, 136–137
El Olimpo: caficulture and, 19–20;
national literature and, 26–28;
Soto Hall and, 32; *See also* caficulture; *criollo exótico*
El Salvador: civil war period (1970s–
1980s), 77, 78–79, 243n1, 243n3;
in literature, 202–203; national
government, and international investment, 170–171; population of,
169; Spanish entrada and, 85–87;
women's history, 80–81; writers
in, 82. *See also* Salvadoran transnational migration
"El Salvador at a Glance" (Avilés),
181–183
*"El Salvador: De movimiento campesino
a revolución popular" [El Salvador:
From Peasant Movement to Popular
Revolution]* (Cabarrús), 81
El Salvador (Monografía) (Dalton), 77,
85–86; and struggle for control of
historic record, 86–87
Elvir, Lety, 224
Empire in Green and Gold (Wilson), 51
employment: loss of, as loss of identity, 209–210; in Washington,
D.C., 209, 227–228
Epicentro, 164, 225
Escudos, Jacinta, 225
"Estética del cinismo" ["Aesthetic of
Cynicism"] (Cortez), 232–233
Estrada Cabrera, Manuel, 32–33
estrecho dudoso, El (Cardenal), 5–6
ethnic identity: clothing as, 122, 125;
in *The Tattooed Soldier*, 122

Fallas, Carlos Luis, 54
feminist discourse, 150; in film,
145–151

Feria de los Añiles, 91
Fernández, Carole, 158
fiction of peace and progress,
200–201, 208; in "And We Sold
the Rain," 204–207; in *Milagro de
la Paz*, 202–204
*Fire from the Mountain: The Making
of a Sandinista [La montaña es algo
más que una inmensa estepa verde]*
(Cabezas), 144
First Amendment Rights, sanctuary
movement and, 156
FLACSO (Facultad Latinoamericana de
Ciencias Sociales), 198
Flor de banana (Beleño), 47, 67, 72–75
Flores, Francisco, 169
Fonseca, Carlos Amador, 145
food, immigration and, 176–177
"Forjando un sólo pueblo" (González,
L.), 193–194; solidarity culture in,
193–194
Foucault, Michel, 78, 79, 228–229
Fragmented Ties (Menjívar), 133
Free Trade Area of the Americas
(FTAA), 7
Fregoso, Rosa Linda, 147
FSLN (Sandinista National Libera-
tion Front), 141, 150; international
volunteers and, 142–143
FTAA (Free Trade Area of the Ameri-
cas), 7

Gagini, Carlos, 20, 29–30; ideas on
writing, 34; influenced by Martí,
26. *See also* Costa Rican literature
Galich, Franz, 224
Galindo, Martivón, 135, 136–137, 138,
142, 225
*Gamboa Road Gang [Los forzados de
Gamboa]* (Beleño); racism in, 69.
See also Canal Zone trilogy
García Márquez, Gabriel, 18
García Monge, Joaquín, influenced
by Martí, 26
Gargallo, Francesca, 80
gender stratification: clothing and,
147; *los hermanos lejanos* myth and,